THE WICKED WORLD
OF WOMEN

Erin Pizzey is well known for her work with battered
wives and their children. She has had a successful
career in magazine journalism and is now a full-time
novelist. Her previous novels include *First Lady*, *The
Consul General's Daughter*, *The Snow Leopard of
Shanghai*, *Other Lovers*, *Morningstar*, *Swimming
With Dolphins*, *For the Love of a Stranger* and
Kisses.

ERIN PIZZEY

The Wicked World of Women

HarperCollins*Publishers*

HarperCollins*Publishers*
77–85 Fulham Palace Road,
Hammersmith, London W6 8JB

This paperback edition 1997
1 3 5 7 9 8 6 4 2

First published in Great Britain by
HarperCollins*Publishers* 1996

Copyright © Erin Pizzey 1996

First published in US by G P Putnam's Son's 1966

The Author asserts the moral right to
be identified as the author of this work

ISBN 0 00 649623 7

Set in Linotype Postscript Sabon by
Rowland Phototypesetting Ltd,
Bury St Edmunds, Suffolk

Printed and bound in Great Britain by
Caledonian International Book Manufacturing Ltd, Glasgow

DEDICATION

This book is dedicated to my skipper, Ottavio Piccolomini. To his first mate, the beautiful Christian Pompucci, and to my little angel Luca Cansarani. To all the dolphins that swam with us to Greece and escorted us back safely. To Ian Murrell and Sharon Brackly at Lloyds Bank, the bank that really listens. To my second home in the Savoy, and to the Byron Hotel in Forte dei Marmi, Italy. To Rachel Hore and Lucy Ferguson at Harper-Collins who have worked on this book with me. Also for Debbie Collings and her husband Mark, who proved that men can still be romantic. For Roberto Capelli with thanks for an exceptionally wonderful white truffle festival in November. The food and wine were superb and the weather warm and sunny. For my friend, writer and philosopher, Romano Battaglia. Thank you for a wonderful annual literary festival at Versillia. Two months of daily meetings for the public to attend. Romano presents the books, journalists, politics and musicians to the public in a pine forest in the evenings. Thank you also Arnold Bernard for your book on Rilke. Also Nicla Morletti and her books. For the staff of Fortnum and Mason and Stella Burrows at Harrods who supply me with the things I cannot find in Italy or the Cayman Islands. To my white knights: David Morris, John Elford, John Levey and Alan Cohen, who attempt to keep me out of trouble. For Graham Harper of Ash Green Travel Services, who has rescued me on land, at sea, and in the air. Finally to Luana Bianchardi who read this book in manuscript. For her daughter, Nicoletta Lazzeroni, who thrilled us with a scholarship to the Sorbonne in Paris. To Lia, Mauro and Rocco Machetti, my next-door neighbours and friends. Finally for Susan, J.C. and Beatrice at their bar in Bagnia Vignoni. Come and see us there.

ERIN PIZZEY
Cayman Islands, November 15th 1994.

I am sure the emancipated man is a myth sprung from our hopes and eternal aspiration.

DORIS STEVENS, 1900

There has been much accomplishment, and more than a few years have passed. But the resentment of men has not disappeared. Quietly it has grown and deepened.

MARGARET CULKIN, 1935

And when women do not need to live through their husbands and children, men will not fear the love and strength of women, nor need another's weakness to prove their own masculinity.

BETTY FRIEDAN, *The Feminine Mystique*

Chapter One

Helen had never experienced pain like this before. Yes, she knew that she would be leaving a man that she believed had never really loved her. But still, lying here in this mean little room in a shabby road in Shepherd's Bush, she still didn't understand where the pain was coming from. She was curled in a fetal position under a very scratchy brown blanket. Her landlady was a kindly Irish woman, who had advertised the flat as 'fully furnished'. It was certainly that, but Helen felt hundreds of despairing single-parent mothers had moved in before her, leaving behind their sorrow and miseries. Wanly she tried to smile, I hope those women used this place as I am and moved on to better things, she thought, though for now, Helen couldn't for the life of her imagine how she would ever get out of this trap.

Helen had imagined that once she had escaped Paul and his bitter, vicious tongue, she might lose the fear of him, but she had discovered that that hadn't happened yet. 'Give it time,' her now distanced friends from Swiss Cottage advised over the telephone. To begin with when she moved into this flat with Toby, her son, there were frequent telephone calls from her women friends, but now the calls were fewer and Helen really had to make an effort not to pitifully hit the telephone and try to hold on to gossamer bonds of friendship that now hardly existed.

Sometimes she felt as if her former friends felt her fall from grace was catching, like a measles virus. Certainly when they dropped by with forced, polite smiles and shifted uncomfortably in the dingy kitchen, Helen tried not to let the anger well up into her throat. After all, she was the wronged one. She had been a good and faithful wife – or had she?

No, for many years now she had not enjoyed making love to Paul. She was too aware of his impatience with her love-making. The whole ritual had become like a marionette performance. He, stiff-limbed and awkward, never able to offer the tenderness or soft caresses that she had dreamed about as a young girl. Far too often his approaches came after yet another fight. 'Why can't you remember to buy my cornflakes? You know I can't eat any other brand of cereal, and I certainly don't want to eat that goats' food that you and Toby eat every morning.'

Helen winced at the memory. Then, shopping was lists compiled by Paul, with her running like a distracted stoat around the shelves in Waitrose. 'I'm sorry, Paul, but there simply were no cornflakes; they'd run out in the shop around the corner and I just didn't have time to go into town to do the shopping. I'll go first thing tomorrow.'

'That won't do. I have to have my cornflakes. Why don't you go down to the all-night Seven–Eleven now?' Paul stared at his watch. Helen looked across at his thin, hairless wrist. The one thing she found unreassuring about Paul was that he had so little body hair. When he was young she had consoled herself with the hope that as he grew older he would look less like a naked rat when he was undressed, and that he would grow a sufficient quantity of body hair to at least make her feel he had some testosterone in his system.

'What are you thinking about?' Paul had broken into her thoughts.

'Oh, nothing, darling,' had come her quick, guilty reply. 'Paul,' she straightened her shoulders, 'I really don't want to go into town at this hour of the night. Apart from anything else, it is dangerous for a woman to be around those Seven–Eleven shops. Drug addicts hang out at places like that.'

'You've been watching too much television,' Paul had replied in his usual contemptuous tones. 'It's all that rubbish you watch. Of course it's not dangerous. Are you seriously saying you're not going to go?' Paul's voice was incredulous. Helen, his wife, was actually trying to disobey his orders. 'What the fuck has happened to you?' Paul's voice rose to its familiar high shriek. 'I know what it is. It's all that old trendy women's-libber stuff you keep reading in your nasty loony-leftie newspaper. Ugly old harridans telling women what to do.' He grabbed Helen by the front of her dress and pulled her up to his chest. His face was close to her face and she could see the little pink rims of his eyes. She felt herself trembling inside. On the subject of the women's movement, Paul was merciless. He seemed to think that the entire movement had been personally invented to get back at Paul.

'But I have nothing to do with that movement, Paul, you know that. I never go out at night. I'm always here with Toby; and the only people I know are your friends and a few women along the road that I have in for coffee or visit in their houses. That's all, honestly.'

'So you won't go and get my breakfast cereal?' Paul let go of her dress, hoping he had frightened Helen enough to make her capitulate.

'No, I won't, I'm going to bed.' Helen had turned on her heel and fled.

This had been the first step in her rebellion against her husband, and then full war had been declared between them. Paul, vocal, vicious and verbally violent, took the high ground. Helen, subterranean, quiet and timorous, lay quartered in a bunker in her head. The more Paul shouted and screamed, the further she withdrew, until she felt she was an autistic mouse down a very deep shaft.

Toby, she knew, felt the changes in her. He often came home from school and put his arms about her. 'Is Dad

3

bullying you again, Mum? You look so miserable all the time. Come on, let's go out for a walk.'

Helen knew she had lost weight and that there were black shadows under her eyes. She hated the fact that she was emotionally dependent upon her young son. It wasn't fair to put him in that position.

'Don't talk to Mum like that,' Toby had tried to defend Helen.

'You mind your own business, Toby,' was Paul's reply. 'Maybe if you did better at school and stopped bunking off and smoking dope, your reports wouldn't worry your mother so much.'

'I don't smoke dope,' Toby said desperately. These attacks from his father were now more frequent. The three of them in this big, generous house seemed to lie like splinters of steel on the floor that seemed paved with destruction. Now, he brought his few friends home less and less.

'Mine fight like dog and cat,' Peter, his friend, tried to commiserate. 'I don't know why they stay together. I guess it's for our sake, though we'd be better off on our own with Mum.'

Toby was surprised by that admission from the very superior Peter. In a way it did comfort Toby that other families fought like his.

Then the day came when Paul, shifting about from leg to leg, told Helen that he was going to leave her and live with Laura, his latest mistress.

During dinner that night, the night of the confession and the beginning of the end of Helen's life, Paul had been drinking even more than usual. His face had been flushed with maudlin self-pity. 'I have something to tell you both,' he'd said, his voice loud and trembling. 'I have decided to move out and live with Laura.' There had been a moment of absolute silence, and Helen had felt as if Paul had punched her in the stomach.

4

'Laura,' she had said, fighting for control of her feelings.

'Yes, Laura.' Paul had glared at Helen. His usual defence was always to attack.

'But Paul,' Helen hated to hear the whine in her voice, 'you promised after the last time . . . ?'

'I know I did, Helen, but things haven't got any better between us have they? You still can't even remember to buy the kind of cereal I like. Other things aren't much good either,' he mumbled, looking across at Toby who sat rigid and white in his seat. Helen had known what Paul meant. The ocean of silence in their bed. The dry-dock of their emotions. No, things certainly hadn't got any better.

'Are you leaving us for good then, Dad?' Toby's face was softer now. 'We'd be much better off. You go off with your little tart.' There had been a sharp sound of Paul slapping Toby's face. Helen had put her hands into her mouth. Toby had stood up and flung his dinner-plate full of food at his father.

This can't be happening, Helen had thought, removing her hands from her mouth. 'Stop it, stop it, both of you.'

Paul had got to his feet and left the room. They'd both watched in silence as he left the house a few moments later with two suitcases. He must have packed already.

'Good riddance,' Toby had said, his arms around his mother.

'Oh, Toby.' Helen's face was buried in her son's shoulder. 'What on earth are we going to do?'

'We'll manage, Mum, don't you worry. We'll manage without the bastard.'

Now, as she lay defeated in bed, Helen remembered those words spoken by her son, and all she could feel was the usual overwhelming feeling of failure.

* * *

Next door to his mother, Toby lay miserably staring at his ceiling. His sod of a father had abandoned him. He'd left the house to join his new woman, Laura. God how he hated the bitch. He didn't know he could hate like that. It even altered his prayers at night. He prayed to discover charity, but he felt his innocence was lost. He clenched his fists until his nails bit into his palms. Neither his mother nor his father, in the fury of their tearing each other apart, seemed to have considered the losses he had sustained.

The last two years for Toby had been a nightmare. The first thing he had noticed was the tension between his mother and his father. They no longer chatted together in the kitchen. His father no longer took his mother's hand and kissed it when they disagreed and he wanted there to be peace in the house. For as many years as Toby could remember, both his mother and father liked to cook together. Now Helen seemed to find his father's presence in the kitchen a nuisance. She cooked alone, snapping at Paul when he was clumsy. Toby watched them both wearily.

'It's like they've flown off to different galaxies,' he explained to his girlfriend, Louise.

'If your mum is grumping at your dad in the kitchen, then I'm afraid it's all over, Toby. My mum always says when you love a man and he stands on your feet you think it's cute. But when he stands on your feet and you push him away, then it's –' Louise made a face and pointed her thumbs down to the floor – '*finito*,' she said.

Well, it was definitely all over between himself and Louise. She had been his first real girlfriend. His only love, and now she too was gone. Their love, or at least hers, hadn't survived his abrupt removal from Swiss Cottage to Shepherd's Bush, Hammersmith. He'd tried inviting Louise to the new flat but, even as he opened the door with a feigned air of pride, he knew it was over. His heart

6

sank into his Dr Marten boots. His mother's drab little flat could not compare with their old home in Swiss Cottage.

His old house had had a small, very blue swimming pool, set like a jewel in a wide sweep of green lawn. Now another boy, almost the same age as Toby, inhabited his old bedroom. He could still clearly remember the white patches where he'd taken down his posters. His father had brought cardboard tubes home from his advertising agency so Toby could roll up the posters for transporting to his new abode. 'Your mother and I can't seem to make anything work, old chap,' his father had said, handing Toby the tubes. 'Can't go on like this.'

'You mean you want to go and live with your mistress. Don't make it Mum's fault.' This was the first time after the explosion that Toby had directly confronted his father. Taking down his Level 42 poster was the hardest thing he'd done so far. Mike Lindup was his idol, and Toby knew he wanted to be a rock star. He was now angry, really angry. Why should his life be destroyed by Laura? Laura with the long blonde hair and the silly giggle. 'Have you thought about Mum in all this? About the fact that I shall have to leave my school?' Toby could feel his eyes burning.

'Yes, I have, Toby. I've spent nights talking to your mother, and about your future and hers.'

Toby could see that his father was upset. Paul very rarely showed emotion, but now his eyes were misty and his hands were shaking. 'But why, Dad?' So many of his friends' fathers bogged off with younger women. 'Why? You loved us once, didn't you?'

'I still love you, Toby. I'll always love you. You are my son.' Paul tried to brush Toby's hair with the palm of his hand but Toby flinched away. 'You don't love Mum any more, that's what you're really trying to say, isn't it?'

He remembered now the weary way his father had hung his head. 'Yes, that's what I'm trying to say.'

Toby had taken his posters out to his mother's battered old car and they had driven off for the last time. He took one long last look at his bedroom window and his heart felt as if it had been kicked clear through two distant goalposts.

After the first few miserable days, Helen had suggested that he should invite Louise to dinner. Although Toby'd talked to her endlessly on the telephone, he was wary of inviting her to the flat. He knew his mother felt guilty about his loss of friends, but massive amounts of guilt couldn't hide the fact that they were now living in what Toby considered genteel poverty. Not the terrible poverty described by Charles Dickens; even that might be preferable to this. No, it was a sort of sour-smelling, brown-formica kind of poverty that disgusted Toby.

'Perhaps you can invite her over for Saturday afternoon and take her to Portobello Market? It's all so ethnic. I used to go there when I first came to London and I met your father. We used to spend the mornings there.' She smiled at Toby. Then she glanced down at her plate and her face reddened. She didn't add that they'd rushed back to bed in the flat she had shared with two other girls.

Where had all that love and lust gone? Why, when you were so much in love, did no one explain that one day the whole thing would just evaporate? How could she ever have guessed that she'd be left with this cold-rice-pudding of a feeling that she now felt about Paul? She smiled at Toby. 'Now we are on our own, I expect Louise will notice the difference. She'll find us much more relaxed.'

Toby tried to smile at his mother but he couldn't. He was much more relaxed before he came here to this dump. Even when his parents had quarrelled and fought, he had been all right. OK, he didn't enjoy it much when they fought, but he had his friends and, to tell the truth, ever since he became fifteen he'd sort of cut himself off from what was happening. Now there was no escape; he had his mother around his neck every evening. She didn't try to go out; maybe he should humour her and ask Louise to come round.

'All right.' Louise sounded relaxed about the whole thing. 'But not Portobello, it's not a cool place any more.'

'I just want to warn you, Louise, that this isn't like where we used to live.'

'Of course not, idiot, women always get the thin end of the wedge. Have you been to your dad's new place yet?'

'Nah, and it's not his place anyway, it's hers. She's making a lot of money in advertising. Dad's joined her firm. Anyway, he says she's a fabulous cook, so maybe she gets something right. I'll see you on Saturday morning, I'll collect you at twelve, OK?'

'That's really good of you, Toby, you know how I hate travelling on my own.'

'Of course I do, Louise. Anyway, I'm dying to see you. We can talk on the bus . . .'

'Toby,' Louise's voice was hesitant.

'What is it, Louise?' Toby felt a moment of intense fear.

'It's nothing, Toby, it's nothing at all. I'll remember what I wanted to say when I put the telephone down.'

Toby lay back and hoped so desperately that there was nobody else. His love for Louise had come as a complete surprise. They had hung around each other in a gang of schoolfriends. Louise was a good athlete. When they had been called to play mixed doubles for the school, at first Toby had been intimidated by Louise. Louise had a serve that failed to rise from the court, ever. He was a steadier player but she played to win. There was a kind of ruthlessness about her playing that intrigued him. Ruthlessness was one of his father's favourite virtues. 'Never get any-where without it, my boy.' This piece of advice was usu-ally followed by an amiable guffaw.

Toby remembered the moment he had fallen in love with Louise. She of the tip-tilted nose and the deep grey eyes. He'd squashed his finger in the classroom door at school. A crowd had milled around him as he furiously sucked his finger and wished he were alone so he could cry.

'I'll kiss it better for you, Toby,' Louise had said. He'd felt her soft lips fold over his finger and then looked down into her beautiful eyes that seemed to be watching him so carefully. There was a question in her eyes but Toby didn't know the answer then. Upon seeing no answer, she had smiled at him. 'Does that feel better, Toby?'

Toby had gazed at Louise as if he were seeing her for the first time. The sun was shining gently on her chestnut-brown hair. It was the beginning of the summer. He knew that his house was up for sale and that his parents were going to separate, but at this moment all he wanted to do was to take this girl into his arms and kiss her. For a moment it had seemed as if Louise bent her head submissively to his subliminal wish. He had felt her mouth again, this time not on his finger but on his lips. 'How did you know?' he breathed.

'I can always tell,' she had said, drawing away and smiling. 'See you for tennis later?'

'Oh yes,' was all that Toby could manage. His whole body shrieked with sexual longing. That was how his love-affair with Louise had begun and now he felt very surely that it was about to end.

Chapter Two

Nothing had changed when Toby took the bus to collect Louise. To get to her house, the big red bus lumbered down his old street and past his house. Now it was late autumn, and the leaves lay thickly on the ground in his garden.

Straining, he could see that the swimming pool was now covered. Drained of water, empty for the winter. That used to be his work. Obviously the boy who now lived there didn't have to rake the leaves on the grass. He'd loved that job. The piles of golden leaves, once raked, left light-green new-grown grass where they had blanketed the earth.

The stretch and the sweep of his arms as he had raked the leaves only last year had assuaged the sexual longings that constantly tormented him. Was he the only oversexed about-to-be fifteen-year-old in Swiss Cottage? he'd wondered then.

'Not Swiss Cottage any more,' he reminded himself, sitting on the bus. Shepherd's Bush and coming up for sixteen but still randy. Buses made it all the worse. All that grumbling and shuddering.

He had consulted his best friend Peter about his virginity when it first seemed that Louise was going to go all the way. 'Going all the way' had been a source of conversation with Peter for many years. Peter had 'gone all the way', when he was twelve. 'Marie-Claire,' Peter proudly announced, 'went all the way last night while Mum and Dad were at the school parents' meeting.'

'Marie-Claire?' Toby was struck dumb with envy. Marie-Claire had figured largely in Toby's sexual fantasies. She was Peter's au-pair. She had arrived from France to look after Peter and his three sisters. Now she had taken such good care of Peter that he was no longer a virgin.

'What was it like, Peter?' Toby blushed as he asked, waiting keenly for an answer. The wait seemed interminable. Just like the years that stretched behind Toby, when sex had been only a fantasy. But now he felt as if the experience was within his reach.

'It's hard to say, Toby.' Peter's voice seemed different now that he'd gone all the way. Sort of deeper. 'It's not like wanking because somebody else is there. I don't know what to say really. It's sort of great but not that great.'

'You mean that you were disappointed?'

'Well, not really. You see, we were in the living room and we had to do it quickly because Rebecca and April were due back from the library. It happened all of a sudden.'

'Do you feel any different, Peter?'

'I thought about that when I woke up this morning. I'm not in love with Marie-Claire, of course. But yes, I do feel different. I don't feel that sex is such a mystery any more. I do feel connected with Marie-Claire. When we were having breakfast, she touched my foot with hers under the table. Boy, I felt as if I was going to explode. Maybe that's what's bothering me. Before last night I thought about sex all the time. Now I know what it feels like, I want to do it all the time.'

'Did you use ... You know, what we were taught in social studies?'

'Actually,' Peter blushed, 'Marie-Claire had one with her. I made an awful mess of getting the damn thing on. She had to help me.'

'Is Marie-Claire very experienced then?' Toby felt as if his heart might stop still. Peter had all the luck, but then he didn't have Louise. Toby's great fear was that when the moment came and he had Louise in his arms, he might somehow fail her. He didn't feel he could ever look at Louise again if he failed her.

So many things could go wrong with sex. First, as a small boy, he had scoured his father's shelves for information about the subject. Unsuspectingly, Paul had left a book on sex and sexual diseases in his sock drawer. Toby read the book like a bible for months. It was a scholarly tome and gave a riveting description of various hideous infections. There were detailed drawings of both the penis and the vagina. Toby thought the vaginas looked beautiful. Like sea anemones. Those beautiful purple and red tentacle-waving marine lives that splayed under him when he lay on his face in the water at Lyme Regis.

The technical drawings of the erect penis gave him a complex. So far, with his sandy colouring and blue eyes, he showed no sign of becoming hirsute like his father, who had hair all over his back and had to shave twice a day. He also had a very long penis. Toby was used to his father's state of undress in the mornings. His father was as blatant sexually as his mother was modest. Even though his mother's modesty was a joke for his father, he, Toby, was glad of it.

Peter's mother and father were madly modern. The whole family walked around with nothing on whenever they felt like it. In the early days of his friendship with Peter, Toby had arrived downstairs one morning after an overnight stay and had been mesmerized by seeing Peter's mother's naked bottom at the stove in the kitchen.

'Hello, darling,' she'd said, turning around. Toby remembered closing his eyes firmly. Hers was the first full-frontal nude body he'd ever seen, and she laughed at him.

'Peter is no longer a virgin,' he had informed Louise at school break. Louise grinned with all the confidence of her fourteen years. 'Neither will you be for long.

13

Let's catch a bus for Hampstead Heath after school.'

Toby had broken out into a sweat. 'Don't we need one of those things?'

Louise smiled serenely. 'I've got a packet of three in my satchel.' She had kissed him hard on the mouth. The bell had rung and Toby had found himself wondering how many times she had done this before with other boys?

He knew she was not a virgin, but then he realized he wanted to kill every boy who'd been near her. He was unused to this choking feeling of rage. His father could scream and shout but he was much more like his mother. Rows frightened him, as did any sort of physical violence. He stayed away from the boys at school. He was known as a swot but he learned to talk his way out of trouble, to tell jokes and to pretend to be clumsy and stupid. This way life was safe for him.

He had Louise, who was aggressive enough for both of them. She protected him. She squared up to any boy that attempted to tease him about his relationship with Louise. The boys in the school were in awe of his relationship with Louise. This fact made Toby proud to be seen beside her. Everything about Louise made him proud. Just the fact that she could want him with her, even though she was almost two years older. Anyway, she was vastly more experienced than he was at everything.

She lived on a nearby council estate. Toby knew she hated the place. Her father had long since absconded. 'Drink,' Louise said with disgust. 'Drink and womanizing: that's all you get from a man.' Toby didn't like the way her mouth hardened and her chin became pointed. It was as if too much life had been stamped on her face too young.

Toby had written an essay feverishly all that afternoon. He'd found it impossible to concentrate. The thought of lying on his back with Louise on top of him kissing him passionately was foremost in his mind. That was mostly what they did when they were alone. Occasionally she had let him put his two fingers up inside her body. She felt like silk. Her warmth and her wetness held his mind still while his body thrashed against her.

She moved to her own rhythm. He was usually spent long before she lay still. 'Is that all right?' he always asked her anxiously. 'That was lovely,' she usually replied. He loved to gaze at her satiated face. Her eyes now at peace and her mouth relaxed. Sometimes her sexual ferocity frightened him.

Maybe once they had really made love he would be less unsure? He didn't know the answer to that, but the big round clock ticked away the minutes and the hours in the schoolroom.

When they had eventually made love it had been all he'd imagined it would be. The sun had been hot on his back when he'd rolled on to Louise, who had taken off all her clothes except for her black petticoat. As she'd removed her school blazer and then her tie and blouse, Toby had realized he had never seen her totally naked. Most of the time they had been swaddled in various bits of clothing. But Louise had discovered a small dell in the hinder parts of Hampstead Heath which seemed to belong to another time and place. There were no signs or sounds of the city. There were no people sitting in clumps or men walking dogs. The little sanctuary lay green and confident, awaiting lovers just like Toby and Louise.

'Have you been here before?' Toby had tried to make conversation.

'Yes, but there's no need to get jealous. I know the Heath like the back of my hand. I pretend that it all belongs to me and that when I go back tonight I'm going back to a house that's as big as Buckingham Palace.' Louise had pushed Toby down on to the ground gently and put the tip of her tongue in his mouth. Toby liked the way her tongue fluttered in his mouth. She seemed to gauge so accurately his feelings. 'You're afraid,' the tongue said. 'Don't worry, just lean back and let me take care of you.'

After that, Toby didn't have any more control over the situation. Louise had helped him remove his trousers and his underpants. He'd been aware of his insignificant erection. 'I'm sorry,' he'd said. Louise had smiled at him. 'Don't be,' she whispered. 'We all have to learn some time.'

She'd unrolled the condom she had in her hand and gently pushed him away so she could put it on. Toby decided to let her take the lead. It was all he could do to stop himself from coming. He tried counting sheep and thinking of his latest chemical equations. At last she was ready and she guided his hand between her legs. He felt the soft fleshy mound between her thighs. He gently parted her lips between his roving fingers. This was a path he knew well. This had been his salvation during the dreadful months of his parents fighting. Between Louise's thighs the world lay suspended. Nothing existed except for this joyous, lucid moment. Not only did his fingers paint moist snail-tracks on the inside of her tender thighs, but his erection made its way unerringly to its goal.

'I've waited for this moment all my life,' he had said, choking on the words. He'd felt himself slip deep into his beloved's body, and then an unfamiliar rocking motion overtook him. He vaguely realized that, unlike his solitary love-making where there was only his body involved, now he was conjoined with another.

They had found a rhythm together that raised his level of feelings, heightened their intensity until he held on to Louise in fear. He had heard his own voice shouting, 'I'm coming, I'm coming,' and then there was silence.

He had opened his eyes. Nothing had changed. Louise was lying under him, her eyes closed. The landscape had not moved. In the background the trees waved a greeting. The dusty bushes stood on guard. The grass was dry and welcoming.

'So, that's what it's all about?' Toby had felt himself grinning. He'd felt as if he were full of champagne. Not just as if he'd been drinking the bubbles, but as if they coursed through his veins.

'Was that all right for you?' He had known the question sounded silly, but he had to ask.

'That was lovely, Toby. You'll make a good lover.'

'Only for you Louise. I mean that.'

'I know you do, Toby, but you'll get over me. Really you will.'

'Louise, we've only just made love and you're talking as if we're finished with each other.'

Louise's eyes were shaded. 'Did you enjoy that, Toby?'

'Oh Louise, you know I did. How can you ask such a question? It's the nicest, most exciting thing I've done in my life.'

Louise stretched. 'I feel as if I've been wrapped in a huge velvet roll of clothes and I've just been unravelled.'

'Louise,' Toby asked, 'how did you get so good at making love?'

'There's not too much to do on a council estate in the summer holidays. It's not like the life you live with your friends, going to Spain and Portugal.'

Guilt had gripped Toby. Of course, he and his friends all went away for the summer. If not to a cottage in Lyme Regis, then to Spain, Italy or France. 'I promise I'll take you with me. I'm sorry. I'll take you on lots of holidays.'

'Toby,' Louise's voice was solemn. 'I don't think there's going to be any holidays for you for a while. I think your poor mother is going to be very broke.'

'I don't care, Louise, as long as I have you. Nothing else matters. I love you, Louise.' As he said it, Toby knew that whatever happened in the rest of his life, this moment would always remain in his memory. Apart from his love for his mother, Louise had taken his heart and now it was hers for ever.

Chapter Three

Now, watching Louise's face as she entered his mother's flat, he knew with a dreadful certainty that his love for Louise was going to continue as a one-sided affair.

'Hello, darling.' Helen's voice was nervous. 'I'm afraid we're slumming.'

Toby bit his lip. 'You may think it's slumming, Mum, but for most people this is how they live.' His reproving voice sounded hollow in the underfurnished kitchen.

'Well at least you're near the shops.' Louise looked at Toby under her long curling eyelashes. Toby loved her eyelashes. They reminded him of the big black theatrical false eyelashes that film stars wore in the fifties. There was something so sexy about the way they rolled back over her long, flat eyelids.

'What's for dinner, Mum?'

'Well, I know Louise loves roast veal with a peach sauce. I've also made some melon and prosciutto as a starter, and then to finish, brandy and cream.' For the nth time, Toby wished his mother wasn't so dreadfully middle class. Couldn't she see that they had both fallen overboard? There was no place for either of them now. They had nothing left that defined that mass of people who were left behind in Swiss Cottage.

Why, when he heard his mother sigh for the umpteenth time, as she put down the telephone, didn't she realize that the women she had left behind had no intention of visiting her in her grotty flat in West London? She was finished, washed up at thirty-two, and he hadn't even begun his life yet. He felt his life was over before it had even begun.

'That sounds lovely, Mrs Beckett.' Louise's smile was polite, but there was no warmth behind it.

'I'll give you a tour of the flat,' Toby suggested. 'It will take all of two minutes.' Toby was longing to hold Louise. To stretch her slim body against his own. He didn't mind that they could not make love here. He just wanted the warmth and reassurance that she wouldn't betray him.

Even as he recognized his need, he knew his quest was hopeless. Louise had never made any secret of her fear of poverty. Now he was one of the poor. His mother's earnings from her new job in the City paid for their daily living. His father covered the rent and Toby's clothes.

Now he learned to switch off the lights when he left a room. To monitor his telephone calls. To carry their clothes to a launderette on a Saturday afternoon. All the things he never wanted to know. Learning, he knew, was hard, but unlearning was even harder.

'Toby starts his new school in a few weeks' time.'

'I know,' Louise nodded. 'Peter told me. By the way, Toby, he says do you want to come to his party next Wednesday?' There was that same hesitation in her voice.

'Sure, I'd love to. Tell him I'll be there. What time?'

'Eight o'clock, I think, but I'll get him to call you.' Louise knew the game well. Peter could afford telephone calls. Now Toby and Louise were on the same side. Only it wasn't a question of sides. It was simply the have and the have-nots. Louise, however, had only one method of escape. From being a have-not she had chosen to be a have. To find a man who would help her up the ladder from his position on the top rung.

Toby had no choice now. He had been a have, and now he was a have-not. He knew his only choice was to fight to get back to that top rung.

'This is my bedroom,' he said, throwing open the door.

He pulled Louise into the room and put his arms around her. He closed his eyes as he searched for her mouth. He felt a passionate excitement rising within him. 'Louise, I know things are rough now for us, but I promise you I'll get a job and Mum and I will get back on our feet. I'll take you away for a holiday next summer. Maybe Spain, what do you think?'

'Toby, I don't think so.' Louise's voice was resigned.

A solid wall of pain hit Toby in the face. He dropped his arms to his side. 'Is there somebody else?' he asked, trying not to burst into tears.

'No, not yet.' Louise looked at him coldly. 'Toby, there won't be any holiday next year. Your mum will have to pay the bills like the rest of us. People like us don't even think of holidays. There's just days when Mum's on the dole and she stays at home or there are days when she's at work. Our family haven't had a holiday since I was little. There's always the bills.

'Bills,' she went on, and Toby had never heard such bitterness in Louise's voice. 'There's a jar for the electricity, a jar for the rent, and then there's the slot meter for the gas. They're taking those out of the council houses so the likes of us – I mean people like us,' she corrected herself, 'can't bugger up the meter. Pity, I'm good at that, and there's not a telephone kiosk that I can't plunder.'

Toby tried to buy time. 'Maybe you could teach me? I could do with some lessons on survival.'

'Nah, Toby.' Louise smiled her old warm smile for a moment. 'You're too decent a bloke. You've got to be born criminal like me to get out of the ghetto. I will get out, you see.'

'But not with me?'

'No, Toby, not with you. But I like you, Toby, I really do.'

'I love you, Louise.' He knew the words sounded theatrical in that dank little flat, but he had to say them one

21

more time and then relegate the words to a cemetery somewhere next to his heart.

Louise kissed him lightly on the lips. 'Come on, let's go and eat your mother's supper. She's a really good cook.' She slipped her arm through his and marched him back to the kitchen.

So that's how love dies, Toby observed as he watched Louise tucking into her veal. It doesn't wither away like an old Victorian pot-plant in the wrong part of the room. One day it exists, and now for Louise I exist no longer. I'm just Toby and she likes me. What a crater between the word 'like' and the word 'love'. The first word brings with it warmth and friendship, and the second pain and betrayal. For now he tried to suspend all feeling and just rejoice in the fact that Louise was here at his table. Later he would grieve.

He escorted Louise back to the end of her street. He had never seen her house. All he knew was that she lived in the middle of the terrace of houses that looked like a set of rotten teeth. The night was cold and sleet was falling. 'I'll see you on Wednesday then. Eight o'clock?'

'Sure. I'll have a friend with me.' Louise's voice was openly defensive.

'I understand,' Toby said. Not understanding anything at all, except that he must jump on the next bus or she would see him crying.

'OK. I'm glad you understand.'

'Of course I understand, Louise.' He looked behind him and saw the warm friendly shape of a big red London bus. 'Goodbye,' he yelled.

He watched her running down the street, her head bent against the wind and the cold. Toby never realized that a heart could physically break in two. He'd heard the songs. He'd crooned them himself. He'd read books about heartbroken men and women. Scarlett O'Hara broke her heart over Rhett Butler in *Gone with the Wind*. All his crowd had jeered at him when he'd admitted he'd read the book, but he had loved it. Now he knew what she must have felt. 'I'll never fall in love again,' he promised himself on the bus back to Shepherd's Bush. He passed the old familiar road to his house. Somewhere a boy his age was fiddling with the books on Toby's bookshelf. His mother had forbidden him to take all his books. His collection had been pared down to several crates of his favourite books.

There were his baby books. His set of Dickens he won as a prize in school. His Sir Walter Scott adventures, and Shakespeare. Most of his books had been given to the local church hall for the next jumble sale.

Somewhere a boy now probably owned his collection of *Dandy*s and *Beano*s. They had originally belonged to his father, but his mother wouldn't hear of their intrinsic value. 'Toby, we're going to be terribly short of space, and comic books just can't come with us. Anyway, you read far too much. You must get out and get on with your life,' she said. Well if Shepherd's Bush was her way of 'getting on with life', they had not much to look forward to. So far, Helen and Toby rewarded themselves with a Chinese takeaway on a Friday night. The bus rattled to a stop and Toby got off. He pushed his hands into his pockets and tried to look as if he was having a good time. His mother didn't need a long face at this moment in her life.

'Wasn't it wonderful having Louise here?' Helen's voice was light and cheerful.

'We've broken up, Mum.' Toby tried to keep his voice neutral.

'Oh dear.' Helen looked carefully into his face.

Toby slid into a chair by the fire. He wished that the landlady had left the original coal grate in the fireplace. The mock electric coals were hideous. 'I think I'll go to bed now, Mum. I'm really tired.' He got up and bent over his mother to kiss her good-night.

'Things will get better, darling.' Helen tried to smile at him but he could see her eyes filling with tears. He felt guilty yet again, but tonight he couldn't deal with her pain. He just wanted to get away from all of it and lose himself in a book.

'Good-night, Mum.' He knew his voice was gruff but he was good at hiding his emotions from his mother.

'Good-night, darling.' Helen looked up at her son. 'Don't be too upset, darling. She was your first girlfriend and you'll have plenty more. Don't be silly like me and marry your first love. Look where that got me.'

'I won't ever fall in love again,' Toby said, shooting out the words like bullets into the room.

'You will, Toby.' He heard the resignation in her voice as he left the room.

'I bloody well won't,' he yelled as he kicked open the door of his room and then slammed it shut behind him.

Left to herself, Helen felt lost. Maybe Louise didn't want to know them, just as her other so-called friends didn't want to know her. Now she could no longer afford her account at John Lewis. She still kept an account with Harrods, but she had let her credit card at Fortnum and Mason go.

Laura, Paul's mistress, had the advertising account there, and Helen felt a sense of distaste at being anywhere near or involved in any way with the woman. She knew it was uncivilized of her. Paul had explained it to her on countless occasions. 'Sweetie,' he said in that unctuous tone he used when he spoke to her, 'as we both share custody of Toby, it would be far better if we bury our differences and you accept Laura and myself as a couple. After all, I don't mind who you have as a lover. In fact, I'd welcome the chap. I'd feel much less guilty if I knew you were being properly looked after.'

Helen gave a small grim cough of a laugh. She knew he meant that he'd like there to be someone else to pay the rent so he could get off the hook. 'Thanks, Paul, but I'd really rather not have anything to do with either of you. If you want to say anything to me, just tell Toby.' That was the last conversation they'd had. The one where she'd lost the fight to keep Toby at his original school, even if it meant a long bus ride there and back.

She stood up and flexed her long dancer's legs. She lifted her right leg and then stretched it from the knee. Maybe she'd go to some exercise classes. Think about getting out in the evenings. Hopefully, once Toby started his new school, there would be new friends to fill the flat. She would like that. She bent to the ground and was pleased that she could still put her palms flat and keep her knees straight. 'There's life in the old dog yet.' She felt cheered. 'I'm going to go to the cupboard and drink that bottle of red wine I bought last night.' Half of it was left. She felt wicked and guilty at such an indulgence. Life with Paul had not allowed for the finishing of bottles late at night. Their regime had been rigid. People in for supper. All dishes marched in line to the kitchen. Paul in his pink gloves did the washing-up and handed each plate to his wife as if they were sacred.

Come to think of it, Paul looked more and more like his mother every time she saw him. Now, with his mistress firmly ensconced on his arm, he positively beamed bovine contentment. Well, Helen wasn't content. Life wasn't fair. She took a swig out of the bottle and then several more. She felt like a naughty little girl. She giggled. Things were going to change, and for the better. 'There's nowhere to go but up,' she said, and then she grinned as the bottle chinked on her front teeth. Dreadful as the flat was, living without Paul and his Nazi dictatorship gave Helen a sense of new freedom. Somewhere out there was a new world to explore. She had been locked away too long. She put the bottle in the sink, along with the dirty plates from dinner. Paul and his despotic mother could go fuck themselves, she thought self-righteously.

Chapter Four

'Hello, old chap. Welcome to the pad.' Paul tried ineffectually to hug Toby. Toby stood stock still within the confines of his father's treacherous arms. Behind him, Laura's head bobbed uncertainly. 'I do hope you like calves' liver Toby. I've made a special dish from Northern France. It's liver cooked with Calvados and cream. It really is delicious.'

Toby didn't want to tell her he hated liver. His mother knew that he couldn't stand even the smell of it cooking. But with both adults looking at him so hopefully, he tried his best to smile and assuage their guilt. He wanted to say, 'Laura, you ruined my life', but he couldn't bring himself to say it. He wanted to scream at his father, 'How dare you take away my home, my bedroom and my friends, just so that you could go fuck your girlfriend?' Though now having made love to Louise, he felt a certain sympathy for his father. Looking at the man, Toby tried not to sneer.

Laura was twenty years younger than Paul. Paul was now trying to lose those extra years of his life. Today he wore American jeans and a T-shirt that said 'SHIT' across his slightly bulging belly. He wore sneakers with splashy flashes on them. Toby held his father's gaze. This was the first time he'd been invited to his father's new place. Up till now he had taken Toby out with Laura to expensive restaurants. They had had very little to say to each other, and conversation had been forced. It was not helped by the fact that his father seemed to need to neck with Laura every ten minutes. 'Come on, Dad,' Toby said at their last dinner date. 'You're not a teenager any more.'

'Ho,' his father replied, kissing Laura's hand. 'It's not only lads of your age that know about the birds and the bees. By the way, Toby –' and here Toby blushed for his father – '*do* you know all about the birds and the bees?'

'Yes, thank you, Dad.' Toby wished very much that he had real parent-parents. Not the two he had, who seemed so much younger than he did. Maybe there was no such thing as grown-ups. Maybe it was all a ludicrous lie made up by people who just grew older in years.

Now, standing in the middle of the huge loft, Toby looked out at the river Thames. He felt himself washed with the unfairness of it all. There was his mother sitting in their flat on her own, and here was his father, the guilty party, living it up like a lord. 'Well,' he observed, his metaphysical hand taking notes once removed, 'the wicked do flourish like the green bay tree.'

'Darling, let's pour the boy a glass of wine.'

'No thank you, Laura. Dad, do you have any Coke?' He knew Laura wouldn't have Coke in the loft. She wouldn't have Cocopops in the cupboard or bars of chocolate in the fridge. His mother did, of course. Helen cooked chocolate-chip cookies for Toby and his friends. Now, of course, he didn't have any friends. There were people along the road that nodded as he went past.

There was a black boy with long hair draped over his shoulders that called out, 'Hi man', the other day. Toby hadn't answered back because he was too shy; and besides, he didn't know any black people. There had been none in his area of Swiss Cottage, and certainly none at his old school.

'I'm sorry, Toby, I don't have Coke.'

'That's OK,' Toby reassured Laura. After all, it wasn't her fault she'd fallen in love with his deceitful father. It wouldn't be long before she was discarded or, if not discarded, at least cheated on. Toby knew his father's view of women, and all of it was bad.

'Come on and I'll show you around the place.' Paul put a protective arm around Toby. Toby smiled. He had noted in his permanent notepad that Laura referred to the loft as her place, so maybe she wasn't as hooked as Toby had first thought she was. He watched her walking away to the fridge to get him a glass of iced water. She had a fridge like the one in his old house. It was big and black and shiny. An American fridge that spat ice and water at you from the door. He grinned at the fridge. One day he would buy his mother a whole loft, bigger and better than this one. He'd be a famous rock star and bestrew her with diamonds and laden her with gifts.

'Yes,' he thought, 'Laura is sexy,' and he watched her bottom jiggle as she walked to the open-plan kitchen. Paul threw open their bedroom door. 'And she's dirty and untidy,' Toby noted.

The room was wide, with a massive double bed strewn with clothes. A yellowed pair of knickers hung off the dressing table, which was littered with bottles and pots of make-up. Toby looked at his father with a question in his eyes. The question was, 'How do you stand the mess?' His father had always been the most fastidious of men. Paul shrugged, seeing the question in his son's eyes. 'It's good for me not to be too much of a perfectionist,' his father said. 'Your mother spoiled me with her immaculate housekeeping. Besides, Laura has a full-time job.'

'So does Mum now, but the place is still clean.'

'Laura's from a different generation, Toby. Women now don't expect to cook and clean for a man. We share the chores equally.' He knew his father was sounding and feeling defensive, but then Louise was also from a different generation. She took Toby's virginity and then, when she realized he had no money or prospects, she had dropped him. Politely, of course, and no doubt with certain regrets, but he had been dumped just as his mother

29

had been dumped. The thought caused his chest to shrink. 'Let's eat, Dad. I'm hungry,' he said.

Paul walked back to the kitchen, trailing Toby behind him. He went up to Laura and began to nibble her neck. Watching his father, Toby suddenly realized that his father was jealous of him. Jealous because he had his whole life in front of him? Jealous because of his age? Yes, that was it.

He watched amused as his father checked out Toby's face. Having realized that his father was in some sort of competition with him, Toby kept his face carefully masked. 'Nice pictures you've got here, Laura.' For the rest of the evening, Toby talked exclusively to Laura. Paul tried to intervene, but Laura was into Level 42 as well and she promised Toby that they would go to their next concert together. 'We'll leave Paul behind, Toby. Your father doesn't like that sort of thing.'

'I should think not,' Paul blustered. He'd had too much wine to drink and his cheeks were red and flushed. 'Dreadful stuff.' By the time Laura served pudding she was happily talking about reggae. 'You must come to dinner more often, Toby. We've got so much to talk about.'

Toby smiled. He was developing a full-blown sunburst of a smile that hid his evil sexual thoughts. Maybe he could make out with his dad's girlfriend: that would be a laugh. He looked back over his shoulder while he was helping Laura with the washing-up. His father had offered to do it, but Laura had hushed him. 'You go and have a snooze. I want to talk to Toby about music. My kind of music. You know, Toby,' she said, taking the dish-towel from his hands. 'It's quite lonely sometimes, being here at night. Your father doesn't really like to go out much, and he goes to bed about ten o'clock, so I'm really all alone in this big barn of a place by myself. Sometimes I put on a record and just dance alone,' she sighed. 'Can't you come and stay some weekends?'

'I'd love to.' By now he sincerely meant it. 'But I have to stay with Mum. She's all alone in the flat and I know she'll be frightened if I'm not there at night.'

'You're a good boy, Toby, and a credit to your mother. It's a pity we can't be friends your mother and I.' Toby nodded, but then he understood his mother's feelings. He wasn't looking forward to seeing his own ex, Louise, at Peter's party. Even less was he looking forward to meeting her new boyfriends. He didn't know if his mother felt as murderous towards Laura as he would feel towards Louise's new boyfriend, but then maybe women didn't feel jealousy the same way men did? He made a note to ask his mother when he got back.

'Mum, how do you feel about Laura?' Toby was sitting by the fireplace watching his mother, who was curled up in a tight ball in her chair opposite him.

'I don't know, to tell you the truth,' Helen admitted. 'Sometimes I envy her. She's young and pretty and her thighs aren't flabby like mine, but then she knew Paul was married to me and she grabbed him. Yes, sometimes I am jealous of her, but then other times I think of her as my liberation.

'I know this bit of our lives can't be much fun for you,' she said to Toby, 'but for me I have a freedom now that I haven't had in years. I don't have to go to bed early any more. I can stay up and not have the television on ever. You have no idea how much I hated the nightly diet of the television. Your father watched such awful crap. I know he worked hard all day and needed to unwind, but it was dreadful. Also, I was never allowed to play my own music. You know I don't say these things to criticize your father. It really was my fault for letting him bully me. My problem is that I just can't get angry over things. Life's too short ... When you were little I used to take you out to the parks with your friends and give you hot baked potatoes to eat in the snow. Do you remember that?'

'Sure I do, Mum. You're the best mum any boy ever had.' Toby gave his mother a huge smacking kiss. He went off to bed, partly guilty for liking Laura, and partly glad to have been able to talk to his mother. Peter could never talk with his mother the way Toby did with his. He heaved a sigh before he fell asleep. He was too tired to come tonight.

On the whole, Helen decided she was glad that Toby liked Laura. No doubt some day Laura would make her way to Helen's door like so many other of Paul's mistresses. Helen smiled. She was aware it was a cold, wintry smile but then she knew Paul very well. He couldn't stay faithful to one woman. Illicit sex was the only way he could satisfy himself. He had to have the one woman at home to fulfil his need to be mothered, and then one to pursue. Once conquered, the triangle became fractured and the vanquished outsider quietly dropped. Not all of them went quietly. Helen remembered a brick through their sitting-room window. 'I don't blame you,' she had comforted the distraught girl. Maybe Paul was trying to hang on to his youth by fucking young women, but then age was never chronological: sex was all in the head.

When she'd first met Paul she had thought of him as the oldest young man she'd ever met. Now he was just old – and boring with it. She filled her glass again and lifted it up. 'Here's to my new life. Here's to my dance class.' She pointed her toe and admired her small, neat feet.

The next time Toby was away at his father's place, Helen dressed in her old black ballet tights. She put on a black jersey and a fashionable scarf. There was a big dance studio just down the road. She enjoyed sauntering into the big classroom and just looking around. This was the new her. The one that might feel shy but wouldn't show it. 'Who do I ask about classes?' she asked an intimidatingly beautiful black woman.

'Over there.' The woman pointed at a cubby-hole. 'His name's Fats.' She straightened out her body which seemed to be looped into as many coils as a snake. 'You new in the area?'

'Yes, I live up the road with my son Toby.'

'Sure, I've seen him on the street. Tall with reddish hair and very blue eyes?'

'Yup, that's Toby.'

'My boy Junior saw him and said hi, but I guess Toby's scared around here. Most of the Bush people have been here all their lives. We know when somebody new comes into the area. My name is Marcia. Hi.' She held out a long slim hand. Helen took it and then gazed at the whiteness of the palm against the velvet blackness of her skin. Marcia laughed. 'My people are from Africa, not from the islands.'

'I see, does that make a difference?'

'Yes. See, my nose has no bridge and my blackness is dark, man, real dark; not like the white honky niggers.'

'Oh.' Helen found herself short of breath. She didn't know people spoke that way about black people.

Marcia seemed indifferent to what she was saying. If she'd come to one of Helen's dinners in Swiss Cottage and said a sentence like that, there would probably have been a hideous silence. But then black people didn't get invited to smart dinners there, unless they were in the diplomatic corps, or had plenty of money, which was always guaranteed to cover a lot of racial prejudice.

'You go over there and talk to Fats, honey, and then come back and I'll buy you a cup of coffee.' Marcia waved Helen away and resumed her exercising.

When Helen returned having put herself down for some

dance classes, Marcia was waiting for her with a cigarette in her hand.

'I'm getting a divorce.' Helen answered the inevitable question and made a face. 'I've been a fool for far too long, but Toby needed his dad and I made the usual women's excuses for my husband's bad behaviour. And you?'

Marcia grinned. 'I don't have no truck with men, Helen. I've got my kid and my place and if I feel like a fuck I go out and get one, but not in my place. I don't want no one in my bed or my bathroom. They are my places.' She grinned an enormous grin, and Helen felt suddenly light-hearted.

Chapter Five

Toby scanned the room at Peter's party. He could see Louise standing next to a very tall boy. The boy's Adam's apple was even bigger than Toby's, and he wore distinctly American clothes. All around him Toby's old friends clustered in groups, talking. For Toby the first half-hour had been a torment. As he'd tried to join groups, and friends smiled at him, he had realized that he had absolutely nothing to say.

'Ah Toby, lovely to see you,' was Peter's greeting at the door. No attempt to punch him on the shoulder, or to ruffle his hair. It was as if by leaving Swiss Cottage and going away, Toby had committed some dreadful crime. Events now went on in his friends' lives without him.

He tried to talk to some of Louise's old friends. 'Hi, Nicole, how's things?'

'Great, Toby. How about you?' He could sense a tension in the room and he thought it was probably that they were all waiting to see his reaction to Louise's new boyfriend. He decided to put an end to that tension by walking up to Louise and giving her a hug. For a moment she held on to him, and then she broke away. 'Toby,' she said. 'This is Grant.'

'Hi, Grant.' Toby extended a barely shaking hand.

Grant's hand was wet with sweat. 'I've heard a lot about you, Toby.'

'All of it good, I hope?' Toby knew by the swift look that passed between Louise and Grant that his love life had been discussed. Suddenly Toby was sick of it all. The house was the usual middle-class, comfortable, family-sized Victorian building. For a moment he felt a pang of regret that he was not in his little flat in Shepherd's Bush. At least the flat was real. The streets outside the flat were full of people moving about with a purpose. The street outside this house was deserted. He could hear voices all round him chattering inanely. 'Nigel won the school prize for literature this year.'

'Oh I say, how fab.'

'Brill, darling.' That was fat Joanna. 'Where are you going for hols this year?'

'Mummy and Daddy have James down for Winchester, but he wants to go to Wellington. They're all rugger-buggers like James. So we can't go to the Caribbean. It'll have to be boring old France again.' Was he ever one of these people, Toby wondered? Did he say fab and brill and all those other words that you had to use to be cool?

No, he decided. He was never one of these people. Even as he minded being excluded from their lives, he was glad to have escaped that tired, worn-out cliché-ridden way of life.

Most of the people in the room were under eighteen, except perhaps for Grant. He looked about twenty or thereabouts. Watching him with Louise, Toby knew they had slept together. Grant had a way of putting his hand on Louise's arm that bespoke of nights between her legs.

Toby felt great rushes of hot, acrid jealousy pouring over him. Time to go, he told himself furiously, before you start heaving bricks through the window.

'I've got to leave, Peter.' Toby squinted at his friend.

'OK, Toby, see you around.' Peter had his arm around a pretty blonde and he winked at Toby. Normally Toby would have winked back, but he couldn't. He let himself out of the house and stood shivering in the wind. No Helen in a comfortable car to pick him up. No, but she had been at her new dance class tonight, and Toby felt pleased that she would be at home by the time he got back; he needed her. He waited for the bus at the bus stop. He blew warm breath on to his red, chapped hands. He sat as the bus wound its way out of Swiss Cottage, down the roads, until Toby could see the streets filling up with people again.

Women in saris pushing prams, with children attached to their skirts. Rastas, black faces. People: normal, ordinary people. Toby leaned his forehead against the window of the bus and let the tears run down his face. It was all over now. That was the last event. That was his past life. Shepherd's Bush was home now.

When he let himself into the flat, he had stopped crying. Helen took one look at his swollen eyes and took him into her arms. 'Darling,' she said. 'Did you see Louise?'

Toby let himself rest lightly against his mother's slight figure. 'Yeah,' he said. 'She's found a rich American and I know they're sleeping together. Mum, I feel so angry and so jealous. I hate feeling this way. I know Grant hasn't done anything to hurt me, but I want to kill him.'

'I know, darling, jealousy is a very evil emotion, but it's common to us all. In time you'll get over it. I can promise you that. Time is the only healer. Toby, loving hurts. That's the problem.'

'Did you have a good time, Mum?'

'Toby, I had the best time I've had in ages. You know that woman I told you about? Marcia? She's invited us both to her flat for dinner on Friday. You'll meet Junior, Marcia's son. He's the one that waves at you. Marcia's going to cook chicken rice and pease for us.'

Toby was pleased to see the colour in his mother's cheeks. 'Look,' Helen bent down to the floor. 'I can still touch the floor with the palms of my hands, see?'

'Mum,' Toby smiled at her, 'you're not only the best mother in the world, you're the most beautiful as well. How about fixing me a big sandwich? After all that jealous rage I'm starving.'

'OK, let's go into the kitchen and I'll tell you all about

Marcia and you tell me all about your evening.'

Toby screwed up his face. 'Well, I just looked around the room at Peter's house and at all those people who were my friends and I thought, What on earth am I doing here? I don't belong here and I never did.

'Grandma and Grandpa come from Hove. You grew up on a beach with a rowing boat. Dad's people were posh, but you're not and I don't want to be like that either. We can go on holiday together, but not to villas with other English people like we did with Dad. You know, I'd like to go camping somewhere, like Greece.'

'You know what I'd really like to do, Toby?' Toby shook his head. His mouth was full of ham and cheese. 'I'd like to sail to Greece.'

Toby looked surprised. 'But Mum, we don't have enough experience to sail a boat.'

'I sailed my little dinghy all over Sussex. Oh Toby, imagine if we really could do it?' Toby watched his mother's face light up with the idea of an adventure. He didn't argue with her. He was just pleased to see her happy.

He could see that the months since she left his father had done wonders for her. She looked years younger. She was trim and fit and her hair and her face contributed to giving her a fresh, innocent look. Toby was aware that at times he was more the adult than she was, but he didn't mind that.

Peter's mother and father were both promiscuous. 'I don't mind Dad having his dolly-birds, as he calls them. But when you find your mother in bed with your dad's best friend, I think it's the pits.'

'It must be,' Toby said sympathetically when Peter first confided in him. 'Fortunately my mother isn't like that. In fact, I know that Dad's the only man she's ever had in her life.'

Now, watching Helen smiling and planning her great

adventure, he knew that at some time there would be another man in her life. Toby felt a pang which he knew now was jealousy. He would make it his business, though, to see that any man in his mother's life would be worthy of her. He would see to that.

Chapter Six

Toby was very relieved to meet Junior. He was even more relieved to discover that Junior still attended his new school, since he was retaking his GCSEs. 'What's it like?' Toby asked upon being introduced.

'Rough, man, real rough, and you'd better get rid of that accent: they'll kill you. The dark have a big bad attitude and they rule the school.' Junior swung his locks around his head and then pulled on a cap, knitted green, red and gold.

'Rastafari,' he said, grinning. 'My mum's African: the real thing. Anyway, you call me Cricket. Only my mum calls me Junior, after my Jamaican dad.'

'What's so rough about the school?' Toby was not much cheered by Cricket's information.

'Well, it's Mince Meat and his gang. We have these poncy white ding-a-lings of teachers, and they shit their pants when he comes by. He's bad news. Most of us try to stay out of his way.'

Toby knew how difficult school life could be, but at his old school he'd carved out a place for himself by generally keeping his head down but being the class clown whenever he'd been threatened. Somehow he didn't think that either of these defences would automatically carry much weight in Peebles Comprehensive. Maybe he should urge his mother to beg his father to find him another school. But then Toby knew there was no hope of that. His father no longer cared what happened to his son, or wife, for that matter.

He listened to Helen discussing with Marcia her idea of a trip. To his amazement, Marcia was equally enthusiastic.

She and Cricket had sailed when they'd lived in Jamaica for a few years with Cricket's father. Marcia suggested they look in sailing magazines, which often advertised for people to crew boats down to the Greek islands.

'We could have such fun, Marcia. I've been locked away being a housewife for so long that I need to break out. Just recently, with all this lovely time on my hands in the evenings, I've been reading the newspapers and watching the news. I feel as if I've come alive again. Of course, I'm glad of those years that Toby and I had together. I never wanted to go out to work. I never understood all those ranting women who screamed we all had to have careers. Looking after Toby and a husband *was* a career as far as I was concerned. Even if the local so-called feminist women refused to talk to me at dinner parties, I didn't care, I just believed that in a liberated world women should have a right to make any choice they wanted to and I was fed up of being bullied by Jill Tweedie and her cronies.

'It would be so good if the boys could see other countries. Do it properly; meet local people.'

'My main concern,' Marcia said, pouring out a thick vegetable soup into four soup bowls, 'is to keep Junior out of reform school. So far he's been out of trouble, but it's hard and the police are unfair. They pick on the blacks here in Shepherd's Bush. The other day I had to go and get Junior out of the police station. He'd just been arguing with Rollo, who's in his group, and when he argues he argues loud. Anyway, somebody called the police and they took them both away in a black maria. Imagine, a squad of police for two teenage boys.

'Trouble is, they don't understand our culture. Helen, your idea sounds great. I'd love to see Greece. I'm sure they're much more like us. Passionate. I watched Zorba so many times. Can you imagine dancing on the beach. Here, sit, boys, and have your soup.'

41

Toby, spooning the highly scented food into his mouth, mumbled appreciatively. 'Mum, you got to learn how to cook this stuff. It tastes marvellous.

'Cricket has a group and I can play with them. I've just tried out his guitar. It's a Fender, Mum, can you believe that?'

'He's a lucky boy. How'd you get that, Junior?'

'Call me Cricket, Mrs Beckett – everybody does. I'm called Cricket because my legs are so long. My dad got it for me off an American musician. It's the best thing I own. We've been looking for a white boy for the group, and Toby'll be just fine. We're putting together some demo tapes to take round the recording studios. See if we can get some free time to record and then send them to the music companies. Rollo has a girlfriend in one of the big recording companies, so we might just get lucky.'

Toby sat at the table in Marcia's cheerful kitchen and felt he was lucky. Nothing like this happened in his former life. Yes, he played his guitar with different friends, but it was always a desultory sort of effort. They played at each other's parties, and once or twice at a gig in the country but with Cricket, his new friend, he felt there was a real possibility that they might end up as professional musicians.

That's what he wanted to do with his life: to make music. Helen had been a violinist. She also sang. She'd told him that she'd turned down the possibility of a professional musical career because she wanted to get married and have children.

Toby couldn't imagine doing that, but then men didn't seem to have to make those difficult choices. His mum had chosen to go to business school for a year, and thank goodness for that. Now she worked in a solicitor's firm in the City to help pay the bills.

* * *

The next day, Toby walked to his new school with Cricket. Cricket had to attend an appointment with his maths teacher. Standing by himself in the playground, Toby felt very nervous. All round him milled a multi-racial mix of children. Many of the boys in his class had the beginnings of moustaches over their upper lip. Toby felt puny and colourless, lost in the crowd of boys that pushed and shoved and swayed.

There were also girls everywhere, openly flirting and chatting up the boys. Girls hung out of the schoolroom windows and screamed insults at their friends below. 'Coon!' a white girl shrieked. Her voice carried loudly and Toby winced. The boy addressed as 'coon', yelled back, 'White honky bitch, snowflake!'

Toby was suddenly aware of a big black hand on his shoulder. 'So you're the new boy on the street with a posh accent.' He felt himself swung round, and then his face was up against a big round face with fierce teeth, the mouth drawn back in a scowl. 'I'm Mince Meat. I hear you hang out with Cricket?'

'Yes, well, he's my friend.' At this Mince Meat growled loudly and Toby realized that he felt afraid, really afraid.

'What's your name, fuck-face?'

'Toby. My name is Toby Beckett.' Toby tried hard to keep the fear out of his voice. He hoped that if he could keep Mince Meat talking he could stave off the inevitable fight. At his old school, fighting had never been part of the curriculum. Anyway, there had always been two masters on duty in the playground, so bullying was almost non-existent.

This all felt very different. An air of menace hung over the playground. To his left he could see two Asian boys watching with what Toby felt was sympathy.

Mince Meat was surrounded by his friends. Most of them wore black leather bomber jackets with tight black jeans, and they all wore gleaming white T-shirts. They also all wore wrap-round black glasses. Toby found he was sweating, and he tried to control his knees from shaking. Mince Meat reached forward and grabbed the hair on the back of Toby's head. 'Say pardon, snot-rag.'

Toby felt like complying, but he knew with a world-weary sense of finality that if he allowed himself to be bullied, then that would become the pattern in this murderous school. 'Fuck off,' he said quietly. He rather enjoyed that swift hiss of the henchmen drawing breath around him.

'Nobody tells Mince Meat to fuck off.' Mince Meat's nose pressed into Toby's face.

'Fuck off, then,' Toby shrieked, and then he felt the first blow tear into his face. He felt his left eye puff and a haze of redness settled over his vision. He struck out as hard as he could and was pleased to feel his fist hit the bridge of Mince Meat's nose. He followed it up with a head-butt, and heard a gasp from Mince Meat, who fell back for a minute. Another blow fell on his shoulder, but by now Toby had lost all sense of fear or time. He sensed a primitive circle surrounding the two of them, but for the moment his only reality was to do as much damage as he could to this figure tormenting him.

He was not only fighting Mince Meat, he was also cleaning himself out. He was scraping the barrel of hatred, revenge and jealousy, exorcizing the feeling that his life had so betrayed him. That his father had caused this hurt to himself and to his mother and now he was in this mess because his father couldn't keep away from women.

He heard himself screaming wildly, and then there was a momentary hush. He felt a whirlwind come in beside him. 'Come on, Toby, let's go.' It was Cricket. Toby turned a bloodstained face towards his friend.

He watched as Cricket launched himself, feet first, into space. The boy was no longer human. He was a flying object with heavy, metal-tipped boots. The boots struck

Mince Meat in the face and threw him back. 'Stomp him
... stomp him ...' the crowd roared. Toby paused for
breath. He held out his hand to Cricket. 'No,' he said,
'leave him alone.' He gazed down at the stupefied Mince
Meat.

'The man's down, Cricket.' Toby leaned over Mince
Meat and put out his hand. 'Fight's over,' he said. Mince
Meat lay curled up in a ball holding his face. He looked
murderously at Toby, and then he spat a long dirty plug
of nicotine-stained phlegm at Toby.

His henchmen hurried to lift him up, but Toby was
aware that now there was a different attitude in the playground. Various girls were simpering at him. He didn't
want to know them. 'Well done,' said one of the Asian
boys.

'Nothing to do with me.' Toby tried to smile through
his cracked mouth. 'It was Cricket who saved the day.'
He beamed at Cricket. 'Wherever did you learn to fly like
that?'

'Fats gives martial art lessons. It's his religion. But man,
you really destroyed Mince Meat, shaking his hand and
all that. He'll never live it down. Never. Hey, I must
remember what you did. Fight's over now, man, let's
shake hands.' He put on a mock posh accent. 'Heavy
duty, dude.' He was whooping with delight.

A teacher came bustling into the playground. 'I hear
there's been a fight.' The teacher was short and thin. He
had buck teeth. 'You been fighting then?' He stared at
Toby. Toby nodded. His mouth was now too swollen to
speak.

'I see you've 'ad a 'and in this, Cricket. I've told you
before about fighting. Take 'im to see Matron. We don't
want no fighting in the playground.' The teacher hurried
off to placate Mince Meat. 'Fucking nerd.' Cricket pulled
Toby's arm. 'Come on, let's go and find Matron.'

Toby grinned through his puffed lips. He was amazed

45

that he felt so good. Good and clean. Rimmed out, like the inside of the barrel of a gun. A bad attitude was definitely something he was going to develop – and fast.

Chapter Seven

'What are you going to give your dad for Christmas?' Cricket was crouched on his chair. He usually sat with his knees under his chin, his long arms around his legs. Toby tried to sit the same way but couldn't. He wasn't double-jointed like Cricket.

'Oh, I don't know. Dad's really difficult to give anything to. I mean, he has everything he wants. I used to try to get him a tie or socks, but he usually puts them into the back of a drawer and I waste my money. Anyway, this Christmas there isn't any money. I'm going to give Mum a poem and a painting. She says she'll get me a shirt for school and a black leather bomber jacket so I'll look cool. Or I'll try to look cool. I think it's difficult for white boys to have style: we're so colourless compared to you lot.'

Toby smiled at Cricket. They'd just finished rehearsing their new track. Rollo had left to get a takeaway. 'You know, I'm really getting used to living down here. When I go to visit Dad, it all feels so tame. Dad wants me to go to his Christmas party on Christmas Eve. I asked him if you could come and he said yes. Do you want to go? It will be dreadfully boring.'

'What's your dad's place like?' Cricket seemed to like the idea.

'Well, it's posh, I guess. Sort of upmarket. The people Dad knows are embarrassing, if you know what I mean?'

'Yeah, I do know what you mean. All of them hanging out and trying to get with-it twenty years too late.'

Toby hooted with laughter. 'And, man, his music is

terrible. They all try to dance like this.' Toby imitated his father's habit of very stiffly wagging his bottom. 'He's still trying to do the twist.' His father always swung from side to side, his feet rooted to the ground and his arms and elbows shooting back and forth, like the pistons of an old train. 'Dad will dance,' Toby went on glumly, 'and Laura will gyrate. She dances like a bitch on heat.' He saw the surprise on Cricket's face. 'I'm sorry, that sounds evil, but then this is Mum's first Christmas on her own and I don't want to leave her on Christmas Eve by herself.'

'She won't be by herself. My mum's having people in from the dance centre. They're all your mum's friends as well. You're both invited to our yard. We can go, take in your dad's do, and then split for home. Mum's parties are a gas, and the music is good. Rollo'll sing and he's brilliant, and then we can gig when we get back.

'I don't have your problems, Tobe. My dad split long ago. Black men don't tend to hang about their women once they split up. I don't think I'd recognize him if he came up and shook me by the hand.'

'Has it always been that way?' Toby had not liked to discuss this subject, but he was aware from his first few months at school that many of his West Indian friends had only mothers at home, whereas the Asian kids came from much more traditional families. There were problems there, too, though. In fact, sometimes he wondered if any families existed anywhere in the world without massive problems. Maybe his new life with his mother was the happiest he could ever be?

'Do you mind not living with your dad?'

'Nah, sometimes I have dreams of a dad who would take me to football, but then,' Cricket shrugged, 'there's always the downside. Mum won't put up with shit, and most men I know are shits. I guess I don't want to be like that. I want to grow up and have kids that I can love and be with. It's not easy when there's no jobs and no money to keep a woman and kids. How many black men do you know who don't earn anything at all?'

'I don't know, Cricket. I don't know any black families except for you and your mother, but certainly if you just watched the telly you wouldn't think black people did anything but tell jokes against themselves.'

Cricket unfolded himself and he wandered off to the refrigerator. 'Want a beer, Tobe?'

'No, thank you.' Toby wished he could drink beer, but it made him sleepy. He also, so far, had resisted dope. He felt bad about that. Sitting with friends or with Rollo and Cricket, he felt he ought to take a draw. But he knew his mother would be upset. 'Go on, Tobe,' Cricket urged. 'Ganja's good for you. Good for your chest. It's better for you than alcohol.'

Toby envied Rollo. He had watched him many a time take a draw and suck in the smoke, then exhale slowly. The smoke spiralled round his head. Then there was the moment when his eyes would cloud over and he'd withdraw into a silence.

Cricket said he'd never be a pot-head like Rollo. 'Man, I want my music too much to ever want to be out of it. I really got into it when we lived in Jamaica with my dad. My music is the most precious thing JA ever gave me. It's up to me now to make my band, The Henpeckers, famous.'

Now, sitting with Cricket and contemplating the bleak future, with Christmas staring him in the face in an unfriendly fashion, Toby thought, What the hell, I'll give it a try.

'Cricket, you got any dope in the house?'

'Yeah,' Cricket grinned, 'I found my mum's stash the other day. She won't smoke in front of me. She says kids shouldn't smoke with their parents.' Toby knew that Marcia smoked, and that she let Cricket smoke as long as he smoked in his own house or with friends he trusted.

'Weed's funny stuff,' she once explained to Toby. 'If you're not feeling good it can make you paranoid. Only smoke with friends and people you love.'

Then Toby had said, 'I can't smoke dope, Marcia, my mother would be too upset.'

Marcia had gazed back at him dispassionately. 'Don't tell her then, Toby. You're a big boy now and you don't have to tell your parents anything you don't want to. Besides, it wouldn't hurt her to have a smoke herself. She's too uptight about that bastard of a husband of hers. Look, I know he's your father, but he's no good, and she's got to stop punishing herself for marrying him. I hope our boat trip will get rid of his ghost once and for all.'

'I hope it will too,' Toby had said. It really seemed as if the wild scheme might get off the ground.

Now Cricket was rooting about in the cupboard in the kitchen. Toby watched him carefully roll a joint. He didn't think he'd ever be able to create such a neat pencil of weed. Cricket lit the joint and then drew the smoke into his lungs. 'Long and slow, Toby, just like good sex.'

'Don't get that much of that any more.' Toby took the joint gingerly in his fingers. He put the rather soggy end in his mouth. He tried to imitate Cricket and sucked hard. The harsh weed hit the back of his throat and he coughed. Cricket hit him on the back and gave him a sip of water. 'Keep going, man,' he encouraged Toby. 'Just keep goin'.'

Toby nodded his head in agreement. On the third hit the wallpaper in the kitchen seemed to decide to have an independent life of its own. 'Wow.' Toby felt a dreamy softness flood inside his chest. 'That feels great, Cricket.' His voice was coming from very far away. Warmth melted his stomach and ran down his legs. He lay back in the chair and took another heavy drag. 'Leave some for me, Toby.' Cricket was giggling. 'Greedy bugger. But it's nice, isn't it?'

'Sure is. Gosh, just think, I've had sex and smoked dope. Dad would have a fit. About the dope, I mean, not about sex. He gave me french letters on my thirteenth birthday.' Then he remembered that he'd promised himself that he'd never say 'gosh', again. It was a very uncool word, and definitely belonged in Swiss Cottage.

Cricket gazed at Toby through a cloud of smoke. His eyes were red and heavily veined. 'You're not a boy of fifteen here in the Bush, Tobe. Fifteen is a man round here.'

'I know that, Cricket, but I've got a lot to learn yet.'

'Sure thing,' Cricket nodded. 'But you're getting there.'

For once Toby did not care that he no longer lived in Swiss Cottage. He was glad to be here in Marcia's kitchen. He giggled when he thought of his mother's face. She must never know. He'd have his first secret from her. He giggled again. 'Oh Cricket, I'm starving.'

'How does fish fingers and baked beans sound to you?'

'Yeah.' The hunger made his voice rise. 'And lots of it. Piles and piles mounds and mounds and miles and miles of fish fingers.'

'Best munchy food I know.' Cricket reached for the frying pan just as Marcia walked in. 'Cricket,' she said, looking at Toby, 'you've been at my stash again.'

'Sure thing,' Cricket said, gasping with laughter.

'Here, boy, give me the chip pan or you'll burn the place down. You OK, honey?' Toby heard Marcia's warm brown voice and was comforted. Keeping your first secret from your mother was a little lonely. It sat there in his subconscious, beating its hands on the wall, demanding to be let out.

No, Toby told his little secret. I'm going to grow into a man and I don't have to tell my mother about smoking dope. Maybe Christmas won't be so bad after all.

Chapter Eight

'I'm sorry, Cricket.' Toby was indeed very sorry they'd come at all. He'd expected the party to be awful but he had forgotten just how awful these events were.

'Don't be,' Cricket grinned, his big brown eyes alight with mischief. 'I'm going to find myself some white pussy. There's plenty of it about, and they do so love black boys.'

Toby envied Cricket. He had no doubts about anything. He often turned up in Toby's bedroom in the early hours of the morning, stretched out on Toby's floor and fell asleep until Helen tripped over him with Toby's early morning cup of coffee. 'Don't want to wake up my mum,' Cricket had explained the first time Helen went flying.

'How do you do it, Cricket? I mean how can you stay out all night fucking and then stay awake at school?'

'Sex is pure energy, Tobe,' Cricket explained.

Now, watching Cricket prowling around Laura's living room, Toby was aware of many a hot, lustful glance following Cricket's bum-hugging jeans. White boys of my age don't stand a chance, he told himself miserably. I look so thin and weedy.

'Toby, could you come and give me a hand?' It was Laura, looking flushed and miserable.

'Dad's up to his old tricks,' Toby thought as he followed Laura into the kitchen area. 'Those are beautiful brioches, Laura,' he said, staring in admiration at the little lobster canapés. She had obviously taken ages to make the table look elegant, and two long wax candles smouldered, lighting up the silver and the gold plate.

Laura made a face. 'Yes and I did it all myself. Your father spent most of the day in the bathroom, titivating.'

Toby well remembered his father parading in front of the mirror. Thank goodness those years were over. And parties like this one. Earlier on he'd escorted his mother to Marcia's house and into her kitchen. Fats, from the dance centre, had been at the stove cooking goat curry, and Marcia had been singing with Rollo. Now he very badly wished he was back there. There was an uptightness about the people in the room that he had forgotten.

Yes, he last felt it at Peter's party. But he was the one that had changed, not them. Now, hanging out in the Bush with Cricket, he was unused to the repressed anger he felt in the room, and it depressed him. In the Bush, if someone were angry, like as not they'd yell obscenities or punch someone. Sometimes mad people went by, cursing the skies and a government that refused to care for them. At first Toby had been afraid, but now he took it all with ease. Nowadays it was events like this that disturbed him. The unsaid, the undemonstrated. It felt so abnormal.

'Do you think your mother would talk to me if I went to see her?' The words tumbled out of Laura's mouth. She was staring intently at Toby. He knew to ask had cost her an effort. He could also see that she'd been crying.

When he'd first met Laura he'd been struck by her smooth, shining face; now there were faint shadows under her eyes. 'Sure she would. She's not cross with you, Laura. She reckons that you did her a big favour taking away Dad. We're so much happier now.' He tried to change the subject and get her to smile.

'At the end of April, Mum and I intend to go with Marcia and Cricket to Greece. Marcia found an advertisement asking for a crew to sail a boat from Elba to a Greek island. Mum loves the sea, and so do I. It's going to be a gas. Cricket used to go sailing – when he was little in JA.' Toby didn't believe for a moment the trip would take place, really, but he wanted to cheer her up.

'Sounds wonderful.' Laura's voice was wistful. 'I'd love to do that, but Paul always chooses our holidays, and he seems to prefer resorts geared to English tourists.'

'Yes, I used to hate our holidays. What a bummer, all those English people sitting drinking gin and tonics. Nobody to talk to and just Dad showing off and yowling to a guitar.'

That made Laura smile. 'You know him well, don't you?'

'Too well. I must buzz off and see what Cricket's doing.'

Laura watched Toby dive into the crowd. Since she'd known him, she was amazed at how he'd blossomed since he left his father. Yes, to begin with she had felt guilty. Having an affair with Paul knowing that he was married was not normally her style. But Paul was so determined to leave Helen for her, that she had been swept up in his moment of passion.

Now, far too late, she realized that Paul had left Helen because he wanted to feel young again. She was just an excuse. She was also confused. To begin with they had made love almost every night, but now it was once a week if she was lucky.

He no longer brought her flowers, or even bothered to speak to her very much. He usually came home late, wolfed his food down, and then spent the evening watching television. She retaliated by spending more late nights at the office.

Still, maybe talking to Helen would give her a better idea of how to cope with Paul. She sighed and moved around the room, collecting dirty glasses. Paul was standing surrounded by a crowd of admiring women. 'Helen and I . . .' she heard him say. Why is it, she asked herself, that men always talk about their first wives as if they'd never left them?

'Toby, this is Anne.' Cricket had his arm around Anne's waist. 'She's invited me back to her flat for a drink.'

'Wonderful,' Toby said noncommittally. 'See you tomorrow?'

'Earlier than that,' Cricket whispered. It was clear he intended to bonk her, leave and come back to the party.

Toby felt a pang of envy that Cricket had scored. But Toby knew it would be a very long time before he ever tried to make love to a girl again.

'Having fun, old man?' Paul's voice was loud and slightly slurred.

'Yes, thank you, Dad.' Toby didn't mean to sound priggish, but his father embarrassed him.

'Not found a girl yet?'

I'm not looking for one, Dad, he wanted to say – not like you, old goat; but as usual he didn't. His father's behaviour around women disgusted him. Paul always made Toby feel that he thought women were slightly less than human. They were there to be used. To cook, wash and clean like his mother did for all those years, and then to be dumped when they passed their sell-by date.

Toby didn't want to live like that. Cricket's attitude was also one of loving and leaving. Later he'd sit up grinning and recount the night's adventures. Toby always listened, but he knew he'd never be able to be that casual about sex. Even the time he had with Louise made him realize that, for him, making love was too exotic and sensual a pleasure to be thrown away lightly on complete strangers.

He felt restless now with Cricket elsewhere. He wanted to be back in Marcia's warm shabby kitchen, or even in his own flat with his guitar. He wanted to be back with the warm, smiling faces and the smell of goat curry in his nostrils.

Here the faces were guarded and the laughter forced. Here in Laura's big loft there were too many unhappy vibrations. Toby wanted to run out into the night and to scream, 'You're all fucked . . .' But of course he didn't.

'Goodbye, Laura,' he said politely at the door, kissing her gently on the cheek. He noted that she no longer smelled of Opium, her favourite perfume. Helen always used Femme de Rochas now, liberally. It meant to Toby that she was happy once again. He shook his father by the hand and left the building. He wished he had the money for a taxi but he hadn't.

So he waited miserably for a bus; but at least the evening was now over and he could go home. Tomorrow was Christmas Day. He found he was very much looking forward to his mother opening his present under their small gallant Christmas tree in their sitting room.

He smiled as the bus blundered into the light from the streetlamp. Shadows played on the faces of the people queuing behind him. Lean faces with long noses; the sound of feet stamping to keep warm. There was a pushing and a shoving and cheerful Christmassy words floated around Toby as he let himself be hoisted into the hot interior of the bus. People sat and stood smiling, their arms full of packages. It was Christmas and then the old familiar Christmas excitement seized him. 'Happy Christmas,' he said to an old crone that sat next to him. 'Bah,' she spat back. 'Humbug,' Toby teased her, and he thought he could see the beginnings of a smile.

Chapter Nine

Toby heard the lilting reggae running down the street and enveloping him in its warm arms. The music spoke to Toby's lonely soul; it spoke of sweet-smelling trade winds. Of nights with warm water lapping softly on white beaches. He tried very hard not to think of Cricket in Anne's arms but failed; tried hard to believe that the promised adventure in Greece would come to anything, but couldn't.

He pushed open Marcia's door feeling miserable, with a half-failed erection. Then he saw his mother's happy, shining face and his mood cleared.

Helen sat next to Fats who had both his massive arms on the kitchen table. 'Darling.' She motioned Toby to her side. Eagerly Toby smelled the nose-tickling incense of the curry. West Indian curries were not at all like Indian curries; they were gentler and more perfumed, though the little Jamaican red chillies peppered the pot with a subtle, biting aroma. Toby was now really hungry. This was real food, not the fancy stuff prepared by Laura. He sat beside his mother and watched Marcia stirring her pot.

In all the time he'd known Marcia, there had never been a moment when there was not something bubbling in her pots. He wished Helen would learn from Marcia, and was pleased that now his mother did try out different dishes. 'Curried goat?' Marcia raised her chin. Toby loved to watch Rollo and Fats talking. Only to eat or smoke did Rollo put down his drumsticks.

Now he sat on the other side of the table, talking about his beloved reggae. His arms whirled like windmills. The room was booming with the sound of voices. Toby heard a snippet of sound from a Fleetwood Mac album. One day it would be The Henpeckers playing on Cricket's sound system. Fats chewed loudly. 'Great food, Marcia,' he said, reaching for some salt cod and ackee. Toby loved ackee. The yellow mound of pulped nuts gave a warm splash of colour to the table. What a difference, he thought. A big fish was laid whole on its plate, lightly sprinkled with spices and a splash of red vinegar. The curry was a warm brown pool of delight. Bottles of red wine stood open on the table, and Fats had a Special Brew in his hand. 'OK, Toby?' Fats said. Toby found himself blushing.

Ever since Toby had joined Fats' fighting classes, he was aware that Fats looked out for him. Not in any showy way, but rather with a hand on his back or a special smile at the end of the class. Fats had given him his first reggae hat to wear over his ever-lengthening hair. Now he felt 'cool', and he knew to be 'cool' in life was the only thing worth living for.

The first lesson that Fats taught him was never to show emotion. 'You have nothing to fear but fear itself,' he said on the first lesson. That made Toby think. For so long he'd been afraid of everything. One day he was a safe little boy living in a beautiful house with a swimming pool, and then abruptly paradise threw him out.

The second lesson was that there is no blame attached to anyone. Anger means attachment. So if you are angry at someone it means that you are tied to them in an unhealthy way.

The third lesson was that he should light a candle every night and sit cross-legged in front of it. He should close his eyes and draw the light from the candle into his heart. 'Soon,' Fats instructed his boys, 'you will see the light from the candle in your heart with your internal eye. Don't strive. Jive with it. Take time.' Fats had a mellow, low voice; it sounded like malt falling over hot brown stones. Toby just liked to hear him talk.

As he chewed the curried goat he felt his loyalties split in his mind. One side of his head belonged to his father's tight middle-class world. There were no comparisons to be made between the party at Laura's loft and Marcia's kitchen. They were both from two disparate worlds. Slowly, as the weeks had gone by, and Toby gained more confidence during the time spent in the Bush, he had realized that this colourful world that included Marcia, his rock group and Hammersmith was far more attractive to him than the white sterile world of Swiss Cottage. 'Come on, Toby, let's sing. Marcia hasn't heard our new mix yet.'

Marcia beamed. 'Go on, boys. I'd love to hear it.'

'Fats will have to stand in for Cricket.' Rollo handed Fats Cricket's Fender.

'Sure thing.' Fats moved his great bulk to the back of the room. He grumbled and grunted while he adjusted his great belly behind the guitar. Toby fussed over the mike and Rollo picked up his sticks with great reverence. He wiped the sticks carefully with a black silk square. 'Four, three, two, one,' Toby instructed them. 'Don't want your idle chatter, don't want your baby talk . . .' Toby had written this lyric for Louise. It calmed the wound to talk about her in music. 'The lies in your eyes,' he continued. Helen winced, she could feel the hurt in her son and it was agony for her. But Toby, with his head back and the music pouring from him, was thinking that Swiss Cottage might have taken his virginity, but Hammersmith had handed him back his soul.

Chapter Ten

Marcia was not afraid for her son, but she knew that even though he was a good boy and did not steal, he was prey for the police that sauntered around the Bush.

Not all policemen were racially prejudiced, but many were. She learned to lie in bed awake until she heard Junior come home. If he intended to sleep in his own bed, he was always in by one o'clock in deference to her. Now, if he decided to stay out later, then she knew he'd go to Toby's house. Helen was a deep sleeper and the boys didn't wake her, even if they took over the kitchen and made huge hamburgers and baked beans in the early hours of the morning.

Tonight, with the sink bursting with her newly washed dishes, Marcia lay on her back, her long arms resting behind her head. She thought about Helen.

There are many ways a man can beat on a woman. Marcia knew that well. In her time she'd encountered emotionally violent men. On the whole, she observed that among black men, the violence seemed to be outright and explosive. It was the white men who seemed to be so sexually neurotic and perverted.

Marcia never fancied white men. Too pallid, too pale-eyed. She knew of their behaviour from other women and now, of course, from Helen.

'Honey, you should have got shot of that mean man many years ago. Why did you stay?'

'I thought I had to, Marcia. The women in my road were all miserably married in one way or another, but we were trapped by being middle-class. We had school fees and big mortgages and houses and cars. All the things we knew we would lose if we left. I felt I couldn't do that to Toby. So I waited like a hamster on a treadmill, and then the day came when Paul opened the door of my private concentration camp and threw me out anyway.'

Marcia smiled at the memory of Helen's glowing face at the dinner table. Toby too, with his new-found confidence. Briefly she worried as she lay there waiting that Junior was safe in the dark streets. Marcia had taught Junior to be extra polite to the police, but sometimes that didn't help and Junior arrived home bruised and shaken. Marcia knew better than to complain. She could only lie in bed and pray.

Junior's dad had been a handsome artist and a musician. She knew once Junior was born that she would have to get rid of him, even if he was the best lover she'd ever had. She didn't want Junior growing up with a father who was never without a spliff between his fingers. Who lay in bed all day and then took off into the night to make music. She wanted more for Junior than her little flat in Shepherd's Bush Road. She wanted her son to have a career. To wear a three-piece suit and a Homburg pulled low over his wide brow like his grandfather.

Marcia smiled. It looked as if Cricket was going to follow his father's footsteps but without the violence. She remembered the little council house on an estate on the edge of Bristol where she'd grown up. Times had changed, and not for the better either.

Marcia's first memories were of feeling cold, of lying in a basket of some sort staring at the frayed rushes. She remembered the scratch of worn sheets. As she grew older she played with the bobbles in the sheets with her fingers.

Her mother had had permanently black rings under her eyes. She looked as if she'd been beaten, but Marcia's father was actually a gentle, kindly man. He was six feet tall and he adored his little daughter.

There were virtually no other black families on the

estate, and Marcia remembered one time when her mother was pushing her on a swing in the nearby park and a little girl with big blue eyes and two pigtails tied with pink bows pointed at her and shouted, 'Does it come off?'

'What come off, Mam?' She saw her mother's eyes fill with tears.

'Nothing, darling, it's just ignorance. Pig-ignorance.'

That was the first afternoon that her mother spoke openly and vehemently to her father at the tea-table. 'Harold, I can bear it when people say racially prejudiced things to me, but not when they attack our child. The little girl meant no harm. She must have heard those words in her own home, but I fear for us sometimes. I feel so alone and exposed.'

It was so unusual for her mother to show anger that Marcia began to cry. 'Rosalee, we do have white friends who aren't prejudiced. There's the vicar at St Botolph's and his family, and Luke and Jessie. They love us and we love them.'

'I know that but Luke and Jessie are from JA. If they get fed up they can always go back home. We don't have a home. We're from Ghana in Africa.'

'From Africa?' Marcia remembered feeling very surprised. She was seven years old and at school now. She was the only black child in her class. She never told her mother how the other children touched her hair and told her she was a nig-nog. She didn't know what a nig-nog was, but it didn't sound very nice.

Once, on a bus into Bristol, a man called her a monkey under his breath. She didn't tell her mother that either. There were lots of things she didn't tell her mother. Especially that Mr Saunders in the sweetshop fondled her behind when she was six and pushed her against the wall. There was a lump in his trousers and she never went in there by herself again.

Sitting in their small but comfortable kitchen, with her

father on one side and her mother on the other, Marcia had felt the world was a safe place once inside the front door. But Africa?

She knew where Africa was because she looked at it on the school map. It was a huge country and had lions and tigers and giraffes. She very much wanted to go to Africa. Where everybody had black skin and brown eyes like her family, except for the men with white faces and pale blue eyes that seemed to lead black men carrying everything on their heads in long lines. It was obviously better to be white anywhere in the world rather than black even in Africa.

'Are we African, Dad?'

'Yes we are. All I know is that we are from a very old tribe in Ghana. That's on the Gold Coast. Our people were royal and we were kidnapped by the Ashanti Tribe and sent away as slaves. Your great-great grandfather worked in a big house in Bristol. The family were meat-packers and very rich. They were quite kind to him, and finally he bought himself out and moved with his African wife, your grandmother, to Bristol.' Harold smiled at his daughter's small, intense face. 'I want you to get a good education and do something with your life,' he said vehemently.

At fifteen, Marcia had been raped by a gang of white boys on her way back from school. The terrible moments of pain and humiliation never left Marcia's mind. From that moment on she'd found it hard to trust white people. But when she met Helen and Toby, she felt instinctively that Helen had suffered too.

Paul, her husband, was a mean rat of a man. Marcia intended to see that Helen slowly got back on her feet. For the moment Helen was still very frightened and alone, but gradually, as Toby settled in the Bush and made friends and Helen settled into her dancing classes, Marcia could see the difference.

Yes, the past had been hard. Fortunately she had not got pregnant as a result of the rape. Her father had made the hard decision not to go to the police. He knew the subsequent damage of a trial would just compound the harm done to his child. Later on she fell madly in love with Junior's father, and so she didn't do anything with her life but live in Shepherd's Bush on welfare, dreaming in her turn that she would see that Junior took his chances. Now, mixing with Toby who was an excellent student, Junior's school results were better. Toby insisted that they share their homework and endlessly corrected Junior's spelling and grammar. Yes, the future definitely looked brighter with Helen and Toby almost within the family. We're like a tribe again, Marcia thought, smiling. A little tribe of lost, uncertain people. Some of us with broken hearts and vanished horizons. But we will get all that back on the boat. Marcia came slowly back to the present.

Chapter Eleven

'I've got to go clear.' Philip heard the desperation in his ex-wife's voice.

'Not again, Elliott,' he said. 'You've only just got back to Houston.'

'I know, Phil.'

Philip winced at the denuding of his name. He felt as if Elliott was belittling him by lopping off the last two letters of his name. Why, he wondered, settling down to listen, do Americans assume an immediate familiarity with names? The non-names like Randy and Rusty or Butch made him feel even more keenly alienated in this strange land. Though it was scarcely strange really: he'd lived in Houston for the last twelve years. Even if he did have intense moments of homesickness, he was wedded to America, as he had been, at one time, to Elliott.

'Darling,' he said gently, 'what's the matter?' He knew very well what the matter was: during their years of tumultuous marriage, he had made the mistake of not only being her husband but also her therapist.

Once they divorced he continued his work, becoming Elliott's unofficial therapist and occasional bed companion. The trouble with Elliott, he thought, was that she had never really stopped being three and a half.

For much of the time she was good fun. Sexually inventive and a pleasure-seeker, Philip knew he was hooked on her. Where they parted company was when she acted like a child and threw tantrums. But she was beautiful. In the way that women in that part of America were staggeringly gorgeous. She was tall, with a thick mane of blonde hair falling down her back and the bluest of blue eyes. She had expressive hands and small, highly arched feet. Philip was into women's feet and Elliott's were the most beautiful he'd ever seen, partly because she'd rarely worn shoes and her feet had none of the unsightly corns and bunions that bedecked so many other women's feet from years of torturing their feet in high heels.

'It's Mom again, Philip.' The problem was always Mom. Philip shrugged. His ex-mother-in-law was a beast of a woman. 'What's she done this time?'

'She says she'll cut my allowance if I don't go to Florida with her.'

'Maybe if she did cut your allowance you'd have to get a job and work like the rest of us.'

'You know I can't get up in the morning, Phil.'

'You never tried.' There was the usual silence. There was no arguing with Elliott. The father-damaged, abandoned child in the woman refused to take any responsibility for her behaviour, and when her wealthy Greek tycoon of a father left Elliott's mother, he left sufficient money in trust to see that his daughter should want for nothing.

All that Elliott had of her adored father were some blissfully happy memories and a note that she read when she was older that said, 'One day I will come back into your life.'

Philip could never decide whether the note was the most destructive thing in Elliott's life in that it made a promise that sent Elliott looking for her father in any man that was interested in her. It was a note that gave her hope that she had not been entirely abandoned and that one day he would come back for her. Either way, Elliott had been in some sort of therapy all her life.

Philip considered that most American therapists did little other than get paid to listen to an endless amount of whining. He didn't allow that for his patients, and now he decided to level with Elliott.

'Darling, you know I love you and you know I'm the one person who will tell you the truth. You have to make a break from your mother. You are thirty-two years old now and it's far too old to be playing Mummy's naughty little girl. Your mother has no intention of letting you go. She's got nothing in her life except you. Running away yet again because you can't have what you want won't help.'

'I know that.' Elliott's voice changed. 'Gee, Philip, you always make such good sense. Want me to come round tonight with some guacamole?'

Philip smiled. 'I'd love you to come round. You make such wonderful guacamole.'

'OK. I'll be at your place at seven. I'll have a plan by then, I hope. A sort of hit-the-road-toad plan. I'm not going to fucking Florida with my mother. She's obscene. She picks up the most disgusting men and she still thinks she looks sexy in her bikini. She looks like a dry old mango, especially under the arms. Ugh! See you later, honey.'

Philip shifted his weight in his bed and sighed. The sun was just rising and Elliott would just be taking to her bed, while he had to get up and go to work. Tonight not only would they share the food and the wine, but also a fairly hectic schedule of love-making. They both knew each other's bodies well. He loved her slender waist and her surprisingly full bottom. She said she loved his prick; she had been the first woman to unashamedly stroke and caress him. Unlike many other women he made love to who, he feared, lied when they said they enjoyed oral sex, Elliott loved to make love to him with her mouth.

What held her to him in spite of all the childish behaviour, was her ability to willingly and whole-heartedly indulge in all sensual pleasures. 'You have a massive mound of Venus,' Philip once teased her. He was reading her palm. 'You betcha,' Elliott said. Her eyes had twinkled and they'd gone back to her beautiful apartment in downtown Houston and made love.

He remembered those early days and he sighed. A whole day of neurotic women clutching their equally neurotic children. Too much time and too much money on their hands. Absent husbands. Shopping malls instead of relationships. America. He sighed. She's a beautiful, lovely, tempestuous whore. But at least tonight would be filled with pleasure.

He rang the bell for the first patient to be shown in. Loyola, his secretary, stuck her head around the door. So far Philip had resisted her advances. 'Never shit on your own doorstep, son,' his father had advised him. So far, he had obeyed his father, though with great difficulty, since Loyola took being a woman very seriously indeed. But then American women must be the most sexually aggressive women on earth.

'You give such good head.' Philip was awash with gratitude. He felt embarrassed because he knew he had an idiotic grin on his face in his darkened bedroom. The duvet slipped to the floor. Elliott was lying happily on his bare chest. She too was smiling.

'It's what I like best,' she said simply. 'Sex is the only thing I'm good at. Mom always hated sex and, as far as I can remember, she always complained to me about Dad. "Sex is all men want." ' Elliott imitated her mother's high, whining voice. ' "All men are beasts, including your father." ' Elliott drew herself up on to her knees. Sitting back on her heels, she gazed at Philip with her big eyes.

Philip knew this mood well. He always felt very helpless when Elliott became so vulnerable. 'If only I'd been old enough to understand why he left. For so long I thought it was me who had sent him away. But then you taught me that it was normal for children to feel responsible when a parent absconds.' The dim light that seeped through the curtains from the street shone on her face. Big fat tears were sliding down her face.

'Why, darling,' Philip stroked her smooth brown thighs, 'why when you're particularly happy do you end up crying? You're too old to miss your father the way you do.'

'I'm not, Philip. You don't understand. For a girl to lose her father, the first man in her life, is a never-ending tragedy. Lots of my friends lost their fathers. Either they divorced their mothers or they ran off like my father. None of us is whole. Some of us are insane and some of us do dreadfully destructive things to ourselves.' Philip tried to take Elliott into his arms, but he knew it was time to go.

Elliott was going to hit the bottle and slide from the fun and laughter of the evening into an alcoholic binge. He would then become the butt of her anger. He didn't want that. It was the rage that had finally driven him out of her arms, but never out of his life. Deep down, Philip loved Elliott and always would, but now he was afraid of her. 'I must go,' he said. He gently kissed her on the top of her head. 'I know you must,' she said in a desperate little girl voice. They had a pact that when she got destructive, he had permission to leave. It was the only way they could stay friends and lovers.

Now, she was going to 'go clear' as she called it. Run off before she was forced to accompany the freak of a mother to Florida.

'Why don't you just take your mother to Florida without a fight? Yes, she is difficult and no, I don't envy you, but do it for once. We all have to do things we don't want to do sometimes. You've always avoided it because you have money. You never have to face problems because you know you can throw money at them.'

Philip knew he was lecturing her like some old aunt, but no one else dared tell her the truth. She was surrounded by a ring of men who adored her and women who envied her. 'Yes, Elliott and no, Elliott. You're right, Elliott. Three bags full, Elliott,' that's what she was used to hearing. There was a moment's silence and then a small sigh. 'I did enjoy tonight,' she said. 'I've blown it again, haven't I?'

'No, you haven't blown anything except me, and I'm leaving. What are you going to do?'

'Take Mom to Florida, I guess.' Her voice sounded so forlorn, Philip felt that his heart would break, but still he knew he must go.

Elliott burned men up. She tore them apart and then she threw the bits away. She was too dangerous for his equilibrium.

Chapter Twelve

'OK, Phil, I'm just ringing to say goodbye. I'm off with the old bitch to Florida. Tampa is where we're going. I'll pick up some well-hung guy and have myself a ball. Mom can chase men thirty years younger than she is and I'll get paid off and take a trip by myself.'

'You don't always have to find a man, Elliott,' Philip said in exasperation. It was four in the morning and Philip had just climbed into bed in his own apartment. He didn't feel much like having a long conversation with Elliott. He was tired. He'd drunk too much Californian wine and he didn't like Californian wine.

Besides, he still felt slightly randy. He'd been making love with his present girlfriend Yvonne. He hadn't enjoyed it much: his release had been perfunctory and she had been unwilling. Besides, having two young children sleeping next door made him feel nervous. Yvonne came like she cooked, often but without much enthusiasm. 'Elliott,' he said hopefully. 'You don't want to come over here, do you?'

'Nah, I'm bushwhacked. I've been shopping all day and my feet are dropping off. Why, darling, feeling horny?'

'How did you guess?'

'You've been with your little girlfriend. You're always horny after you've been with her.'

'How do you know that?' Philip was always amazed at Elliott's spy network. She should work for the CIA, he teased her. 'No, I'm not coming over to fuck you just after you've been with her. I'm jealous and I don't like to share my men.' There was a moment's silence and regret hung heavily on the telephone wires. Philip spoke first. 'OK, see you when you get back from Florida? Take care of yourself, and why not try to have a good time?'

'I'll sure try, Philip, but you know what she's like.'

'I do. Believe me, I do.' He had this horrific vision of Mrs Stearforth sitting in her vulgar drawing room wearing a bright red swimsuit and dark glasses.

This had been his first vision of her. 'Just catching the rays,' she'd said, proffering her hand. She had licked her lips suggestively. Philip found her reptilian hand repulsive, and that was part of the reason he had fallen in love with Elliott. Nobody should be exposed to such rampant evil. Beside her mother, Elliott shone like a white light in a wicked world. Pity was not the right reason to fall in love, but Elliott had looked so embarrassed at her mother's behaviour that he had felt his heart concertina for her. Now she had to put up with at least a week of her mother's company. His prayers went with her.

If Elliott had known that Philip's prayers were going with her it would certainly have helped. 'What are you doin', honey?' Her mother's nasal whine cut through Elliott's soul like a knife. 'I'm sitting on the john smoking a joint if you must know,' she yelled through the door. Smoking was the only way she could keep calm enough to deal with her mother.

She knew without looking that her mother was prowling about her bedroom dressed in her usual tiny black bikini. Elliott wished she was not so disgusted by her mother, but she was and that was all there was to it. It was positively indecent to have a mother picking up young men and balling them loudly in her bedroom. Elliott often pulled a pillow over her face to try to block out the noise. She supposed her mother screamed and yelled loudly to prove something to Elliott. To have a mother in constant competition was the bane of Elliott's life. Nothing escaped her mother's eagle-eye. Now when she bought a new dress she refused to tell her mother where she'd bought it, otherwise her mother would buy an identical outfit. Elliott used to feel a fool as her mother tottered beside her in impossibly high heels, claiming they were lookalikes. 'Everybody thinks we're sisters,' her mother would lisp. 'I hope not,' would be Elliott's stock reply.

The air in Florida was humid. Sweat dripped off Elliott's arms. It wasn't the good clean sweat from a hot day, but rather the bitter-smelling sweat from an irritated and irritable body. She swallowed the last hit and then she dropped the joint down the toilet. She stood up and expelled the air. Hopefully the fan would blow out the smell of the joint. She didn't want the cops to come sniffing, but then maybe she did: at least it would be some form of excitement.

For one week she would be prepared to listen to her mother. To take her out to dinner and then walk along the pontoons staring at the boats. Elliott had a love-affair with boats; most of the men that interested her had boats. Big, swanky, exotic boats. While she was married to Philip they had had a small dinghy.

She had loved the boat with a steady, unwavering passion. Not Philip, she used to tease him, but his boat. She was called *Gazelle* and she danced on the waves. She pranced up and down in the worst weather. She was a boat that liked to sail rough. She would dive her prow into the deepest hollow of the sea, and then surge triumphantly up a sheer wall of white water. With the wind behind her she rose at a gallop until she strained like a leashed dog. Elliott would imagine her back would break, but then with a triumphant toss of her small sail, she would settle back into the water again.

Elliott's main happy memory was when the little blue sail shook itself out in the wind. A sudden gust and she bellied pregnant with the wind. The sail pulled *Gazelle* along, and with her Philip and Elliott.

Why, Elliott wondered, as she ambled back into her hotel bedroom, did she have to lose the man she so loved? She didn't know the answer. She did know that the only reason she was here with her mother was to please Philip. For him to know that she could do something responsible. Swine, where was he when she had to put her drunken mother to bed?

Her mother had made pass after pass at Philip. Elliott sometimes thought that her mother couldn't understand that there was an age difference of twenty-five years between them. Her mother thought of herself as Elliott.

She dressed like Elliott, she spoke like Elliott and she walked like Elliott. The only thing she couldn't do was to hold her drink like Elliott could. 'Come on, Mom, let's go poolside.' She'd developed a sort of shorthand for talking to her mother, as if she were a child.

'Oh,' her mother squealed, her bright red lipstick smeared across her buck teeth, 'how wunnerful, I can't wait to see the pool. Here's the brochure.' Elliott winced. The way her mother pronounced the word brochure made it sound as if she were talking about something to eat. 'The brochure says it is the biggest pool in Tampa. There should be lots of great-looking guys.'

'I'm sure there are, Mom. Florida is famous for its gigolos. You can pick a new one every day.'

'Wunnerful,' her mother breathed. 'We can ball all night and catch the sun all day. Perfect, Elliott. Isn't it wunnerful we're such good friends?'

'Yes, Mom.' Elliott tried not to let the resignation in her voice upset her mother's finely tuned ear. 'It's great.'

Chapter Thirteen

Elliott was on her way back from Florida on the aeroplane when she bought a copy of the *Herald Tribune* and, idly flipping through the back section, saw the advertisement. 'Three women wanted to crew a yacht from Elba to Greece in the spring.'

'That's it,' she breathed, 'that's exactly what I want to do.' It meant that she would have to hang about Houston for the winter, but then she would have the trip to look forward to. Suddenly the world did not seem such a desperate place after all.

The week had meandered by. Elliott had switched on her internal radio and managed to ignore her mother most of the time. She had fastidiously stayed away from the men who stalked her around the swimming pool, and just turned up her television when her mother was entertaining.

When she got back to her apartment, she stripped off her clothes, threw them on her bed and began to unpack her bags. For the week she had been with her mother she had made a point of walking about fully clothed. She deeply resented the way her mother wandered about, cigarette in hand, naked. 'Goodness knows,' she muttered to herself, 'it's not as though I'm a prude.'

She decided that the problem was that she always felt smeared by her mother's body. She was aware, or thought she was aware, that there was a horrible look of envy and sometimes lust in her mother's eyes when she stared at Elliott.

Sometimes, when she was much younger, her mother had called Elliott to her bed. 'Come and give your mom a cuddle,' she'd whined. Elliott grimaced at the memory. She tried very hard not to let her feet touch her mother's pubic hair. She wriggled away as fast as she could but often, after a fit of drunken crying, Rosie would clutch her and imprison her in her arms, and then there was nothing to do but to wait until she fell asleep. Then, like a thief in the night, Elliott tiptoed out of her mother's bed and back into the safety of her own.

Now, all these years later, Elliott was conscious that her own bed was a must in her life. She had to feel safe in it. Even when she married Philip, she had asked to have a bedroom of her own. He had persuaded her against it; recently, during one of their long, rambling telephone calls, he'd agreed she had been right to ask. 'You were probably quite right, Elliott,' he said. 'The rich in England often have their own bedrooms, and the men also have dressing rooms. Thinking about it, that's how you can keep some mystery in a marriage.'

'Ha!' Elliott was triumphant. 'You've actually admitted that you're not perfect.'

'Far from perfect, my love.'

Elliott had heard such sadness in his voice, and she remembered this conversation as she unpacked her clothes on to the floor, kicked the pile into the air and bounced on the bed. The apartment was clean and everything was beautifully arranged. Norma, her housekeeper, had taken the opportunity to tear the place apart. Elliott grinned. 'It's mine, all mine.' She lay naked on the bed and picked up the telephone. 'Do you know what I'm doing?'

'No, but I can guess with that tone in your voice. Darling, I've got a patient with me.'

'Well get rid of her. It is a her, isn't it?'

'I'll ring you later.'

Elliott made a face. Philip was always so punctilious about his patients. 'Goodness knows,' she muttered defensively, 'I've been away for a whole week.' Frustrated and bored, she got up and went to the bathroom to run a bath.

There was only a postbox address for the advertisement she had seen in the paper. As soon as she dried herself, she went to her computer and typed a reply:

'I would very much like to crew your boat with two other women. I have been sailing all my life. [That was true, though she had no qualifications.] I am a fully experienced skipper. I look forward to your reply.

'If you have already signed up two other women, I would be happy to write to them so we can make our plans for the trip.' The last bit of information seemed to sound good and businesslike. She threw on shorts and a T-shirt and went to post the letter.

On the way to the postbox she passed the Houston House of Women. Here she stopped and went in. Debby was sitting at the desk in the front office. 'Hi, Debs. Anything new happening?'

'Nah, I haven't seen you for a while. Where have you been hanging out?'

'In Florida, with my mom, would you believe?'

Debby made a face. 'Yes, I would believe. I've got one of those too, remember?'

Elliott grinned. Debby's mother was even worse than Rosie, her mother. Debby and Elliott regularly had dinner and compared notes. Now Elliott stared at the job offers on a large board on the wall. 'I need to occupy myself before I take off on an adventure in the spring.'

'Any men involved?' Debby perked up.

'No, not interested. This is to sail with some other women from Elba to Greece.'

'Elba, where's that?'

'Where that guy Napoleon was exiled. You remember? The one who said, "Not tonight, Josephine, I've got a headache and my piles are killing me."'

Elliott scanned the board. 'Hum, they need help in the soup kitchen. I could give that a try. Last time I worked there I got lice. Still, it beats the women's collective. No men. Not interesting. They're putting out such outrageous fascist stuff. If they were men they'd be sent to jail for discrimination.' She sniffed. 'OK, Debby, I'm off to post my application. I'll keep you posted.'

When she got back to her apartment, there was a message on her answering machine. 'I'll come round for dinner at eight o'clock. Love you, Philip.'

There's nothing in the house, Elliott thought in a moment of panic. Philip was so keen on having decent meals. I'll have to run out to the deli and stock up. Elliott was aware that she was pleased that Philip was coming to dinner, but then they were always like this. Apart they yearned to be together, and together they tore each other apart. She sighed. Would it always be that way? Probably, yes, she decided.

Chapter Fourteen

'Marcia, I've got a letter from a woman called Elliott Stearforth. She says she is the third member of our crew. Isn't that exciting?' Helen stood in Marcia's kitchen with snowflakes melting on her hair. Her cheeks were flushed and her eyes were shining. Marcia looked up. 'You look lovely, Helen.'

'Thanks. I feel great.'

Marcia was bent over her stove stirring a wonderful-smelling dish of island stew.

Helen inhaled the incense and smiled again. 'I'm starving, Marcia, can I have some of your stew? You make such good food and the flat always smells so wonderful. I'm not going to be able to get into my swimsuit at this rate. Look, I'm even getting fat. When I first came here I was just like someone out of Belsen.'

Helen plonked herself down at the kitchen table. 'You know, for so long I never thought I'd be happy again. Now I even love the flat. I've spent most of the New Year painting it. Toby is in the school football team and also in the school play. He's much happier now but –' she frowned – 'his relationship with his father is no better. Toby mentioned that Laura wants to come round and talk to me. What do you think, Marcia?'

'I'd slap up any bitch that tried to take my man away from me.' Marcia stood by the stove, one hand on her hip and the other holding a dripping spoon.

'Yes, I understand that, Marcia, but if she hadn't taken Paul off with her I'd still be stuck with him, and I'd be a basket-case by now. He tried to rule my life. Men are such control freaks. I don't think I'd ever want to live with a man's irritation again. Women aren't that way. I know I can get cross and impatient but it's very rare. I hope I'm right,' she laughed. 'We'll have to see how we all get on when we're on the boat. Weeks all stuck together in very cramped quarters. I hope you'll still be my friend.'

Marcia put the spoon back in the stew and gave it a few swirls. She put two soup plates on the table and put on the kettle for a cup of tea: they always seemed to get through gallons of it. 'Don't be such a goose, Helen. Of course you'll always be my friend. Though I have to admit I didn't ever believe that I'd end up best friends with a white woman. All the women I drink with in the bar are women of colour, except for Maisie. One day you'll meet Maisie. She's really funny. Anyway, the whole point of a friend is that you know all about her and love her anyway, even when she's being a bitch. Men just can't have friendships like that. They do have friends, but more for drinking or smoking with, not for truth-telling like we do.'

Marcia leaned over and studied the writing on the letter that Helen had in her hand. 'Hmmf,' she said. 'Very childish.'

'I'm thrilled to hear that I've been chosen to sail with you. As soon as I hear from you I'll book myself into The Savoy and give you a call.'

'The Savoy,' Helen said, thunderstruck. 'Can you believe that? She must be rich. I've only had tea there once.'

'And I've only walked past it. Boy, imagine what a meal must be like there?'

Helen paused. 'I'd order the things I used to eat in restaurants when I was well off. Smoked salmon, lobster thermidor. Then I'd finish with chocolate profiteroles.' For a moment she hurt. 'I'd order chicken rice and pease and then fried yam and the waiter would say no nigga food.' Marcia laughed and there was pain also behind her laughter. 'No, I bet that's the one place you can get any food you want. When I was there there were all sorts of people taking tea. I bet you a fiver if we get to see Elliott at the hotel we'll ask her to ask the *maître d'*.'

'Done, and that's one bet I'm not going to let you forget.'

'OK. I'll rush straight home and write to her now. Toby's in the flat with Thelma: she's a very nice girl he met at school and they're doing homework together. I'm much happier about her than I was with his first girl-friend. She was such a knowing little thing if you know what I mean. She really hurt him a lot. I know one has to learn through painful relationships, but she was only after money; wasn't interested when we moved. Thelma is sweet and a little old fashioned.' Helen finished the remainder of her soup and then wiped out the bowl with a piece of bread.

They sat in silence for a while, then Marcia remarked to nobody in particular, 'Life's a bitch and then you die. Who said that?' Whoever it was had had the same luck with men she had. 'Well,' she said to Helen, 'this black nigga is going off to sea in a boat.' She was glad Junior was so thrilled with the idea.

Marcia moved to the window and looked out at the slush-filled streets. She put her arms around her slim body and leaned up against the casement. 'It's so cold now,' she murmured. She hated the cold. She loathed these grim bitter months. People starving out on the streets. The homeless. The battered women's shelters she saw on tele-vision, especially after Christmas when the violent men were bored at home and had had too much to drink.

Thank goodness her father had been a good, kind man. There was no excuse for her attraction to bastards. Maybe it was just that most men were bastards at heart, and it was just a question of staying away from all of them.

Not all of them, but the bastards were often the ones that had the most fun. Not Paul, she opined, he was a real bastard and boring with it. She used to watch him getting out of his car to say goodbye to Toby. She watched Toby pull away angrily from his embrace. They'd usually been fighting. Sometimes Paul chased Toby into the house shouting at him and then Helen went to the front door and timorously tried to defend her son. The last time that happened Paul slammed back into his car shouting, 'You spoil the little brat, Helen!'

Now, standing watching the people with bowed heads trudging by, Marcia smiled. Helen and she had come a long way, and Marcia was going to see that they kept on going. Any more lame-dog men that came their way, Marcia would kick them out of the way.

'Mum, what's for dinner?' Junior erupted into the room.

'Stew, pork stew with green chillies.' Marcia smiled at her son, now so much taller than she. How odd it was to see his father's face so firmly stamped on the son. Sometimes it took Marcia's breath away with longing. 'We're all right now, aren't we?' she said anxiously.

'Sure we're all right. You're the best cook in the world and the best mother and I'm the best son.' Cricket put his arms around her. 'One day, when Toby and I are rich rock stars I'm going to take you back to Africa. To Ghana, to find our folks.'

'Sure thing, honey. Now eat.' She sat and watched Junior spoon the food into his mouth, just as he had when he was a little boy. 'How on earth did I give birth to anything so big?' she wondered, and then she lit a cigarette.

Chapter Fifteen

'Marcia, Laura just called. She wants to come round now to see me. What should I do? I got into such a panic that I told her I'd ring her back because I had something on the stove.'

Standing by her telephone, Marcia grimaced. She hadn't heard that childish note of panic in Helen's voice for a long time. 'Honey, she can't eat you. She's probably just in trouble with that rat of a husband of yours. What do you really want to do?'

'I don't know, Marcia. I'm frightened. I just don't want her to open up all those old wounds. Not now, not when they're just beginning to heal.'

'Then tell her no. I'd have no time for her myself.'

'But half of me wants to help her. If he's fucked her up as badly as he did me, she'll need all the help she can get.'

'So OK, help her.'

'You're not going to make the decision for me?'

'No, Helen, it's your decision and you must make it. Remember what Fats taught us. You make a decision after you have considered the foreseeable consequences. Of course, there are unforeseen circumstances. But if you have made your decision with love to all things in your heart, then the consequences will be for the good.'

She heard Helen give a sigh of relief. 'Thanks, Marcia, that's stopped the feeling of panic. You're a brick. I will try and help. It's a lot less negative than saying no to her when she's asked for help. She did sound so desperate. I'll ring her now and see her this evening and get it over with.'

Helen found herself fussing around the flat. She tidied the place and then washed the kitchen floor. In her head she heard herself rehearsing her conversation with Laura. 'Well, it's like this, Laura. Paul's an arsehole. A mean, selfish bastard.' She hit the floor with her mop to emphasize her point. These were all the things she would never say to anybody but Marcia.

She smiled as she put a clean red-checked tablecloth on the kitchen table. She'd fixed the appointment for seven o'clock. Drinks. If she remembered rightly, Laura drank gin and tonic. Fortunately she had some gin left over from Christmas, and she'd bought a six-pack of tonic on her way back from work.

Toby promised to go over to do his homework with Cricket just before seven. Normally Marcia preferred to let the two boys study in her flat. Marcia let them have the television on and their music blaring. Helen failed to see how anybody could study anything with that amount of noise.

I know it's silly and middle-class of me, she thought as she plumped the cushions, but then I've got precious little else other than my standards. Goodness knows her mother had schooled her well enough in the running of a house; that she knew she did well.

Now, with the sudden nose-dive in lifestyles, her standards were her bedrock. They were a set of rules that helped her live one day at a time. The getting up in the morning. Cooking breakfast for herself and Toby. Seeing him off to school and then catching the tube for the City and work. Reverse order on the way back.

When the bell rang, Toby was just on his way out. 'Hi, Laura,' he said, giving her a kiss. 'How's Dad?'

'The same as usual.' Laura smiled a wan white-lipped smile. 'He says he's taking you to a football match on Saturday?'

'I guess so. He's so bloody embarrassing to be with.

85

He sits on the bench dressed in his tweed jacket shouting, "I say, well done that chap." He's such a terrific nerd. Still, if it keeps him happy and he's off Mum's back, I'll feel useful.'

Toby ran off, slamming the door behind him. Helen jumped at the loud bang. 'Toby,' she hollered, 'come back here and shut the door properly.' Then she smiled at Laura and shook her head. 'He's impossible now. Six foot tall and trips over his feet all the time.'

'Helen.' Laura was wringing her hands. 'I think it's really good of you to talk to me or even to agree to see me, but I do want your help.'

'Come and sit down, Laura, and I'll get you a drink. It's gin and tonic, isn't it?'

'It used to be, but now it's more like a straight vodka. You see,' Laura could no longer hold the words in, 'we've got this new woman at work and she's after Paul. I mean, she doesn't even bother to hide it. She brushes past him and then she looks at me. We have this big open-plan office –'

'How does Paul take it?' Helen interrupted.

'He's delighted. At first I thought it was just a bit of office flirtation. It isn't, though. The other day he confessed he was desperately sexually attracted to her. Oh Helen, I thought I would die.' Laura put her head in her hands and began to cry.

Watching the bowed head and seeing the tears leaking through the girl's hands, all Helen could feel was a violent rage. She tried to control her trembling hands, then she took a deep breath. This was no time for a panic attack she told herself firmly. She let the breath out slowly through her nostrils. Her anger was a mixture of feeling the pain she'd felt when Paul confessed his affair with the woman who was now crying in front of her, and the rage that yet again Paul was screwing up a woman's life and getting away with it.

'The trouble is, whatever Paul does, his mother is right behind him.' Helen handed Laura her vodka. 'I'll knock back some mother's ruin,' Helen said bleakly.

'Ah yes, Paul's mother. With Mummy he's her adorable little boy, and with all other women he's a fiend. He pays us all out for the rage and anger he feels towards Mummy, who spoiled him rotten and let him throw tantrums. You can't even begin to get him to look at himself. After all, Laura, he's PP. Perfect Paul,' she explained. 'What are you going to do, Laura?'

'Was this what it was like for you?'

'Yes, mostly. In the honeymoon period we were happy, but that didn't last long. Now I realize,' she shrugged, 'it's like that for millions of women all over the world. Men, once they hook you into marriage, take over your life. I guess it's in the genes. Not much has changed since they hit us over the head with tree-stumps and took us into their caves. And not much is going to change until sufficient numbers of women are prepared to do without men and just get on with their lives. At least, that's what my friend Marcia and I think. It's just not worth the loneliness and the misery of marriage. Men all want to control women. Well, maybe not all.' She realized she was sounding really bitter. 'They want to tell us what to do. What to wear. How to behave. Keep the house spotless. Wash their socks. Be whores in bed. Though how you're supposed to be a whore in bed when you've been up the night before with your sick child I'll never know.

'Yes, Laura, my life with Paul was a misery. Sure it hurt when we separated, but now I've rebuilt my life. I'm happy and contented. Toby's fine and it will be a long time before I look for another man in my life again. I'm having too much fun now. You either accept Paul as he is because he's not going to change, or get out while you're young enough to make another life for yourself.

You are beautiful and you are talented and somewhere out there is a man who will really love you.

'And if you find him, give me his brother's address,' Helen laughed. 'I'm having another gin. How about you?' I'm chatting banally with my husband's mistress, she thought suddenly. Why aren't I saying, 'You deserved this misery, bitch?' She supposed because Laura didn't deserve Paul, no woman did.

'I'd love another vodka, but I'll have to lay off at home. I just get mad and yell at him.'

'Ya, it's OK if he does the yelling, but if I dared raise my voice . . .' Helen shuddered at the memory.

'Really? He's always going on about how you never quarrelled with him, and how you cooked and kept the house clean.'

'Standard ex-married-man's game. Keep the first woman nervous about his second woman, and then tell the second woman how good the first one was. Men never leave their first wives in their hearts. Of course, they run off and chase other women, but it's always the first wife they think of on their death-beds. I know that sounds melodramatic, but that's what Marcia says and she's usually right about anything to do with men.'

'She sounds like a good woman.' Laura finished her drink.

'Yes, she's sussed.' Helen was proud of her advice and her new-found slang. Laura put down her glass. 'Well, I guess I'd better go home and think about all this. You know, just recently I dread him coming home. I never know what mood he's going to be in.'

'Yes,' Helen agreed, 'that was always the worst for me. I was afraid to open the door and look at his face.' There was a profound silence, broken only by a long sigh from Laura. 'Goodbye, Helen,' she said. 'And thank you.'

Helen found herself smiling affectionately at the younger woman. She was amazed that she felt no jealousy towards her. What she did feel was a sense of protection for this vulnerable woman beside her.

'You know, it's a dreadful cliché, but sisterhood should be powerful. It's such a shame that a handful of journalists and media thugs ruined the women's movement for us all.' They were moving to the door.

'I know. The only thing that movement did was to give men the right to do anything they want. Paul gets a great kick out of teasing me about being a liberated woman. I earn more than he does and that gripes him. But I don't care who earns more than whom. I'm just pissed off that he won't lift a finger in the loft when I'm working harder than he is. What's for dinner? he says when I come through the door at eight or nine o'clock.'

'Well, Laura, we can be good friends in spite of him.' Helen now knew what a real friendship with another woman was. Her friendship with Marcia was the most important relationship in her life after Toby. She leaned forward and gave Laura a hug. For a moment Laura clung to her like a child. Helen felt her eyes fill with tears. Paul, like so many men, only gave physical affection if he were roused. Poor girl. She remembered the original Laura. The bright shining hair and the general air of fashionable grace. That had all gone.

Men, Helen thought as she shut the door on Laura. They could do it to you, all of them.

'What did Laura want?' Toby asked the next day when he got home. 'Isn't it a bit naff for Dad's bird to come and visit you? I like her, but that's a bit rough on you.' Toby stood bareheaded in the kitchen, looking anxiously at his mother. His rasta hat was still in his hand and now his lox looked more serious.

'Don't worry, darling.' She wished he could be more relaxed about her feelings. 'I'm a lot stronger now. I'm sorry for her, actually.' Helen felt a bit guilty talking about Laura to Toby, but there was no one else at the moment she could talk to. She ought to go round to Marcia's house, but she needed to make Toby's dinner. Not that he couldn't make it for himself. He was an enthusiastic cook. But it usually meant she'd have to clean the kitchen up after him, and she'd had a hard day at work and she was tired.

'No, Toby, I don't want to make you feel bad about your father, but he's up to his old tricks again. I at least had you on the many nights when he was out playing around. She has no one; she sits in her lovely loft waiting for him.' Helen shook her head. 'Oh, those awful nights.'

Toby walked across the kitchen. 'Forget them, Mum. Those days are gone for ever.' His face brightened up. 'By the way, before you got back from the office there was a telephone call from the American lady, Elliott. The one that's sailing with us. She sounds loads of fun. She'll be at the Savoy next Friday. She wants us to have dinner. I told Cricket, but he's worried because the only suit he has is the one he wore for his confirmation. But Marcia said no problem, he can go out and buy a new one. Can I wear my dinner jacket? I never thought I'd get a chance to wear it again!'

Helen thought her heart would break right there and then. Why, oh why did Toby keep so much to himself? How awful to think that he believed that for the rest of his life he'd be so poor and life so dismal that he would never wear his dinner jacket again? She cleared her throat. 'Certainly, darling. I'll get it out and see if the trousers need lengthening. I remember I had to take them up when we bought it.'

'Thanks, Mum. I just need to finish off some English homework. Cricket's already split to buy. Marcia said he's to buy a proper sensible suit, but Cricket says he's going down to the Bush to get a black leather suit. He's seen a really cool one. I'm glad I'm not going to be there when Marcia finds out. She'll tear his ears off.'

Helen laughed. 'She will indeed. I'll hear her yelling from here.'

The monthly alimony cheque hadn't arrived yet again. Helen made herself a cup of tea and then steeled herself to ring Paul in the office.

'So, what have you been saying to Laura, Helen? She's difficult enough to cope with, without your encouraging her.'

'What did I tell her, Paul?' Helen could hear that Paul was in a belligerent mood. She wasn't surprised that Laura confessed her visit: Paul had apparently learnt his methods of grilling from the KGB.

'She told me you said that I would never change. Though why I should consider changing, I don't know.'

Helen made a face. 'Oh Paul, fuck off. Don't tell me what to do.'

'Stay cool, don't blow it.' She could hear Marcia's voice in her head. Laura took a deep breath. 'Anyway, while we're on the phone, I need my money to arrive on time.'

The mention of money sent Paul into a whining mode. 'Actually,' he said, 'I'm having a bit of a hard time myself.'

'Your problems are nothing to do with me, Paul. I just need to buy a new shirt for Toby.' She didn't tell him it was a dress shirt for the Savoy. He would have a nervous breakdown if he thought his money was being spent so frivolously! Whenever she sent Toby off to spend time with his dad, she made sure his clothes looked suitably shabby. She never discussed this ruse with Toby, but she knew he understood. Little ways of protecting each other without letting on.

'I'll see what I can do, Helen, but I don't like your tone of voice. I don't expect to be sworn at.'

'No, Paul, you don't. You don't expect any woman to stand up to you, and if they do you just move on to the next one. Now if you give me any more problems over paying, I'm going to come down to the office with Marcia and we will picket you. You know Marcia, so don't think we wouldn't do it, because we would.'

'Are you sure that these strange friends of yours aren't giving you some dangerous ideas? Since when have you learned to be so belligerent? You're not on something, are you?'

'Certainly not.' Helen felt furious, then she realized how absurd he sounded and had to stifle a giggle.

Paul was still talking. 'You know that young friend of his, Cricket,' Paul said. 'Where he comes from they think pot is rather a good thing, don't they?'

'Cricket is an Afro Caribbean, Paul. He was born here and he is black and proud of it. Why can't you give up this dreadful fascist PC stuff?'

'I can't be bothered to go on with this conversation, Helen. I have to earn money.'

'I want the cheque here by Monday, Paul.'

'You shall have the cheque by Monday.' Paul put down the telephone.

Slimy bastard, Helen thought. Silly, pompous, bastard. She felt a lot better. 'I must get angry more often,' she thought. She began to hum as she fried Toby's fish fingers.

Chapter Sixteen

Toby waited rather breathlessly for Cricket to arrive with Marcia. He hadn't been able to resist finding out what Cricket had finally bought that was 'so cool'. 'Did you get the gear?' he asked later that night. 'Gear is for dope, stupid. Yeah, I got it. It's a neat suit.'

'What did your mum say?' They were in Cricket's bedroom and Marcia was slamming pots around in the kitchen. 'She screamed and slapped me around the head, but I can run faster than she can. So I just ran around the kitchen table until she was exhausted.'

Toby smiled. Cricket was laughing his usually goony laugh. It came from somewhere out of his head, and was not so much a laugh as a series of shrieks and gurgles. Toby loved the way Cricket was completely oblivious to everything around him. If he was thinking about music he would wander through the traffic. Only God, Toby thought, must have a very firm hand on Cricket. Often Toby had to jump out of the way of a bus thundering towards them. He tried countless times to pull on Cricket's jacket, always to no avail. Once, however, on a never-to-be-forgotten occasion, a taxi did swerve and hit Cricket. Toby crouched over the still form of his friend. The cabbie was screaming and swearing, 'You fucking little bastard.' Toby glared at him.

'Am I in heaven?' Cricket asked, opening one eye. 'No, you idiot.' Toby was furious. 'You're lying on the ground in Hammersmith Broadway. Get up.' He hauled Cricket up by the shoulders and then realized his heart was pounding in a panic. It was then he realized how much he loved Cricket. 'Don't you ever do that again, you goon,' he screamed, shoving Cricket on to the pavement. 'And you can sod off,' he yelled at the cabbie. He shook his fist at the man and then, to his surprise, he watched himself dance up and down on the pavement in a rage.

'Hey, Tobe, cool it, man.' Cricket took Toby's arm. Now, waiting for Cricket to arrive with his mother to go to dinner with Elliott, he remembered that day. At least he could stand up for his friends now, if not for himself.

'My, Helen, you look lovely.' Marcia came into the kitchen wearing a tight red dress which set off her magnificent slender figure. She pulled at the front of her own dress. 'Just the right amount of tits and arse,' she said grinning, spinning round the kitchen table.

'I know this is a bit of a stuffy dress,' Helen said nervously. 'I just don't feel me in anything else. I know it's sort of nineteen-fifties.'

'You've got great legs, Helen, you ought not to hide them.' Marcia smiled at her friend. Helen blushed. 'I used to have great legs, Marcia, but not any more.'

Toby was trying to keep a straight face. Cricket looked really bad. Not just bad but wicked. The black leather suit looked as if it had been sprayed on to him. He had huge wrap-around glasses that completely disappeared around the top half of his face. There was an alarming bulge in his crotch. What on earth was it? He couldn't have a hard-on, could he? Toby wondered.

Cricket looked mean and hard and probably, to people who didn't know him, with his flying dreadlocks hanging down to his chest, very frightening. While both women were making travel plans, Toby sidled up to Cricket. 'What's that?' he said, pointing between Cricket's legs.

'Just bragging,' Cricket said, grinning. 'It's a pair of socks. Might get lucky in the Savoy, you never know. I fancy me a suite and a rich bint.'

Toby looked at himself in the mirror before they left the flat. 'I look dull and boring and very British,' he told his reflection. 'Nobody would want to pick me up.' He felt a sadness but also a sense of relief. He, unlike Cricket, could concentrate on the food. These days, thanks to Paul continually carping on about money or the lack of it, they didn't go out to restaurants.

'Do I look dull and boring?' he whispered to his mother before they got into the taxi.

'No, darling, you don't at all. You look young and handsome and I'm really very proud of you.'

'I hope Elliott Stearforth is as nice as she sounds.' Helen sat back in the taxi and smiled at the two boys who were sitting on the twin jump-seats. 'I hope she's very rich and we get to drink champagne.' Cricket was bouncing with excitement. Toby thought he looked like Tigger from *Winnie the Pooh*.

The taxi pulled up and they got out. For a moment the four of them huddled on the pavement, unsure of themselves. Around them, uniformed doormen continued to greet the incoming cars and taxis. 'Come on.' Marcia pushed Helen in the back. 'Follow me.' She swept into the main foyer as if she'd lived there all her life.

Cricket bounded in after her and then looked round the chandelier-draped hall. 'Ahhhhh,' he said in wonderment and delight. 'The Saveloy. I'm home.'

For a moment Toby froze with embarrassment, and then he laughed. The staff were smiling too. Toby realized that they were enjoying the pleasure it gave Cricket to be there. 'I could live here for ever,' Helen said quietly to Toby.

'One day, when I'm a great rock star, you shall,' he told her. 'And that is a promise I intend to keep,' he said to himself.

Toby wished Louise was here to see him now. 'I need to pee,' he said wildly to Cricket. Why on earth must he be taken short and embarrassed like this? It was then he realized how nervous he was. 'No problem.' Cricket sauntered across the marble floor. He leaned over the curved mahogany front desk in a confiding manner. 'Where's the karsy?' he asked the head porter.

'Over there, sir,' the head porter replied gravely.

Toby was entranced as they walked over the soft, silken carpets. 'How on earth do they keep it all so clean?' He felt bewildered. Beautifully coiffed women passed by, leaving soft, subtle, sexual smells as they moved on. Men in well-cut suits stood about, waiting for women, Toby assumed.

'One day I'm going to have a permanent suite here.'

'You can have a suite right next to my mum, Cricket. I'm so glad we came. She's really enjoying herself.' Feeling relief wash over him Toby went into the cloakroom with Cricket.

On the way out, they heard a loud American voice. 'Well, you must be the girls?' A tall blonde woman with wide blue eyes had an arm around Helen's shoulders. 'Are these your boys?'

'Yes,' Helen said with pride. 'This is Toby and this is Marcia's son, Cricket.'

'Hi, boys.' Elliott gave each a big hug. Toby felt her firm breasts against his chest. 'Boy, she's tall,' he thought. But he liked her bright happy face and her wide open laugh.

'Come on, let's go down and eat. I could munch on a moose.'

As Helen sat looking out of the big bay windows, she was silent with awe. The river flowed on, oblivious to everything. Even though the room was packed with people, for a moment she heard nothing at all but the song of a small bird that sat outside on a tree. What sort of bird was it that it sang in the cold and the damp? She didn't know. He must have stayed up specially late just to sing to her, she thought romantically. He whistled and carolled and then gave a delicious warble.

'What do you want to order?' Elliott was looking at Helen. Helen looked down the menu and nearly fainted at the prices. 'It's all so expensive,' she said, feeling guilty that Elliott would be paying the bill. She would be lucky if she had enough money to pay for the first course.

'Don't worry about the bill, Helen. There's a perfectly good cheap little seafood bar upstairs, but I wanted to treat you all, and the River Room is my most favourite place in the world ... Have the smoked salmon, it's excellent.'

Elliott grinned at the boys. 'Before my bastard of a dad split and left me and my mom, he used to bring me here when I was a little girl. I feel at home here. I sometimes think that everything here is big, like in Texas. The beds, the showers, and of course the lovely fluffy towelling robes. Other English hotels don't understand Americans. We love our luxury and all our creature comforts. Not for us your tiny little bathrooms and your miserable amounts of hot water.'

You're right, Helen thought, remembering her rusty little water tank and her tiny cold bathroom. 'Still,' Elliott went on cheerfully. 'If we're lucky with the weather when we go to Greece, we can forget all that misery for a while. I'm really looking forward to our trip.'

'Goodness,' Helen exclaimed as she gazed down at the pile of smoked salmon on her plate. 'That's more smoked salmon than I've ever had in my life.'

'I'll organize several sides for the boat,' Elliott grinned. 'I intend to take at least thirty-six bottles of Rosso di Montalcino, so hopefully we won't run out of wine.'

'That sounds like a great idea. Toby and I will take a crate of Special Brew as well. Can't do without the brew. Hey, Toby, that's a good slogan. We should write a rap and sell it as a commercial.'

'While we're away, Rollo is going to take our demo discs round to some places and see if we can get somebody to give us money to make a single.' Toby's face was very young and very earnest. Helen watched him and felt a pang. Now, living where she did, she knew of so many young people driven by a lust for fame and fortune. Maybe one per cent of them would end up singing. Toby certainly didn't seem driven by the fame, but he was driven by his need to take care of her, and this made Helen guilty. A boy should not have to bear the burden of the welfare of his mother on his shoulders . . .

'What's Greek food like?' Cricket was firing questions at Elliott.

'Great. The yoghurt is wonderful and so is the roast lamb.' She looked across at the waiter. Marcia watched Elliott. She was hiding behind a haze of smoke from her cigarette. Marcia knew that she was not sophisticated like Elliott. She couldn't command a waiter's attention as if she had X-ray eyes.

'Time for another course, everyone?' Elliott was happy. She was enjoying herself. These were neat people. 'Choose what you want and don't worry, I'm a Rich Bitch Trust Fund Kid. That means Mom's been left a lot of money and she pays for everything.' Elliott gave a short sharp laugh.

Helen felt as if a razor had sliced her hand. Why was Elliott so bitter? she wondered. Three crippled women and two hurt boys at sea, she thought. Then she cleared her mind. Put away the notebook and the pencil, she ordered herself. 'I'd love – I mean, I'd really kill for – a lobster thermidor.' She could hardly breathe for longing.

It had seemed that the days when lobster thermidor was taken for granted and she regularly cooked the dish in her kitchen had disappeared into the ether. Now she was poor, and it seemed as if she'd always been poor. She was used to totting up figures on the backs of envelopes, trying to make ends meet.

Sitting on the plump little gilded chair, Helen realized

she hated being poor. She hated seeing Toby's face pinched and cold in his unheated bedroom. She couldn't afford to heat the other rooms. They kept the mock coal fire on in the kitchen, and they lived there for the winter months, as did everybody else that she knew.

So far they had both managed, with the help of their hot-water bottles, to stay in their beds, but if it got any colder, Helen resolved to bring the beds into the kitchen. Anything was better than that he suffer from the continual sore throats and colds that beset his friends at school.

It was a nonsensical middle-class idea that working-class children were used to the cold. She knew you never got used to being cold. Street kids got a lot sicker than Toby's friends in Swiss Cottage, who were dressed in warm clothes and surrounded by central heating. Most of what she'd learned while she was married to Paul would have to be unlearned. Helen hoped that they wouldn't always live this way. Maybe they could live in a little whitewashed Greek cottage?

'Elliott, do you know where in Greece we are going?'

'Sure, the guy who owns the boat told me we have to sail her to Ithaca. We put into port at Cephalonia because we'll be at sea for a couple of days. Fill up with gas, fresh water and stuff, and then go up to the island.

'I asked him why women and he said women sailors tend to be more responsible than men. They don't go on benders and chase sex.'

'I intend to chase women: he's quite right.' Cricket was tucking into a thick red steak. It was striped from the grill, and little bits of rosemary gave off a lovely smell. 'I hear Greek women are especially game.'

Toby looked up from his veal. 'Umm. Mum,' he said, 'could you make this at home? The sauce is ace. Here, try some.' He put a piece of the meat on the end of his fork and then carefully dipped it in the yellow sauce. He handed her the fork.

'That's Marsala and lemon juice,' Helen said.

'You'd better watch out,' Toby advised. 'Greek men are very jealous and guard their women carefully.'

'Not *so* carefully that I can't catch one of them. You watch me.'

'Junior, please don't talk rude like that. It's not nice.' Marcia felt herself blushing.

'Don't bother on my account, Marcia, I fully intend to catch me a beautiful Greek boy.' Elliott drained her wine glass. '*Mmmmmm,*' she hummed. 'That's really fine wine. This is the Altisina from Buonconvento. I have it at home, too. I persuaded Mom to have it shipped there. I don't like American wine much.'

Helen sat there watching Elliott. Jealousy was not a normal feeling for Helen, but now she realized that she did feel envious. Elliott could talk about shipping wine across an ocean. She could afford her easy-going attitude to money. Come to think of it, her attitude to men sounded fun too. Helen knew she could never be that casual in her relationships with men.

Anyway, after the damage Paul had done to her, she had had enough of men. She reluctantly finished the lobster. 'That was lovely, Elliott,' she said. 'Thank you.'

'Think nothing of it, honey.' Elliott waved away the thanks. Somebody's sure done a hatchet job on this poor woman, Elliott thought. She knew the signs well. She smiled at Helen's nervous, apprehensive face. Now Marcia looked like a much tougher broad. You'd have to get up very early in the morning to get even with her. 'OK, folks, pudding time as you say in England. I'm a chocolate freak, how about the rest of you?'

All heads nodded enthusiastically. 'Great.' Elliott was in her element. 'My problem,' she said as she summoned the pudding trolley, 'is that I'm addicted to chocolate, champagne, white truffles and bad men.'

'Sounds OK by me.' Marcia laughed. 'I've always been attracted to bastards.'

'I'll agree to all the rest, but not to bad men. I don't want anything to do with bastards ever again.' Helen's voice was bitter and she wasn't laughing. 'Once in my life is enough.'

'It's OK, Mum,' Toby said. 'He can't hurt you any more.'

Helen very much wished that were true. Elliott felt a lump in her throat. Oh why, she wondered, don't I have a beautiful son like that to touch me so tenderly when he knows I'm hurting? But then she knew why. One of her lovers had given her a virulent dose of syphilis which had rotted her ovaries. She could now never have children. Only now did she mind. Still, she comforted herself, this trip looks as if it will be fun. She would see to it that they worked hard and played hard.

'To our great adventure.' They all held up the remains of a bottle of champagne in their glasses.

'And to our intrepid Skipper Elliott,' Marcia said. 'From what you've been telling us tonight, you know what you're doing at sea.'

Elliott flushed at the toast. 'Sure,' she said. 'Bottoms up.'

Chapter Seventeen

After everyone had left, Elliott wandered back to her suite. She lay across her bed and reached for the telephone. 'They're a really great bunch of people.'

'Who are?' Philip's voice was lost in sleep but he was pleased to hear from Elliott. 'My new crew,' she giggled. 'They all think I'm a wow of a sailor.'

'But you can't sail, Elliott. Only the dinghy.'

'I know, but I didn't tell them that, silly. You know, Philip, I think I like women's minds and men's bodies.' She was thinking lustfully of Philip's wonderfully cuddly behind.

'Well, I'm glad to hear it's not the other way round.'

'Do you miss me?'

'Of course I miss you, Elliott, but you sound a lot happier and much less depressed than you were before you left Houston.'

'That's because I'm away from my mother. I feel I can breathe again. I can laugh and play and there's no disapproving silence or competition. If men make passes at me she's not there to be jealous. Jealousy is such a petty emotion, don't you think?'

'It is, Elliott, but you don't have much to be jealous about. You're beautiful, rich and talented. Not many women can say that for themselves, so they try to hold on to what they have.'

'And I'm great in bed?'

'That too, darling . . . but I'm sleeping, Elliott. Couldn't you one day think about time-zones?'

'You know I don't understand time-zones, honey. It's

the same time all over the world for me. It's only humans that divide it all up to suit themselves.'

Philip sighed. He really didn't want to get into this argument while he was trying to catch some sleep. 'OK, have it your own way. Now good-night, and thanks for the chat.' He put down the telephone and lay back, now wide-awake. When God designed Elliott, he forgot to give her a logical brain, he decided. He got out of bed and shambled to his fridge. One packet of dried cheese. Some milk. He smelt the carton. 'Whew,' he muttered. Shopping with his new girlfriend Yvonne was like shopping with a fiend. Her fridge was always packed to the gills with bottles of champagne, wine, beer and packages of cold edible delights. He gazed forlornly at the white emptiness in front of him. His empty fridge made him feel lonely. Maybe he should marry Yvonne and get taken care of. Or maybe not. If only Yvonne had some of Elliott's wildness, and Elliott had Yvonne's gentleness and housewifely talents, he'd be a happy man. But that would never happen. He'd waited for years hoping Elliott would mellow, but she only got worse. He got himself a glass of water and went back to bed.

Elliott lay in the huge bathtub and contemplated the ceiling. The ceiling was covered in mirrors. She lay listening to the sound of the suds popping. *Femme* bath-oil. She lifted a leg, smooth and glistening. 'What a waste of a beautiful bath,' she thought. 'I need to go find me a man to share the suite.' She soaped herself delicately between her legs. 'I think I should go down to the bar and hunt for a man,' she told her pubic hair. She was glad that her pubic hair was the same colour as the hair on her head. She had friends who dyed the hair on their head and their pubic hair to match. 'Sure,' she reassured her breasts, 'what a good idea.'

She opened her cupboard. Hanging from a thickly

padded fleshly pink hanger was a dark blue dress. The bodice was slashed to show off her breasts to their best advantage. She grinned. If Marcia and Helen could see her now! She slipped the dress over her bare body and was pleased to see that her breasts needed no support. My bazookas, as she fondly called them. Well, tonight she'd fire with both nipples. She lavishly applied perfume under her arms and around her neck. She flashed a little mascara under her eyelashes, and a touch of bright pink lipstick to her lips. '*Mmmmm*,' she murmured at her reflection in the mirror. She wiped away the steam that had clouded the mirror and said: 'Mirror, mirror on the wall. Who's the fairest of them all?'

'*Moi*,' she answered, and giggled again. She pulled on her soft silk shawl and sailed out into the empty corridor. She took the little gilded lift to the mezzanine floor, and then she walked into the foyer of the hotel.

It was late but she could hear the jazz musician still playing. She looked around her nonchalantly. She was aware that every member of staff in the foyer was staring at her. She knew them all from her frequent visits. She waved her hand and smiled. '*Ciao*,' she said. A barrage of greetings followed her down the wide stairs to the bar and tea-room.

As she walked down the stairs, she swayed to the time of the music. She heard the jazz player stop for a second. Then he let out a long, low whistle. 'Baby,' he said, 'where have you been all my life?'

'What a corny line. If you must know I've been in Houston waiting for you. Why don't you play "Smoke Gets In Your Eyes". It's been a long time since I heard that song.' She stepped into the little pagoda that housed the piano. She felt his body stiffen. 'What's your name?' she said softly, her pink lips very close to his ear.

'Barry,' he said simply. 'My name is Barry Martin and I'm from Chicago. It's the most beautiful city in the world.' He began to play the old familiar melody, and Elliott felt the song washing over her. With the song came lovely memories of her life with Philip. She felt herself relaxing and a dangerous self-pity threatened to flood her. But she wouldn't let it. 'Wanna drink?' she said, slurring the words.

'Sure, I'd love a vodka and tonic.'

'I'll have mine straight.' She beckoned a waiter and ordered the two drinks.

Barry looked at her sideways. 'You a serious drinker?' he asked.

'Uh-huh.' Elliott nodded. 'It gets me into a lot of trouble.' She wrinkled her eyes and watched as the waiter brought the drinks.

'Thanks . . . ?'

'. . . Elliott,' she said. 'Are you doing anything after you finish playing for the night?' she asked.

'No,' he said. His eyes were grey, she noticed.

She looked at him directly. 'Would you like to come to my suite for a nightcap?' she asked.

Barry took out a packet of Rothman cigarettes. He offered her one and she took it. He lit both the cigarettes and then resumed playing. 'Just a nightcap?' he asked.

'We'll see. It's early yet.' Elliott checked her watch. It was five past twelve and the bar was almost empty. 'Where's everybody?' she asked with interest.

'All gone home to get a good night's sleep. Tomorrow's another day.' Barry grinned.

Elliott nursed her vodka. This man interested her. He was attractive and he played the piano well. He went on to play all her old favourites. 'To Catch a Falling Star', 'Sipping Soda': that was an old song of her mother's generation; she liked it because it was so innocent. It had been composed in a time when a girl and a boy would indeed sip soda sitting at a soda fountain, instead of snorting coke and getting smashed on vodka. She downed another drink and Barry ordered her another one. 'Boy, you can put that stuff away,' he said with admiration.

'Irish ancestry,' she laughed, 'but we'd better get upstairs before I get rat-drunk and pass out. You'll have to sling me over your shoulder and put me to bed.'

'We can't let that happen.' Elliott summoned a waiter and signed her bill. 'Come on now, little darlin'.' Barry mimicked a cowboy accent. 'I'm going to lasso you like a little heifer and we'll go upstairs.' He took Elliott's elbow and held it firmly. Elliott smiled up at him. They sailed through the foyer.

'Barry's struck gold again.' The doorman smiled tolerantly.

For once Barry didn't feel cynical. This woman was obviously rich and certainly very beautiful. She sure picked up a man without any qualms. But there was a certain sweet innocence about her that he found endearing. Hopefully, they could become friends. He found himself thinking of great places to show her in London. They reached her suite and she pulled out her plastic card.

'Here,' he said, 'let me do that for you. They are very difficult to use.'

Hmm, Elliott thought. He's done this a lot of times before. 'Thank you,' she said gracefully as she stepped through the door.

The lights had been dimmed by the maid. 'Do you want me to fix you a drink?' Barry gazed at her. His hair was shoulder-length and curly.

'No, not really. I'd like to touch your hair.' Barry bent his head obediently and Elliott ran her hand over the soft blond locks.

'How old are you?' she asked.

'Twenty-seven,' he said, and then he smiled.

'You have the most beautiful mouth,' she said in a whisper. She stood on tiptoes and gently kissed him. He pulled her to him and then kissed her warmly and deeply.

'There,' Elliott said with deep satisfaction, 'I knew that would be nice.' She giggled. The sound of her giggle reminded her of the water going down the plughole in the bath next door. Maybe they'd make love in the bath another time, but for now Elliott was feeling tired.

'Are you sure you want this?' Barry asked.

'Sure as I ever am about anything.'

Barry lifted her into his arms and carried her gently into the big bedroom. He put her down on the huge double bed and then slipped her dress off her shoulders. 'You're so beautiful,' he said. 'So very beautiful.'

'I know.' She smiled up at him. She raised her arms and wound them around his neck. He tried to take his clothes off in between kissing her. 'Just a minute,' he said, and removed the rest of his clothes. 'Do you want me to shut off the light?' he asked, slipping into the bed beside her.

'No, I want to see your face when you come,' she said. She pulled his now naked body on top of her. He felt her slim waist and her surprisingly strong thighs take possession of his body. She came before he did, and the last thing he saw was her big blue eyes staring intently at his face. He moaned and then he climaxed and slumped on top of her. 'How was that?' she asked.

'Beautiful,' he said. 'Bloody beautiful.' Elliott pushed him aside. She smiled down at his exhausted body. The vodka was running through her veins like ice. She loved the moment when a man came in her arms. For her it was power, pure power. She lay back on the big square pillows. 'Good,' she thought. 'He can take me around London.' Life was definitely looking up. A new crew, a new lover, and some new clothes tomorrow. She grinned and then flipped the light out. Barry was already asleep. Tomorrow was going to be a great day.

Chapter Eighteen

Elliott was not surprised to find that Barry had gone when she awoke the next morning. In fact she was quite relieved. She liked her bed to herself in the morning. Having to share a bed was one of the things that had broken up her marriage.

Lying beside her glass of water by the bed was a note. It read, 'Unless you have other plans, here is my telephone number. I'll pick you up at two o'clock. Don't ring unless you need to change the plan, man.'

Good, she thought as she slowly stretched her satiated body. More sex, lots of days and nights just fucking. 'Ah me,' she said out loud, 'it's good to be alive.'

She pulled on her big fluffy towelling robe and strode into the bathroom. The old pipes carrying the hot water to the bath ran under the marble floor, making her feet comfortably warm. She examined her face in the mirror. Lots of fine lines running from her nose to her mouth. 'Well, if I am going to be wrinkled, at least I can be interestingly wrinkled and have terrible tales to tell when I'm eighty.' She wondered if nuns had fine lines running down their faces? Or did doing without sex keep the skin young? She knew that nuns had a much lower rate of cervical cancer, but then so did Jewish women.

She thought about Marcia and Helen and the two boys. 'Interesting, very interesting,' she murmured to the black television set. She didn't want to watch the morning television news in England. England, she decided many years ago, only wished to push out the bad news. Watching television in England was enough to give you a massive depression. The television set assured her that murder, kidnapping, rape and torture awaited her as soon as she set foot out of the door of the Savoy.

She ordered coffee and waffles. She was always hungry after making love. She brought her own brand of coffee from Houston and gave it to the floor manager: the coffee served in England was abysmal. Then she went back to bed with the newspaper that hung so elegantly from the doorknob.

She had her second cup of coffee of the morning in the executive suite at Harrods. Her personal assistant beamed at her. 'Welcome back, madam,' she said, smiling. Elliott was reassured to see Sally. They both got on so well together. As usual, Sally had organized a vast pile of clothes for Elliott to choose from. 'I always take far too much on holiday,' Elliott confessed.

'You can never be too well dressed, madam. Look at this little bathing suit: it matches the colour of your eyes.' She held up a tiny thonged swimming suit. 'This cashmere wrap is one of our nicest. Wonderful for a cool evening on a boat.'

Elliott watched Sally carefully pack all her purchases. 'Can you send the parcels down to door two and I'll pick up a cab from there? I'm just going to pop down to the food hall to get some nice eats for tonight.'

Elliott left Sally filling the big green Harrods bags and took the lift to the food hall. The big green bags were gifts for her mother, who carried them proudly around Houston.

From when she was a child she loved the food hall. The wheel of fish and the big blowsy displays thrilled her. She bought some prosciutto, and some pecorino cheese and grapes. Then she saw some fat, bursting, juicy purple figs. They looked so ripe and so sexy she had to buy them. The idea of the taste of the sharp, slightly pungent pecorino cheese with a melting bite of the bulgingly seeded figs made her smile. She hoped Barry thought food was as erotic as she did. A few fat-dotted slices of salami and then she wandered off into the bakery. 'Unsalted Tuscan bread, please,' she said.

She wished she could live in London full time, but then she remembered that it could only be a daydream. She couldn't leave her mother. Her mother would never settle in England. Houston was her life. She adored her white air-conditioned Rolls Royce. She lived in a big white apartment block, full of abandoned old women like herself. They went to the hairdresser's together. They visited the cinemas, played bridge, and generally hung out complaining loudly about men.

The English were nothing like as gregarious as Texans. In Texas everything was outsize. Especially the Texan men. They were loud, big, and adored their bossy wives. Here nobody wished Elliott a happy day. The people in the shops looked miserable. Probably because they watched English television. But Elliott was happy. Harrods was full of people from all over the world, all colours. It felt like a huge rich bazaar in the middle of a city. She always felt a sense of loss when she left Harrods. She felt safe when she was either in her suite or in the food hall. Men might let her down. Her mother might make her life extremely difficult. She might play dangerous games with unknown men, but these two places were eternally unchanging in her life.

At lunchtime she phoned Helen – 'Do you feel like coming round for tea Monday?' – hoping she would say yes.

'We'd love to come. The boys will be home from school at four, and I'll leave work early so it will have to be a late-ish tea. Shall we say five by the time we get there?'

'Wonderful.' Elliott put down the phone and wished she could have offered to pay for a taxi, but she knew she mustn't. She'd learned that kind of tact from Philip.

When she first met him she had poured money on him, and he'd resented it. In fact, that had been another nail in the coffin of their relationship. Her money, or rather her mother's money.

Now she would spend the time until two o'clock putting away her new clothes. Promptly at two o'clock she heard a knock on the drawing-room door. 'It's me,' Barry said, standing in the doorway. She opened the door. He had a big bunch of spring flowers in his hand.

'Boy, you're punctual for a musician.' Elliott took the flowers and kissed him.

'I'm not usually on time, but I'm in love,' he answered. He bent down and pulled Elliott into his arms.

'Hey,' she said, pushing him off, 'if you go on like this we'll never get out of the hotel. I want to see some of London.' Then Elliott stared at Barry. There were shadows in her eyes. Warning shadows, tinged with black. 'Don't fall in love with me, Barry. I'm not for love. I want to have a good time with you and go on being friends. I like to have a man in every capital city in the world, but no one permanently. Do you understand that?'

Barry could feel the hurt in Elliott. He nodded. 'Sure I understand, Elliott. We'll just keep it light. I thought of taking you for a walk. Down by the river at Hammersmith. It's beautiful. Wrap up warm and we'll go.'

'OK, but I have to be back by five o'clock.' She'd told him about the trip the night before. 'Oh Barry, it's going to be such a blast.' Elliott wrapped herself in a black cashmere coat. She'd left her mink in the cupboard. Although she'd never wear the fur of an endangered animal, she could not see why for the life of her a coat made from a specially raised mink was any different from the leather obtained from cows to make boots and shoes. Still, there were more important things in life to argue about. The amount of bruised women Elliott saw when she came to England, for instance. At least in the States there were huge government grants for shelters. Judging by what she saw in the streets, not enough was being done in this country. But then, English people had always preferred their animals to women and children.

Outside the revolving door, Barry's little Renault Four stood gleaming in the winter sunlight, standing its ground defiantly while surrounded by sporting Jaguars and big rounded Rolls Royces. Elliott laughed out loud. 'Gee, she's pretty,' she said.

'Don't.' Barry put his finger to his lips. 'It's a he and his name is Hieronymus after Hieronymus Bosch, the artist.'

'My, you do know a lot of things, Barry. I'm dumb, really dumb.'

'No you're not. We just don't have as much history as Europeans. That's why I live over here. Except for Boston, there's not much around America. Yeah, we have lots of immigrant stories, and tales of how we founded the Wild West. Did you know that the West was founded by women, Jews and freed slaves? Most of the men coming down on the wagon trains were killed by the Indians. The slaves went west for the big tracts of free land, and the Jews were kicked out of the East because they were too successful. They all moved down and founded Santa Fe, New Mexico, and then on down to California, where they founded the movie business.'

They drove in a companionable silence along the river.

'There's the Tate Gallery.' Barry pointed to an imposing building. There were queues of people winding down the stairs.

'I've heard about the way the English all line up to get into places. Look at them all: it's so orderly.' Elliott watched them. There was no pushing and shoving. No, 'Hey bud, you watch it.'

'Yeah, it makes for a much calmer society than ours, but I find the English very menacing. You always feel that they'd like to break out but don't know how to. It's as if they all do as they're told, like chickens.'

'You don't like the English? My Mom brought me up to adore everything English.' Elliott was surprised. She'd never heard England criticized before.

Barry made a face. 'No, I don't much like them. They're a complacent lot. The people who work in the hotel are mostly Italian and fun. The working English have a good sense of black humour; it's the people who think they're top dog that I dislike. The people I have to play for night after night in the hotel. Most of them remind me of braying donkeys. They're the sort of people who supported Hitler and Mussolini. No, I don't like the English. I like the Irish, Scots and the Welsh but I'd nuke the flabby South.'

'Oh Barry, do let's talk about something else, honey. You're spoiling my dream.'

Barry smiled down at her. 'Elliott, you can't be a little girl, forever gazing into shadows with your finger in your mouth.'

Elliott giggled. 'How do you know I do that?' she said.

'I watched you from the first moment I met you. I saw you coming down the stairs and you had your finger on your lips. I looked up and I thought, "Now there's a mouth I'd like to kiss." And then –' his eyes were teasing – 'you picked me up.'

'Does that happen to you often?' Elliott was curious.

'Yep, but it's not often that I find somebody like you.'

'Are you married, Barry?' Elliott had wanted to ask that question ever since she awoke. She liked him, she realized. Sometimes after making love with a strange man she minded the smell of the man in her bed. But Barry smelled nice. A sort of new-mown-hay smell. She strained to hear his reply.

'Separated,' he said shortly. 'I have a little girl I love more than my life, but I can't stand my ex-wife. She won't divorce me, so I'm kind of stuck in limbo. I'm not the sort of man that can't do without a woman. I've always been very self-sufficient. I can clean, cook, sew . . .' He stared at his hands on the wheel. 'But I need to get Patricia out of my life. I need to get my sanity back. You have no idea what it's like to be sucked down into somebody else's madness.'

'I do,' Elliott's voice trembled. She felt that they were both on dangerous ground. 'My mom is like that. My dad ran off and left me with her. Just like you're doing to your daughter.'

'Maybe he left because he had to save his own life. If I'd stayed any longer I'd have ended up by beating her up. She was a holy terror. She'd scream and throw things. Dance in front of me naked and tell me I was a homo-sexual.' There was a terrible sadness in Barry's voice. 'The problem is that I really loved her. With all my heart. I want my heart back again. Do you know how to do that?'

Elliott put a comforting hand on Barry's arm. 'No, I don't, but I feel like that about my ex-husband. I drove him away with my bad behaviour. I screamed and I shrieked. I couldn't cope with his love for me. Maybe it's because he's English. But I do really love him. Still, we are able to be good friends, at least.' She stared at the mean streets around her. 'Where are we?'

'This is Hammersmith. Don't worry, it gets better when we get to Chiswick. Unfortunately, we've had lunatic architects for the last twenty years and they've fouled up the city. Soon we'll get back to classic architecture. Chiswick is pretty, and that's where I have an apartment.' He laughed. 'I've now learned to call it a flat. When I first arrived it took such a long time to learn English-English. I still haven't quite got the hang of it yet.'

'Is your ex-wife here or in America?'

'She's here. She lives in Ealing which is down the road, and I have the kid for the weekends. I have to take her back in the evenings because I'm working, but we have a great time together. She is learning to play the piano and she's very musical.'

Elliott watched the way his eyes shone as he talked about his daughter. She felt a deep sense of peace sitting beside this man. Maybe because he was a fellow American. Certainly he was lovely to look at. He had a big chunky body and firm hands which guided the car carefully but well. There was a fluent ease about him that interested Elliott. Most American men were socially insecure. They either hid their fear by a show of belligerence, or they dithered and ducked, trying to pretend they were in control. Barry was in control of himself, both in bed and out of it. She wondered if they'd make love in his apartment. Flat, she corrected herself. Then she grinned.

'What's the joke?' Barry asked.

'I was wondering if we get to make love at your place?'

'Before the walk or after?'

'After, or we might never get to walk, and I need the exercise after yesterday's huge tea and delicious dinner. And I've got tea again with the girls and two boys I'm going sailing with. It should be a very happy time for us all. I need an adventure. I get so restless if I don't get out and live a little. It's a break away from all the problems I have with Mom.'

'OK, we're here.' Barry turned down a small road and parked outside the door of a very English public house. They climbed out of the car and, after locking the door, they began to walk.

The river wall came up to Elliott's shoulders. She peered

over the wall and gazed down at the dirty river, and at the flotsam that had washed up on the river shore. Old plastic bottles. A doll's head and long wrinkled French letters. 'What a shame they don't keep the river clean. It's so beautiful but so dirty.'

They strolled down the pathway that led into an open grassy space, and then passed some beautiful, well-kept houses with manicured grounds. 'England's so strange.' Elliott's voice was wondering. 'There's little pockets of beautiful houses and shops, and then so much poverty.'

'Well, you know what they say about England? Most of the wealth is in the hands of a very few people.'

'Really? It's not like that in Houston. I've got girl friends who own their own businesses. I got girl friends that run bit charities. When I get back I'm going to work in a soup kitchen. I've done that before and I enjoy it. The place is full of bums and prostitutes but they're straight.'

Barry put a protective arm around Elliott's shoulder as they walked along the river. Then, without saying much, they returned to the car and set off for Barry's house. Elliott felt relaxed and cared for. This is what she missed out of marriage. Yes, lovers were a fine distraction, but being actually committed to another human being had a great comfort to it.

They made love slowly and carefully. Barry was a good lover and he was gentle. So many men thought of themselves as sexual athletes in bed. For many, Elliott knew it was a way of hiding their inability to orgasm. What was happening to men these days? she wondered. Certainly Barry was a lucky find. She looked at the picture of a little girl with big eyes and a face as delicate as a spring violet. 'She's a honey, Barry,' Elliott smiled at her lover.

'Yes, I know, and she has to live with that bitch.'

'Still, she has you, and that's more than I have.'

Barry hugged Elliott. 'Well now,' he said, opening the

front door of his little flat, 'you have me. I'll be your lover and your friend.'

'Somebody in England to hug and to kiss.' Elliott's sombre mood was broken.

Chapter Nineteen

Toby didn't want to go to tea with Elliott. It was not
Elliott's company he minded: he liked her. It was the quiet
hush of the hotel and the formality of it all. Also, it was
a life he'd left behind him, and he was uncomfortable
with reminders of the past.

'Do I have to go, Mum?' he pleaded plaintively when
he came in from school. 'We've got a gig tomorrow night
at the Hammersmith Arms and I need to practise.'

'Yes, you must come, Toby. We need to get to know
Elliott, and besides, I think she's probably lonely all by
herself in London.'

'Elliott's not lonely, Helen,' Marcia was laughing.
'She's got some man in her suite hot for her. Helen, grow
up and don't be such a baby. Women like Elliott are
wolves for men.'

'Wolves are faithful to each other, Marcia; besides, I
don't want to think ill of Elliott. I don't have a dirty mind
like you do, Marcia.' Helen was tired of Marcia teasing
her.

Toby gazed at his mother with surprise. He knew she
came in from work tired. She was such a competent
mother. He hated the way she always looked strained.
He hated the way she had to patch his clothes. His granny
had taught her all these things, and it was just as well.
Now Toby and his mother automatically put extra
water in the washing-up-liquid bottle to make it last
longer. They used white vinegar to clean the flat instead
of expensive branded cleaners. They used clear plastic
bags from the supermarket to cover the food in the fridge.
Toby never wanted to see a dented tin of anything again.

They bought tins that were wrinkled and suspicious at knock-down prices.

Marcia showed them the shops in the Bush where they could buy cheap fruit and vegetables just before closing time. The butcher believed they had a large dog, and gave them free bones, which Helen turned into nourishing soups. They were surviving, but only just.

Toby knew that it was his mother that needed Elliott's company, not the other way round. But he was her security. She had so enjoyed her dinner out. Toby had watched her all through the other evening, trying to still the hatred for his father in his heart. It was at times like that that his gorge rose and almost choked him.

Hatred, he decided, staring at his mother now, was the bitterest of biles. 'OK, Mum. I'll come. I just need to change. I don't want Cricket and I looking as if we're Black Panthers invading Elliott's posh hotel.'

'Hey dude, we look cool. I'm not changing.' Cricket was slouched against the wall by the kitchen door. These days slouching against walls was the cool thing to do. Cricket hardly ever stood upright. Toby shook his head. 'No, Cricket, I'm not you. When whites try to look black in a situation it doesn't work. I'd just look silly. It's OK in the Bush, but not at the hotel. I'm changing into my tweed jacket and grey trousers, and then I'll feel OK.'

Slowly Toby was finding his own style. He no longer followed Cricket with slavish devotion. Their friendship survived disagreement. They balanced each other out. When they practised their martial arts with Fats, Toby could take Cricket on, flying feet and all. Cricket had the long spidery arms, but the weight now belonged to Toby. He'd filled out and he'd learned to use his weight properly.

Concentrate, project your light and then jump into it. One of Fats's rules for survival. Toby used the light more and more. He knew his mother needed him to accompany her; he could feel her uncertainty. With Fats's help he learned to be compassionate towards his mother; instead of his former irritation he felt love. Try as he might he could not refuse her. She was so defenceless and so very vulnerable. It was his father that had done that to her. All that damage in the twelve years of marriage. He remembered her when she was much younger. A laughing, plump country girl. She tasted of the sea that she loved so much. They spent so many holidays running on the sands and playing in the little boat.

Still, he comforted himself as he went off to change into his Savoy gear. They had the holiday ahead of them. That was the one thing that kept the light in his mother's eyes. If he saw it fading, he brought the subject around to their sailing adventure. Now she could spend tea-time with Elliott discussing her favourite subject.

The atmosphere at tea-time was quite different from dinner. It was more relaxed and more cosy. Both boys sat on the edge of the little chairs, struggling to hold the dainty tea-cups with their large fingers.

'What have you been doing since we saw you last?' Helen was making conversation.

'I went to the river.' There was a sexy smile in Elliott's eyes, and even Helen realized that Elliott had not been alone. 'The walk was beautiful and we had an early cup of tea at a place called the Maids of Honour. It was such a cute place.' Helen thought that Elliott was like a glass of good champagne. She bubbled and frothed. Her energy gave her an aura of excitement. She was going to be fun to travel with. Helen began to relax.

'Tell us a bit more about the boat.' Helen sat back in her chair and frowned at Cricket who was stuffing brown fingers of smoked-salmon sandwiches down his throat. Marcia sipped her tea and wished Helen didn't look so much like an expectant child. Helen was wearing a pure wool dress. She had a Peter Pan collar around her neck and long puffy sleeves. Why did English middle-class, middle-aged women dress like teenagers, Marcia wondered?

Laura, Paul's mistress, was of a younger generation. When she'd first seen the woman, Marcia had thought she looked really glamorous. Now she didn't look much different to Helen. Maybe Englishmen drove their wives back into their childhoods. Helen must have been incredibly dependent on Paul. When she'd first moved into her flat she had been unable to change a lightbulb or even put a plug on her iron. Really, English women were hopeless when it came to men. Helen needed to toughen up. But then Marcia softened when she watched Helen's eyes shining. 'Does the boat have a proper stove so I can cook?' Helen asked anxiously.

'Sure, I checked with the owner. We have a fridge with a nice compartment so I can have ice with my vodka. I drink gallons of the stuff, by the way. What do you two boys drink?'

'We drink gallons of Special Brew.' Cricket snorted with laughter. 'And we get plastered, don't we, Tobe?'

'No you don't, Cricket,' his mother frowned.

'Yes I do, Mum.'

There was a moment of embarrassed silence. Elliott broke the silence with a laugh. 'Deal is, boys, that nobody gets drunk on board. What we drink or do elsewhere is our own business and nobody else's. OK? Cricket?'

Elliott put a cigarette in her mouth. Cricket leaned forward and snapped open his black Zippo lighter. Elliott gazed at him through the flame. She crossed her leg high at the knee. She leaned forward so that Cricket could see the tops of her big breasts. She smiled as she watched his hand shake.

'The boys are both underage and in England they are not allowed to buy alcohol.' Marcia's voice was cool and level.

Cricket sensed that Elliott had put down the Queen of Hearts on the tea-table. 'Sure thing, Elliott,' he said pleasantly. He would let the card lie on the table under the watchful eye of his mother.

'Don't throw a hissy fit, Marcia. I'm only teasing the boys.' She too would let the card lie on the table. Time enough ahead of both of them. Besides, boys of that age could be difficult. Hard to lose and Elliott wanted fun. Lots and lots of fun and no regrets. She sucked hard on her cigarette and thought of Barry's long slim hands on her belly. 'More tea anyone?' she asked.

Chapter Twenty

Slowly Toby began to get to know Fats. Inside this warm, ebullient man sat a very shy child. 'My mentor is coming from Tibet,' he confided in Toby one day. 'He's a monk called Gaylang Rimpoche, but he won't use the Rimpoche.'

'What does Rimpoche mean?' Toby asked.

'It means that you no longer have to be reincarnated. You've finished your task on this earth and you can leave behind your fleshy envelope and move on into the universe. Isn't that an exciting idea?'

'I don't know,' Toby said doubtfully. 'It means that you die, doesn't it?'

'There is no such thing as death in the Western sense, Toby. Nobody dies; you just move on. You are not only responsible for your birth partners because you get to choose your incarnation, but you are also responsible for how you die.'

'How do you know that for sure?'

'Because I had a vision when I was a child. I haven't told anybody about it because they would think I was nuts. Here, come with me and I'll show you my paintings.'

'I didn't know you painted, Fats.'

Fats smiled at Toby over his shoulder. 'There's a lot you don't know about me, Toby. I keep to myself. I've learned the hard way.' Toby didn't feel he should ask any more questions. Whatever Fats had learned the 'hard way', it had obviously left him scarred. We are all of us scarred in one way or another, Toby thought as he followed Fats. They walked into the back of the army drill-hall where they had their lessons. Fats pushed open a big door and Toby followed him into the room.

'Gosh, Fats, they are beautiful.' He walked up to the row of canvases that faced him. He gazed at the beautifully painted scenes of men and women in traditional Chinese robes. 'They really are marvellous,' Toby said, stunned. He could feel a sense of peace emanating from the room. 'It's so peaceful in here, Fats.' Toby felt as if his ribcage was being squeezed. All the rage and violence in his body seemed to be warring; he heard a dull roaring behind his ears.

'I'm going to teach you how to meditate, Toby. Here, sit in this chair and look at the flame on this candle.' Fats moved to a sideboard and brought back a long slim candle. He stood for a moment, his head hanging down and then, having said something to his soul, he lit the candle.

He lowered himself into a chair in front of Toby and said quietly, 'Now look at the light of the candle. Half close your eyes and empty your mind. Breathe from your stomach and try to get the light to leave the candle and enter your heart.'

After a few minutes of silence Toby said, 'Fats, I can't get my mind to stay still.'

'That's perfectly normal. Humans, especially Westerners, have minds like breadbins, full of crumbs. Now imagine taking a little brush and a tiny dustpan and start sweeping up all the crumbs. As you sweep, leave only darkness behind.'

Toby sat entranced. He did succeed in leaving only darkness behind for a few sweet moments. 'I did it,' he exulted. There was no sound from Fats. Toby watched his face in the candlelight. Fats must have some West Indian blood in his veins, Toby thought. He was white-skinned but he had 'natty hair', as Marcia called it. The silence was not aching, but Toby felt a peace steal over him. For the first time in many months he felt as if life were sweet again. His father was in a faraway place where he couldn't disapprove of him. His mother was fine and he saw a vision of her smiling face. Life was whole again. He smiled in the darkened room and he felt love for the candle and its brave little light.

'Better now, Toby?'

'Much better thanks, Fats.' He was silent for a moment and then he said, 'Are you my mentor, Fats?'

'Yes, Toby. I've known you and your mother for a very long time. Aeons, in fact. That's why we are so comfortable together. Now you are going on a long journey together and you will discover things about yourselves that you need to know. Remember my first rule. Harm no living thing.'

'Yes, I always will.'

'Then learn the next rule. Your life cannot be dominated by passion or lust. The soul must lead the body into the light. Stay on the path, Toby. Others will try to come and steal your light. Don't let them. Only you can travel your path. People can join you for a while, but when they want to deviate from the light, let them. You must bear the pain and the sorrow of their leaving, but nothing lasts for ever.'

Toby sat and let the words pour over him. Nothing lasts for ever. Not his life in Swiss Cottage, not his love for Louise, or his parents' marriage. Life was like a broad flat stream, endlessly flowing. Like the river Thames. All history slid down that river. Kings and Queens on huge Tudor barges went to their deaths down that river. The river never acknowledged them. It just carried its terrified charges to their fate.

'What about fate? The things that happen that I can't help or avoid?'

'There is no such thing as fate, Toby. You choose; everything that happens to you is a consequence of that choice. You have free will, and that's the most terrifying thing about this world. If you decide to populate your world with bad people, then bad things will happen.'

'I see,' Toby said slowly. 'Or at least I think I see.'

'Meditate every day, Toby, and next week the grand master will be here and you will be in the presence of great learning.'

'I can't wait, Fats.'

'Now go, Toby, and remember that anger creates attachment.' Toby knew he was referring to his anger against his father. 'Anger is very bad for the body. Anger wears out the muscles and creates little crystals in the joints that will eventually cause all sorts of arthritis and rheumatism.'

Toby got to his feet and walked to the door. 'Thanks, Fats,' he said slowly. He left Fats sitting with his candle and walked home.

'I've learned such a lot from Fats, Mum. Today he taught me not to be so angry and bitter with Dad.'

'Good, Toby. Your dad can't help being what he is, and in his own way he's trying to reach out to you.' She didn't have the heart to tell Toby that his father was trying to get the alimony reduced. His young heart was already too bruised, and she did not want to add to his burdens. 'Give your wrinkly old mum a hug, darling,' she said.

'You're not old, Mum, you're beautiful and I love you.' The words brought a warm ray of sunshine into Helen's heart.

Chapter Twenty-one

'Woe, he's seriously big,' Toby whispered to Cricket. They were both sitting on the brown-scarred floor of the gym. Behind them were rows and rows of people, also cross-legged. Gaylang sat, huge and seemingly made of stone.

'What have you come to see?' he asked the audience. 'Do you think I can do any good for anybody but myself?' He raised his hands and spread them, palms facing outwards. Toby gazed at the strongly marked hands. They were big with large knuckles.

These were hands that were used to study fine books and hold delicate pens. These were not hands that had slaved and toiled. Even so big, there was a delicacy about the hands.

Gaylang left a very long pause between his words. Toby felt as if he'd been sitting cross-legged for years. Maybe for all his life. He felt a fluttering of excitement in his heart. His cheeks were red. He watched Gaylang very carefully. The man was raking the room with his eyes. Toby believed that Gaylang could see right into his lust-filled heart. He blushed. I'll never wank again, he promised God. I'll keep my thoughts pure. Then he found himself smiling. Of course he'd wank again.

'What makes you smile, child?' Toby jumped. 'Er . . . nothing. I just thought of something funny.' He was now purple with embarrassment. Cricket was whooping with laughter beside him. 'He's thinking about girls,' he spluttered. 'He's always thinking about girls.' Gaylang smiled. He had a wonderful moon of a smile. It rose from his mouth and climbed up his face until his eyebrows shot up into his bald head. 'Ha, ha, ha,' he guffawed loudly. Several purists in the audience gasped in disbelief. Grand masters, in their opinion, should always be impassive. 'Sex is good for the soul and for the body.' Gaylang beamed cheerfully at the thought. Obviously celibacy was not one of his disciplines.

Ohhhh. Cricket was rolling on the floor. Drumming his heels. He spun on one hand and then flipped over. He was beating the floor with his fists. 'I like this guy, he's super cool,' Cricket yelled.

'Shut up, Cricket.' Toby was embarrassed by Cricket. But then Cricket often embarrassed him. The rest of the band were as loud and as careless as Cricket. Rollo sitting behind them was also convulsed with laughter.

'Quiet now.' Gaylang held up his hand. 'How do you feel now, boys, after the laughing?'

'Great,' Cricket said cheerfully.

'And you, child?'

Toby tried to smile but he felt more like crying. There was such a tender quality about the man. He felt for this unknown man an emotion he'd never felt for his father. He blinked away his tears. 'Fine, thank you.' He knew he sounded prim and very English, but he was afraid that if he let go he'd put his head on the floor of the gym and cry for the rest of his life, the pain was so bad.

Gaylang sat looking into Toby and Toby sat letting him look. It was as if, for so long, Toby had had to wear a shield over the rejection from his father. At times the shield made him feel desperate, but he knew trying to reach out to Paul emotionally would only result inevitably in Paul lashing back at him. Toby's crime, unspoken and judged, was that he had chosen to love his mother. His father would never forgive him for that choice. Toby was not born a Beckett, he was his mother's child and in looking at his son, Paul saw his wife's face. Indeed, Paul's mother had hinted widely that Toby was not Paul's child but another man's bastard (though the word 'bastard' would never disgrace his paternal grandmother's lips).

'Fats,' Gaylang turned to Fats, who was sitting behind him, 'you take care of this boy and you teach him.' He grinned at Cricket. 'Also that rascal. He likes girls too much.'

'Ohhh, I really do,' and Cricket was off again.

Toby left the hall on a tide of rising happiness. 'Let's go back to my place and make music,' he said. He saw Fats in the doorway. 'How about coming home and cooking curried goat for us?'

'Sure thing, boy,' and Fats hurried to get his coat.

Chapter Twenty-two

Toby felt he'd found a new friend in life. He attended the teaching sessions every evening. He loved the evening meditations. He particularly enjoyed his quiet moments just kneeling beside Gaylang. He was aware that the monk had opened Toby's mind to a far wider horizon than he'd ever thought possible.

The first real breakthrough in Toby's thinking came when he asked Gaylang why there was so much tension between his father and himself. 'Because, Toby, you don't have any respect for your father. Without a man creates respect in other people, there is no ability to love or to be loved.'

During the rest of the session, Toby withdrew into his meditation. He watched the candle very carefully. Soon he forgot the other people in the room. Some were shuffling. There was a cough in the distance but he was lost in the meaning of meditation.

He found himself swallowed up in the word respect. Somewhere between the letter s and the letter p he had a glimmer of understanding. His father didn't love anybody except himself. When that thought was made conscious, he felt an icy blast of loneliness. It was as if he'd misspelled the word respect for most of his life, and now he could read it clearly.

He shifted his position and then he heard Gaylang's voice internally. 'Well done, Toby,' his voice said.

'So you can talk to me from the inside and the outside?' Toby was amazed.

'Yes, because there is no inside and there is no outside. They are all one and the same thing, Toby.'

'I don't understand,' said Toby, puzzled.

'It's all a matter of perception,' Gaylang patiently explained. 'Most people only live in the external world. Your friend Cricket is an example. For the moment his life is centred around his music and sex. But you have an exceptional ability to live in your internal world. It will bring you great rewards, but you will suffer more intensely.

'It is far easier to live only for external happenings. To feed the needs of the body and not of the soul. Your soul is ageless and eternal. The strength of your soul is in its capacity to love. You have a very big capacity to give and to receive love, that is why your work at the moment is to love your father unconditionally. He is unlovable. You are his son. Learn to accept him as he is and not as you want him to be.'

Abruptly, the voice ceased its internal dialogue and Toby slowly came back to the present moment. He turned his head to look at Cricket. Cricket was fast asleep, his head on his left hand. It was a very Cricket pose. Cricket was lucky, Toby thought, sitting cross-legged in the gloom. Nothing bothered him much, except chasing girls. That and loving his mother.

'Mum, Gaylang said that I must learn to love Dad *because* he's unlovable. That's a new idea for me. I've always tried to love him because I want him to change and be lovable.'

Helen held her breath. These conversations were always very difficult for her. She wanted to say: 'Toby, your father is a complete shit and Gaylang is right.' She knew she couldn't do that. She'd attended enough sessions with Fats and with Gaylang to recognize the truth of leaving negative things unsaid. Better for Toby to find his own way to the truth of his father's nature. To bad-mouth Paul would only cause her internal world to become sullied and blackened.

'Hopefully, Toby, you will in time understand the things that went on in your father's life to make him what he is. I'm not making excuses for him. Nobody has a perfect childhood, and at some point we have to take responsibility for our own behaviour and not blame everybody else.' She sighed. 'Laura is in a complete state. She's on her way over. She says she is sick of him and his women, but I don't think she's ready to leave yet.'

'Laura is different to you Mum. You have a world of your own. We lived alone most of the time because he came in late and then went out to the pub. You read your books and did the garden. Do you remember when you went through a phase of stripping all that pine furniture: our hands were wrecked!' Toby smiled. 'I can think of lots of happy times we had together. You don't need to have a man in your life. You're much more like Marcia. Laura can't manage if she doesn't have somebody to love and kiss her is how she put it to me.'

'But then, if she'd had a good mother and father like I did, she would have had sufficient love as a child not to go looking for it.' Helen shook her head. 'It's so sad, this generation of women. They told men they were equal in every way. They let men into their homes and their beds, and in return men ran away from all responsibility.'

'Not men like Fats, Mum. There are good men around. Especially Gaylang. He told me that he would be with us always, and that if we needed him we would hear his voice. I've already done that and it's exciting.'

'Gaylang has helped me find a lot of peace.' Helen's voice was gentle. 'I've got back a lot of feeling and am less resentful. What I learned this week, and I needed to learn, was that I got lost in that whole material trip with Paul. It mattered to me that all the plates matched. Boy, Toby, what a madness. Yes, I do like my silver tea-set, but not because it's valuable. I just love the shine of it.

That's OK. It's when you lay the table to impress other people that it's wrong. You should lay the table because you want to impress yourself.

'Give me some time with Laura and then I've got to check out the roast beef and make Yorkshire pudding. Elliott, Marcia, Fats and Cricket are coming over for dinner.'

Toby wandered off into his bedroom. He liked the room now. His old posters were still in place, and now others had been added. He also had a big Samurai sword, a present from Fats, on the far wall. He'd booted out the old bedframe and in its place he had a double mattress on the floor with a black duvet and sheets and two black pillow cases. The room looked really cool. He'd bought a second-hand sound system from Rollo. He had an old reel-to-reel and could tape and edit his songs on it. 'Yeah,' he breathed, 'it's cool.' Then he smelt the gently simmering roast beef wafting from the kitchen. He was suddenly deliciously hungry.

Helen ran around the kitchen, trying to set things to rights. It was not that Toby was particularly untidy; he was just a boy. Boys never seemed to understand that things needed to be put back in the same place. Now Helen was looking for her scissors. Toby probably borrowed them to rewire something in his sound system. She muttered and tutted to herself, waiting for the doorbell to ring. When it did, she popped the kettle on the stove, wiped her hands on her blue and white checked pinafore, and opened the door.

Laura, as usual, looked distraught. 'Oh Helen, I'm so confused.'

'Have a cup of tea, Laura, and tell me all about it.' Helen knew the confusion Paul was capable of creating in any woman that tried to love him. Paul was an expert in keeping everyone in a hysterical uproar.

Laura flopped into a chair at the end of the kitchen

table. Her hair was lank and untidy. 'Who is it this time?' Helen inquired.

'Oh, it's some little woman he met in the pub. I knew he was at it again because he always buys himself new shirts and ties. He's into wearing fashionable jeans and American T-shirts. I tried to tell him he looks ridiculous, but there's no point.'

'But he was dressed like that when you knew him. Men always seem to need to find a woman at least twenty years younger when they hit forty, and then they think somehow they can be young again.'

'Yes, but then . . . Helen, I didn't know that he'd spend so much time sleeping, and if he isn't sleeping he's watching the television or eating. I tell you, there's precious little time for making love.' Laura paused and looked embarrassed. 'I'm sorry, Helen . . .' her voice trailed off.

'Don't be, Laura. Paul was no different with me. I was his mummy tucked up and at home, and the rest of the world was full of wild adventures. Women to be snared and tormented. Women to be manipulated so that they might fight over him.' Helen made a face. 'That's why I didn't fight. There seem to be two types of unfaithful men. One type bonks about and confesses each time to his wife. He expects it to be a big drama, and then to be forgiven and bonk his wife once again. That's Paul.

'The other type of man keeps the whole thing a big secret. He gets off on the fact that he's having illicit sex and his wife doesn't know about it. Those men can have affairs all their lives and the poor woman never guesses.'

'Men are such bastards.' Laura picked up her mug of tea.

'No, Laura.' Helen's voice was cool. 'If there were no treacherous women, there'd be no unfaithful men.' Helen stared at Laura. 'You wouldn't have been in this mess if you hadn't gone for Paul. You see, at some point you have to learn not to define yourself only through a man. If you do you're going to end up bitter and hurt.'

'Yes, but Helen, I want to get married and have children. You're OK, you've got Toby.'

'Yes, because I was never confused by what I wanted. I wanted to fall in love, get married, have children and live happily ever after.' Helen sipped her tea. 'I often wonder how many lives Lipton's tea-bags have saved? Certainly mine. If I'm miserable I make a big hot mug of tea. Add some milk and sit here with my feet on the rungs of my chair and just watch the steam rising. It's so wonderfully comforting.'

'I wish I could be comforted so easily. What shall I do, Helen?'

'If you tell someone what to do in their lives, you block their path, Laura. I can share what I did with you. But what you do must be your own decision. Fats taught me that.'

'I know what you did, Helen, but you're a strong woman.'

Helen laughed. 'Why do people always call a woman who takes action "a strong woman"? Poor Marcia is always being told that. Actually, Marcia's no stronger than any other woman. We both agree we're both shit-scared of everything but not frightened of anything. That's our new motto. Laura, I got out. What you do is up to you.'

'I love him so desperately, Helen. I can't imagine life without him. We have so many things we enjoy together. Music, poetry, books.'

Helen sat quietly, just listening to the litany. Thank goodness, she thought, that's not me sitting at the end of the table saying exactly the same things. It had taken Helen years to realize that Paul was not the least interested in books. Yes, he'd read a Booker Prize entry so he could mention it in dinner-party chats, or read all the book reviews and sound as if he'd read the actual books.

As for music? He had plenty of classical and jazz CDs, but actually he watched television. Endless amounts of television. Nights filled with the sound of American voices. Guns, screams. Helen usually lay on their bed and read her books. Laura would find out in time. Paul was in no hurry to boot Laura out. She had a beautiful loft and money. Two things that made sense to Paul.

'Laura, I've got to cook dinner. I've Fats and other friends coming over.'

'You're lucky, Helen, I've got no friends. Paul leaves me at home and goes out.'

'I'm not lucky, Laura. Nobody's lucky. I just rebuilt my life and took responsibility for myself and my child. I'm not lucky. It was bloody hard work, and you're right. I had no friends but I do now.'

Laura got to her feet and wordlessly hugged Helen. Helen felt again the desperate clinging of the woman. 'No wonder men take advantage of her,' Helen thought. 'She's another needy woman and they can feel it.' She kissed Laura and gently pushed her out of the door.

Sitting at his mother's kitchen table, Toby began to feel at peace with himself. He watched Fats eating. Fats was a good man and he felt a surge of affection for him. There were precious few men like Fats and Gaylang in Toby's life.

'Gaylang took a real shine to you, Toby. He told me that he is expecting great things from you.'

'You mean, he's going to be rich and famous,' Rollo interjected.

'No, Rollo,' Fats said patiently. 'Being rich in cash is unimportant. He means that Toby will have a valuable spiritual life.'

'Oh.' There was a terrible disappointment in Rollo's voice. He was a huge boy with big feet and an enormous smile. The girls in the gigs raved over him. He was much the most popular boy in the band, but completely uninterested in the girls that surrounded him after the gigs. Rollo loved to practise karate; he was already a black belt. Although he'd only been with the group for a short time, everybody loved him. Helen in particular adored him, and in return Rollo loved her back.

'More roast beef, Rollo?'

'Yes, mam.' Rollo lifted his bare and empty plate and gazed at Helen.

'Don't call me mam, Rollo. My name is Helen.'

'Yes, Mrs Beckett.'

'Oh, Rollo, you're impossible. Why can't you call me Helen?'

'Because my aunt don't like for me to talk that way to a lady. It's not respectful, and my aunt says respectful is what I got to be all the time.' He grinned as Helen piled the meat on his plate. 'I don't often get to eat real beef. My aunty is real poor.'

'So are we.' Helen smiled at the boy. 'This is a treat for Elliott.' She looked across at Elliott who was deep in conversation with Cricket. 'We'll leave from Elba and then go through the Straits of Messina. I've never done this trip before. I know the Florida waters and the Cayman Islands. They can be treacherous, but the Ionian sea . . . ?'

'"The wine-dark Ionian sea,"' Helen quoted. 'I wish I could remember who said that.'

'Have you ever been to JA? I remember it from when I was a child.'

'Sure I go there all the time, Cricket.'

'What's it like now in JA?' Cricket was leaning forward to hear Elliott's reply.

'It's beautiful, Cricket, it's really beautiful.'

'D'you know any Rastas?'

'Yeah, I go up into the mountains and smoke with them.'

'You smoke dope with Rastafari?' Cricket's voice was incredulous. 'Wow, that must be exciting. Do they all want to go back to Africa?'

'Some did, and found that the Africans would not accept them. So they came back sadder and wiser.' Cricket let out a long, slow whistle. 'They must have been really turved.'

'Turved?' Elliott looked puzzled.

'Yeah, topsy-turvy,' Cricket explained. 'Sort of upside down, disappointed.'

'What language is that?' Elliott was laughing.

'It's street. We all talk it, and just as other people suss what we're doing, we change all the words again. Like the police used to be called Rads, now we've changed the word for the police to Control. That's what they do. They try to control everything in the Bush but they don't control anything. They just think they do. We control the Bush. It's our yard.'

Elliott watched Cricket's face and she saw a very hurt young boy. 'Your British police are nothing like as bad as our state troopers. Mind you, I had a boyfriend who was a state trooper and he was great, but on the whole they are very violent because they have to be. Everybody in America carries guns. The state troopers know it's either kill or be killed. It's no way to live.'

'Why is America so violent?' Toby joined in the conversation.

Elliott shrugged. 'I don't know,' she said.

'But I do know that men are violent to women at home in a way you don't see here.'

'Maybe it's because you American women stood up for your rights long before we did?' Marcia gazed at Elliott through a haze of cigarette smoke. 'Also, all we see on our television sets are American programmes about men beating, torturing and raping women. It's no wonder the children grow up violent and disturbed.'

'Sure, and of course we have that awful American puritanism to deal with. You'd be appalled at how grey and bleak life is in America. It's like one huge great shopping mall. They have crack shoot-outs behind my block of apartments. No kids playing in gardens like you see here. It's too dangerous. They get kidnapped and sold off for porno movies.'

'It's getting like that here.' Fats smiled shyly at Elliott. 'My kids are telling me that some of their yards are being run by hooligans. Men who call themselves Rastas but aren't. They are bringing coke and crack into the schools. Rasta men are non-violent. Their religion is peaceful. They are originally farmers and don't eat meat.'

'Down my way I don't have no trouble because I'm big,' Rollo explained. 'But I hate it when they spread you over the police car. I get humbled.'

'They do that to us too, Rollo.' Toby was filled with compassion for his friend. 'At least in the Bush everybody gets done over. I used to think the police were there to give directions and tell you the time. That's when I lived in Swiss Cottage.' Toby blushed at the memory of what a nerd he'd been. 'Still, Cricket taught me how to run like the wind.'

Dinner was finished, and after long, lingering conversations over the coffee cups, Elliott left. 'Next time I get to see you guys,' she said, 'it'll be Easter, and we'll be on the boat.' Through a chorus of hugs and goodbyes she left. Helen watched her leave the house. The streetlight clung to her expensive black coat.

'I don't have any money, but I'm happier than Elliott is, even if she's loaded with money.'

'Dosh isn't what makes you happy,' Toby replied. 'Come on, Cricket, you're in my house and we have to do the pots.'

'I still don't feel it's cool for a man to stand at a kitchen sink, Cricket,' Fats interrupted.

'Don't be such a wally. Men can do anything in the house a woman can do.'

'No they can't. They can't have babies. Only women can do that. Housework is women's work.'

'That's bull, Junior. I don't make you wash up because you destroy everything around you. I want some pots left.' Marcia made a face.

'I help my aunty or she'd box my ears.' Rollo looked very solemn. 'She boxes hard, too,' he said, 'though she's only a little thing,' he grinned.

'I used to box Junior's ears, but he's grown too tall.'

'You wash, Cricket, and I'll dry, and Rollo can put everything away.' Toby very much wanted to go into his room to meditate.

Chapter Twenty-three

'What do you think?' Helen was relaxing with an early cup of coffee in Marcia's kitchen after work.

'Think about what?' Marcia said.

'Elliott, silly.'

Marcia was preparing the evening meal. 'I don't know, Helen, but I don't want her to have a fling with Junior. He's bad enough with women as it is.'

'She wouldn't do that, would she?' Helen sat straight in her chair, her hands clenched around her coffee cup. She knew all about the toy-boy syndrome that infested the tabloids, but she realized now that she was shocked by it.

'Oh Helen, don't be such a baby. Of course Elliott would. Elliott's the sort of woman that takes any man who offers.'

'How do you know that?'

'It takes one to know one, honey.' Marcia's brown eyes sparkled. 'She gives off heat does Elliott, and Junior's definitely interested.'

'How are you going to stop them? I'm sure – at least I hope – Toby doesn't even think of making love to women of that age.'

'Of course he does, Helen. Boys of their age think of nothing else but sex.'

'Are you sure, Marcia? I certainly didn't when I was their age, but then we didn't have the magazines and television blaring sex. As for the sex education classes at Toby's school, they weren't about sex education as far as I understood it, but about how to have sex.' Helen put her cup down on the kitchen table. 'I don't know if I'll ever understand what happened in the last ten to fifteen years. I was technically a virgin when I married Paul. All I'd been into was heavy petting at parties. Now Toby's no longer innocent at fifteen. My mother didn't believe homosexuals existed. I knew they did because I had a girl friend at school who told me about herself and her friends. But it was a private matter, and now they get called "batty men", on the streets and in the Bush.

'Maybe I was innocent because I was brought up in Hove. Life was so easy then. Boys respected you and you could say no. Now they think they can jump into bed with any woman; and where has that got women, I'd like to know?'

'Nowhere as far as I'm concerned. I don't hand myself over like Elliott does any more.' Marcia's voice was sad. 'I realized far too late that the only liberation that happened in my time was liberation for men.

'We got stuck with the babies and the bills. Still, I'll make sure that Junior takes care of his woman if he ever settles down. As for abortion, I told him, "Those are my grandchildren you're talking about." If he gets a girl pregnant I told him I'll take the child. Yeah, I can see abortion is a way out for some women but, for me and mine, I don't see it. So far I've been lucky: in all his bragging he's been careful, and none of the women have got pregnant. The trouble with Junior is that he's in competition with his father's reputation as a womanizer. I don't want him to be a bunny rabbit like his dad. But then all I can do is wait and see.'

'Toby's not like that, but then I feel guilty sometimes about his first girlfriend, Louise. The girl he's with is nice enough, but he fell for Louise so hard. She came at such a bad time for him. To lose her because I separated from Paul . . .' She could see Marcia's eyebrows raising dangerously. 'I know, Marcia, I know; but even if she would have left him in the end, it was the way it happened for

Toby. And I know my guilt will make you furious, but I can't help it. I just have this awful albatross around my neck. I'm hoping that this boat trip will give me a chance to hand the albatross to its rightful owner. Hopefully he'll rise from the sea and hold out his hand and I'll cut the bird loose and give it back.' Helen laughed uncertainly. 'I suppose I don't make any sense as usual.'

'First answer. Give Toby time. He's a quiet boy but he'll find his feet. Yes, I do get angry with your guilt trips. They do no one any good, least of all yourself. Third answer. Yes, I do think the boat trip will be good for you because you'll have to make your own decisions. Even now when I hear Paul on the phone bullying you, instead of telling him to fuck off, you say, "Yes, Paul," like a small child, and go and do whatever he wants. You've got to stop, Helen. You've got to get a sense of self. You're not just an extension of other people's needs.

'Anyway a boat is such a confined space, we'll all find out a lot about each other. If there are any problems I don't intend to leave the boat. Finally, it's Gaylang's last night tonight and we've been invited to go with Fats.'

'Poor Fats.' Helen remembered his face when he told her that he'd been found abandoned as a young child in a paper bag at Charing Cross railway station. 'You know, Marcia, Fats really loves Gaylang. He first met him when he was in a hostel and he was sixteen years old. On drugs and in trouble with the police. It was Gaylang who rescued him, not his social worker.'

'Hmmmph,' Marcia snorted. 'Last year the school social worker called me in about Junior. She said he had an attitude problem. She was the one with an attitude problem. She looked like a man and smelled bad. A bath, I told her, would do her no harm, and a face transplant.' Marcia grinned at the memory.

'You told her that?' Helen was lost in admiration.

'Marcia, you're brave. Those social workers terrify me. They behave as if they own everybody.'

'They do,' Marcia said grimly. 'They make a point of bullying the black community. Taking away our children and stuffing them into foster homes and children's homes. Our kids are fodder for their loony revolution.'

'Marcia, isn't that a bit extreme?'

Marcia shook her head angrily. 'One day, Helen, you'll get there. No, it isn't a bit extreme. There's been a plan kicking around the Department of Social Services to make sure that our kids remained uneducated, unemployable and delinquent. This way the ghetto gets bigger and bigger. More and more jobs for the boys and girls who run the schools, the social services, the children's homes and the prisons. I'm part of the ghetto. Junior and me. That's why we understand it all so well. Them's the runnings, as they say round here. Come on,' she took Helen's arm and then gave her a hug, 'let's go and meditate. Anyway, if Paul gives you a hard time, you can always count on me. I'll shriek at him.'

Helen smiled. 'Thanks but no thanks, Marcia. That's something I've got to learn to do for myself.'

Helen left Marcia's flat to change her clothes. She walked out into the clear crisp evening air. It was now early February, and the pavements were still hard and iron-clad with frost. London reminded Helen of an old lady with a bonnet clamped to her grey hair. Frost studded the windows of the houses around her. Hers was a supposedly poor area in the Bush, but for Helen now it was home. It was at times diverse in its ethnicity, and often perversely violent, but she no longer felt afraid.

Years ago, it seemed, she lived that other life. The life where she talked of Peter Jones or she shopped for Cash's name-tapes for Toby's school uniform. Looking back at all the talking she did with her friends, she now knew that they had never had anything interesting to say.

Now with her new friends she had issues to sort out. Did she believe in abortion? In Swiss Cottage she would have said absolutely not, but now she wasn't sure. Now she knew women who had no choice but to have abortions. Fats helped women to have abortions. He listened and he counselled them. Now Helen knew that she would still not have an abortion herself under any circumstances, but she would willingly help other women if they asked for help.

How could she have lived so cut off from what was happening in the real world? It was easy, really. Thousands of women lived like she did. Behind the glossy front door, a middle-class paper in one hand. Reassuring discussions about the problems of the poor and unfortunate in the centre pages. The message was always there. The message was subliminal: This sort of thing doesn't happen to our sort of people. Now Helen knew why she had been so abruptly dropped by her 'friends'. She was no longer Quite One Of Us, Dear. She'd moved down the scale to join those women and their children who interested her friends at dinner parties. The hotly discussed issues. Female circumcision in Africa with the first course. Date rape and sexual harassment with the second course. Any disease of the immune system for pudding, followed by a huge row with the men at the table about single-parent motherhood. Well, single-parent motherhood or fatherhood sucked. She could attest to that.

Before she left the house this morning, Paul telephoned. Yet again, Laura was threatening to throw him out. How is it, she wondered as she let herself into her flat, that you leave your ex-husband and suddenly he thinks he's got a free therapist. 'If she throws me out I'll have to take my rent out of your alimony payments,' he whined.

Helen had a bus to catch. She didn't want to arrive at work all upset. 'Let's cross that bridge, Paul, when we have to,' she said as sweetly as possible. Now, switching on the fire in the freezing sitting room, she paused. The world was divided into bullies and the bullied. Paul was a bully, but he couldn't bully her if she refused to be bullied. Who the hell wants to spend the rest of their lives fighting their corner to keep from being bullied? Men seemed destined to bully. It was probably all that testosterone in their genetic make-up. Better, she reminded herself, far better to stay friends with men. She pulled on a grey pair of slacks and a thick grey jumper. Once a man went to bed with a woman, he seemed to think he owned her. She left the flat and ran to the gym.

'I'm here,' she whispered to Toby, and slipped him a bar of chocolate.

'Thanks, Mum.' His voice was grateful. He sat quietly beside his mother. The first bite of chocolate stilled the pangs of hunger and satiated his nervousness after a day at school, but above all he felt an overwhelming feeling of gratitude to this woman who loved him in such minute detail. Only Louise called up the same overwhelming feelings. Day by day the loss of her was lessening. He supposed that one morning in the future he would awake and she would not be his first thought, but for now that hope seemed very far away.

Beside Toby, Cricket sat cross-legged. He gazed at Gaylang who sat massive and contained in front of his pupils. Gaylang was the only man Cricket respected, but then if your own dad didn't think you were worth bothering about, it was difficult for Cricket to hide the hurt. He pushed the pain and the betrayal deep inside him. Only by pulling as many women as he could did he feel wanted and loved. Sure his mother loved him, but his father did not. No, he didn't feel bitter about his mother telling his father to fuck off. Cricket saw enough of the violence to know that, for his mother's safety and sanity, his father had had to go.

Now, watching Gaylang's face, Cricket felt a deep sense

of love for the man. At times Cricket was sure that Gaylang was hardly human. Then, at those moments, Gaylang would read his thoughts and look across the room at Cricket and smile. 'Yes, I'm human, Cricket. I'm very human and I fail all the time. So never think of me as anything other than human, just like yourself.' When Gaylang spoke directly to Cricket like that, it embarrassed him but it also thrilled him.

'Goodbye, my children,' Gaylang began quietly. 'As you know, this is our last evening together. I leave you in the care of my brother Fats. When you hear I've moved on, don't mourn for me. Promise? I need to move on into eternity from whence we all came. Remember my teachings. Follow your paths with heart. Those of you that choose the path of the hearth and the home, don't be put off by cynics who insist that the path of the hearth and the home is a false one.

'Mostly women choose that path, and some men. But I tell you that, until an adult holds the child of his children, until a mother holds her child's child, the world makes no sense. Only at that moment does the word immortal fall into place.'

Helen found herself nodding vigorously. 'Yeah, yeah,' she was crowing. All those dreadful nights when she was scolded by the women in Swiss Cottage. 'You mean you don't have a career? You mean you don't go out to work? What on earth do you have to say to interest your husband?' And hardest of all when Paul left. 'Well, of course, no wonder he left you. You had nothing to say.'

'Above all, beware the people who need to gather in groups. Throughout history they gather first to praise and then to destroy. Learn to live on your own. Learn to treasure peace and silence. Particularly now, in a world gone mad.

'Remember the only man who came to this earth to fulfil his mission. His name was Emmanuel. He was a

Jew and he alone overcame the world. We are all potentially divine. Made in the image and likeness of the supreme intelligence.

'Our lessons here have been on listening to our inner voices. Understanding our inner lives. Trusting that the supreme intelligence loves you. If you struggle towards a total understanding of the universe, you will find joy. If you insist on being enmeshed in the snares and the delusions of this world, then you will sink without trace.

'There is no hell. There are no fiery furnaces. Only the absence of God's face. The darkness where no light shines. Watch my face,' Gaylang instructed.

Toby watched carefully. He'd been wondering about joy. Only with Louise had he felt pure, unalloyed joy. He wondered miserably if he'd ever feel it again. Slowly, Gaylang's face seemed to recede into the darkness. Toby could no longer see Gaylang's features. Instead Toby saw the beginning of a glimmer of light. Just a little ridge across where Gaylang's nose had been. The light got brighter and he could hear a few gasps in the audience. Then the light got even brighter. Now it seemed like hot honey, falling from Gaylang's face on to his lap. It spilled on to his hands and then down his knees on to the raised platform. The light trickled over the first row of people. There were sighs and sounds of happiness until someone behind Toby burst into tears, and cried, 'I can't bear it.'

'Peace, my child,' Gaylang comforted the sobbing woman. 'Happiness is fragile. Happiness is very delicate. Now all of you can feel my peace and my joy. Take care of it. Keep it within you, and when sorrow comes, and pain, take out my gift to you and examine it. For pain and suffering in this world has a purpose. These emotions help us to grow.'

Slowly the light drew back. It drew back to Gaylang and then his face began to reform. The crowd sat stunned into silence. Fats put on the lights and Gaylang still sat there, beaming.

Toby looked at his mother. Her face was shining. All their faces were shining. Fats came up to Helen and Toby. Helen saw that the light around Fats was very intense.

'Did you feel Gaylang's peace and his joy?' Fats asked Helen.

'Oh yes, I did.' Helen enveloped Fats in a big hug. Then she laughed. 'Oh dear, I'm sorry, Fats. I don't know what came over me.'

'I do,' he said, smiling. 'Gaylang calls it universal love.' For a moment they both stood staring into each other's eyes.

'Hey, Fats, going to join us for a pizza . . . ?' Cricket interrupted the moment, but Helen tucked it away in her heart.

Chapter Twenty-four

Arriving back at Houston Airport, Elliott found she was feeling a little lost and depressed. Quite why, she hadn't understood until, sipping a glass of champagne, she realized that Marcia, Helen and the boys almost felt like the family she had never had. Fats, she thought, was the father-figure to the group.

This was the kind of closeness she had never really known. Mostly she stayed away from women with children. They bored her with their endless talking of nappies and bottles. Then, later, when their children were teenagers, her friends seemed to have forgotten their nefarious backgrounds and they yammered at each other about their children's sex lives and drug addictions.

Elliott, who was more into sex than she was into drugs, had nothing to say. If she reminded any of her now virtuous matronly friends that they had all shared joints and sniffed nosefuls of coke, they drew back from her presence with a horrified rustling of skirts. 'Poor Elliott,' she imagined them murmuring among themselves. 'Gone to the dogs.'

Now only Elliott was left among her contemporaries. She still did sex, drugs and rock and roll. She watched her friends climb in and out of their station-wagons piled with children. In the early days, when she was in her twenties, they had all driven beat-up Caddies. Then the future had looked as bright and shiny as the huge bumpers of their various cars. Now it was as if the windows were misted over and the future unclear.

All her friends, the men included, developed the most

convenient memories, and were now assuring everyone that would listen that they had never had sex in the back seat of their cars, or smoked dope or dropped acid. She'd tried laughing them out of their unreality, but it was too late. Now they had conveniently put away their past behaviour; some of them even donned suits and ties to attend church on a Sunday morning.

It wasn't the going to church that bothered Elliott, it was the hypocrisy of it all. She sighed and finished her drink. American women had so much to live up to. What she really enjoyed about Marcia and Helen was that they had nothing to hide. Marcia was tough; she understood street life. It gave Marcia another dimension in Elliott's eyes.

Marcia had suffered in the hands of men. Helen had only suffered through one man, but Elliott knew that the first was always the worst. That was a rhyme she'd contrived when she lost her first boyfriend. Nothing ever hurt as badly as that again. She felt for Helen. Paul was her first and only relationship, and Helen was still raw and bleeding. But then, Elliott surmised, most men, given half a chance, would bully and abuse women. The trick was to take no shit.

There were exceptions, and her ex was one of them. And as far as she could see, so was Fats. Barry, her jazz pianist, had been fun. He was for weeks in London in the winter. A romp in bed. Nothing more.

Elliott put on her seatbelt for the descent. One of her favourite hotels was Raffles in Singapore: there she had Seth Chang as a lover. He was half Chinese and half American. He was beautiful. He had a long slim body. His eyes were a curious blue and his nose curved. His black straight hair looked as if it had been lacquered on to his well-shaped skull. He taught her how to have continuous orgasms. Yes, Seth was very special, but then so was Courtney Barnes.

She had found Courtney in the Peninsular Hotel in Hong Kong. He worked for the Hong Kong and Shanghai Bank. He was a straightforward lover. She enjoyed walking into restaurants on his arm. He was tall and very English. Courtney made an entrance. She especially liked the shrew-like faces of the women in those restaurants. Most of them knew Courtney, and they suppressed a barely concealed loathing for her. Elliott, yet again, was the woman who had the most desired man in Hong Kong to herself.

All the men in her life kept her busy. Courtney taught her to read. He gave her books. Plays by Ibsen. Mystical novels written by Hermann Hesse. Elliott never pretended that she was any sort of intellectual, but with his guidance, she was able to read the plays by Ibsen and struggle with Hermann Hesse.

Before they left for the boat, Elliott decided that she would write to Helen with a suggested list of reading. She noticed the piles of books in Helen's little sitting room. While she was at sea, Elliott promised herself she would try to improve her mind. She had already partly ruined her body with good wine, bad men and sexual adventure. She wondered if it were possible to encourage Helen to live a life of debauch on this trip. Probably not, but it would be fun trying.

She remembered Barry's mournful face as she waved goodbye at the Savoy. 'Can't I visit you in Houston?' he had asked.

'No, Barry, but you can be my London lover. I keep a lover in every port. What's good for sailors all these years is even better for me.'

'How many lovers have you got?' was his jealous reply.

'None of your business, sweetie-pie.'

Now she was looking forward to telephoning Philip as soon as she got back to her apartment. She was carrying half a side of smoked salmon and a jar of Beluga caviare in her suitcase. She'd missed Philip's warm solid body, and tonight she didn't intend to sleep alone.

Chapter Twenty-five

The hard winter earth was softening up, and Helen felt that she could afford to lose her wintry smile. After Elliott left, the world seemed a less charmed place. She brought with her such a careless enjoyment of life.

Would it really harm her to behave like Elliott and take men to her bed? What would Toby feel about his mother if she did that? When she consulted him with her questions, she was momentarily nonplussed at his evident enthusiasm.

'I'd love you to have a boyfriend, Mum. Why not?' He stood in front of her, taller than ever, and looked down into her face.

'But you said you were glad I wasn't promiscuous, Toby. Do you remember?'

'Sure I do, but that was when I was much less cool about things. Marcia has boyfriends. She doesn't bring them home, and Cricket says that's fine with him as long as they treat her right and don't try and boss his brains.'

Helen tried not to wince at his accent. It was now pure Shepherd's Bush. 'Darling,' she said tentatively, 'you used to speak so beautifully. There's nothing wrong with the Queen's English, you know. English is such a gorgeous language: you do murder it, you know.'

'Yeah, but it ain't OK talking posh.' Toby was teasing her. 'Seriously, Mum, if I talked proper English I'd get beaten up and called a poofter or a nerd. Don't worry about it. When I need to I can slip back.'

'Toby, are you serious about me finding a boyfriend?' She realized how silly the word 'boyfriend' sounded now she was in her thirties. 'I haven't anybody in mind,' she said hurriedly.

'Don't worry, Mum. I'll instigate a search instantly. What nationality?'

'English, of course.' Then Helen caught herself and laughed. 'You know, Toby, there's two me's now. The lady that lived all those years in Swiss Cottage and never knew anybody but your father's friends and mothers from your school, and now the other me. The old me sits on my shoulder and whispers, "Helen, you're making a fool of yourself." But the new me knows that, of course I could love a man from any country in the world. You search high and low for me, darling, but just make sure it's a man who wants to take care of me for a change. Oh, and he does have to have a fabulous sense of humour. That's important. That's what I missed most with your father. It's so odd, Toby. You know, when we first got married he was such fun. When I met him I didn't really like him at first. I thought he was an old stick-in-the-mud. But then I could see all sorts of good things inside him. Sort of hidden, like a secret garden. I thought, idiot that I was, if I loved him enough he'd uncover the secrets and bring them out into the light.

'Instead, after a while, he retreated into those secrets. I think the only other person who shares them is his mother. I couldn't reach him any more, and then slowly he began to disapprove of me more and more until I think he really hated me.'

'Dad reminds me of a black and white photograph. He can suck the colour out of any situation. I know what you're talking about because I thought I could help Louise. Change her, love her enough so that she wouldn't need to sleep around and want material things. But I failed.' There was a moment's silence between them, and then Toby broke the silence. 'Anyway, talking about Dad's disapproval, he's coming to the Lion Heart tonight to hear us gig. Oh man, how uncool can you get?' Toby groaned.

'He can and he will get very uncool,' Helen smiled.

'I hope he brings Laura and not another woman. I feel so terrible when I see Laura. She never says anything, but I can see the question in her eyes. If only she could catch him actually with another woman she might get the courage to boot him out and keep him out.'

'She won't catch him out. He's not going to risk living on his own. Your father can't even boil water, let alone look after himself.' Helen was glad that her tone was less bitter, but she still acknowledged that her breath quickened at the thought of seeing him when he came to collect Toby. She was still afraid of him even after all this time.

Later, sitting at Marcia's kitchen table, Helen consulted her watch. She so enjoyed her deep, intimate talks with Marcia. 'Toby and Cricket will be into their gig by now,' she said.

'Yeah, and Junior said that Paul was thinking of turning up.'

'I expect he will, he's desperate about growing old. The trouble with Paul is that, the harder he tries to look young, the older he looks. He reminds me of those old whiskery coconuts in the Bush market.' Helen laughed. 'Paul diets so much, he looks as if he's dying from the inside out.'

It was a delicious, if a guilt-inducing moment for Helen to feel that she could be unkind about Paul. For so many years she had presented herself as a quintessentially happy housewife, and that had been a lie.

'Why do you think I stuck all that misery for so long, Marcia?' This was a question that went round and round in Helen's brain.

'If I had an answer to that, honey, I'd be a millionaire many times over. There are so many reasons: first, white women are trained from birth that they have to have a man. Black women know that men are trouble. Most black men want you to keep house while they go out after other women and gamble. White men are just the same, but they pretend harder.'

'Oh dear, Marcia, this is such a depressing conversation. We know that all men aren't like that. Your dad and mine were fine; but I want to believe that somewhere or somehow God will send me a special angel.'

'More like a Special Brew,' Marcia said, laughing. 'You can trust a bottle.'

'I already do too much. I wonder if all women drink like me to get to sleep because they are on their own at night and have nothing to do?'

'What was it like when you were married?'

'No different. He was out all the time, and if he wasn't out he watched the television. I hate television. Not the news or a good programme, but the idea that somebody should watch it all the time . . . Paul sat and flipped from channel to channel while I sat in silence, seething inside. You know, it's good for me to remember the bad times with Paul. It's easy to romanticize the past and forget the really bad bits.'

'That's the difficulty. There were good bits with Junior's dad and that's what hurt so much. With others there were no good times and they are quickly forgotten. So with those men I don't have regrets. Just that I was such a needy arsehole and tried to find a man to solve my problems. But then I got Junior.' A lovely warm smile came over Marcia's face. 'And my life changed for ever. I don't need a man. I don't need anything. Just to hold my child's child. That's all I ask the Lord these days.'

'I know how much you really loved Cricket's dad, Marcia.'

'I did. Too much. No man is worth that much pain.' Marcia's voice silenced Helen.

Helen leant forward and touched Marcia's arm. 'We

have each other,' she said lightly, then added, 'I wonder how the boys are getting on?'

'I wonder,' Marcia said. Helen knew she wasn't talking about the boys.

Toby was just beginning to relax when he saw a familiar shape at the door of the gig. The pub had an old-fashioned, brass-hung, mahogany-lined bar. Toby loved gigging there. The audience was usually made up of young people his age. The men were drinking their Special Brews, while the girls drank Diamond White if they were young and innocent, or Malibu and Coke if they weren't. The older men drank their deep pints of English bitter in the back of the bar, sitting in rows against the plush red velvet banquettes. In the mirror that ran along the wall, Toby could see the reflections of the backs of their heads. He liked to check on who had just had a recent haircut. Often in answer to a demand, he would play an old loved song like 'The White Cliffs Of Dover', much to Rollo's disgust. He was doing one of these old numbers when he saw his father standing in the doorway with a much younger woman at his side. She certainly wasn't Laura: she was black. On a small square of a dance floor, several couples were swaying in time to the ballad 'Smoke Gets In Your Eyes'. This was a favourite of the pub owner Crinkly Hinkley. He was dubbed Crinkly by Cricket because his hair lay in black greasy marcelled strands across his balding pate. He considered himself the Lothario of Shepherd's Bush, and there were reputed to be several little Crinklies running about the surrounding area as far as Turnham Green.

Toby watched in horror as his father approached Hinkley. 'A G and T for the lady, mine host, and a Campari for myself. Hey, Toby, I'm over here,' his father bellowed. Paul took Hinkley by the shoulder and squeezed hard. 'That's my boy over there,' he said, waving his hand.

'Oh no,' Toby groaned. 'Cricket, he's here.'

'Man, if this isn't the funniest thing I've seen for weeks. Your old man with a dark doin' his Swiss Cottage slumming act.' Cricket let out a piercing wail on his synthesizer. 'Wheeewhoooo.' The instrument sounded like his laughter.

'Smoke gets in your eyes ...' Toby ended the song prematurely. All he wanted to do was a faithful imitation of Gaylang when he described how it was possible for Jesus Christ to pass through the crowds who wished to persecute him. He knew how to dematerialize, and so far Toby hadn't yet learned to do that.

Toby wondered if things were going to get worse. Firstly, why the hell was his father with this woman? Paul had always been racially prejudiced. Not that he had ever said anything out loud, but Paul and his friends simply existed in a world that failed to notice anyone that wasn't white. Now, as he broke into a new number, Toby's voice warbled with tension. His father pulled the girl on to the floor and started doing a full-length smooch.

Cricket giggled. 'He might as well ting her on the dance floor.'

'Who is that turd?' Rollo leaned forward and whispered into Toby's ear. 'He's trying to dry-hump that young chick on the floor. Dirty old man.' Rollo enunciated the last three words carefully.

'That's my dad, Rollo,' Toby said in an agonized whisper.

'Sorry about that.' Rollo's voice was full of sympathy. 'He's not cool, man. He's not at all cool.'

'You can say that again. Look, let's play something fast and see if we can get him off the floor. Toby adjusted the mike and then shouted, 'OK, folks. Let's hit the beach.'

'The beach, to the beach, sun's in the sky and I wanna lie ...' This was one of their fastest rap numbers, and

159

they had been asked to make a demo of it by a major DJ for a record company. This was the record that they all sweated nights over. Now, for Toby to see his father gyrating in a sixties effort to make the twist fit his lyrics and his music, was an unendurable horror. Why couldn't somebody, preferably the police, come along and put Paul away? The girl was in her twenties. She had big tits and a small fat bum. The sort of pneumatic woman that his father liked. She moved well to the music and seemed embarrassed to be seen with Paul.

Slowly the other dancers left the floor, laughing. Then everyone sat quietly. Finally there was a rising chorus of titters and chuckles. 'Go man, go,' teased a young rasta. Paul, convinced he was a great success, waved his hands in the air and began to rock and roll. The girl, unable to follow his directions tripped him up. He lay on the floor with his legs in the air. By this time, Crinkly Hinkley was hysterical with laughter. Toby put down the mike and fled from the bar. The others would have to carry on without him.

He raced down the street, around Hammersmith roundabout, and down the endless length of Hammersmith Road. At the end, by the petrol station, he turned into his own road. Breathless, and with tears streaming down his face, he inserted his key into the front door. He ran up the stairs, opened the door to the flat, and entered the kitchen, where his mother was reading at the kitchen table.

'Toby, what on earth is the matter?' Toby pushed past her in an effort to get to his bedroom. 'He came to the gig, didn't he? Oh Toby, what did your father do?'

'He made an absolute arsehole of himself, as usual.' Toby talked through gasps of rage. 'He brought a black girl, young enough to be his daughter, to show how with-it he was, and then . . .' Not for a long time had Toby collapsed into his mother's arms, but now the familiar smell of her scent, the warmth of her comfort was a necessity for Toby.

'Shhhhh . . . darling,' Helen smoothed his hair with the familiar stroking movements she had used since he was a small child. 'Come, we'll sit down together and we'll have a glass of wine. I'm drinking a rather good St Emilion at the moment. Have you eaten?' The familiar motherly question helped him to regain his composure. His breathing became normal again.

'I'd like to kill that bastard sometimes,' he said more quietly.

'I know the feeling, darling, but your father has always been an idiot. He was once a lovable idiot, but now he's just a sad, lost man. Laura doesn't really want him any more, and the young women he picks up just want a night out. Don't be too cross, darling.'

They both jumped when the telephone broke into their conversation. 'I'll get it.' Helen knew it would be Paul.

'Where on earth is Toby? Really, Helen, it's so inconvenient of him to run off like that. Gail wanted to meet him.' Paul was using the same petulant voice that used to drive Helen crazy.

'Toby's here and he's fine. You made the usual fool of yourself and he didn't want to stay there and be embarrassed.'

'I don't believe you, Helen. You're just jealous that I'm out having a good time and you have nowhere to go. Tell Toby to come to the phone.'

'Fuck off, Dad,' Toby screamed from the kitchen table. 'You tell that bastard that I'm never going to talk to him again.'

'Toby says to tell you to fuck off and he never wants to see you again.' Helen's voice was prim. She tried not to giggle.

'Well, I never . . .' Paul's voice was aghast. 'I don't believe that my own son would ever talk to me like that.'

Helen smiled. She could hear the music and the people talking in the background of the pub. 'I think it's those . . . those dreadful . . .' Paul's voice faltered.

'Those black people, Paul? Isn't that what you want to say?'

'Certainly not, I don't have a racially prejudiced bone in my body. I'll have you know that Gail is –' he paused – 'a woman of colour,' he said.

'Oh Paul, it's far too late to have to deal with your crap. Get off the phone and leave us alone. Toby will ring you when he feels like it.'

'I'm not happy about this, Helen. I'm not happy at all.'

Helen heard the old menace in Paul's voice that used to make her shake and go weak at the knees. 'Tough titty,' she said, and put the phone down.

'Here's to us,' she said, lifting the glass of wine. Toby lifted his.

'To our new demo disc,' he said. Helen was glad the colour had come back into his face.

Chapter Twenty-six

'I wonder if I ought to change jobs, Marcia? What d'you think? I've been lying in bed and I can't sleep. My life seems to be one long, unrewarding slog. I get up in the dark, I catch the bus, I go to work. When I get in, I make coffee and the tea for the senior solicitors. Then I take dictation and go to my desk. I work until one o'clock, and then I eat lunch at my desk. I can't afford to go out to lunch, but I do pop out to do the shopping for the house.

'Sometimes I feel as if I don't exist. I look at my reflection in the window on the bus and I see no one. That's a frightening feeling. Do you think I'm being neurotic?'

'No, I don't, Helen. I've been watching you getting thinner and thinner and I've been worrying about you. You see, my life at the dance centre is busy and warm. I can walk to work and there we all know each other. I get plenty of hugs and kisses and good strokes. We all need those things, honey. I know you've got Toby and me and Fats as friends but you are working in the white middle-class Protestant world and that's death. Believe you me, white honky is dead honky meat.'

Marcia grinned cheerfully. She was soaking dried salt cod in milk. Helen now knew how to cook salt fish and ackee with rice and peas. 'I'm sure you ought to change jobs,' Marcia continued. 'There's a job in our bar down the road up for grabs. You wouldn't have to pay bus fares, and what with the tips and the little extras in food and wine you can bring home, I reckon you'd be just as well off. That, and you can do the job under the counter and collect the social like everybody else.'

'Oh no, Marcia, I couldn't do that. It would be dishonest.'

Marcia shrugged. 'Some of us have no choice. The deadbeats that run social security have made it impossible to live without collecting the social. If you get a job, you lose your benefits, so women with kids don't have much choice. I hate going down there every week, but when Junior's dad left I had no option. Don't think that we are all social security scroungers like the papers say. Most of us cringe when we feel obligated. People didn't come to this country to get supported by the state. Most people came here to get their children an education and to better themselves.

'Look what's happened. Everywhere us black people are in chains. No jobs, no housing. Black people are on the bottom of the pile of discrimination. Our kids on the streets, hustling to survive. No, Helen, black people are tired and sick of how they are being treated. You get yourself a job at the pub and you'll find a new way of life. More real. More like the life you are learning to live here. The problem for you is that you are half in your other life at your job, and half in your street life in the Bush.'

'You know, I never thought about it like that.' Helen's face brightened. 'That's exactly what has been wrong. I get up in the morning with the same feeling of dread. All those men with their wrinkly baggy suits. Whether the senior partner will take his tea with sugar or with lemon is about the biggest decision I make all day. Or whether Mr Simpson will arrive in a foul mood and I'll make him cross.'

'Helen, why do you care if he's cross?'

'I don't know, Marcia, I just get scared and I start to shake.'

'You know what Fats says, honey?' Marcia's eyes were concerned. 'We all create our own realities.'

'Yes, I know but I'm too stupid to understand what he's trying to say.'

'Helen, you're far from stupid. Have you ever considered that you seem to have a need to attract people to you who disapprove of you. Paul, for instance?'

'I see what you mean.'

'Helen, stop being so damned humble. You'll make people want to kick your teeth in. Quit cringing. Go out and change your life. Only you can do it.'

'Well . . .' Helen's voice was hesitant. 'I'll have to ask Toby if he minds me working in a pub. Then what on earth do you think Paul will say?'

'Helen! First, Toby is your son. You don't ask permission from your son before you choose a job. If you don't stop leaning on Toby, you'll make him into your surrogate husband. Stop it. He's still a young boy. Second, it's none of Paul's business what you do. You don't have to tell him anything. You're no longer his business and he is no longer your business. Next time he rings to whine about Laura, put the phone down.'

'You really mean I should put the telephone down on Paul? That's awfully rude, Marcia.'

'Sure thing Helen. Life is rude, it's dirty and it's mean. Grow up.'

Helen sat on the other side of the kitchen table, feeling scorched by Marcia's anger. But in her heart, she knew Marcia was right. The ground-rules of her life had been terminally changed when Paul dumped her for another woman. There was no point in hanging on to her concept of English middle-classness. She hadn't come from there in the first place. Anyway, even while she had tried to live in that stuffy contained wardrobe that seemed to her to be how Paul and his friends liked to live, she always felt suffocated. She missed the easy informality of life in Hove. The fishmonger, her friend, who helped her choose fish with her mother. The butcher with his haunches of meat impaled on savage hooks over his head. The bakery where she and her mother collected big round sugary doughnuts to take home and dunk in the tea. The English middle-classes didn't even dunk biscuits in tea, let alone sugary doughnuts.

All her street in Hove celebrated babies being born, and attended funerals. In every closet in each of the houses so neatly shackled side by side hung a wedding dress in white, a dress for a christening, and then a black dress for deaths. Helen could never decide which event was the most exciting. Probably the deaths. Awful sobbing shook the bereaved and the mourners. Even if Helen didn't know the person so well she cried. Especially if a baby died. Helen's mother knitted booties for the new babies and sat with the dead and the dying.

How she'd been living with Paul accounted for nothing. It was time wasted but for Toby. He was the one jewel out of that débâcle. Marcia was right. She did not have to consult Toby. Anyway, in her heart of hearts, she knew he wouldn't mind. Now she must learn to make her choices out of strength like Marcia did, not out of weakness.

Marcia lifted the big silver fish out of the milk. The thick white flesh was now smooth and plump. She ran the tap and then washed the fish carefully under the cascade of water. 'There's a shipment of fruit coming in from JA this afternoon. Want to come down to the market and buy some?'

'I'd love to. Saturday afternoon is such fun there.'

Wandering along beside Marcia, Helen watched the brightly lit stalls twinkling in the evening air. Piles of flowing oranges and apples; so very many different types of apples. England had the best apples in the world, Helen thought. Yellow bananas smelling sweet and slightly rotted. She'd always thought of bananas as very erotic fruit, but she realized she hadn't thought about sex for some time now. Too cold and too tired, she told herself. She was conscious of her cheap shoes and cold feet.

Marcia packed her basket with prickly pears and mangoes. 'They're much too expensive for me to buy, but I'd die without mangoes. They are made in heaven. I believe that they are grown under the wings of angels. Look, Helen,' Marcia pulled a small round mango out of her thatch-palm basket, 'this is a rose mango. Smell it.'

Helen inhaled deeply. 'That's wonderful,' she said. Her voice was happy and light. 'Why don't you come over tonight and I'll cook shepherd's pie and we can talk to Toby about my new job?'

'OK, but you *tell* him about your new job. Don't ask for his advice, you hear?'

'I promise.' Helen was laughing. 'On the way back we can pop into the pub and see if the job's still on offer.'

'Atta-girl, Helen.' Marcia put down her basket and gave Helen a warm hug.

They continued to wander down the busy lanes filled with jostling people. Helen smiled at the pretty little West Indian children with their can-rolled hair. She couldn't plait like that for the life of her. Sometimes, when she was at the dance centre with Marcia, Marcia tried to teach her, but Helen found it impossible. Marcia's quick, nimble fingers made it all look so easy.

The elegantly clad Asian children walking so quietly and so obediently with their parents enchanted Helen. Their huge brown liquid eyes reminded her of the wheels of licorice that she bought in the sweet shop around the corner from her mother's home in Hove. In fact, she thought as she followed Marcia's determined back, this is about as far away from life in Hove as she could have found. This weekend she was taking Toby on one of their now less rare visits to his grandparents. When she'd been married to Paul, her visits had almost stopped because Paul hated the simple life her parents lived. He sneered at their reverence of the local bank manager. He disliked the open coal fire. 'So very working-class,' was his final condemnation of her parents and their way of life.

'What's wrong with that?' she countered. 'Most of England is working-class.'

'Vulgar,' he said, and then refused to visit ever again. So her visits had become fewer too, but now she was slowly rebuilding her bridges back into her parents' world. Her mother was more understanding about those icy gaps; the years that they saw little of their beloved grandson. 'I never liked him,' was all Rosalee would say of Paul. But Helen knew her mother understood. In the way that women understand the subtexts of situations all over the world.

Her father was just pleased to see them both back in his house, and he was especially proud of Toby. Now they were just a few yards from the pub. Helen began to feel nervous. 'Do you think we should ask today, Marcia? Why not wait until tomorrow?'

'Helen, we do it now. Come on, just follow me and I'll do the talking.' Marcia marched up to the bar, where several men were sitting on the high barstools with their pints of beer in front of them.

''ave a pint, sweethearts,' a thin man with a white face and blackened teeth leered at them both.

'Fuck off, fuck-face,' Marcia said amiably.

'Just asking, just asking,' he said, backing off.

'You don't take any shit from anyone in this place, Helen,' Marcia told her.

'OK, Marcia, message understood.' Helen wondered if she'd get a mouth on her like Marcia. Probably not, but then she could always say: 'Get thee from me, thou lickerish lout.' Lickerish, she discovered when she opened her dictionary to find out how to spell licorice, meant lecherous; also eager to taste or enjoy.

'What can I do for you today, Marcia?' Crinkly Hinkley's voice was full of charm. He'd crossed Marcia once before when he fondled her behind as he passed her in the bar. The mark of her stiletto heel could still be seen on his bare foot. Her remarks upon the meanness of his genitals thundered through the crowded pub, and the ensuing laughter kept him well in hand. He would love to get her whippet black body into his bed, and then he'd show her what he could do with his equipment, but that was not going to happen in this lifetime.

'I want you to give my mate a job.' It was not a matter of discussion, it was a command.

'Anything you say, sweetheart.' Crinkly smiled ingratiatingly. 'When would you like to start, Helen?' He'd seen Helen many times sharing drinks with Marcia. Not much of a looker to his mind, but she had a nice smile.

'Monday,' Marcia said firmly.

'I can't, Marcia, I've got to give in my notice,' Helen said anxiously.

'No you don't, you twit. Tell them your aunt's died suddenly and you have to go and look after your eleven cousins.'

'But that's a terrible lie, Marcia. I can't do that.'

'Helen,' Marcia's voice was ominous, 'we do not live in Swiss Cottage, honey. Needs must, as you so often remind me. I can't bear to see you looking so miserable; and besides, you're drinking too much all alone at home every night. Good to get out in the evenings. Have people to talk to. Join the real world.'

Helen thought for a moment. Well, she was spending the weekend with her parents. That would be the first time she'd gone anywhere except for her visits with Fats and Marcia. 'OK.' She smiled at Crinkly Hinkley and he smiled back.

'None of that, Crinkly.' Marcia frowned. 'You lay a hand on her and you'll become a eunuch overnight.'

'Wouldn't dream of it.' Crinkly very much wanted to cross his legs. 'Come on, Helen, let's go and find a real man.' Marcia cast a contemptuous eye across the bar and grinned as the men sitting there gazed into their beer mugs. Helen swept out behind Marcia. Sweeping about was fun, Helen decided. She must learn to do more of it.

Chapter Twenty-seven

'You're sure that you want to work in a bar, darling?'

Helen's mother's voice was cautious. Helen knew her mother wasn't happy with the idea, but that she was trying not to step too heavily on the delicate bridge they had thrown across the chasm of their relationships with each other.

'Yes, I'm sure, Mum. I need to stop all the travelling. I spend far too much time on buses and tubes, to say nothing of money. Sometimes I get really frightened coming home in the dark. Hove is still a safe place, but the London underground isn't. Often men follow me and I have to run.' Toby was sitting beside her, busily devouring his breakfast. She saw his eyebrows rise. She had never discussed her fears with him.

'You didn't tell me you had men following you, Mum,' he said reproachfully. 'Anyway, I think the pub is a good idea. I can always walk you home at night.'

'Thanks, Toby,' she said, and hugged him.

Her father, his face buried in the local newspaper, just grunted. 'Let the girl do what she wants, Mother. She knows what's best.' He put the paper down, his round face beaming with approval. 'Don't pay any attention to your mother, dear. She'll not move with the times. Do you good to work nearby. You'll get to know a lot of nice people.'

Upstairs in her own little bedroom, she sat for a moment on her pink shiny satin quilt. She inhaled the smell of her childhood. Clean pillows and sheets smelling of wheat. Her pictures of cats on the wall. The tall, now fashionable, pine dresser and matching wardrobe.

And of course, the net curtains, the bane of her life.

She remembered Paul when he had first stepped into her bedroom. 'I see,' he'd said, one eyebrow lifted. 'Net curtains. How endearing.'

'What's wrong with net curtains?' Helen remembered her defensiveness.

'Nothing if you live in a row of other houses,' he'd said.

She hadn't known what to reply, but she'd taken them down regretfully and folded them in soft billows in the bottom drawer of her cupboard. The windows looked bleak and bare, even with the curtains shut. Now the curtains were back, and had been since the first day she had come back to the house with Toby and without Paul.

She gazed at them and then she felt a stab. Mostly the pain had left her, but sometimes it came back in full force and left her winded. She was amazed at just how physical the pain was. She lay back on her bed, her eyes full of tears.

This had been the bed they had shared after they came back from their honeymoon. Helen had been a little embarrassed the first morning they had both emerged together. She remembered sitting at the dining-room table, waiting for her mother to bring them bacon and eggs. She wondered if her parents would hear them making love? Probably not, but she hadn't wanted to make love to Paul under her parents' roof. He had insisted. 'Don't be so silly,' he'd hissed fiercely into her ear. She was slightly drunk. Too much of her father's homemade barley wine. A surge of lust swept over her. An unquenchable lick of fire between her legs. No time to do anything about it now: she had to go down for lunch.

When, in the early days, they had made love, it had been so perfect for her. Then, he had been a gentle lover. Later he became brutal and demanding in bed. How many other men out there, she wondered, would rape a woman in marriage? How many men so mother damaged, that they were the walking wounded. They took their malice and spite that rightfully belonged to their castrating mothers and spilled it into the innocent laps of their partners. Too many, far too many. She stood up and took a deep silent breath. Still, she was safe and far away from those terrible days. She would see that she was never again trapped in a relationship with such a man.

She gazed in the mirror and tried to practise a confident smile. All she saw was a quivering, wounded face staring back at her. 'It'll change,' she whispered to the mirror. 'Not long now and I'll be on the boat.' She saw her face radiate with happiness again. 'The sea,' she murmured. 'To the sea.' Her face didn't look so bad after all.

She left the room and ran down the stairs. As she ran, the years fell away and she felt as if she were her twelve-year-old self running downstairs to Sunday dinner. Now, of course, it was lunch, but then she called to her mother, 'Is dinner ready?'

Toby sat opposite his mother at the table. 'Grandma,' he said, 'I love your food.'

'I know you do, love, and I love cooking for you. That's what grannies are for. None of this modern nonsense of going out to work.' She blushed. 'I'm sorry, dear, I didn't mean that to sound rude. You have to go out to work.'

'Yes, I do have to go out to work. I didn't for many years because Toby needed me at home. But now he's in his teens I can go to work without feeling guilty. If he's sick at home, it'll be much easier working in a bar where they will give me time off. All this talk about women working . . .' She made a face. 'If I dare ask for time off at the office, I have to pretend I'm ill. They wouldn't hear of taking time off for children. Anyway, I like working out of the house. I don't have a cleaning lady any more. Toby and I sort of manage to keep everything together.

173

I don't enjoy cleaning and housework like you do.'

'Thank you, Grandma.' Toby watched as his grandmother put a steaming plate of roast beef and Yorkshire pudding in front of him.

'Let me see you clean your plate, young man.' His grandmother retired to her seat and smiled benignly at her family. Helen smiled. Her mother repeated the same sentence every time Toby came to Hove to see them. The words comforted her. Like her bedroom, they were familiar and known. Helen didn't like the unknown. She didn't want to stare into the future. The here and now was all that she wanted.

On the way back to London, Toby was very quiet. 'A penny for your thoughts?' Helen smiled at him.

'Not worth a penny, Mum. I was just wondering how you and Dad managed to stay married at all? Life is so different with Grandmother Beckett. I mean, they sit at the table with all that silver and cut-glass. With Nan we sit comfortably and eat even better than they do. Sometimes I feel as if I'm in lots of different plays. When I go to Grandmother Beckett's house I try to remember what to do with the knives and the forks. When I'm with Nan I try not to say anything rude. When I'm at our house I'm OK. Then at Cricket's yard it's quite different again. Do you understand what I'm trying to say?'

'Yes, I think I do,' Helen said slowly. 'Life for me used to be easy. I grew up in Hove. I was a small-town girl. Then I met Paul and slowly learned how to talk posh. How to behave at the table; all the things I hadn't learned from Mum and Dad.

'At first it was really difficult, because I made Paul embarrassed and cross if I made a mistake. Then, as the years went by, it became automatic. I know I hurt Mum and Dad with my new ways. I made them feel they weren't good enough for us, but that's over now. Actually, most of Paul's way of life is a load of crap. It really is, a lot of pretentious nonsense. People who need to be on show all the time are dreadfully insecure about who they are. Really posh English, like the old duke and duchess who lived outside Hove, always looked like gardeners. In fact, the old duchess used to sail in and out of the shops with huge ladders in her thick woollen tights!

'Anyway, darling, we've had a lovely weekend together. Hopefully there'll be some news of your new demo when we get back. I love the song, and you've got such a fabulous voice.'

Most of the way Toby dozed. There was a flicker of excitement in his heart, but he tried to pour cold droplets on to the flame. He and the group had been working so hard and so long on the label that he didn't want to get his hopes up, only for them to be dashed again.

He wished he could find a girl that really interested him. There were girls at school and of course Thelma, the girl who did homework with him. Some of the girls he fancied, but he was still too raw to risk any deep relationships. Besides, he had met no one who could match Louise. Occasionally he heard news of her. He remembered with sweet regret the times they used to sing together on the Heath in Hampstead. She had a beautiful soaring soprano voice. It reminded him of larks in a high vaulted blue sky.

He also wondered about himself. Why had he fallen so deeply in love with Louise? Cricket was constantly in 'lurve', as he called it. He could bounce from one affair to another. 'What happened to Georgina?' Toby asked him before he set off to visit his grandparents.

'She? Blood clot,' Cricket said, exaggerating his West Indian accent.

'Don't you ever get stung, Cricket?'

'Na. Yo bitch, I say, and they come running.'

Maybe Cricket just hid his pain better than Toby did. Toby lay in the car seat with his eyes shut and then he thought, Maybe Cricket is one of the lucky ones who doesn't feel much at all. His Dad was like that. He only felt anything about Laura when he knew she might boot him out of her yard. She ought to do that. Toby vowed he'd tell Laura so the next time she came round to visit him. 'Fumans,' he thought, using one of his baby words. 'Fumans, who'd have them anyway?', and he fell asleep.

Chapter Twenty-eight

Elliott lay passively under a man who was labouring to his very belated climax. Why were so many American men virtually impotent? she wondered. Here she was with a fantastically good-looking dude and it felt like hours since she'd come.

Elliott was bored. This was now a fairly familiar scene. Handsome man, dinner for two, back to her place to bed, and he couldn't make out. Usually, Elliott felt a stab of pity, but this time she found she was not only bored by this non-event, but also angry.

'Why,' she said, rolling him off her body, 'can't you just tell me that you have a problem and we could discuss it?' She looked down at his attempt at an erection. 'No wonder you can't come, Chet, you can't even get a hard-on.'

Chet rolled on to his stomach and buried his face in her pillows. 'I know,' he mumbled, 'I can't do anything about it. I've seen lots of medics and quite a few psychiatrists. They say it's all in my head.'

'Maybe it is but it's stupid to go on balling me and just making me sore. How long have you had this problem?' Normally Elliott would move into her Mother Earth role and try to help him. Tonight was different, or maybe she had just decided rather late in life that she was not responsible for rescuing impotent American men. 'OK,' she said briskly, 'let's get out of bed and go eat. I'm starving.'

'That sounds great.' Chet's voice was a hundred per cent relieved. Elliott bounded out of bed and went to the kitchen. She opened the fridge and stared into the familiar empty space. 'Shit,' she said loudly. 'I forgot to go shopping. How about we smoke a joint and then eat baked beans. Baked beans are a must when I'm high.'

She opened the can of baked beans and put the can directly on to the gas hob. 'Saves washing up,' she said, smiling again. Chet came up behind her and put his arms around her waist. 'Are you disappointed?' he said.

'No, it happens to everybody sometimes, but if you have a problem like that you need help. Us girls share sexual information at the drop of a tampax, but you guys don't know how to talk to each other. It's time you all did. Too many of you nowadays are no good in the sack. It's not just me who has trouble. All my girl friends are complaining.'

She stirred the beans and then fished out her plastic bag of weed. 'Wanna joint?' she proffered.

'No thanks.' Chet blushed. 'I don't do drugs.'

'What do you do then?' Elliott lifted the joint to her lips. She regretted the remark she had just made. 'Sorry, Chet, that was mean.' She inhaled a long thick stream of smoke. The weed hit the back of her throat and rasped. She felt as if someone had run a toothbrush over her palate, but when the weed hit her it soothed her irritation. 'Boy, that's good,' she said. 'Try some?'

'I'm scared,' Chet admitted. 'It used to make my mom and dad real mean when they were smoking.' Nevertheless Chet put his hand out and put the joint in his mouth. He had the inexperienced look of a small boy about to try his first cigarette. He inhaled and then coughed.

'Don't give up. Take a few deep breaths and get the stuff into your lungs,' Elliott instructed.

Chet tried again. This time he coughed less. She watched his face, narrowing her eyes against the harsh kitchen light. She saw him visibly relax. He took another drag and then handed the joint back to her. 'Go back to bed and I'll bring us a plate of beans and two spoons. You'll be surprised at how good it tastes.'

When he'd gone, Elliott gave a big sigh. She would much rather hit the phone in her stoned state and talk to her new English friends. Now she'd have to sort out Chet's sexual problems. But by now she'd become quite fond of him. He was such a big child. What was happening to men in America? Was it women's fault, Elliott wondered? Usually, when men had problems, the answers were all to be found on women's doorsteps. They were all too loud, too aggressive, not aggressive enough. The list was endless. Elliott sometimes felt that a woman like herself had to be a full orchestra to fulfil the needs of the new American male. Take Chet as an example. Chet wanted Mummy sex. Just to suck at her breast. She would probably finish the evening jerking him off and sending him home with a smile on his face. She sighed again. The dope had done its work and she was feeling lightheaded and giggly.

'OK, Chet honey, here I come,' she said.

Later, after kissing Chet at the door, she poured a vodka on the rocks and telephoned Marcia's house. Since she'd been back she'd phoned Marcia and Helen several times a week. She enjoyed hearing Cricket's cheerful tone.

'That you, Elliott? How's things?' Elliott loved joking around with Cricket and Toby. Cricket was teaching her London street language. 'Your street cred sucks,' he had told her in their last conversation.

'I know,' she admitted. 'I'm the child of the flower-power generation. I'm sort of stuck in the sixties stuff, where my Mom comes from. Now Chet, the guy who's just left, he's in his early twenties, so he's kinda away from all that stuff. He's so clean he squeaks.'

Tonight she wished to talk to Marcia. Marcia was so calm and so quiet, but she knew about men in a way that Elliott did not. Marcia sexually educated Elliott, and Helen disciplined her mind. Now she had all of Ibsen's plays by her bed. The guy really didn't like women and that's for sure, she had complained to Helen.

To her surprise, Helen had agreed with her, and Elliott had felt pleased. 'I think there are several reasons for that,' Helen explained. 'One answer could be that he was just a misogynist, but I think it was more than just that. As an intelligent and passionate man he detested the sort of women who surrounded him. Women in those days were trained to be providers for men. To simper and play the little girl child. Norah, certainly, in *The Doll's House*, played the role to the hilt. Ibsen was sending her up, actually, but so many so-called intellectual women of that time were too stupid to realize that.'

'Wow, Helen, you really are clever.'

'Not really, Elliott. I just read a lot. Now I have time to myself I can think things through. Before, when I was married, I was always so rushed. The house needed cleaning, I had the cooking to do, the washing, and making beds. All the sort of stuff that contributes to brain-rot . . .'

Elliott's mind came back to the present and the less intellectual conversation she was having with Marcia. 'Anyway, Marcia, I guess I just don't have an answer to Chet's problem, or any of them. I know that when a man takes his clothes off and says, "Gee, I hope . . ." my heart sinks and I think, not again.'

She heard Marcia's quiet chuckle. 'I know what you mean.' Marcia's voice was amused but serious. 'I don't think women ever imagined that when they told men they were going to take the initiative in the sexual field, men couldn't take the challenge. If you think about it biologically, they are designed to force the female to submit, and women won't do it any more.'

'So what's the outcome, Marcia?'

'Your guess is as good as mine. But it's something that men should be thinking about.'

'Yeah, but since when did men ever talk about their

sexual problems? Chet can barely talk to me even though he sleeps with me, or tries to. He had a loony-toons hippy-dippy-do-dah for a mother. His dad wore a nappy on his head and got religion. I don't know, it's all so fucked these days. I can't wait to get away on the boat. I might even try celibacy for a while, who knows?'

'Chance would be a fine thing, Elliott.' Marcia's voice was wry.

'I only said might,' Elliott reminded her.

Chapter Twenty-nine

Helen was slowly ambling back from her first day at her new job. She remembered with a smile the senior partner's voice when she telephoned to say her aunt had died and she must go away for a month and help her young uncle take care of her many nieces and cousins. She knew he wanted to hear the details. Other people's lives in his office belonged to him, but she refused to give him the satisfaction.

'Oh, well then, we can't manage without a secretary for a month. We'll have to get somebody else, won't we?'

'I suppose so.' Helen felt guilty but then shook her fist at her meek little dormouse self. Don't be so silly, Helen, she told herself firmly. He doesn't care who makes his coffee and sharpens his six pencils every morning before he comes in.

'I am so sorry, could you see that I get my P45?'

'Surely, Mrs Beckett.' His voice was now unctuous. 'Thank you for all your hard work.'

'And thank you, sir.' She put the telephone down and did a little jig. 'It's all over,' she carolled. 'It's all over and now I'm going to be a barmaid.'

Tonight she took her time walking back to her flat, in the dusk of a winter's day. She particularly liked the earthy squares that surrounded the tall plane trees that grew down Hammersmith Grove. In fact, she loved Hammersmith Grove. How could she be so unfaithful to Swiss Cottage, where she had lived all her married life? Easily, was the answer. Swiss Cottage was a drab little man with a bowler hat on his pimpled head, and an umbrella permanently unfurled in case it rained. Life in Swiss Cottage was a series of strategies devoted to surviving the fierce competition with the neighbours.

Nobody in the Bush cared if it rained. The children wore big woolly hats. Big knitted bonnets with brims in greens and golds and red. The colours of Rastafari. They strutted down the roads. They swung their hands and danced imaginary dances. Big groups of young people with happy, shining faces.

At first Helen had been intimidated by them. But they all knew her face, as they did Toby's. Now she saw her son surrounded by a sea of different nationalities. She was happy to live like this in the real world. Instead of living among the pale children of the middle-classes with their secret drinking and drug-taking.

Parents who pretended that their lives were as clean as their kitchen floors. Two doors down from Helen's house, a child had been found swinging from a rope from one of the big, expensive, imported antique beams in his bedroom. There had been an even bigger silence that day in the normally silent neighbourhood. It was as if death were catching. Too many of Toby's friends swallowed pills, had miscarriages and abortions. Stayed high on drugs and drink to stay away from the pain of growing up among their highly ambitious parents. Their unrelenting needs to make their children famous.

Helen knew as she peered at the base of the trees that the Bush parents were also ambitious, but she felt the ambition was mostly healthy. These parents wanted their children to 'better themselves'. To have a wider choice in life. These ambitions were based in a reality. The parents took a keen interest in the children's schooling, particularly the mothers. Yes, some of the children were scruffy and ill-kempt. These were largely white children, Helen noticed. The Jamaican children for the most part were very well dressed and extremely polite. As were Toby's

Asian friends. Toby now practised a very pronounced South London accent. He faithfully mimicked Cricket, and mostly talked a very jumbled language that she often failed to understand.

'Darling,' she tried a few times, 'couldn't you just say, "Hello, Mother" instead of "Yo, Mum"?'

'Nah,' Toby answered, and laughed. 'I don't wanna talk posh.'

'Toby, it's not posh. It's the Queen's English. English is such a beautiful language, the finest in the world, and you're murdering it.'

'Them's the runnings, Mum.'

'The what?'

'That's how things are,' Toby patiently explained.

On her first day at the bar she arrived shaking with nerves.

'Put the wood in the hole, there's a duck.' Maisie, the big busty barmaid she knew vaguely from her evenings in the bar with Marcia, flashed her a cheerful grin.

'I was ever so pleased to hear that you was coming to work 'ere.' Put the wood in the hole, Helen discovered, meant 'shut the door'.

'Really, Maisie, you really mean that?'

'Sure I do. Hinkley says he's goin' to call you the Prof, 'cos you got an education. Marcia did good at school, but I left when I was fourteen. Pregnant, of course. Still, I'm good with me punters.'

Helen did know that Maisie had a second job. She was a prostitute. Helen had at first been shocked. Prostitutes were ladies of the night. Figures that vaguely lurked in the shadows. Sometimes she'd seen cars drawn up against the pavements and a woman leaning into the driver's window. She'd been surprised to meet Maisie and see she was a big, happy, motherly type of woman.

The only other prostitutes she'd known had been in literature. Moll Flanders or Polly Garter in *Under Milk*

Wood. Romantic women willingly handed themselves over for free. Anyway, at dinner parties all her loony-lefty friends insisted that all prostitutes were poor downtrodden, abused women. There was nothing abused about Maisie.

Maisie untied her apron and removed her bright pink rubber gloves. 'I got you a pair of yellow gloves,' Maisie said. ''Ere, try 'em on.' Helen pulled the faintly powdery gloves on to her hands.

Maisie giggled. 'Last night I 'ad this punter. 'E gave me a lot of dosh for dressing up like a schoolgirl and wearing gloves. Schoolgirl stuff.' She wrinkled her nose and laughed.

It felt curiously indecent to laugh, but Helen was riveted with curiosity. 'What on earth did he actually want you to do?' she asked. 'Chastise him?'

'You know, beat 'im on the bottom with me whip. Mind you, I'm not one for serious violence. Not like some of the other girls I know. A little tap here or there. A bit of a spanking and that's me down. If they want anything more, I send them to Lace.'

'Lace?'

'Yer, Lace. She'll do anyfing. Anyfing anybody wants, and that includes wimmin too. I don't do wimmin. The men are bad enuff. But when the wimmin start getting difficult, it's time to get out.'

'I think I'll have a coffee before I start with the washing-up,' Helen said faintly.

'OK, you do that, and I'll start sweeping.'

Maisie made Helen a big creamy cup of coffee. 'When you've finished that I'll show you the back of the kitchen. We do the glasses behind the bar. The rest of the stuff you takes back into the kitchen and wash up. Don't forget your gloves.'

Helen felt slightly silly. She had never worn rubber gloves before. All her married life she must have dropped at least two dinner services' worth of plates, and stacks of glasses. Now, with slippery rubber gloves, she was frightened she'd do the same here.

Maisie noticed Helen's hesitation. 'Don't worry, luv,' she said, beaming. 'We're one big 'appy family 'ere. All me mates come down for a drink, and me boyfriend. 'E's a bastard. I can't 'alf pick 'em, I do. But I love 'im, an' that's wot counts.'

'I'm taking a rain-check on bastards these days,' Helen said smiling. 'My husband – my ex-husband –' she quickly corrected herself – 'was, is, and always will be, a bastard to women.'

''E'll get his comeuppance, don't you worry.'

'I hope he does. Otherwise a lot of other women are going to get hurt. Funny you know, Maisie.' Helen followed Maisie's back into the kitchen. 'You can't guess when you fall in love that the man is going to turn into a complete bastard.'

'Nah, you can't, but then most men are spoiled rotten by their mums and they hand the mess on to us.'

Helen smiled. She'd had this conversation so many times with Marcia.

'God love us, Helen, is that the time?'

Helen spent most of the day with her hands buried in the sink. Maisie dashed in and out, grabbing whatever she needed. The music blared in the bar and Helen was totally happy.

'God love us,' she mimicked Maisie as she studied the bare-armed trees outside the kitchen window for early signs of spring. God surely loves us, she comforted herself. And it won't be long before we're sailing away for Greece.

Tonight, she promised herself, I'll open a bottle of wine with Marcia and we'll study our sailing books. And I want to celebrate the fact that I didn't drop anything. A tiny bud of confidence began to grow in her forest of despair. Anyway, you can learn everything from books, even sailing. The trees waved their branches in silent dissent.

Chapter Thirty

Marcia was relieved and happy that Helen seemed to have found her feet again. When she'd first met Helen she had thought of her as a woman who had lost not only her feet but her hands too.

So many years of being bullied had taken away all her self-confidence. Marcia remembered her own years of despair and felt a deep bond and sympathy with Helen.

Marcia knew from experience that the first man to break a woman's heart inflicted the most damage. After that it became more of a case of 'here we go again'. Now long out of the fray, Marcia was glad that she had made that decision.

The months of quivering hurt during which she had comforted Helen had just served to remind her that men weren't worth the price or the pain they caused. True, she missed making love. Junior's father had been a good lover. The best of all her men; but even he had extracted too high a price.

Now Marcia was content to live each day at a time. She was looking forward to her sailing holiday. She was practising her barre stretching when Fats came out of his office. 'Hi, sweetie,' he said, giving her a smacking kiss. 'How you doin'?'

'Just fine for one old nigger woman.' Marcia felt a surge of happiness. 'Not long and we're off on our boat, Fats.'

'You must be raving mad, Marcia. Neither of you knows how to sail a big yacht. It's dangerous, I can tell you.'

Fats had been painting his office a fierce shade of yellow and he had a large blob of colour on his nose. 'Why don't you come with us, Fats? You know how to sail. We need you.'

'Marcia, honest to God, I'd drown you within the first week. Women are bad luck on boats, you know that. I'd sooner share my boat with rats than with women. All that fixing and fussing. No, sailing is men's business.'

'Well, we'll pick somebody to help us. Anyway Elliott says she's a good sailor, so she can teach us as we go along. Both of us know boats. I sailed as crew with Junior's dad, and Helen had a dinghy in Hove. So we're not neophytes. Elliott will teach us all to sail. Helen will improve our language, and I'll keep Elliott out of trouble. At least I'll try to keep Elliott out of trouble.'

'Huh, Elliott's all mouth and trousers. Or rather, designer jeans.' Fats laughed. 'How is she, by the way?'

'She's fine. She says she's given up on her sex life for the moment. I really like her, Fats. She's so warm and generous. I think we'll have a great time.'

Fats nodded in agreement. 'I'm particularly pleased for Helen. Toby's doing fine, but Helen needs to get right away where she doesn't hear from that bastard of an ex-husband of hers. I can always tell when he's been bullying her. Her eyes go wet and watery. She's so closed off, that one. I know when you're not all right because you tell me–' he grinned – 'and usually at the top of your voice.'

'Yeah, I do rant and scream, Fats, but at least I let it all out. Not like Helen. Her feelings are all inside her like a cancer. Maybe if we get completely caught up in getting this boat to Greece, she'll let go some of the hurt.'

'Try to get her to visualize the hurt. Tell her to think of it as an old smelly bundle that needs to be thrown away. Then she can imagine dropping it over the side of the boat before you leave to come back to England. Get her to wave goodbye to it and then tell her to visualize feeling clean and empty and ready for more adventures.'

Fats moved his bulk down the room. It was a long time since he'd had a real-world physical adventure. He didn't need to leave his meditation room. He could wander to his heart's content anywhere in the world.

Fats knew with a certainty taught by Gaylang that to live in the light was what he was here to do. Not many people understood his philosophy. The cost of living in the light was external and internal excellence. He did not believe in denial of the joys of life. Of sex, food and good wine. Those people who chose denial of the light's abundance did not understand the concept of eternity. The supreme intelligence has designed all good things for people. The fleshly rewards are to be enjoyed in moderation. Ah me, Fats sighed. Moderation, that was the fatal flaw. He loved his food and his wine. In making love he found a wonderful and profound communion. Fortunately, he had plenty of romances. But for now he felt empty.

The Bush was a special place to him. Now he had no more coming back to earth to do. His time was finished. Gaylang had gone on. Because it was his last manifestation on earth, Fats led his life with special care. Not to harm any living thing. To lend his heart and his soul to the young and the needy.

The seasons carried with them an exceptional nostalgia. He looked back over his shoulder. Fats could see Marcia laughing happily with a friend. As he went back to the little office, he realized that he was carrying a strong feeling of love for her. They had been friends for a long time. Marcia knew him very well. She also knew that Fats had a special interest in Helen but was waiting for her to be healed before approaching her.

Marcia was cleaning the floor of her kitchen later that night when Cricket finished playing his guitar and came into the kitchen. There was a moment of welcome relief from the strident music. 'Mum,' Cricket said. 'Are we going to be the only darks in Greece?'

'Why, Junior, does it bother you?' Marcia was surprised at the question.

'No, not really, but here I'm with other black people. I can't imagine being somewhere without other people like me. It's like being in Swiss Cottage when we visit Toby's dad. Everybody in the room has the same pale skin and when I come home I have to look in the mirror to check my face.'

Marcia lit a cigarette. 'I remember those feelings when I was a little girl in Bristol. I was the only black kid in my school. I used to try and plaster my hair down on my scalp like the white girls,' she laughed. 'Actually, it was no laughing matter. For years I drew myself as white. I had no way of knowing I was black, and my mum and dad certainly didn't talk about colour. They just ignored the subject. Coming as we did from a slave family, my mum and dad were humbled by everything.

'Now I was different. From a very early age I decided to take no lip from anyone, and I didn't. Your grandma and grandpa were horrified. Before I left home, my mother warned me about being too uppity. Needless to say I didn't listen.'

The telephone interrupted Marcia's reminiscences. 'It's Elliott for you, Mum. I love you, Elliott,' Cricket said down the receiver before he handed it over to his mother. 'I love you too,' she replied.

While he was watching his mother talking to Elliott, he realized that he did indeed love Elliott. She was only a few years younger than his mother but there was something exuberantly child-like about her. Cricket smiled at the memory of Elliott sitting in this room sparkling with laughter and giggling at his jokes. Yes, he did like her, and sometimes at night, in the safety of his own bed, he fantasized about what it would be like to make love to her. The fantasy, while exciting, made him feel guilty. After all, she was old enough to be his mother.

After one evening gig, Cricket had said casually to Toby, 'What do you think of toy-boys, Tobe?'

'Disgusting, bloody disgusting,' Toby had said firmly. That had sort of hit the nail in the coffin of his fantasy.

'Why is it OK for a man to be twenty years older than a woman and not the other way round?' Cricket had tried again.

'Because it isn't,' Toby had said firmly.

Marcia got off the telephone. She looked at her son, and knew from experience he had something on his mind.

'Mum,' he began, 'Toby says toy-boys are disgusting. What do you think?'

'Toby is so straight about things, Junior. He shouldn't judge so harshly. Life can be very perverse at times. And I don't know the circumstances you are describing. Age isn't chronological, you know. It certainly is physically but not internally. I've known people, especially women, who never seem to age. The best thing you can hope for is to be a child and then to grow into a wise child. The whole idea that there is such a thing as an adult world is just a myth. There is no such thing as an adult. There are only those children who grow in wisdom and under-standing, and those who don't.'

The doorbell rang. 'That'll be Toby,' Cricket said.

Toby came in, red in the face and fuming. 'My fucking father's walked out on Laura again and she's round at Mum's crying her eyes out. Mum's tired out from work-ing at the bar and she doesn't need the aggravation.

'Maisie's just had dinner with us and she's been telling such funny stories about her clients and making Mum shriek with laughter. Now Laura is depressing the hell out of her. Dad would have a fit if he knew we'd had dinner with a prostitute!'

'Your dad doesn't like you coming round here, let alone

having dinner with Maisie,' Cricket said.

'Well, your father is a leftover from the sixties,' Marcia pointed out. 'White honkys threw everything away in those years. The world they thought they'd made when they could do anything they liked didn't last. Your father lost his light many years ago. Now he just crumbles.

'Toby, try not to think too many negative thoughts about your father. The negative feelings will just depress you.'

'I do try,' Toby said, 'but it's so difficult. He lives so much in the past. He loves to go on about how life was in Swiss Cottage. He seems to remember it all as a very happy time. I don't remember it like that at all. I just remember Mum crying a lot and Dad yelling at her. I remember it was a terrible time for me. I was miserable, but the awful thing is I didn't know I was miserable until I got away.

'Mum says it's like Plato's cave: you don't know you're chained to the wall in the cave until you escape. The fire at the back of the cave makes everybody in there think that the flickering shadows on the walls are real life. When you go back and try and tell them about the real world outside, they don't want to know. It's like Cricket and me trying to tell Mince Meat and his henchmen that there is a world that doesn't involve crime and violence. To him, that's shit. He likes his violent way of life.'

'Sure, and in time Mince Meat will die as he lived – violently,' Marcia said slowly. 'My rule is to give a psychopath enough rope and he'll hang himself.' There was a moment of cold silence in the room.

'Come on, Tobe.' Cricket broke the silence. 'Rollo's waiting for us at the club.' He kissed his mother on the cheek. 'Don't wait up, Mum, I'm going visiting,' he said.

Marcia sighed. 'Oh, Junior. You are so like your dad sometimes.'

'Sure, and I'll reform when I'm a hundred.'

'Get on with you.' His mother pushed him away and laughed.

Chapter Thirty-one

'I always think of Plato as such a golden writer; he really understood what a glorious world we live in.'

Toby smiled, when his mother was in a philosophizing mood it meant that she was happy. 'I'm just going to telephone your father and see if he will give us a little extra for your sailing clothes. We will all have to wear slickers, of course. That's what Elliott calls oilskins. Elliott says we need to have bright colours so that if we fall off the boat people can spot us. What colour do you want?'

'Yellow, I'd like a bright yellow oilskin like the one I had when I was three. Do you remember it?'

'Sure I do, and you used to make such a fuss about wearing the hat. Doesn't it seem strange? You were wearing oilskins and a sou'-wester when you were little and now we're going out to buy them for ourselves again.' She picked up the telephone and heard it ringing in Laura's loft. Yet again, Laura had let Paul back into her life.

Although Helen had never been there, she'd listened to Cricket and Toby discussing all the fabulous pieces of artwork and the pale suede furniture. She looked around her own little room. Well, she comforted herself, I was never one for pale suede anyway.

'Hello.' It was Laura.

'Hi, Laura, it's me, Helen. Is Paul there?'

'Yes, he is, I'll just go and get him for you.' She could hear Laura's high-heeled shoes tapping across the floor of the loft. She wondered if Laura bent and kissed Paul before handing him the telephone like she used to do? Probably not, Laura was not such a sentimental idiot.

'Hello, Paul,' she said as cheerfully as possible. Inside her chest her heart was beating hard. She felt frightened of Paul's possible refusal. She heard Fats's reassuring voice. 'Don't panic, take deep breaths from your stomach. Remember, you have nothing to fear but fear itself.' Even Fats couldn't help; she *was* afraid of Paul.

'What do you want?' Paul's voice was its usual ungracious self. However charming and sensitive his act, his voice always betrayed him. It was high and light and had a whine in it.

'I need a little extra money to cover clothes for Toby's holiday, Paul. Not much, I can do most of it myself. About seventy-five pounds would do it.' Helen deliberately said seventy-five pounds because that's what Paul spent on his last meal out with Laura and Toby.

'I'm afraid I can't manage anything this month, Helen. I'm completely broke. If I overdraw I'll have to pay interest on the money, and I can't do that.'

'But Paul, I'm always overdrawn. How can you say that when we're trying to eat? I can't worry about interest on money. I have to see Toby has a decent meal.'

'Helen, you shouldn't have left your *proper* job. Here you are, working in a bar. What am I supposed to tell my mother? Her grandson has a mother who is a barmaid?'

The thought that she could appal Paul's mother cheered her up. 'Oh well, Paul, if you won't help, we'll just have to do it ourselves.'

She watched Toby's face and wished she'd made the telephone call when he was out of the house. She could see the muscles grinding in his left cheek. She made a 'never mind' face at him, and waved a hand. Toby came over to where she was standing and took the telephone from her. 'You fucking bastard,' he said. 'I never want to see you again.'

He slammed down the telephone. 'Don't worry, Mum. I can take on a paper round.'

'You don't have to do that, darling. Now I've got this new job, I get tips. I'm so pleased when somebody likes me enough to leave me some money. If you suffer from a need to please everybody, then running around being a waitress is a really good idea. At least I get paid for it . . . I'm sorry Paul was so beastly, Toby, but don't worry, we'll muddle through.'

'I know we will, Mum, but I want something better for you. I hate to see you come home so tired and your feet so hurt.'

'I know you hate to see me so tired, but now it's a happy tired. I sit in the bath and examine my feet. I didn't know that you could bruise your feet from the inside out, did you?'

'No, I didn't.' Toby tried not to let her see that he was nearly in tears. The whole unfair situation made the back of his throat sting. Here he was, going out for expensive dinners with his dad and Laura, and his mother, he knew, hadn't got the money to buy herself a new pair of shoes.

Despite what he'd said on the phone, Toby made one last attempt to approach his father for the money. Of course his dad said 'no' to the oilskins. Paul was furiously jealous that they were going off to Greece. 'I think it's a damned silly idea, if you ask me. Three middle-aged women on a boat: they'll sink it.'

'No they won't.' Toby's voice was hoarse with indignation. 'Elliott's sailed boats before, we all have a bit; and besides, Cricket and I can leap about and do the tying up and all that stuff. Mum can just relax and enjoy herself.'

'Your mother relax? That'll be the day. She'll spring-clean the boat and open a restaurant.'

'I know she will.' Toby's voice was dreamy. 'She's the

best cook in the world. I can't wait until she cooks Greek food. All that charcoal. Elliott says they cook delicious lamb with garlic and lemon juice.'

Now Toby was back in the flat with his mother. He put his arm around her, bent down and gave her a kiss. 'We'll be all right, Mum, just you see.'

Later that night, when she recounted her telephone call with Paul to Maisie, Helen was comforted by Maisie's angry response. 'What a bleeding bastard,' Maisie said, her eyes blazing. 'Why don't you let me get my bloke to go over there and duff him up?'

'Because, Maisie, Paul's the sort of man who'd call in the police and sling the book at your Garry. He loves exacting revenge.'

'I'd exact 'im 'an all, I would. Nobody'd know, Helen. Garry just waits for a dark night. The old brick in the mailbag and then *boff*, let 'im 'ave it. All over in two seconds flat.'

'No, Maisie, I don't think so. It's a nice idea, though.' Helen smiled. She tried to change the subject and collected five wine glasses carefully by the stems, the rims hanging upside down from her hand. 'Look, I can carry the glasses like you do, Maisie.'

'You can an' all, ducky. Hinkley's taken a fancy to you, you know. He thinks it's ever so flash to 'ave a lady in the bar that talks posh like you.'

'Well, I don't know about that, Maisie, but I do know that I'm really happy here. The bar feels sort of like a refuge. When I was married to Paul, I couldn't go to a battered wives' refuge because I didn't have any bruises. You know I'd have been lucky if he had hit me. He hit everything else. The walls, the cooker, the fridge; anything that annoyed him. Once he took a huge spanner to the car because it broke down before we got home. I sat there, terrified. Lots of people passed by and just stared at him. I could see women whispering to their friends or husbands, but nobody thought of asking me if I was all right.'

'Nobody does nothing for nobody these days, dear. Just you get used to that idea.'

'It's different down my road though, Maisie. Everybody knows everybody down my road. If I see a woman with a black eye, I go up and ask her if she's OK. Of course I can't do anything about it, because if her fellow knew she'd told someone he'd punch her again, but at least she knows that I know and I care.'

Helen felt a lump forming in her throat. 'You know,' she said, 'I'm surprised more women don't die from the cruelty of men?'

'Many more do than you read about, Helen. Specially in my game. If the coroner's office know you're on the game, they don't bother. You just go down as a suicide, or drugs if your punter is rich and famous. They all get away with it, do the rich.'

'That's terrible.' Helen was shocked.

'Yeah. I've 'ad friends murdered in snuff games. You get called in to identify them on ice, and then it's Bob's your uncle. They let you 'ave her for burial and down the 'ole she goes in a cheap coffin. When Muriel, an old mate, died, Lace 'ad a whip round and we got 'er a good coffin. Muriel was a special mate of Lace an' me. We were all on the game together. Lace always said Muriel would come to a bad end. She was a wonderful woman, though.' Maisie sighed; her bosom lifted consolingly. She slipped on to a chair and beckoned Helen to sit down.

'You got to understand that with us girls we're well – we're real family. They're all I got. My mum and dad died young. There's all the diseases and the poor on the National 'Ealth don't get treated like the rich do.'

'I'm not rich now, Maisie.' Helen felt defensive.

'I don't mean you, dear. I mean all those naff people who come with their children and look down their noses at me. They can eat and drink what they like. We can't. We know our kids don't get the vitamins they should. You are what you eat, you know. It says so in the *Reader's Digest*. And what we eat is shit, so we end up feeling like shit. Look at my feet. It's bloody disgusting. I can't afford a pair of shoes that fit me proper.' She thrust her feet at Helen. There were two big bunions deforming both feet.

'That must hurt,' Helen said, wincing.

'It do bloody hurt, but me plates of meat is all I got to make a living. An' me teeth are false.' Maisie thrust a plate out of her mouth . . . 'Anyway, back to me story. We buried Muriel. It was a bitter cold day. The vicar tried to make us 'ave a cremation but we didn't want that. We didn't want to think of Muriel or what was left of Muriel being burnt. The vicar started to say that Muriel had led an immoral life, but Lace shouted for 'im to shut 'is cakehole and that Muriel was a better woman than 'e was a man. So 'e shut up and said nice things about 'er. I went 'ome that night and cried and cried. I'd lost a sister. We pulled our first tricks together. Muriel had a fantastic sense of humour. She'd take a Polaroid of her John and then when he was too drunk to see straight she'd take one to show me. Next morning she'd come round to my 'ouse wiv 'er pictures and I'd show 'er mine. We'd laugh fit to bust. You know, if those bossy old biddies at the social ever heard us they'd wet their knickers. Oppressed, they call us. Well, I'm only ever pressed against a mattress, and that's for a lot of money. More than the likes of them will make in a million years.' Maisie was laughing again.

Helen envied Maisie's ability to slip from mood to mood like an agile circus performer. 'I guess I'll have to face the death of my mother and my father. They're quite old now. I was a late child and I had such a happy childhood.' Then Helen felt guilty. She knew that Maisie had had an appalling childhood.

'Helen, sometimes,' Maisie said slowly, 'sometimes you're better off learning the facts of life early on. It's people like you that get knocked for six when you hit a problem. I can see that rat of a 'usband 'as really KO'd you. I'm used to men being bastards. Sure, you do meet a few who aren't, but then they're married. I've 'ad hundreds of men in my life. Not all of them punters and not all of 'em bad. But take it from me, no man is worth giving you grief. You die young of men. They're like a disease. Once they get in your knickers, you can't get them out. It's like leeches. They suck your blood.'

Maisie rose to her feet. 'Best lay 'em and make 'em pay. That way the line is clean between the two of you. I've never 'ad trouble with punters, but once I let a man into my life . . .' Maisie sighed dramatically. '. . . It's all over. First the sweet-talk and the 'oneymoon and it's all down-'ill from there. You mark my words, dearie. Marriage is made for men by men. That's why I never married.'

'You're wise, Maisie. I did, and now look at me!' Helen laughed. 'Actually,' she confessed, 'I'm happier now than I've been in years.'

'Leaving that bastard took ten years off your face, didn't it?'

'It sure did,' Helen answered with her best American accent. 'Come on, let's finish the washing-up.'

Chapter Thirty-two

'Are you always this cynical about men?' Elliott had had a hard day and she wanted smooth, slurpy sympathy from Marcia, not a lecture on doing without men. 'I don't want to be without men in my life, Marcia. I like men. I know the last one was in the closet and I got hurt again. But now I've learnt not to get too worked up when gay guys go on about homophobia. There's just as much hetero-phobia around, but we liberals don't dare say anything.'

'You might love men, sugar, but you can't afford the sort of men you attract. You go for bastards, in or out of the closet. They can smell your scent. "Please abuse me, I'll do anything to please you." You've got to get a grip on yourself, or one day you'll come up against a man that will be really dangerous.'

'Are there any other kind?' Elliott tried laughing, but a shiver ran down her spine.

'Sure there are,' Marcia said firmly. 'But they're few and far between. Besides, the best ones are married. Their wives have potty-trained them and taught them to flush.'

'Yeah, but at least if they're married they don't move in with you. You only have to share your bathroom when they're in town. The trouble with single men is that they want to move in with you.' Elliott could hear Marcia laugh at last. 'Were you feeling down when I telephoned, Marcia?'

'No, not really. You have no idea how grim and grey England is in the winter. I'm taking Junior down to see my mother and my father. They live on a huge council estate in Bristol. I hate going back there. I took so long to escape from that place. At least here Junior is surrounded by kids his own colour. I was so lonely as a child, but then Mum and Dad love it there. Dad has his roses and Mum her church. So I guess I'll just quit belly-aching and go down there.'

'Look at it this way, Marcia: it won't be long before we're on the boat. Are you excited?'

'Yeah, in a way. But to tell you the truth, Elliott, I'm too tired to feel excited yet. What sort of fruit do they grow in Greece? I so much want to eat real good fresh fruit, like we used to have when Junior and I lived in JA.'

'Sure, when I was down there it was September. I picked fresh figs off the trees. I also lived in the middle of an orange and lemon grove. The smell of the fruit in the evenings as I sat in the little cottage was overwhelming. I was with a German guy who was obsessed with buckets. He had a blue bucket for water and a red one for washing his clothes. What a nerd. Oh yeah, although the guy was a total washout, the grilled lamb on a bed of rosemary at the taverna was *fantastic*.'

'What I'm really looking forward to is getting to Elba.' Marcia's voice was dreamy. 'I always loved history at school. I read all about Napoleon. He had his own private court in Elba. Did you know he kept his elephants there?'

'How do you know all that stuff, Marcia?'

'I read a lot: that's the only thing to do when you're a poor nigger kid. You go to the public library and get out books. At the moment I read in bed. We can only afford to heat the kitchen, so I make a hot-water bottle and lie under the blankets and read. Only the tip of my nose is cold. They don't make nose warmers yet, but Helen and I are thinking of going into business and making our first million.'

'How is she?' Elliott asked.

'She's fine. She loves the bar and she looks so much better. I go round on a Friday evening and have a drink with her. She's making friends, and Maisie has taken her under her wing. Paul is spitting his guts out. He doesn't want Toby to mix with the likes of Maisie. He'd better watch his tongue: Maisie has a lethal temper. I mean *lethal*. She bottled a bloke once in the bar. Sliced off half his chin.'

'Sounds as if Maisie could well deal with Paul.'

'She may have to. Paul has taken to going round to the pub to argue with Helen. He doesn't want his BBC friends to know that his ex-wife works in a bar.'

'Tough,' Elliott said feelingly. 'My mom dies if any of her friends find out that I work in a soup kitchen. I love every minute of it. OK, I'd better get off the phone and get on with life. Give Helen and Toby my love and give Cricket a big hug from me.'

Marcia put the telephone down. What was she feeling on hearing that she should hug her son for Elliott: jealousy? She decided then and there to have a warning talk with Junior. But she knew it probably wouldn't do any good. Junior was a dog when it came to women, just like his father. But then she couldn't altogether blame him. Women did throw themselves at him, and also he was young.

Marcia sighed, she was feeling old and lonely this evening. Never mind, she told herself. She poured herself a glass of Special Brew. Tomorrow is Friday and it's my night out at the pub. She checked the little box she kept for loose change. Two pounds and ten pence. Hummmm, she mused. Enough to buy herself a drink. Helen drank on the house. One of the advantages of working in a bar.

It was such a bitch being poor. Marcia didn't envy Elliott, but sometimes she wished she could have the money Elliott spent just telephoning her. She minded the cold most of all and now, packing Junior's case for the weekend, she was careful to put in very warm jumpers. Both her mother and her father were immune to the cold.

* * *

On the way down to Bristol in the train, the wind whistled and pulled the carriages irritably backwards and forwards. Marcia sat back with her eyes closed and tried to remember the fabulous times she'd had with Junior's father on the boat in JA. She felt that those years in JA had spoiled her for living in London.

Would the Greek blue skies be the same colour as the skies in the Caribbean? She rather doubted it. The blue Jamaican skies couldn't be bluer. The water was a wonderfully drinkable green. Parrot fish, that's what she remembered most. Blue and white striped, and so playful. They'd gathered around her in shoals. Once she'd swum right up to a big barracuda. ''Cuda,' Junior's father had shouted in warning. Marcia wasn't scared. 'I'm not scared of fish,' she had shouted, 'only men.'

She had made the decision that Junior's father had to go when he'd decided to colonize her life. 'Go mash some other women,' she'd said furiously as she threw him out. The sound of his bags hitting the pavement made her smile even after all these years.

She remembered his face. 'Why'd you do that?' he'd said plaintively, sitting on the pavement next to a large dog turd.

'Because no swine is going to take over my life. I belong to me and nobody else.' She had slammed the door and that was the last she'd seen of him and she packed up Toby and their belongings and headed back to England.

It had been hard on Junior though. Now she watched him through her lower lashes. He was sitting quietly on his seat looking out of the window. Such a surge of love welled in her chest. 'Junior,' she said. 'What do you think of Elliott?'

'I like her, Mum. She's good fun and really very pretty.'

'Don't you think she's a bit old for the way she acts?' Marcia despised herself for the questioning, but she persevered.

'No, not really, Mum. I think she acts like a child because she is a child. She's rich and she plays hard. There's nothing wrong with that, is there?'

'No, I guess not. Junior,' Marcia's voice faltered, 'you're not –?'

'If I am, Mum, it's not your business.' Marcia heeded the warning in her son's voice. He was right, it wasn't her business, but she was worried anyway. Why? She didn't know. Maybe it was because Junior had never been serious about any of the girls he had brought into her life. Elliott could be different. She was jealous, she told herself. But then that was natural. She didn't want to lose her son to anyone, and certainly not to a rich American who might take him, like a souvenir, back to Houston, Texas.

Once inside the door of the little house in Bristol, Marcia felt comforted. 'Not long before we go on the boat,' she told her mother.

'I do hope you'll be careful, dear. I worry about you both all the time.'

'You don't need to.' Cricket helped himself to another piece of fried chicken. 'We've got this American woman called Elliott going with us. She's the sort of woman that can sail anything. She said so.' Marcia looked sharply at her mother.

'I see.' Rosalee's eyebrows flew into her hair. 'What's this Elliott like, dear?'

'She's tall and she's fair, she's complicated and she's great fun. You'll like her. Everybody does. The band thinks she's terrific. Rollo's got a crush on her.' Cricket was glad that he was black and couldn't be seen to be blushing. The truth was that his nights were full of fantasies of making love to Elliott. He was embarrassed but he held his ground.

'She sounds like a paragon of virtue, Junior. Have some more yam.'

Cricket grinned at his grandfather. His grandparents were the most secure thing in Cricket's insecure life. 'Boy, she's beautiful,' he said happily. 'Not as beautiful as Mum, though.'

'Thank you, son.' Marcia smiled, partly mollified. 'Eat up, Junior, we have to catch the nine o'clock train back to London.'

'I wish you could stay a little longer, Marcia. You look so tired.'

'I wish I could, Mum. I've taken on more hours at the dance centre to help pay for the holiday, and Junior is doing a paper round. It's not much, but we are getting there.' She sighed. 'Life's hard on my own, but at least I have my peace.' She gazed into her coffee cup. 'And that's worth plenty,' she said.

'Amen,' said her mother, and got up to clear the table.

Chapter Thirty-three

'I wish my hair was like yours, Tobe.' Cricket was standing in front of Toby's mirror. The windowpanes of the room were rimmed with a late frost. Toby was sitting in a forlorn heap under his duvet. He remembered the days when he was always warm. It was the cold that got to him, made him feel poor. Not only poor but sort of unwanted. Well, it was true his father didn't really want him, except to moan about his mother or to complain about money.

'Your hair is great, Cricket. I wish I had hair that curled in long locks like that. My locks look awful. White hair just doesn't work in locks.'

Cricket lifted up one of his locks. 'I was thinking of straightening my hair.'

'Don't do that, man. That's cheating on your roots.'

'I don't have no roots. Just somewhere in Africa. My dad is from Montego Bay in JA. I left JA when I was too young to remember much of it, though I do remember the boat. Mum keeps saying it's the most beautiful place in the world.'

'One day we'll go there, Cricket. We'll take the band and go and smoke ganja with the Rastas in the Blue Mountains. I'll bring Blue Mountain coffee for my Mum. She loves Blue Mountain coffee and we can't afford it any more.

'Boy, can you imagine getting high and then running down the mountainside with the Rasta men and diving straight into the Caribbean sea? I'm going to pick a whole pile of mangoes and eat them while I float about. Gosh, Cricket, d'you think that there'll be mangoes in Greece?'

'Nah, fool, there ain't no mangoes in Greece!' Cricket pulled on his big tall Rasta knitted cap. 'There's lots of other fruit and girls. I hope there are lots and lots of girls who can't say no.' Cricket mimed stroking a girl's breasts. His hands seemed to have a licentious life of their own. 'I love titties,' Cricket crooned softly.

Toby wished Cricket was slightly less vocal about sex. 'I don't want to get tied down to a girl.' Toby knew he sounded rather prim but now he was dating a girl called Sarah from school and he enjoyed her company.

'I like Sarah, and she helps me so much with my English books. I'd much rather be in Greece with her. She doesn't push and she's gentle and kind. Not like Louise. It's taken ages to get over the mess she made of my head. This time I'm moving slowly. I never want to get trapped in that sex stuff again.'

'You're an old fogey, Toby. Why don't you do like me and just bump them all?'

'Because I can't, Cricket. I don't want to. I want to share love with a girl I really love. I loved Louise and she dumped me. I know I'll get over it. Your problem is that you've never been in love.'

'No, and I don't want to, not after seeing what my dad did to my mum. I thought my mum would never smile again. She's not as tough as people think she is,' Cricket said.

'No, she isn't. I know that. My mum is much happier now she works in the pub. I'm going down later this evening to see her and walk her home. It's dangerous out there. But at least Mum is making a new life for herself. Dad certainly isn't. He just lives in the past.'

Cricket slapped Toby's outstretched hand. 'You take care, man. I'll be back after closing time. Expect to find me stretched out on the floor.'

'Don't you feel the cold, Cricket?'

'Sure thing. Contrary to popular thinking, the poor feel

the cold just as much as the rich. We just get used to having colds and sore throats.'

'I'll get a couple of blankets out of the linen chest for you, Cricket.'

'Linen chest? How very middle-class, Tobe.'

'I am middle-class, Cricket, and I'm not apologizing to anyone for it. If Mince Meat and his gang make life difficult, I know how to fight and I'll fight with them any time.'

'You and your bloody accent, Toby. It's got us into so much trouble.'

Toby laughed. 'Yes, but it gets us out of trouble with the police, doesn't it?'

'Yeah, I guess so. Bye,' and Cricket was gone.

Toby got out of bed and watched Cricket's long legs lolloping down the road. Cricket loved his mother but he didn't have the same protective feelings towards Marcia as Toby had towards Helen. Marcia was so much more streetwise. Toby always felt a familiar feeling of terror when his mother was out at night. All his life he'd been used to having her at home. Her presence in the kitchen or reading in the sitting room, the sound of the wireless, the six o'clock BBC news: he had always thought these things in his life would be immutable, but they were not. It was now all gone. Life had slid into a black chaos.

He went back to his bed and sat down. He could telephone Sarah. She lived with her mother in Hammersmith Grove. Another kid without a father. Now, at this school, there were very few kids with fathers at home. Toby didn't particularly envy those kids who did have a father still. Most men, he reckoned, had bunked out of any responsibility, and behaved like pigs like his father. Paul had been so charming and such good fun around his friends, but what a pig in private. Toby made a face. He had to go and visit his father tomorrow, he reminded himself.

He reckoned that he might as well have a bath in the beastly cold bathroom. He hated the way the top half of his body froze while the bottom half went an unattractive shade of bright pink. Cricket was wrong to dislike his hair or his colour. Toby sat in the bath, thinking.

Cricket's colour was a beautiful velvety black. His skin had a bloom and a shine on it that made Toby envious. Shit, why did he have to have such boring pale blue eyes that looked as if he were permanently about to cry. And as for his sandy blond hair, he hated it.

Two hours later, invigorated by his bath and newly washed hair, he closed the front door behind him and admired the steam which poured from his mouth. He still felt damp and his hair stuck to his scalp. He walked out into the milky cold night.

He loved the way the lamps poured a stream of gold at his feet. One day, hopefully in the not-too-distant future, he wanted to take his mother away from all this squalor. He would load her hands with diamonds and pour riches into her lap. Sometimes, as he felt this soft melting feeling about his mother, he wondered if any girl in the world would be as wonderful as her? Maybe not, but with Sarah he felt warm and comfortable. She sat quietly beside him in class and they worked very hard together. She loved animals and wanted to be a vet.

This was a side of her that Toby really liked. She was at heart a country girl, and she was lost in a city like London. He took her to places like Richmond Park and Syon House. Her favourite place was London Zoo. She loved the wolves. He was made nervous by the wolves. Their backs were hunched in the winter weather, their heads flung back. Their long howls seemed reminiscent of his own feelings after he lost his room and his house in Swiss Cottage.

There were no leaves to kick as he walked along the road to Chiswick High Road. He turned the corner and saw the bright lights of the public house. Chiswick was National Front territory, and he was glad to see the lights.

Marcia had gone to a funeral with Maisie and Lace. The two M and M's, as he thought of them both. Maisie he loved very much, but Lace frightened him. She had eyes that looked as if they'd seen things he would never want to see. How women could sell themselves to men he couldn't understand, but Maisie made him laugh when he was with her and he could do with a laugh tonight.

Once inside the warm fuggy pub he searched for his mother's fair hair. There was always a particular shine about her that he noticed had only arrived since she'd left Paul. He heard a raucous laugh. It was Maisie. She had her arm around Helen and was hitting her knee with a fat bejewelled hand as she came to the punchline of the joke.

For once Lace was silent. She sat staring into her gin and lime. Marcia looked up when she saw Toby walking towards them. She smiled at him, but her eyes were sad and blinded by recent tears.

'How was it?' Toby said simply. He felt so silly. What did one say about a funeral? Hardly, did you have a good time?

'It went as well as could be expected,' Marcia said, shrugging her shoulders. 'It was sad: she was so young. All that was left to identify her was a blue tattoo on her right arm. Maisie had to go to the police to identify her.'

'The only time in my life when I was glad of the filth,' Maisie put in. 'What an 'orrible sight. I'll never forget it. Another port and lemon, Hinkley pet; then I got to go off and earn me rent.'

Toby tried not to blush. He wished Maisie wouldn't talk about 'going to work' like that. It embarrassed the hell out of him to even think about her work. How could a man pay to put his willy into someone as fat and shapeless as Maisie? Maybe she did it for laughs, but when she told long tales of her punters she put her hands on her belly and rocked from side to side like a vast bread-and-butter pudding.

Now Lace was different. Very different. When Lace walked into the pub, everything went quiet. There was a definite air of menace about her. She was slim, dark and quite beautiful, but she made her money whipping her clients. Toby had heard his mother discussing this subject with Marcia.

Helen put her arm around Toby's shoulders. 'It's a sad day for us all,' she said, smiling at her son.

Toby stood looking down at her. What a change in her. There in Swiss Cottage, all the talk had been about Habitat and how the poor were scrounging off the state. Teenage girls having babies on purpose to get welfare money and flats. Now Toby knew it was all a bloody load of rubbish. This world was much more interesting.

'I'll be off then, Helen. I'll see yer tomorrow, OK?'

'Right-oh, Maisie. I'll see you here the usual time.'

'I'm off to the Gloucester Road tonight to roll Arabs. There's a rich fellow at the 'otel, so I'll pick up a nice bit of business.'

'Aren't you ever afraid that a man might hurt you, Maisie?' Toby felt compelled to ask.

'Nah.' She waved a big fist. 'No man'll ever get the better of me. My old man once tried to batter me and I nearly took 'is head off with me frying pan. Men who batter wimmin are all wimps. Hit 'em where it 'urts. Besides Arabs is good to wimmin. Not like the English bastards. All that beating them on the bottom at their schools. It's not good for no one. If anybody gives me lip, I give them a knuckle sandwich.'

'I'm sure you would, Maisie,' Helen said faintly. 'Come on, Toby,' she said, taking off her apron, 'time to go home.' She took Toby's arm. He walked his mother out of the pub and down the long road, feeling a million years old.

'Cor, Mum,' he said. He loved to watch her face when she was cross.

'Toby, you're not to talk like that. You must speak the Queen's English. It's a beautiful language and I won't have you mangling it.'

'Don't worry, Mum, I won't go all common on you.' He grinned. 'After all, we're down the Bush now and I don't want to get the shit kicked out of me for sounding posh.'

'If anybody kicks the shit out of you, Toby, they'll have me to deal with.'

Toby laughed helplessly as his mother clenched her little fists and frowned. 'Oy, we're getting all belligerent, are we?' he said.

'You bet,' his mother said, and grinned.

Chapter Thirty-four

'I was unsettled all day, Elliott.' Marcia was driving Elliott to the Savoy from Heathrow Airport. Helen had lent her her old car. 'I spent the weekend with my parents, and I've spent days thinking how lucky Junior and I are to have such wonderful family. I suppose the idea of leaving them now when they are so much older bothers me.'

'Well, you ought to get them bronzed. The trouble with having lousy parents is that you spend your life trying to get reparented. That's what Philip keeps telling me. He said that I wanted him to father me and he couldn't be my father. It's also why I go for older men.'

'Philip's quite right, girl, he can't father you. Only your father can do that.' Marcia cast an affectionate look at Elliott who was wrapped in a thick fur coat. 'Elliott,' she said, 'haven't you heard of animal conservation?'

'Not when I'm damned cold, I haven't. Anyway, it's been dead for years. It belongs to my mother. She has a whole closet of them. She wore this one for a year and then got bored of it. She's found herself another gigolo and is off to Grand Cayman until I get back from Greece. I warned her not to let him run through all her money. But then,' Elliott grinned, 'Mom's as tight as a tick's butt when it comes to spending money on anybody else but herself.'

'So she's no fool?' Marcia drove smoothly and well, unlike Helen who tended to panic. 'No, my mom's a good businesswoman, it's just that she is so possessive of me. I hate the feeling that she wants to live through me. She interferes all the time. Philip says we have a symbiotic relationship.'

Soon they were swirling around Hyde Park. 'Ahhh,' Elliott gazed at the flag fluttering on top of Buckingham Palace, 'I read somewhere that the British flag is flown whenever your Queen is in residence.'

'Yes.' Marcia followed Elliott's gaze. 'I always like it when I know she's in residence. She's the one good thing this country's got going for it. The Queen and all her family. My mother said that my grandmother prayed for the Royal Family every day. My mum used to keep a scrapbook of the Royal Family. I have it to this day.' Marcia's knuckles gripped the steering wheel. 'The way social workers and teachers are behaving these days, you'd think we lived in a totalitarian state not a democracy.'

Elliott snorted. 'Try living in America, the home of the huddled masses. That's exactly what has happened. The masses are huddled on the beaches and the homeless and the insane crowd our soup kitchens. The social workers have been brainwashing the kids to fail at everything. Teachers refuse to teach them anything, and the rich are just getting richer. I'm glad I'm getting out. I'm going clear. You know like when you've had so much to drink and you're not on the floor yet and you can see everything, I mean inside you and inside everyone else around you? It's like you're an aeroplane and you're going into the stratosphere . . . ? Yeah, I'm glad I'm out of it, if only for a few weeks.'

'Is it really that bad?' Marcia was surprised. 'When I was at this funeral last week I looked at all Maisie's friends gathered together and I thought, Well, here we all are. Most of us broke and single-parent mothers, but what the hell? We're a great bunch of women. We went back to the pub and had a drink and a laugh. Funny really, how men hate women these days. My mum says it wasn't like that in her day.'

'It's frightening in America. If you live on your own

you never open your door at nights. You never walk on the streets after dark. You are frightened to death most of the time. I sometimes think it's because not only did we ask for equality in the workplace but also we asked for our sexual freedom.'

'Yeah, that's what Helen and I think, but then we don't bother with men any more.'

'But you need men for sex, don't you?'

'Oh Elliott, don't be so American. If I want sex I find a lover and enjoy myself. I have Cricket in the house and I know boys can't stand their mothers to be promiscuous. Anyway, I prefer to keep my sex life to myself.'

'Sorrryyy,' Elliott affected an American high-pitched whine. 'I just asked.'

'Don't ask.' The car pulled up at the Savoy.

'Oh boy, I'm glad to be back, Marcia. I could live the rest of my life in this hotel. What I need is a nice big sugar-daddy who can keep me in the style I am now accustomed to. Hello, honey,' she said, smiling at the warm friendly faces of the staff. 'Hi, everybody, I'm home.' Elliott flung out her arms in an expansive gesture. Marcia winced. Sometimes she wished Elliott would be less dramatic. But she had to admit it worked for Elliott. Tired busy faces relaxed and gazed fondly at Elliott. She stood, dripping with diamonds in her fur coat, and Marcia had to agree Elliott could carry anything off. She had nerves of steel and absolutely no sense of self-criticism.

Elliott handed over a large wodge of cash to the bellboy.

'Elliott!' Marcia was scandalized. 'I could live on that for a week.'

'Well, he's a great kid and I love him to death.'

'You wouldn't . . . ?'

Elliott laughed. 'Not in the Savoy.' She tried to forget the piano player. Idly she wondered how he was doing.

She knew he was in Switzerland playing in a hotel for the skiing season. Oh well, the boy had been cute, but he was not her type. 'Forget it, Marcia, let's have a drink.'

'I don't drink at this hour of the morning, Elliott.'

'Well I do.' Elliott went to the mini-bar in the bedroom and Marcia heard her rummaging through the bottles. 'Ah, vodka and tonic. Look, packets of delicious little nuts and, best of all, a bar of white chocolate. It's an expensive way to collect nuts, but what the hell, you're a long time dead.'

Marcia stood by the ornate fireplace and wished she could be honest with Elliott. What she wanted to say was that, while Elliott had plenty of money, Helen and Marcia were going to have to count every penny. She wondered what effect Elliott flinging around large amounts of cash would have on Junior. Toby, she knew, couldn't care less. As long as he had his supply of books and his guitar, he was pretty oblivious to money or girls. The girl he was with now was a dear, shy little thing, and they considered themselves romantically in love. Cricket told Marcia that Toby hadn't even made love to the girl.

But Junior, now Junior was another matter. Junior loved money and he was attracted to Elliott. She could see it in his eyes and the adoring way he looked at her. Well, if he got into a bunk with Elliott he might come out a wiser boy. Still, she didn't like the thought of it at all.

'A dime for your thoughts, kiddo?'

'Not worth a dime,' Marcia said hurriedly. 'OK, let's go shopping.'

Elliott agreed. 'I want a nice big roomy tent.'

'What for?' Marcia was puzzled.

'Oh, just in case I feel I need time out. I've been on boats enough times to know it's a really squashed experience, and I need my space.'

'Oh,' Marcia laughed. So that's how Elliott is going to

entertain her men, she thought. She's no fool. Aloud she said, 'What a good idea, Elliott.' Marcia lit her cigarette. She sucked the smoke through her lips. I wish it were a joint, she thought. The idea of Junior in bed with Elliott was really bothering her.

'Can you stay for lunch?' Elliott raised one eyebrow.

'No, I've got to get back to the dance centre. Fats has another teacher coming to give some classes on mind control.'

'Mind control?' Elliott looked surprised.

'Sure. You see, Fats teaches us that thought creates matter. If you want something to happen, you must think about it to bring it into being. You plan what you want in your mind and then, using a meditation technique, you call for it.'

'Do you really believe that stuff, Marcia?'

'Sure I do, I absolutely believe it.'

'OK, let me see you do it?'

Marcia thought for a moment. 'I'll get Helen to call us in the next five minutes.' Marcia walked over to the telephone which was on the writing desk by the window. She stroked the telephone with her fingers. *Call Helen*, she instructed Helen internally. She cleared her mind and visualized Helen. *Call Helen* she willed again. She felt the need to hear Helen's voice acutely. She waited, breathing deeply from her stomach. She was conscious of the air entering her nostrils and then leaving her in a huge, gasping sigh as she exhaled.

She turned her back to walk away. 'I'm sorry,' she said, and then the telephone shrilled, making them both jump.

'It isn't . . .' Elliott said, laughing, but it was. 'Wow,' Elliott shrieked, 'I don't believe this is happening.'

Marcia smiled. 'Hello, Helen. I'm just giving Elliott a lesson in mind control.'

'You'd better hurry over here.' Helen's voice was tense.

'Junior and Toby have been arrested and charged with robbery.'

'Oh shit!' Marcia felt as if she had been punched in the stomach.

'What's the matter, Marcia?' Elliott saw the look of fear on Marcia's face.

'It's the boys, they've been arrested by the police. We'd better get round there fast before they get the shit beaten out of them.'

'We're gone.' Elliott was running across the suite clutching her coat. They both raced down the corridor and piled into the little ornate lift.

Marcia was shaking. 'If they hurt Junior, I'll kill them all.'

'They won't hurt anybody once I get there.' Elliott's voice was angry. 'London police might think they're tough, but I'm used to taking on American state troopers, and they're the worst.'

'If Sergeant Jameson is on duty, we'll be all right. He's one of the few good cops in the shop. He likes the boys, and he knows they'd never hurt anyone.' Marcia wondered if the lift was going to take the rest of her life to descend to the first floor.

Chapter Thirty-five

The car pulled up outside Helen's flat. She was waiting, her face white and anxious. 'I've telephoned the police station but Sergeant Jameson isn't on duty. I've warned them that if there's a mark on either of the boys I'll sue them blind. I've telephoned Paul. I had to because we use his family lawyer. They're on their way down now. Paul is simply furious and he says it's all my fault.' Helen's voice was trembling with tears.

'I'll deal with that bastard Paul, Helen. Don't give it another thought. The boys will be fine, just you wait and see.' Elliott pulled Helen into the car. 'If we have any trouble, I'll get hold of my friend who is the American ambassador here in London. Leo is a sweetie.' She hugged Helen. 'Come on, honey,' she tried to make her friends smile, 'boys will be boys.'

'I just don't want them hurt, Elliott. Until I lived down here I had no idea how vicious and violent the police could be.'

'It isn't the police force, Helen.' Marcia tried to calm her friend. 'It's just that the police force, like the army, can attract violent men. Most police are decent enough.'

The car pulled up outside the police station. Helen's heart sank. Here she was, trying to get her son released from a police station. Maybe Paul was right, she *was* useless, a total failure as a mother and a wife.

Elliott raced up the steps and burst into the shabby police station. Helen and Marcia followed, Marcia buttoning her purse after paying off the car.

The sergeant on duty looked up wearily. 'What can I do for you ladies?' he said, trying to smile.

'We've come to collect Junior and his friend Toby Beckett. Where are they?' Helen said breathlessly.

'What's the charge?' Marcia asked, her voice shaking with anger.

'Let me see.' The sergeant ran his eyes down a piece of paper. 'Breaking and entering.' He looked up and frowned. He remembered the boys and they were not the sort usually seen in a police station.

Helen felt her heart pounding. 'It can't be possible, my Toby wouldn't do a thing like that.'

'The lads were apprehended in the park after a description was given that matched both of them perfectly,' he said.

'Did they have anything on them?' Elliott's voice was firm.

'No, but they were described as being seen running away from the scene of the crime.'

Footsteps approached the desk. Paul, Helen thought, I'd know that angry, determined, flat-footed walk anywhere.

'I'm Mr Beckett, Sergeant. I've come with my lawyer to bail out my son Toby Beckett.'

'And Junior, Paul.' Helen's voice was light but determined.

'What you do with your criminal friends is up to you, Helen. I intend to get my son out and take him home with me. This is a disgrace. What on earth are my friends going to say?'

'I don't know and I don't care. Anyway, piss off. I'm bailing out Toby and Junior and you and your fucking lawyer can clear off. I thought you'd be a help, but obviously you're just going to be a bloody nuisance.' Helen caught sight of herself in a fly-blown mirror. She had her hands on her hips and the rage felt wonderful.

'I say, Paul.' The family lawyer had strands of black

hair across his balding pate. 'She's a little over the top, don't you think?'

'Always was and always will be,' Paul replied, blinking with embarrassment.

'I want to bail both boys out. Is that all right, Sergeant? Toby lives with me, not his father.'

'Surely, as long as you can pay the bail you can take them both away and we'll let you know the date when the court is going to sit.'

'It's a first offence,' Marcia said. 'Neither boy has ever been in trouble with the law.'

'Yes,' the sergeant agreed. He looked at the two women's shabby clothes. Inwardly he hoped there'd been some mistake. Both boys looked like good lads, and their mothers obviously really cared about them. Not like most of the slatternly women who came into the station.

'I'll go and get them out now.' He left the desk and pulled out a huge set of keys.

Tears fell down Helen's face. 'Get lost, Paul, before I get jailed for assaulting you. I don't want you here when Toby comes up.'

'All right, all right.' Paul was nervous. 'I'm going. Come on, Richard, let's leave.' They walked out of the door.

'Good riddance to bad shit,' Marcia said dismissively. 'Now, where are the boys?'

Helen heard the sound of keys turning in a lock. She winced. It was one thing to watch police stories on television, but quite another to hear the sound of a key grating in a cell lock in reality. 'Toby,' she said, running towards him. He looked so white and strained.

'It's OK, Mum. Please don't make a fuss.' He pushed Helen aside.

Helen drew back, hurt. 'I'm not making a fuss, Toby. I was just desperately worried about you.'

'Don't be, Mum. It's just a silly mistake and we can sort it out.'

'Come back tomorrow,' the sergeant said as Helen signed the bail form. 'We'll run a line up and see if anybody can identify the boys.' Privately he knew that neither of the boys was likely to be a thief. Toby, the younger of the two, didn't look capable. As for the black lad, the most trouble he'd been in was probably truanting from school. 'Are you one of Fats' boys?' he asked Junior.

'Yeah, and he'll be wild when he finds out what's happened,' Junior replied.

'Don't worry too much, ladies. I think it's just a matter of mistaken identity.' Those two women would have a sleepless night. Two more lads without fathers. Thank goodness for his wife and four children. Pie and mash for supper tonight. He smiled at the boys. 'Off you go then,' he said.

When Helen got back to the flat the shock of the event hit her. 'Cup of tea, Toby?' she said, trying not to sound shrill.

'No thanks, Mum, I think I'll go to bed and sleep. I'm whacked.' Toby leaned over her and gave her a soft kiss on her cheek.

Now, as she heard his door shut, she allowed the tears to roll down her face. Her hands were shaking as she put the kettle on for a cup of tea. She could still smell the police station. A curious mixture of sweat, fear and Dettol. Underlying the smell was the stale smell of unwashed bodies and urine. How could the police work in that place year in and year out and not go mad? The sight of so much human misery paraded before them day after day? Well, the sergeant was a nice kind man and the boys had been lucky. Marcia had told her that some of the police in the station put their prisoners under a mattress and then beat them. 'You see,' Marcia said grimly, 'if they use a mattress it hurts just as much but they don't show any bruises.'

The world was indeed a hideous place. Helen took her

tea into the sitting room and curled up in front of the fire. It was nearing the end of the month and there was no money for coal, so she wrapped the blanket around her thin shoulders and nursed the tea to keep her hands warm.

What a prig Paul was. She remembered his flushed face and his pompous friend who had escorted Paul carefully away from the presence of his insane wife. Well, if she *were* insane, she was far better off here in this unheated flat with Toby than she had ever been in their big house and their utterly boring lifestyle.

She was also disturbed by Toby's attitude to her in the police station. '"Your children are not your children . . ."' She recited the poem from Kahlil Gibran's book *The Prophet*. Yes, Toby was her arrow and he wanted to fly. He didn't want his mother clucking after him. One day Toby would be gone for good, and then she'd be alone.

She stared at the backs of her hands, then at the cup sitting on the table. It was a pretty blue cup with a round, warming belly. Helen was particular about her cups. She had a very big cup for her morning cup of tea and another one, this one, for her afternoon cup.

Alone in bed, Toby sobbed himself asleep. Helen, much later, before she went to bed, pulled up the bedclothes and kissed his flushed face lightly. Her heart went out to her son, but he was growing up now and she was glad of it.

Chapter Thirty-six

Toby awoke at dawn with a start. For a moment he lay wide-eyed and shaking. No, he was not in that dreadful, stinking cell. His hands gripped the soft duvet and his aching body relaxed.

He could hear his mother breathing heavily. She didn't snore, but she sounded as if she had difficulty breathing. Probably too much wine, Toby thought. Her drinking was worrying him. This thought made him feel even more guilty. For so many years it had not crossed his mind that his mother was not in control of their universe, and critical thoughts were like urban terrorists in Swiss Cottage: unthinkable.

After he picked up Cricket outside his house, they went to see Fats before going to school. Fats listened with his big head on one side and his brown eyes exuding sympathy. 'Happens all the time,' he said, shaking his head. 'Sounds like a copper needed a fit, that's all. Don't worry, boys, I'll go up there myself. What I think will happen is that they'll ask you to attend a line-up this afternoon, and if nobody can identify either of you, you'll be in the clear. I'll ring your mothers if that's the case.'

'I'm not worried about the police, Fats,' Toby said. 'It's Mum, she's so terrified of everything. By now she ought to have learned to be cool. Then I feel so angry with her and that makes me feel bad.'

'It's OK to be angry with your mum, Toby. She's not like Marcia who knows to let Cricket roam. You have to learn by your own mistakes. That's hard on her – your mother,' he corrected himself. 'Nobody's mother or father can give a child their freedom. The child must take their freedom and tear away from the parents, only then can they come back and be free.

'You see, that's why I said it's OK to be angry with your mum. To feel guilty when you think bad things about her. That's part of you growing up and beginning to see her as a real person.'

'You should have seen me when I got back to my yard with my mother,' Cricket said. 'I had to run round the kitchen table and then she got me with her broom.' He grinned. 'But it made her feel better. Licks don't bother me any more.'

Fats raised his bulk from his chair and picked up the three coffee cups. 'You boys run along to school and I'll go up and see some of my friends up there. They're mostly a good bunch, but when a rotten apple gets in –' he shrugged – 'then it's frightening.'

Sitting next to Sarah at school, Toby felt envious of her. Now he visited her family on the odd occasion. He was embarrassed by their clean, tidy house. By the mumsie mother who bustled and hustled continuously, brushing away crumbs and plumping the pillows in Sarah's small, squat, semi-detached house in the back streets behind his block of flats. They were neat flat-faced little houses with pocket-handkerchief gardens. Now spring was arriving, the thin, spindly branches studded with little shoots of green warned Toby away. 'You don't belong here,' they seemed to say fiercely. 'Here we guard our privacy and our lives. We don't think you're the right boy for our Sarah. She's a good girl. She wants to get her GCSEs. Get a career so she can take care of herself if needs be and then get married and have Sunday dinner one week with her mum and dad and the next week with her in-laws.'

Sometimes, when Toby woke up in his mean little room, he watched the sour air of his beer-lined mouth blowing old froth between his lips. He, too, like his mother, was drinking too much. He wished he wasn't so rude and impatient with his mother, but she made him feel such a fool in front of other people. OK, he was fifteen and he was no longer a virgin. He lusted after girls, even if he kept his randy thoughts to himself. He knew how to drive her car. She didn't know that, but Cricket had taught him how to hot-wire the engine. They took the car off into the night; Helen was such an innocent she never even checked the milometer.

This double life was new to him, and the guilt of it tore him apart. The more vulnerable she became when he was impatient with her, the more vicious he felt. Her hand stretched tenderly out towards him made him scream. 'Can't you ever say fuck off, Mum? Just once raise your voice. Living with you is like living with a desert. I try to pour my feelings into you and nothing comes back!'

'You're my beloved son, Toby. I couldn't shout and scream at you any more than I could fight with Paul. Yes, he wanted me to, but I couldn't. If you're upset about something, I try to listen and to help you. That's all I know how to do.'

'All right, Mum, let's drop the subject.' Toby gave his mother a guilty hug. Both mother and son would stare at each other for a moment, the mother trying to understand the male needs of her son and not succeeding, the son seeing a hurt, defeated woman in front of him with no hard edge to protect herself. She had no mantle to keep her feelings from the cold blast of reality. Women without men, he thought as he turned so often away. Still, Marcia and Elliott were different; maybe in time his mother could learn too.

In the mornings he could hear the sounds of his mother getting up. The early morning rustle of her trajectory to the bathroom. He always waited for her to come out of the bathroom and go into her own bedroom. They were shy of each other. Each was used to a bathroom of their own. His mother shared hers with his father, and Toby had his own thickly carpeted bathroom with a big, deep bath. How he missed his bathroom sometimes. He had had a big American shower and a bidet.

What made him shy with his mother was the unfamiliar smell of her in the bathroom. Her knickers over the shower rail. The towel rail was not heated and their big bath towels soon acquired little bobbles, a nap like barbed wire from being washed at the local launderette.

This morning, before his visit to Fats, he had waited as usual, and had heard the sound of the loo flushing. 'Toilet,' he reminded himself. Cricket warned him that lavatory was on the too-posh list. Toby was weary of remembering what was considered posh or not. 'Karsy' was acceptable, he was told. Why should you risk being beaten for your words? He'd stopped wondering about that. He now just accepted that violence was a reality. Fit in and conform.

He waited and lit a cigarette. Soon her door would close and he would struggle with the shower. A bath was too dreadful to contemplate.

In her own bedroom, Helen felt the sadness of the morning slowly squeeze her heart. She heard Toby go into the bathroom. She knew of his feelings of reserve at having to share a bathroom with her. She wished she didn't have to hang her stockings or her underwear on the shower rail. She hated the mean little shower that trickled so disdainfully over her head. She hated the little pink bulbous shower head. If only she had the money to squander on a big rose of a shower head that would drench her with water and wash away the lack of colour in her life.

One thing she'd learned: that it wasn't the flat, the thin threadbare carpets, or the brown formica that broke her down. Those she could make into projects and, with cheap pots of paints and stripper, she could make her changes. No, it was the shower head. The one she wanted cost far more than her budget could ever allow. It was a luxury and, therefore, now out of her reach.

'What does one wear for a line-up?' Fats had telephoned the bar at lunch-time. 'The boys need to go to the police station after school,' he said. 'I don't think there's any problem. The boys think that's all that will be necessary. If no one can identify them, they'll drop the case.'

Helen was relieved to hear his voice. 'Thanks, Fats,' she said gratefully. 'I don't know where I'd be without you.'

'You'd be OK, Helen, but I'm glad we know each other.' There was a moment's silence and Helen put the telephone down thoughtfully. Fats had a gentle quality she had never found in any other man except her father. In her father she felt the quality was more of a gentle resignation in the face of a world that had not offered him much in the way of opportunity. With Fats it was very different. In his own way he was a quiet dynamo. He ran his gym, cared for his boys. Took cases to court. Watched the neighbourhood carefully.

Back in the flat after her lunch-time shift, Helen picked up the telephone. 'What on earth does one wear for a line-up, Marcia?'

'Your best clothes. They'll get off. If they're doing a line-up it means they haven't got any real evidence, so they'll tie the whole thing up and let the boys go. Look sad and cry if you can. Men hate seeing women cry.'

'I probably shall cry, I'm scared stiff.'

'Helen, don't get too upset. It was just a mistake. It will all be put right. Trust Fats, he knows what he's doing.'

'I trust him. After this I'm going back to meditating every day. I need to have something to centre me. To keep me steady. Otherwise I become sucked into all these horrible worldly events. I forget that, within me, like Gaylang says, there is a quiet centre of peace. I've lost it all just recently, Marcia.'

'So have I,' Marcia said with feeling.

Helen put down the telephone and decided to wear a black skirt with a blue jumper. The nice thing about Marcia was that they both talked the same language. Laura and her friends would find the whole idea of a peaceful inner centre of the soul completely baffling. But then, Helen reminded herself, Laura maybe didn't need a peaceful centre of her soul. She wasn't going to watch her son stand with other potential juvenile criminals in a line-up.

Chapter Thirty-seven

Helen knew she couldn't afford a taxi. She envied the way that Marcia took taxis all the time. She couldn't afford them either but then Marcia was 'cool' about money. Still, Helen couldn't bear to think about being late at the police station, and was too shy to ask what would happen there in case Marcia got cross with her. However, now as they bowled along the littered streets spotted with dog turds, Helen was glad of her decision.

The sign in the taxi asked for people not to smoke. Helen saw the cab driver glance over his shoulder at his passengers. His dislike of them wasn't mitigated in any way by the fact that Cricket was smoking.

'Put out that fag,' the cab driver snarled.

'Fuck off,' Cricket replied amiably. 'We're paying you to drive us, so shut up.'

Helen's hands began to shake. She could not cope with Marcia and Cricket's aggressive responses.

'Fucking racist pig,' Cricket remarked to his mother. Helen could see the back of the man's neck getting red.

Marcia leaned towards Helen. 'Helen, if you don't learn to bully back you'll never be a winner. Don't you understand that?'

'I guess so,' Helen said doubtfully. 'But Marcia, there is a sign saying he'd rather we didn't smoke in his cab.'

'And Cricket wants to smoke. So?'

'All this aggression seems so unnecessary. I mean, why can't you just ignore him?' she asked in a low, tremulous whisper.

'Because, girl, when you see or hear a man give you lip you give it back. He's the sort of man that's racist.

You don't know what it's like to walk down the street and people spit in your face, hurl abuse at you. To lie frozen in fear at night, thinking that the police might have Junior in one of their cells.'

'I didn't, but I do now.' Helen's words came from the bottom of her fearful heart. 'I have never been so afraid as I have been in the last two days.'

'Well, you know, Helen, this time I wasn't so afraid. When Junior's been pulled in on "sus" before, he was usually with his black friends. This time he was with Toby, a white middle-class boy. The police can see that. When Paul came round with a solicitor, that in an odd way comforted me. And Fats helped out too: that man's a treasure.'

The taxi pulled up in front of the police station. 'That'll be five quid,' the taxi driver growled.

'Here, take the money. You don't get a tip. Next time you watch your stinking honky mouth. Listen up.'

'Now I've seen it all. I've seen it all. They were swinging off trees a few years ago, and now they're all here.'

'Yeah, I'm a black bitch with an attitude problem and it doesn't come off in the bath,' Marcia yelled after him, her eyes shining.

'Come on, boys,' Marcia cajoled, turning to them. 'Heads up and hands out of your pockets.'

Helen realized how much she admired Marcia's strength and courage. Then part of her knew that it would never be possible for her. She lived in a permanent state of panic but now, thanks to Marcia, she had learned to hide the fear if not the trembling. She took a deep breath, squared her shoulders, and marched into the police station behind Marcia. Both boys followed them somewhat sheepishly. Cricket had dogged his cigarette and palmed it.

'Line up,' said the sergeant. He pointed to a dirty peeling door.

'What's that, Marcia?' Helen asked nervously.

'Oh, it's just where they hold the line-up. The boys join a line of others. They stand behind a one-way glass partition. Those people that identified Junior and Toby try to pick them out again. If they can't, we're OK.'

'If they can?'

'Then we're not OK; but there's no point in worrying about that now, Helen. Take life one step at a time or you'll frazzle.'

'Oh,' said Helen faintly. She very much didn't want the boys to disappear behind that awful door. She imagined a snakepit full of vipers. Maybe a row of electric chairs. 'Don't be so stupid,' she warned herself.

She remembered old films of Raymond Burr who was always wheeling himself up and down lines of guilt-stricken men. They didn't have one-way glass mirrors then. In real life it was completely different, she thought.

Raymond Burr's police station always appeared so glamorous. The awful smell from yesterday climbed up her nose. Marcia and Helen were ushered into another room. Toby glanced at his mother over his shoulder. He was very white and his face was strained. Helen gave him a rictus of a smile. Cricket loped nonchalantly behind the sergeant, his baseball cap on backwards and his huge Nikes dribbling laces across the floor.

'Where you done time?' Cricket asked the villainous-looking boy next to him.

The boy was shorter than Cricket but huge, with long, pendulous arms. He had a knife slash gashed across his cheek. 'Scrubs,' he replied out of the corner of his mouth. His cold eyes stared at the policeman. Toby noticed that the policeman tried to avoid the boy's eyes.

'Wow,' Cricket said admiringly, also speaking out of the corner of his mouth. 'Big time?'

'Yeah. This goon jumped through the wire mesh stretched across our landing. They said I pushed 'im. Lied, the fuckers. I sort of nudged him. We called 'im chips after that. 'E died. Blood all over the place. Mesh sliced 'im right through. I love the smell of blood.' Toby felt really uncomfortable. The boy's eyes were alight with an unholy glee.

'Weren't you scared?' Toby tried unsuccessfully to talk through the side of his mouth.

'Shut it over there,' the policeman shouted.

'Go suck cunt,' the boy said loudly.

Toby watched the policeman warily. He pretended he hadn't heard the boy.

'Nah,' the boy answered Toby. 'I ain't scared of nuffink. I done it all. Been in Rotherhithe, a piece of cake.'

'Rother'ithe?' the boy on the other side said mockingly. 'Rother'ithe's for pansies and homos. Nah, you got to get to Barlinnie if you really want to do 'ard time. That's a place can kill a man's soul. All those shrinks goin' on about your mum and what she did to you. "Get in touch with your hostility" crap. You goes in there skinny and weak. After three good meals a day and a work-out in the gym you come out fit, and madder than ever.'

'What's your name?' Toby thought he might try to introduce a little sanity into the conversation.

'Junior Madness,' the boy replied. 'And you?'

'Toby Beckett.' Toby blushed at the utter banality of his name. Why wasn't he called something like Junior Madness? Why bloody Toby. 'Why were you er ... in prison?'

'Killed a bloke in a fight. You should 'ave seen 'im. He ran straight on to my knife. I swear to God I wasn't guilty. Fucking careless of 'im, I said to the beak. But he done me anyway. It's the system, you see, 'cause I'm black and I'm poor. My social worker says I'm discriminated against but come the revolution he and his pals are going to overthrow the government and then we can take over the prime minister's house and Buckingham Palace. Mind you, I'm not against the Queen like 'e is, and I like the Queen Mum. She looks like my poor mum and she is on her own. If we lived in Russia we'd 'ave everythink lovely, my social worker says. But we don't live in Russia, we live in this bleeding stinking country. Watch out, there's the bleeding bint wot shopped you.'

Toby could see dark figures moving around outside the glass. The boys straightened their shoulders and stood to attention. Toby felt that most of these boys had spent miserable lives being bullied in one institution after another. No wonder they responded badly. Even stood to attention. 'OK, lads, look straight ahead and no smiling.'

Toby felt his heart pounding in his chest. He stared at the glass and hoped his mother was all right. He didn't like her being put through this ordeal. He didn't want to have to grow this hard shell that meant he couldn't show fear or emotions. He very much wanted to be in the flat, or with Fats learning about another world that was so much more important to him. He centred himself internally. He took a deep breath from his stomach and held it for a count of seven and then let it out.

'OK,' the policeman said after listening to his intercom, 'you can all go.'

For a moment Toby felt exultant. Was this what being a man was all about? During the line-up, Toby had felt a surge of adrenaline flow through his veins. It peaked when the policeman told them to go. He noticed that Cricket's eyes burned with excitement.

When the policeman left the room, Cricket gave a loud whoop of joy and slapped Toby a high five. All round the room boys were dancing and singing. How very un-English. Toby could hear his father's loud sniff of disapproval. 'Fuck you,' he thought. 'This is living and I'm having fun.' He darted out of the door to hug his mother. Helen held him tightly and tried not to cry.

He's not my little boy any longer, she thought. Toby

is really now on his own. He won't want me running after him like I used to.

'What's to eat at home, Mum? I'm starving.'

Helen laughed; at least that part of him would never change. 'Fats says we're to go round to his place and he'll cook us a celebration feast.'

'Aw right, great man. I'm up for that.' Cricket was leaping up and down. 'He knew we'd be all right, didn't he, Mum?'

'Yes, darling, but then Fats knows everything, doesn't he?'

'Yeah,' Marcia agreed happily, 'he does indeed.' Marcia watched Helen's face soften and then she smiled. Helen was beginning to trust Fats and Marcia was glad.

Chapter Thirty-eight

It took several weeks before Helen failed to feel a sudden moment of fear when she heard the scream of a police siren. Now the whine and the screeching of the wheels around corners had a different meaning for her. No longer were her feelings disinterested. No, now she knew that the police didn't only give directions and tell you the time. She watched the dark blue police vans race around Hammersmith roundabout and she too felt the fear in the streets.

'Lace,' Maisie said conversationally one day at the bar, 'she's fucking the 'ead of the 'ouse of 'orrors. That's what we call the station near my 'ouse.'

'Does it give her any special privileges?' Helen was amused. Maisie and Lace seemed to have got their lives really very well sorted out. No man ever told them what to do, unless he'd paid them, and they didn't have ex-husbands whining down the telephone. To say nothing of ex-husbands' mistresses.

Toby's wrongful arrest had given Paul sufficient ammunition to keep him on her doorstep for ages. 'And another thing,' he'd bellowed that morning, 'if there's any more problems with Toby, I'll send him to my old boarding school. They'll make a man of him.'

'Like you, Paul?' Helen had leaned out of the window and screamed back. 'You're fucking impotent most of the time. That's what your school did for you. Fuck off.' The words leapt from her mouth. The feeling of searing anger enlivened her. She didn't care if the neighbours all hung out as well to get in on the act.

'That's what neighbours are for,' Marcia explained

238

when Helen was new to the place. 'They are there to mind everybody else's business. What else have they got to do?'

Well, Helen felt, as she triumphantly banged the window shut, I've given them a good run for their money. They'll have something to talk about for the rest of the day. Paul stalked off, waving his fist in the air like a cartoon baddie. Fortunately Toby had already left for school. Quite why Paul had to come all this way to insult her she knew not. Probably all to do with his meddlesome mother. He'd been telling his mother Mabel all his problems as usual, and now she must have urged him to take action. Helen toyed with the idea of ringing her up and screaming at her, but then she thought better of it. The bitch was old and frail, even if she was as lethal as a New Mexican Sidewinder.

Helen's mind came back to the present. 'Marcia's out shopping today,' she told Maisie. 'She has a long list of all the medicines we need to take with us to Greece. Elliott says we need to get a tube of stuff to fill holes in our teeth. Apparently the island has only one dentist, who specializes in hoiking out the nerve-endings of your teeth if you have a filling fall out.'

'Marvellous sort of 'oliday you're planning for yourselves. Me, I'm off to Paris. Yes, siree, Paris, France. I got an old mate of mine working the Metro. I fancy 'aving a bit of a fling among the Frenchies. They say the pimps are better over there. Not so fierce as 'ere. Mind you, I'd never go wif a pimp. I always takes care of meself.'

Helen shook her head. She was rinsing off rows and rows of beer glasses. There was a special way of washing the glasses so they shone and sparkled under the lights of the bar. Now Helen made sure that all her glasses were clean. She enjoyed setting up the bar as soon as she came into work. It was Crinkly's bar but she organized it.

She took great pride in the long rows of beer and wine

glasses. Off to one side were smaller glasses for drinks like port and lemon, which she'd learned was called a white lady. She wondered if one day she would be clever enough to shake cocktails like Crinkly Hinkley. She hadn't yet graduated to making drinks or running the till, but she was getting there.

No longer was she going to accept the limitations that she had put upon herself. She could no longer just lay the blame for her failed marriage at Paul's door. Fats had seen to that.

'Helen,' he'd said when she was having one of her hopeless crying jags. 'Helen, you must take the responsibility of the fact that you picked Paul. You married him and then you let him drive you into the ground. No, he shouldn't have done it, but you let him, didn't you?'

Helen raised her tearstained face and gazed into Fats' soft, kind eyes. 'I know,' she snuffled, 'but why, Fats, why?'

'That's the question you have to answer, darling, and nobody can answer that except you.'

'I'll have time on the boat to think about that. Lots and lots of time, Fats.'

'And the answer will come to you, just wait and see.' Helen remembered the warmth of his bear-hug. Thank goodness for a man like that.

She plunged her arms back into the warm, popping suds, then looked up to see Marcia burst into the bar.

'Well, I've got enough Pepto Bismol to make sure that none of us ever farts again – even Junior.'

Helen laughed. Marcia was so good for her. Having lived with Paul, who would back out of the room rather than fart out loud, Marcia made a welcome change.

'We'll have to get used to each other's smells, won't we?'

'Sure we will. Junior blows off like a walrus.'

'What do you do, Marcia, when you want to um . . . well, fart?'

'I do couch rumblers. I sit down, let go, and then pretend I've heard nothing. It works, but you need to have a deep old couch like mine.'

'I'll practise,' Helen promised. She went back behind the bar and collected five glasses in the fingers of her right hand. 'See, I can do something well,' she called to Marcia as she went behind the bar.

'You can do lots of things well, you idiot. The only fool thing you did was to marry such a bastard.'

'He wasn't always a bastard,' Helen said defensively.

'Yes he was: you just couldn't or wouldn't see it.'

'I guess so.' Helen leaned over the sink and reached for the washing-up liquid. Behind her the bar rattled and shook as people moved in and out of the crowded room. Hanging over the sink, she realized how much of the time she was just frightened. Before she met Paul she had been shy but little had bothered her. And why indeed should it? She was much loved by her parents, did well at school, and was confident in her ability to work as a secretary; but now all that confidence had gone.

How long would it take to get it back? She didn't know, but she was prepared to wait. Maybe the rest of her life? How could another human being so destroy another? What was it about her that had finally made Paul so furiously angry?

It couldn't be that she'd escaped from his concentration camp. After all, he had wanted to leave her and live with his mistress. It certainly couldn't be jealousy. He had nothing to be jealous about. She had no talent worthy of envy. She had never looked at other men while she was married to him. Come to think of it, she still didn't have anything to do with other men.

Nowadays Toby seemed to have less to do with his little girlfriend. So he too was really on his own. 'I don't want to get hurt that badly ever again,' was all he said about the new distance.

'I know what you mean,' Helen replied. Now, rinsing her glasses, she gazed at the lovely shape of the wine glass. I'm like the wine glass she thought. Fragile, so fragile I could snap. But I won't. I can't, for Toby's sake. I have to stay whole and in one piece. With that thought she took off her pinafore and joined Marcia for a drink at the bar.

'A penny for them,' Marcia said, looking at Helen's drowned face.

'I can't wait to see a dolphin, Marcia. Do you think we'll be that lucky?'

'I'll show you how to call dolphins, honey. My ex taught me how to do it.'

'I didn't know you were ever married, Marcia.'

'There's a lot you don't know about me, honey.' The shadows around Marcia's face deepened. 'A lot,' was all she'd say.

Chapter Thirty-nine

'I think Mum wonders why I've given up my girlfriend. Well, almost given her up. And I'm not looking for another one. I told her, like I always do, that I don't ever want to get that hurt again. Even thinking about those months after Louise dumped me makes my stomach ache. Anyway,' Toby sighed, 'it's just not the same. Nothing is. Kissing Sarah isn't the same: I find I'm pretending it's Louise and then, of course, it isn't.'

'Well . . .' Cricket grinned. Toby watched the smile creep up his face all the way to his forehead. Toby always swore that Cricket was the only boy he knew who could smile with his whole head. Even his ears joined in. It always made Toby feel so deliciously happy. 'You got to get an attitude like me. My mum wonders when I'm going to give my dick a rest. Never, I tell her, and then I run. Sex, Toby, that's what you need. Lots and lots of sex with different kinds of women. You're different. You think too much.' Cricket bunched the fingers of both his hands and pretended to pinch two full breasts.

'The exciting thing is you never know when you're going to score. White chicks, black chicks, they come in all different colours these days. 'Course, you got to use all that new man language. Tell them you cook for your poor tired old mum. Of course mine's doubly oppressed because she's a woman of colour and a woman. Tell them how you wash the floors for her and do the shopping.' Cricket laid a histrionic hand on his heart. '"My mum," he said in a high-pitched voice, "she's in a wheelchair and I push her everywhere." The thought of me pushing my poor old mum around the block works every time.

243

Off comes their knickers. You see, Toby, girls love to comfort fellas. I give them the feeling that I'm such a hard-working good boy and I love my mother so much. It works every time.'

'What happens if a girl meets your poor old mum and she's not in a wheelchair?' Toby was laughing.

'I just say I prayed for a miracle and she got better, but not to mention my prayers to my mum because she hates religion. Sex is God's greatest gift, Toby. Beats football, darts and even dope.'

'I suppose it does if you can do it with people without getting hurt.'

'Toby, you are a dope. Of course we all get hurt, but the trick is to look at it all as if it's a game. You love A and she loves B. You lie in bed plotting about killing B, and then make your move on A. Anyway, even if you don't score, you can always have sex in your head.'

'I know that. That's all I do these days. But at least my right hand won't let me down. Not so far, anyway.' Toby glanced at his hand suspiciously. 'What hand do you wank with, Cricket?'

'I'm ambidextrous.' There was a note of pride in Cricket's voice.

'You would be,' Toby said forlornly. 'I only have one-handed sex. Well,' he said, stuffing his sleeping bag into the rucksack, 'maybe I'll meet the girl of my dreams on a beach on the island.'

'And maybe I'll meet Elliott on the beach without any clothes on and my mum won't know. She'd go after us with a chopper if she ever found out.'

'Are you serious about Elliott, Cricket?'

'Never been so serious in my life. We often talk when Mum's not home. It's funny, when we're together I don't feel any differences between us. Yes, she's much older in some ways, but she has no street smarts. She's just a kid about so many things. She's never been poor, or cold.

244

She's never dealt with any problems. She's always thrown money at anything or anybody that made her mad. But we get on really well. I love being with her.'

'Do you love her, Cricket?'

'There you go again, Tobe. The old romantic. No, I'm not in love with her, but I like her, we have fun. I can learn a lot from her.'

'What can she learn from you, Cricket?'

'Well, Mr Professor. She doesn't really like herself much. She's got that awful bitch of a mother who puts her down all the time. I can help her find out that she's really OK. You know, Fats taught us that if we really like someone and care about them, then making love to them is all right. But then you also have to take responsibility for your relationships.

'I know my mum would freak to begin with, but for now I'm not telling her anything. Remember I taught you that you have a right to your inner life, without always telling your mum everything?'

'Yeah, I do. That's when you taught me to smoke a joint.'

'Uh-huh, that's right. It's like Elliott and I have known each other for ever. The first time I looked at her I connected. She says she feels the same way about me. I know there's a hell of a difference between our ages.' Cricket was quiet for a moment and then he said slowly, 'It's like Gaylang says. Souls don't age, only bodies. And our souls have known each other for a long time. This time round I want to get our relationship right.'

'Funny you should say that. Fats told me that I've been trying to rescue Louise each time round. But I've always failed. He says hopefully next time, if I choose to come back to this earth, I will manage one lifetime to get my relationship right. Or the other possibility is that I turn away from her and don't get hurt. But then, sometimes when I think about her and the past, I'm glad.' Toby smiled. 'After she left, I really had to do a lot of thinking.

'I was frightened by our new lifestyle to begin with, but then, apart from being cold, I'm much happier. Before, all those years before, I was sleep-walking.'

'Elliott's kinda like that. She's got that awful mother and her dad who abandoned her, so she's really got to work through all that. She's spent a mound of money on shrinks, but nobody seems to be able to get through to her. She's got to work through all that being angry with her mum. It means she's still attached.'

'I know,' Toby said with feeling, 'I'm still angry with Dad at times, so I'm still attached.'

'I think the father–son kick is the hardest one of all. You're supposed to grow up being like them, but if they're bastards, why the fuck should you be like them?' Toby heard the note of bitterness in Cricket's voice. It was a tone he'd often heard before. The helpless hurt of being abandoned and betrayed.

'Come on, Cricket, let's go down to the club and gig. There's a guy down there who's got some great Lebanese Gold and some Thai sticks. I could do with a smoke.'

Once enveloped in the gloom of the now empty club in the bowels of Hammersmith Road, Toby inhaled and felt the hash relax his limbs. He was aware, with that peculiar clarity that a smoke always gave him, that he missed sex now more than he actually missed Louise. The hole she'd left was actually beginning to fill, but still he didn't want to risk being ripped open like a fish and left flapping on the ground in pain.

He gazed into the auditorium. Would there ever be a girl out there with big soft breasts who would love him? Louise had such beautiful breasts. He wondered, sucking on the joint, why he loved breasts so much. His mother had small, hard breasts. He remembered as a child often lying in her arms. He missed the pillowed feeling that sizeable breasts gave him. Most of all he missed being sheathed in Louise's warm vagina. He wondered if other girls liked sex as much as Louise did.

During the interval, when they took a quick break, Toby asked Cricket, 'I know this sounds a really silly question, Cricket. Do girls really like sex, man? Louise was so good at it I wonder if I'll ever find a girl that good again.'

'Some.' Cricket was watching the back-up vocalist snort a line of coke. 'Ja man,' he said with disgust, 'we don't do hard drugs in this band.' Cricket walked over to the man and knocked the piece of glass out of his hand. The man immediately fell to the floor and tried to lick the white powder. Toby watched him and felt appalled. He was only a temporary back-up artist, but Toby liked the man and hated to see him debasing himself like that. He shivered. It could so easily be him.

He knew he had the right profile. An abandoned life. A new beginning in a poor area where drugs were rife. But at least here the drugs were in your face. Behind those big square, Georgian houses with their brass knockers, his middle-class friends took drugs in secret. It made it all much more exciting to them.

By now, as far as Toby was concerned, the prisons, the borstals and the remand centres were where you put black people. Most white people got off with a fine or community service.

The man got to his feet. 'Fuck you, you cunt.' He glared at Cricket. 'Boy,' he said contemptuously, 'that was sixty quids' worth of coke.'

'I don't care what it cost, you don't do drugs in this band.' He picked the man up by his collar. 'Get it,' Cricket said. 'Got it?' He threw the man down on the floor. 'Good.' Cricket was cheerful again. 'Don't worry, Toby. You'll find your girl. One day we'll be famous. We'll be singing together when they drop that big silver ball on

New Year's Eve in New York.' He patted Toby on the back.

Toby grinned. Cricket wanted fame so badly he always said he could taste it. Well, so far the tapes were good. Toby was pleased with them. They also had enough material, if the demos were good enough to make a single, to immediately push out an album.

The man on the floor looked up at Cricket. 'OK,' he said.

Cricket stretched out his hand and pulled the man to his feet. 'OK, man,' he said. 'No hard feelings?' The man nodded.

Chapter Forty

'I don't really want to go on a blind date, Maisie.' Helen's voice was troubled. 'Besides, we're off to Elba to pick up the boat on Saturday. Toby's so excited he's already packed.'

'You're going to 'ave to get your oats regular some time, 'Elen. It ain't normal to go without a leg over.' Maisie's brow was clouded with concern.

'Oh yes it is, if you've been through what I've been through. I don't care if I never have sex with a man again.'

'You'll get over the bastard; it just takes time.'

Helen wrinkled her nose. 'It's not just sex, Maisie. It's having to live with a man ever again. I'm used to my freedom now. Toby and I live so peacefully together. He eats when and what he wants, and I do too. I couldn't give all that up again. Men are such control freaks.' She poured herself a glass of wine. She picked up the glass and looked into the dark red liquid.

'You know,' she said dreamily, 'even if I have no money at all, the quality of my life has changed. I know now that you don't need money to be happy. It sounds like a trite thing to say, but as someone who has recently escaped out of a private concentration camp, I really mean it.'

'I know you do, love, but Charlie won't hurt you. 'E's a good man and 'e's got a Porsche.'

'I don't care if he's got a Porsche or not, Maisie, I just don't want him to make a pass at me.'

''E won't make a pass at you, love, not if you don't let 'im.'

'That's the problem, Maisie, I have no experience of men at all, so how do I stop him?'

'Tell 'im straight that you're not interested in sex.'

'I couldn't do that, I hardly know him. He's only been in a few times for a drink and we've chatted. He's bought me a couple of glasses of red wine, but I couldn't say that to a man who is almost a stranger.'

'Don't you tell 'im then, I will. You let 'im take you out for a drink. Get you out of 'ere for a change. Don't be scared of 'im, I've known 'im for ages and 'e won't 'urt you.'

Helen sipped her glass of wine. 'OK,' she said, feeling defeated by Maisie's insistence. 'I'll go.'

'Good girl.' Maisie smiled and her bosom swelled with pride at her successful matchmaking. 'I'll give Charlie a ring and tell 'im you're on.' Helen smiled, watching Maisie's big round bottom sway as she bustled off to the pay-telephone on the wall. Helen thought for a moment. Now Charlie was going to be warned off by Maisie and she didn't have to dread him making a pass at her, she realized she rather liked the idea of going out for a drink with him.

Now she wished she'd worn a nice dress to work instead of her usual slacks and sweater, but the sweater was a nice colour of dark blue and went with her eyes.

She had first noticed Charlie when he pushed his way through the big sweep of the bar. He had sat on a high stool and beamed at her. 'Hi, sweetie-pie,' he'd said, and then he smiled. He had beautiful white, even teeth. She liked his broad shoulders and copper-coloured hair.

'Would you like a drink?' she asked, smiling back.

'Gin and tonic,' he'd said. 'That's all I drink, or champagne, of course.'

'Of course.' Helen had blushed faintly. It was such a long time since she'd had a bottle of champagne. Not since her meal with Elliott in the Savoy. Now she was going to have a drink with Charlie; hopefully he'd be in a champagne mood.

She felt her heart beating with fear and anticipation. A red tide of embarrassment caused her face to flush and then left her feeling white-faced and shaken. 'Don't be so silly,' she scolded herself. 'He was only asking you out for a drink. He's not going to rape you.'

'Scared?' Maisie asked sympathetically. 'Men are like puppies, Helen. Remember what I taught you. Fuck 'em, feed 'em, and they'll be no trouble at all.'

'I don't mind feeding him, Maisie, I just don't want to fuck him.'

'Fine, then don't. Men are funny bastards. If you make them respect you, they'll do you no 'arm. See that 'e opens the doors for you. All that sort of thing. Trouble is, a whole bunch of loony women told men to fuck off and they 'ave. A whole bunch of 'em came nosing round Lace. Asked did she think she's exploited? Lace give it to them back. "Fuck off," she said. "Go and get your dildoes." That sent 'em packing. Ran off like frightened rabbits, they did.' She bellowed with laughter. Behind her Helen saw Charlie's smiling face.

'Brought you these,' he said, pushing a very large bunch of pink roses into her hands.

'Oh, how nice.' Helen buried her nose into the flowers and was amazed to find her eyes filling with tears. Paul had given her her last bunch of roses for her birthday. She wondered why she still minded so much? 'That's very kind of you, Charlie,' she said, looking at him earnestly.

How like a child she is, Charlie thought as he slipped on to a barstool. Not only like a child, but so vulnerable. Not like his ex-wife at all. She was a neurotic bitch. Her whole life was one long dramatic act. Well he, Charlie the mug, paid for it all. She never thought Charlie would dump her. After all, she called herself the artist. She picked him up from the gutter, she never ceased to remind him. She pulled him into her world of art galleries and film studios. She knew everybody there was to know in that world. But her world was completely insane and he was glad to be out of it.

One day he had just walked out of the big, opulent house in Cheyne Walk and left it all to her. He'd divorced her. There were no children, and now he was beginning his life again. Charlie felt reborn. But, looking at this pretty little woman holding his pink roses, he knew she wasn't over the shock and the hurt yet. He remembered the nights he'd lain sobbing in his new flat. It was not for his wife he'd sobbed, but for the loss of the fantasy of what might have been. He'd been sucked deep down into her neurotic illness. It happens to men, too, though you wouldn't have thought it looking at the headlines on women's magazines that festooned his sitting room in his old house. His ex-wife didn't read books but she did devour magazines, and he failed every miserable test the magazine editors devised to prove that all men were bastards and rapists and incapable of giving women multiple orgasms.

The restaurant was off Beauchamp Place. Helen felt very underdressed. Charlie did order champagne. The interior decoration was all white marble and pretty pink table napkins and matching pink lightshades. The first course she ordered looked too pretty to eat. Four fat white scallops on a bed of smoked salmon and a little mound of green spinach. The waiter slivered slices of white truffle over the scallops. Helen laughed: she'd never tasted white truffles before and the smell of rotting socks hung in her nose.

'I've never tried these before,' she said. 'They're fabulous. Here,' she stretched out her fork, 'try some. You'll either love it or hate it. I love the taste.'

Charlie put a big hand over hers and guided the fork

to his mouth. 'Whew,' he said. 'Reminds me of me old man's bad breath.'

Helen giggled and then stuffed her napkin in her mouth. 'Go on, laugh then, Helen. You look as if you could do with a good laugh.'

'I could,' Helen nodded. She put the last forkful of spinach into her mouth. Little flecks of green spinach were left in a drizzle of oil on the plate. 'That was wonderful,' she said, moving the strands around the plate. She lifted a slice of garlic up off the plate on the tines of her fork. 'Vegetables are so beautiful,' she said thoughtfully. 'God is such an amazing architect, don't you think?'

'I don't know about things like that. About God, I mean. Now cars, I do know about cars. But God . . .' he shifted uncomfortably. 'I haven't been a good boy in my time.'

'That doesn't bother God, Charlie.'

'Yeah, maybe not, but I done a bit of bird.' Helen looked puzzled. 'Time,' Charlie explained. 'Not for nothing rough,' he said hurriedly when he saw the look of alarm spread across Helen's face.

'No, there was this geezer that I owed and I couldn't pay, so he done me for fraud. I didn't defraud no one, but then that's life, innit?'

'I guess it is, Charlie. Can I have another glass of champagne?'

'Yes, darlin', you can have anything you like.' He hurriedly poured her another glass, the slim neck of the bottle nearly disappearing in his hand. 'Honestly, Helen, you *can* have anything you like.' Charlie leaned forward across the table, his voice heavy with emotion. 'Helen, from the first moment I set eyes on you, I was in love. Honest, I'm not making this up. I just can't stop thinking about you.'

'Charlie,' Helen was suddenly serious, 'I don't want to get involved with a man at this point in my life. I've had such an awful time for so many years. I just want to be by myself for a while to heal, and to spend good times with Toby, my son. I'm off to Greece on Saturday. We pick up the charter yacht in Elba.'

'I know, Maisie told me.' Charlie sounded glum. 'I'll miss you, Helen.'

'I'll send you a postcard.' Helen smiled at him.

'Will you?' Charlie brightened up. 'Now, what do you want to eat next, me darling?'

Helen inspected the menu. She was enjoying herself. 'Could I have a beef Wellington? Is it too expensive?'

'Nah, nothing's too expensive for Charlie's girl.'

Chapter Forty-one

Helen sat cross-legged in the lotus position on her bed. She took deep breaths from the bottom of her stomach. She held each breath for a count of seven and then slowly exhaled.

> Listen to the reed. It is complaining.
> It tells of separation, saying:
> Ever since they tore me from the reed-bed,
> My lament has moved men and women to tears . . .
> Everyone who is left far from his source
> wishes back the time of union.

The old Chinese philosopher who wrote that thousands of years ago really understood the universal fear of separation. That's what had made Helen's first months by herself so painful. The feeling of being torn out of the ground. Her shredded roots aching with fear and pain; but now things were different.

Helen's body felt loose and supple and her skin glowed. Charlie had kissed her lightly and gently on the lips, but she knew there was more to come. She laughed out loud and climbed off the bed. He had big, sure hands. She felt the warmth of them on her back. He would be a normal, loving man in bed. She was sure of that.

On her last day at work, Helen danced into the bar, beaming. Maisie chuckled. ''E says 'e's coming over to say goodbye to you at dinner time. 'E's got it bad, and by the looks of you, so 'ave you.'

'Well, I don't know what it is that I've got, but it's put a smile on my face and makes my feet want to dance. It's my dance class tonight, so I'll dance it all out then.'

'What you need, my girl, is a bit of rumpy-pumpy. That'll set you straight.'

Helen made a face. 'I know,' she said, 'but I'm scared, Maisie. Suppose he turns out to be like Paul?'

'Nah, you don't 'ave any worries about Charlie. Any man 'oo loves 'is food and 'is drink like 'e does is bound to be good in the sack. I've seen 'im with some right lookers, but he's gone on you, 'e really is.'

'D'you really think so, Maisie?' Helen felt flustered.

'I know so.' She rested her head on her fist and grinned at Helen. 'You know, you look smashing, Helen. You're a lovely-looking woman when you smile.'

'I haven't had much to smile about, Maisie. Not for a long time.' She could feel her heart beating in anticipation of Charlie's visit. She rushed around the bar, flicking her teacloth and twitching the table mats straight. She felt as if a pack of beagles was at her feet, nipping her heels. The time crawled slowly. Many snails must have lived and died before the clock finally heaved its longest finger to point to one o'clock. Would he be late? Would he turn out to endlessly keep her waiting like Paul did? There was so much she didn't know about him.

The time was two minutes past one when she saw his big bulk come pushing through the glass door. He had a way of backing into the door and then using his weight to make it swing open, leaving both hands free, that Helen found endearing.

She loved his big, golden smile. He wore his usual cashmere camel coat with a brown and yellow striped cashmere scarf and brown corduroy trousers. He came straight up to her and kissed her. 'I'm going to miss you,' he said loudly, stopping the conversation in the busy bar.

There was a silent hush in the room. He pushed an enormous box of Italian chocolates into her arms and then two dozen pink roses. 'Charlie,' Helen laughed, 'I've still got all the other roses you gave me when we went out to dinner. You must have telephoned me about twenty times.'

'You can never have enough roses,' he said firmly. 'Besides, I'm not going to be seeing you for six whole weeks. What am I going to do with myself?'

'Shush, Charlie.' Helen took him by the arm. 'Come over here, sit down and be quiet.'

He obediently sat down and gazed at her. 'I couldn't sleep last night, Helen. I spent all my time thinking about you. What it felt like to have you in my arms.'

'Charlie, we mustn't rush things.'

'Why not?'

'Because, Charlie, we might not be the right people for each other.'

'Can I take you out to dinner tonight?'

'No, I've got my dance class, and then I'm having Fats and Marcia and the boys for dinner in my flat. Elliott's here, and it's our last night together.'

'Can't I come too?'

Helen looked at his dejected face and then she relented. 'Of course, you can come too, darling,' she said, patting him on the head as if he were a puppy. 'Now you sit there quietly and I'll get you a gin and tonic and then put these lovely roses in water.' She walked off to the bar and Charlie watched her go. She moved so beautifully, so gracefully, that he felt his heart melting like toasted cheese. It reminded him of that wonderful moment when the cheese slides over the sides and starts to fill the plate with its golden, waxen presence, the smell of it filling one's nostrils. Helen smelt wonderful. She smelt like milk with a dash of honey and maybe a squeeze of lemon.

That night it was Helen's turn to cook. Over the year, Marcia, Fats and Helen had all taken turns. Helen cooked her traditional English dishes, Fats made fancy Indian curries and Japanese sushi, while Marcia specialized in

Caribbean dishes. Tonight Helen had planned to cook a Lancashire hot pot, but now she knew that Charlie was coming to dinner, she decided to cook his favourite dish, toad-in-the-hole.

As she stirred the batter, and lightened it with a dash of beer, she sang to herself. What a world away she was from all that terrible, tormented unhappiness. Why had she allowed herself to suffer like that? Why had she let Paul debase her? Probably because she did not recognize for many long years that his belittling of her and his cruelty were undeserved.

Her mother and her father treated each other with such respect and affection that she often asked Paul why he did not behave towards her that way. 'Your parents are out of the ark, darling,' he said dismissively. 'Now we talk honestly with each other about our feelings. My mother is the one who understands you very well.'

Those were always ominous words, and meant that Paul and his mother had spent time together dissecting Helen and Toby. For the last years Paul's mother (for Helen she had no name, she was just 'Paul's mother'), refused to come to her house. Helen imagined the look on the woman's face, the little ratty face devoid of chin. 'Far too dirty, Paul. I have to wipe the silverware under the tablecloth.' Helen had watched her doing it all those years ago. She'd watched Paul's mother exchange looks with Paul. Looks that meant mother and son were of the same blood. Indeed, Helen often thought that if she'd cut Paul with a knife, his mother would begin bleeding in sympathy.

She banished all thoughts of Paul and began to hum again.

'Hi, Mum.' Toby barged in from school. 'More roses from your admirer?'

'He's coming to dinner, darling,' she said, giving Toby a quick hug. 'I do hope you'll like him.'

'Of course I shan't, I'll hate him. He's my rival. I won't let him pinch your bottom.'

'Toby, how can you say a thing like that?'

'Oh Mum, I was only kidding. Not all men are bastards like Dad. Of course I'll like him.' He gave her a mammoth squeeze and disappeared to go into the shower.

Helen gave a small sigh. How could a boy who was a dirty little ink-stained creature emerge years later and live under the shower? The bills were horrendous.

She poked the sausages into the creamy batter. She added a plop of wine to the gravy sitting on the stove. Gravy, real English gravy. She'd spent several days boiling the free bones given to her by the butcher. Helen always had a pot of fresh stock sitting on her back hob. 'Got a big dog then?' he said.

'Yes, enormous,' she said, smiling at him. He was a sweet man and Irish. He often gave her scraps for free which she turned into nourishing casseroles. Funny how much her cooking had improved, now that she'd had to make it a creative art to feed Toby properly on the little money she had.

Crinkly Hinkley often gave her good bottles of wine to take home, and pies and other items of food. She knew he valued her advice; she also helped him with his business accounts.

'You talk so posh,' he said admiringly.

'I didn't always,' she confessed. 'I used to listen to the BBC news. It's not that I think talking posh is a good idea. It's more that I love the music of words spoken properly. If you really want to hear excellent English you must listen to a Scot speaking. They use the purest English in the world. Words like "durst", for "I dare not". How beautiful!'

Now it was time to make Helen's Bad-For-You chocolate pudding. This was Toby's favourite. Lots of dark chocolate, butter, cream and a dash of brandy. Then, whisking lightly, she beat the egg yolks, folding them into the sweet-smelling chocolate sauce.

For Fats she made a salad. Crisp, green and delicious. She shopped for fresh salad at the top of Hammersmith Broadway. There, picking through the piles of vegetables on the stalls, she had many friends. Particularly the old woman who sold the prawns from the whelk stall. On pay-day she bought a small wet bag of briny shrimps. She held them close to her nose on the way home and she and Toby shared them. Not only did they enjoy sharing the shrimps, but it reminded them both of the years when they ran on the beach at her mother's house and walked along the tideline with the waves breaking next to their feet.

Oh, the sea, she thought, always the sea. The chocolate pudding assumed a life of its own. It grew, it billowed, and it gave off an incense that filled the kitchen with warmth and good feeling.

Chapter Forty-two

Helen sat at the end of her long, dull brown formica table and watched Charlie as he ate. He ate with solid concentration. His mouth filled, his cheeks bulged. Paul would never eat like that. He took cautious little nibbles.

'*Mmmmm*, Helen,' Charlie said with his mouth full. 'You can cook! The only other person who can cook like that is my mother – or rather was my mother, God rest her soul.'

'Oh good,' a small, wicked voice piped up inside Helen. At least we don't have a potential mother-in-law problem. But was it a bad thing to be already thinking about his mother? She didn't know.

'What was your mother like?' she asked. The others at the table stopped talking; even the boys listened. 'She was a hard-working woman. She cleaned her front doorstep just like all the other women in our street, but she died before I made my money.' Charlie's face was sad. 'I've always wished she'd lived long enough for me to buy her a nice house and some pretty diamonds.' He shrugged.

'She was a grand woman and she had a back hand on her that could knock me off my feet. Mind you, she didn't have to use it often. My dad was a boxer and as mean as they come. Still, after him I swore as a small boy that I'd never hit a woman, and I never have. Mind you, I've come close to it several times.'

Helen smiled. Charlie looked so sweet sitting there spooning his food off his plate. In the sink there was yet another bunch of roses, and a bottle of champagne stood on the sideboard. 'For you to take on the boat, darling,' he'd said as he'd kissed her cheek upon his arrival.

261

'My mum gets mean with the broom. She chases me so fast I have to run like a Jack rabbit,' Cricket offered.

'My mum doesn't even have to do that. She just goes silent on me. She knows I can't bear that.'

'I don't do that often, do I, Toby?'

'No, not now you've lightened your act and got the job in the bar.'

Fats nodded. Helen was aware that Fats was watching her very carefully with Charlie. There was a special pleading in his eyes. Helen wanted to say, it's all right, Fats, we will always have our special relationship, but for now I just want to play with Charlie and have fun. To be like a child again. To hold hands and to receive flowers. She smiled gently at Fats. He struggled to smile back. Oh why must life be so difficult, she implored? Why can't God organize it that we fall in love with the people who'll love us back. Instead love was blind; falling in love could be as randomly dangerous as throwing yourself at a heroin pusher.

'The best thing that happened to your mum, Toby, is that she met me.' Charlie was wiping his plate clean with a piece of bread. 'Home manners,' he added unapologetically.

'That's fine, Charlie. I'm glad you feel at home.'

'Just when I find you, you're off. What am I going to do without you?'

'Charlie, don't try and make me feel guilty,' Helen pleaded.

Toby snorted, 'Mum's got GCSEs in guilt. She's getting much better now, though. Fats and Marcia have straightened her out.'

Elliott, who'd been deep in conversation with Cricket, leaned forward, exposing the tops of her very tanned breasts. 'Why don't you join us on our Greek island? I'm sure Helen would love that.'

'No I wouldn't.' Helen was surprised at the vehemence

of her reaction. 'Sorry, Charlie, I don't mean that to sound as rude as it does. I just need to go away and be by myself for a while. I want to walk on the sweet-smelling thyme and think. I've had such an awful few years that I vant to be alone.' She said the last phrase in a mock Swedish accent. 'Do you understand?'

'Sure I do. My ex left me on the floor without a die. People think that women can't be violent. They never met my ex.' He thrust out his arm. 'Look at this, this is where she knifed me.'

'I'm violent,' Elliott offered. 'Philip was such a wimp he would never fight back.'

'Why is he a wimp if he didn't hit you, Elliott?'

'I dunno, I just got bored of the whole thing.'

'Yeah?' Marcia glanced at Elliott.

'Yeah,' Elliott said, shaking her long blonde hair.

'You talk about Philip with such affection, Elliott.' Helen smiled at Elliott but she felt troubled.

'I am fond of him in a way. In a way I'm still in love with him. I'm too neurotic for him, I suppose. He's so terribly, terribly English. His British nanny taught all these blah things like keeping the shower clean. Everything in its place and a place for everything. I can't just pick things up from the floor. It's just not me. I don't want to shop regularly and keep the fridge full. I like to open the door and see it all empty. Maybe a jar of peanut butter or something out of a can. I'll drink beer out of the bottle if I damn well want to.' Her face was flushed and her voice vehement.

Fats looked across the table at Elliott. 'Charlie,' he said, 'you don't understand Elliott as well as we do. She's not the dreadfully tough delinquent woman you think she is. Underneath all that bluster, she's really very soft and frightened.'

'You read my mind. Yeah, I did think that. Helen's much more my type.' He gazed adoringly at Helen who shifted on her chair. 'She's soft, gentle, and so feminine. You need a break, my girl. I know what you mean by finding a space inside. I lived on my own for years after I got rid of that bitch.'

There was no mistaking the fear and intensity in Charlie's face. Helen felt her heart contract. Certainly Paul had never hit her, but he did bully her into the ground, and even now she dreaded his disapproving presence. He would have wrinkled his nose if he'd seen Charlie at her table. He would call him 'working-class'. But then his mother had aspidistras in her sitting room, and that told Helen of her attempt to keep up with several million Smiths and Joneses.

Charlie was perfectly at ease here in her kitchen, and if she did put a bottle of milk on the table for coffee he would not object. Some people were totally socially secure wherever they were, and Charlie was one of them.

Later, much later, when everyone else had gone, Charlie stayed behind to help her with the washing-up. Helen could still feel Fats's warm hug and his whiskery kiss. 'Take care, my little one,' he said so gently that Helen was torn.

'I will,' she said, smiling up at him. Now she was confused again. 'You don't have to help me with the washing-up, Charlie,' she said. 'You can sit by the fire and just talk to me.'

'I want to help you, Helen. I want to see you smile and be happy. It's a long time since you've been happy, isn't it, Helen?'

'Yes, a very long time. I've been very frightened since I've been on my own with Toby.' He watched her face as she smiled a very wan, broken smile that hardly reached her eyes. 'I really hope this trip will eradicate all the ghosts of my past. All those people who pretended they liked me when it was Paul they really wanted.' She sighed, and Charlie's arms went out to enfold her. He pulled her close to his chest and whispered to her.

'Darling, I'll be here when you get back.'

'I know you will,' she whispered back, 'and I'm very glad of that.'

He kissed her gently on the mouth. There was nothing sexual in the kiss. It was a promise of friendship freely given; her lips acknowledged the offer and returned the kiss.

'I'll go now,' Charlie said softly. He didn't trust himself not to ask for more. She looked so lovely in the glow of the kitchen.

When he left the flat, he felt as if a light had been turned out inside him. Helen was such a creature of light. If he'd ever believed in haloes, Helen wore one. A warmth and a brightness shone in her face, even though it was overlaid by sadness.

He felt the scar on his own soul shiver in sympathy. We've all been hurt and betrayed, he acknowledged as he climbed into his car. Soon she would be back. He knew he was really going to miss her. 'Take care of her, God?' he implored.

After Charlie left, Helen found herself aimlessly walking around and around the little flat. It was as though she had itching powder in her brain and roller-skates on her feet.

She tried pouring herself another glass of wine and plonking herself down in her chair by the fire. Charlie had sat in her chair, unaware that the chair was her special place. All her friends knew that. They respected the chair as her safe place in the flat.

Marcia had the same habit, she sat at the end of her own kitchen table in an old Windsor chair. Now the chair was worth a lot of money, but Marcia would never sell it, even when she and Cricket ate sweet potatoes with margarine at the end of the month when money was always tight.

'That's my place in the universe,' Marcia explained to Helen.

'Huh,' Elliott said when she was turfed out of Helen's chair by Marcia. 'You women are a pair of neurotics,' Elliott exploded.

'No, we're not. We just try to live with perfect concentration.'

'I guess that's the stuff that Fats teaches you?'

Marcia had nodded agreeably. Now, in the firelight, Helen curled up and felt the corners of her mouth twitching at the memory. Sure, she thought, and I wish I could talk to Fats now. There was something so instantly calming about his gentle presence.

The restlessness pursued her. The best she could do, she decided, was to have one of her heart-to-heart talks with herself. She walked over to the window and looked across at the sleeping street. Yes, there were three other windows lit by yellow electric lightbulbs. She wasn't the only one sleepless that night.

What's the matter with you Helen? she inquired of her reflection in the window. I'm afraid, she thought, that's what's the matter. I've been alone long enough to have drawn in my boundaries. I am no longer the corpse stretched out on the ground. The night shadows have gone now. The relationship assault squad has been and gone. While they were with me they stuffed my entrails back into my belly and removed the knife from my vagina. Finally, they painted a big white line around my now dead self and I have arisen and tiptoed away. I have left the old Helen where she lay.

I was devastated and undefended by the man who was supposed to love me. I was mutilated and hated by the words in his mouth. Helen took another sip of wine. He still has power over me, she thought. Often, she addressed a particularly dirty corner of the windowpane, if I feel a pang of loneliness, I remember his words. 'You'll end up a lonely old woman. Nobody really likes you.' These words had a prophetic knell about them. Did she really want to risk the possibility of all the cruelty again?

There are no guarantees in this game of love and war. Did all men both love and hate women? Lacan in the Adjudication of Tiresias said, 'If the parts of love-pleasure be counted as ten. Trice three go to women, one only to men.'

Maybe that was why men were so frightened of women's sexuality? Maybe Paul found her ability to reach orgasm with ease and have multiple orgasms whenever she felt like it threatening. His sexuality was precarious. Maybe it was that way with most men? She wouldn't know, but perhaps since women so vociferously demanded sexual equality with men, men couldn't stand the threat and retaliated like wild animals.

Marcia certainly thought men were mostly wild animals. She used men for her pleasure, but she kept her mind and her heart carefully defended. Toby, Helen knew, was more like her, and she trembled for his vulnerability. 'Yes,' she whispered, 'I am afraid. Very afraid. Charlie seems so nice and I am attracted to him. I want him to make love to me.'

'Once you let a man into your knickers, dearie,' Maisie said laughing, 'you can't get rid of 'im. Unless 'e's paying for it, and then you're in control.'

Now she knew that Maisie was right. She was no longer the silly little middle-class woman she'd become after years of marriage to Paul. Even her own parents had been singularly locked away in their own little world by the seaside.

Maisie and Lace led her into a very different world. A world that had big dark shadows, where men lurked who were dangerous. A world of politics, in which men and women used long words to talk about poverty and hunger. She couldn't follow the words and was unimpressed by the people.

Charlie wasn't like that. He enjoyed life too much to bang on about 'the working-classes'.

'I am the working classes!' he'd yell in the bar before she'd first registered who he was. 'Fuck off all of you loony-lefty bastards.' Charlie wasn't frightened of anyone or anything. That was part of his attraction. She loved his rugged face and his self-assurance. She felt safe with him around her. Nobody could harm her, and his care for her was sensitive and gentle. Yes, she was afraid, but now she felt calmer.

You have six weeks to be alone, she told herself. To lie in the sun, read your books; and then you can make a decision. Maybe this trip will be the final move to put the last pieces of the giant jigsaw puzzle together. The jigsaw that was Helen and her future.

She carried the glass back to the sink. She brought her pink flannel nightgown to the warm patch in front of the fire. She always hated the moment that she had to take off her warm day clothes and for a split second stand in the cold, only her shins warm from the fire.

Hurriedly she dropped the nightdress over her thin shoulders. She caught a glimpse of her stippled thighs. 'Oh no,' she murmured. 'I couldn't show my wrinkly belly or my thighs to anyone.'

The nightdress fell to her feet, mercifully hiding the unlovely sight. It fell like the last-night curtain in the theatre. She pulled on her hockey socks and then she laughed.

She heard the genuine joy and excitement in her laugh. Her suitcase was all packed and bulged companionably by her bed. She wandered across her bedroom on her way to bed, hugging her hot-water bottle. It would have to be a man I could really trust, she reminded herself. Then, puzzlingly, she fell asleep and dreamed of Fats, who was smiling tenderly at her as he had during supper.

Chapter Forty-three

Helen hung back as their little group straggled down the long corridors leading to the plane. The boys carried their backpacks and each of them carried two suitcases belonging to Elliott.

'Elliott,' Marcia said, eyeing the suitcases balefully. 'We are only going on a holiday, not a safari trip to Kenya. What on earth have you got in there?'

'Oh American coffee, American cigarettes, vacuum-packed bacon, hot dogs and American ketchup. They don't do proper ketchup like ours in Greece, or anywhere else for that matter. And, of course, loads and loads of sanitary towels. I bleed like crazy.' Helen shot a nervous look at Marcia. Not in front of the boys, she wanted to say. In fact she had hidden her packet of sanitary towels and two boxes of tampax in the side pockets of her suitcase. This was a subject she had never discussed with Toby.

'If you do bleed,' Cricket said, laughing at the loudness of Elliott's voice that had not only informed her party of her bleeding habits, but also the rest of the passengers standing on the rolling escalators, 'you bleed on your own bunk and not anyone else's, you hear?'

'OK.' Elliott was in an amiable mood. 'Come on then, you boys. Haul your asses. Back to the plantation.' Elliott swung an imaginary whip over the boys' heads. A tall thin woman with a high beaked nose and spectacles turned in front of Elliott and stared coldly at her.

'Aren't you being a little racist? I mean, I find your manner of talking offensive.'

'Sure thing, ma'am.' Elliott was grinning. 'I jest came

back from my chapter meeting with the Ku Klux Klan. I'm den mother, you see. Big group in Hemel Hempstead. We're planning to wipe out people like you. The thought police.' She was still grinning, but Elliott's eyes were cold.

'Americans.' The woman sniffed and joined her woman friend.

'Fucking dykes: think they control everything,' Elliott mumbled.

'Elliott, you're not prejudiced against lesbians, are you?' Marcia asked.

'Nah, I just hate the way they've taken it upon themselves to tell us heteros how to behave. In Houston they form big exclusive groups and they hate hetero women. I was into screwing with a woman for a while, but then,' Elliott shrugged, 'I guess I found it boring. Like playing doctors and nurses when I was six years old. Pity, really. At least women know how to look after women. I guess I'm stuck with loving men.'

'Good morning.' A British Airways stewardess stood in the mouth of the plane and welcomed them aboard.

'How the hell does she look so great at this hour of the morning?' Elliott asked Marcia as they squeezed into the tourist-class cabin. 'Gee, there's no room to move down here.'

'Well, Elliott,' Marcia was feeling a little sharp, 'I did say you should go first class and let us peasants sit behind you, didn't I?'

'Aw, come on, Marcia, I'd miss you guys.' Elliott squeezed past Cricket. 'I want the window seat,' she said.

'Oh Elliott, don't be such a baby. Let the boys have the window seats,' Helen objected.

'Cricket, let me sit by the window. Please, Cricket.' Elliott had Cricket's hand in hers and she fluttered her eyelids and giggled.

'Oh, all right then, Elliott, but you'll have to shut up. I want to listen to my Walkman.'

'Done.' Elliott watched while Toby and Cricket stashed the various bits of hand luggage into the overhead lockers. The cabin crew patrolled the aisles. There was such a sense of heightened excitement. Toby, sitting next to his mother, held her hand as the plane taxied off to begin its flight.

'This is the bit that scares me,' Helen confided in Toby.

'I know that, Mum, that's why I'm holding your hand.'

He didn't want to confess to the knot of fear in his own stomach.

'As soon as we're up I'll order a bottle of champagne,' Elliott announced.

'Not for me you won't,' Cricket corrected her. 'I'll drink Special Brew if they have it.'

'So will I,' Toby seconded the idea. There was a moment of tense silence when Elliott was wondering if she should make a fuss. After all, it was nice of her to offer to buy champagne for everyone. But then her face cleared and Cricket raised an eyebrow.

'Not worth a fuss, Elliott,' he said evenly. 'We're playing this trip super cool, aren't we?'

Elliott made a face. 'OK, then two Special Brews and a bottle of champagne.'

'Now,' Cricket announced, 'I'm going to find me a girl to chat up.' The seatbelt lights went off. There was an almost collective sigh of relief from all parts of the aeroplane. They were up, and now red lights dotted the overhead control panels. Noses were blown as passengers cleared their ears. A small child was crying noisily, and Helen winced. She remembered how painful flights had been for Toby who had had constant ear infections as a child. Now she looked at his happy, cheerful face and wondered, not for the first time, if all those years of colds and fevers, blocked eardrums and sore throats were really illnesses or just signs of stress in an unhappy marriage? She didn't know for sure, but even now she was aware that there was a welcome feeling of escape, a few weeks without Paul in their lives, even if he had made Toby promise to telephone him regularly. 'In case that mad woman of a mother of yours does something silly,' he'd said by way of explanation.

Toby watched Cricket wrinkle up his eyes and run his surprisingly pink tongue over his lips and then slip his Bans on to his nose. Toby followed Cricket's gaze. He imagined Cricket's eyes to be two Messerschmitts zooming down a huge plain hunting down an escaped prisoner. In Cricket's case, though, his target was a pretty girl.

Finally, Cricket's eyes focused on a tall dark girl sitting a few rows back. He caught her eyes and then beamed at her. Toby watched as Cricket lifted himself out of his seat between Elliott and his mother. He squared his shoulders, flexed his biceps which bulged under his tight T-shirt, and then he joined the girl. Within minutes he had his hand over her knee and she was gazing into his face, her whole face alight.

Toby turned and watched Elliott's profile. She was staring steadily ahead. But Toby could see her mouth droop slightly. There was an undercurrent between Cricket and Elliott that was running faster now they were on the aeroplane. Toby felt Cricket was sending a message to Elliott that she could take nothing about him for granted, that he had not yet decided whether he was going to be with Elliott after all. Elliott's messages seemed so much simpler. More direct. Toby wondered if all Americans were that way. Elliott seemed to be trying to say to Cricket, Hey, we like each other, why not?

Toby was bothered by the mixed messages between Cricket and Elliott. After the violent currents that passed between his parents, and the unspoken rows, Toby was frightened of things unsaid. When his parents were openly quarrelling, he at least knew what was going on. The bridges and the gorges of the valleys involved in the fighting at least had substance. But when there were silences, words used that meant other things, Toby was then made to feel afraid. Suddenly the valleys and gorges disappeared in a mist of misunderstanding. The rational world became irrational. Toby very much hoped that, once on the boat, he and his mother would not be drawn into any mists of misunderstanding. He very much needed and wanted peace, calm and a chance to laugh. This would be the first time he and his mother would be free of the shadow of his disapproving father, and that meant such a lot to Toby.

Maybe, he thought, as he leaned back in his seat and watched a pretty air stewardess move gracefully down the aisle towards them, maybe there were people like himself and his mother who didn't want to go out into that sexual holocaust that is laughingly called the 'real world'. Maybe it was a better, gentler life to live quietly at home with his mother, do his homework, and just wait patiently for a girl to come into his life and to love him. He wanted a clean, simple love. Nothing neurotic. No shouting and quarrelling like his father. Helen never raised her voice now. Toby realized with a sense of shame that he had always thought it was Helen that did the shouting. These days, hearing his own voice raised as he tried to reason with his unreasonable father, he knew differently.

'Mum, what sort of girl would you like me to be with?'

'One that loves you, cooks and cleans the house and gives me lots and lots of grandchildren,' Helen laughed.

'Mum,' Toby groaned, 'don't ever say that in front of any of my girlfriends. Girls these days go out to work and expect to have careers. You're so unliberated.'

'No I'm not, Toby. Just you remember, I always saw being married and having children as a far more important career than just going out to work. I expected to have a big family, but once we were married Paul refused to have any more children, so I just had you; but I loved being home and watching you grow up. I loved the house and the garden and all the creative things I could do. Sewing, knitting, watercolours. I felt so grateful to Paul that he didn't expect me to go to work like so many other wives down the road.

'I think any girl has the right to choose anything she wants to do or be, but it's only recently that women like me have been labelled boring and unliberated. Remember, Toby,' Helen's voice was urgent, 'when I knew my marriage was over, I tucked you under my arm and left everything I had and got on with my life. I think that's what liberation is about. Not hanging on to a defunct marriage. Not begging and pleading because you can't stand on your own two feet, but getting out.'

'I guess you're right,' Toby said slowly. 'You know, I never thought of it that way. I'm so used to thinking that most kids go home to empty houses. I used to love coming back home after school and sticking my head round the kitchen door to see what you were making for a snack. Our kitchen always smelt so good. Peter's kitchen was always spotless. The au pairs might make him a sandwich, but the place was dead. Something missing. And of course, you're right, it was having a mum at home. Somebody to come back to. Even Dad's miserable now. He complains that Laura is always at the office until very late, and he has to sling an ear of corn into the micro and sit and eat in front of the television.

'Your kitchen smells of rosemary and thyme, while Marcia's kitchen smells of those green bonnet peppers.'

'Drinks, madam?'

Helen looked up at the stewardess. Their moment of closeness was broken.

'Could we have a bottle of champagne and two Special Brews?' Elliott interrupted.

'Certainly, what sort of champagne?'

'Gee, I dunno. Do you have anything from California?'

'How about a Veuve Clicquot?' Helen interjected. The stewardess nodded and moved back to get the drinks.

'You'll have to teach me about wine, Helen,' Elliot said gratefully.

'Sure and you teach me about men.' Both women smiled at each other. Marcia so far had spent her time lying in her chair with her eyes closed. She, like Cricket, was wearing dark glasses. She was also feeling the currents running between Elliott and her son. It was not making her happy.

Cricket kissed the girl on the mouth and came over to join his mother when he saw the drinks arriving. He settled himself next to Elliott and grinned at her. 'Thanks for the beer,' he said. He held the glass in his hand and raised it to the girl who was looking at him. 'Wow,' Cricket said to Toby. 'She's going on holiday to Rhodes. What a kisser.'

Toby watched the girl. She was now sitting without her dark glasses. She looked so defenceless and somehow lost. 'Don't you think you ought to go back and at least sit with her until the end of the journey, Cricket? You have been snogging with her. It's a bit bad to dump her for a glass of beer. You're a shit sometimes, Cricket. You know that?'

'Yeah,' Cricket said, 'but I'm a satisfied shit.' He downed his beer. 'Come on, Elliott,' he said, looming over her. 'Give me some of your champagne.'

'Piss off, Cricket,' Elliott growled, but she handed him the glass. Two small lines creased between Marcia's eyes.

Chapter Forty-four

When she saw the boat swaying on its anchor, Helen was surprised to find her eyes full of tears. After the initial surge of sheer joy at the beauty of the boat, memories of happier times on holiday with Paul in their early years of marriage came flooding in. Don't be so silly, she chastised herself.

The boat had beautiful lines. Her sails were neatly wrapped in blue covers. She had a square stern and space for four people to sit comfortably in the cockpit. The cushions lining the bench seats were also a matching blue, and a generous-sized white canopy kept the cockpit wonderfully in the shade.

Helen was so relieved that the boat matched her dreams. Inwardly she had been afraid that the boat would be all fibre glass and modern. She stood with her suitcase at her feet and breathed in the clean sea air. 'This is perfect,' she said to nobody in particular, 'just perfect.' Then why, if it was all so perfect, did she feel like crying?

Marcia looked at Helen and smiled gently, 'Honey,' she said hugging her, 'it always hurts. It will take a while for you to give yourself permission to be happy. You have been unhappy for so long now. Also, when good things happen it tends to heighten the sense of failure that we all feel when our lovers dump us or we dump them.'

'I know that but,' Helen gave a deep sigh, 'it feels so odd to be on holiday with just Toby and me. I'm used to all the things I used to do with Paul. Like on the first night of our holidays we drank champagne.' She didn't add that they then made love. One of the few times in the recent years that it worked for them.

'Well,' Elliott's voice intruded, 'I can't help you out, but I have brought the champagne – not to mention the red wine. Let's all climb aboard. I get the biggest bed.'

'I brought the champagne that Charlie gave me as well. Maybe the best thing is to unpack and then make plans for the evening?' Helen suggested.

The boat was tied up in a horseshoe-shaped harbour. 'Marciana Marina?' Helen looked at Marcia.

'Yeah, that's where we are. Isn't it spooky to think that Napoleon lived over there?'

While they were struggling with their bags, Elliott was already in the boat. The boys deposited her suitcases on her bed and then went back to help their mothers. Marcia grinned when she saw that Elliott had chosen the fold-down dining table and indeed it made up into a double bed. Well, Elliott could share the cabin with the two snoring boys: there were two bunks by the stairwell. There was a small separate cabin under the cockpit, so Marcia at least got to share the little cabin with the two neat bunkbeds with Helen.

Helen inspected the stove and the fridge. They were new and the fridge had a blue top. She smiled. She was really looking forward to cooking here. She felt herself warming to the little boat. For a moment there she had felt as if she'd been stuck in an icy snowdrift. The feeling of singleness now didn't want to make her cry. She felt an excitement tingling her spine.

'Elliott, first thing tomorrow morning, you'd better begin to teach us how to sail this boat. We're your crew and you'll be our captain.'

'Hey Helen, whoever said anything about me knowing how to sail?'

'Elliott,' Helen's voice was scandalized, 'you told us all sorts of stories about your sailing adventures with all your boyfriends. Remember the one where you held on to the tiller in the middle of a hurricane and you almost capsized, except that you pulled the right rope and saved everybody's lives?'

Elliott was a funny shade of red. The boys had stopped talking and were listening intently. 'Elliott?' Cricket's voice was alarmed. 'Are you telling us now that you don't really know how to sail and that all those stories were porkies?'

There was an appalled silence on the boat. The only sound was the slapping of the waves against the hull and the squeak of the joints in the wooden beams. A terrible hush came over the little party. 'You mean you don't have your master's certificate? That was also a lie?' Marcia was furious. 'That means that if we're going to get this boat down to Greece, we're going to have to hire someone to sail with us.'

'Well, I do sort of know how to sail,' Elliott offered. 'I mean I can raise the anchor and I can steer a course. We'll learn, Marcia. I'll go off into town and find a book.'

'How's your Italian, Elliott?' Cricket was laughing. 'You won't find a sailing book in English in this town.'

'Quit laughing, Cricket.' Elliott punched him hard on his arm.

'Ouch, that hurt, you bitch.'

'Junior.' Marcia's voice was angry. 'That's not showing respect.'

'Elliott doesn't deserve respect, she tells lies. Come on, Elliott, I'll go with you. What's this village called, Mum?'

'Marciana Marina. Toby, you go with them,' Marcia said very firmly. She intended to see that Elliott was never alone with her son. Toby was from this point on designated by Marcia to chaperone his friend. 'While you're gone we'll unpack and put everything in order. Elliott, you can dispose of your clothes when you get back.'

'Oh dear,' Helen groaned, 'what a mess.' She watched the three of them walking down the pontoons, Elliott unselfconsciously holding hands with both the boys. 'Trust Elliott to make it all up and, silly fools that we are, we believed her.'

'Well, it's too late to back out now.' Marcia was unpacking dried salt cod, tins of ackee and red beans, a big bag of rice and several packets of bonnet chillies.

Helen laughed. 'Look at the difference between us. Here am I, an English woman, unpacking smoked salmon, Marmite and Ryvita, not to mention marmalade.'

'Just remember you filled your whole bloody empire with your Marmite and Ryvita.'

'Yes, but we gave you a lot of good things. Our wonderful writers. Thomas Hardy and Jane Austen.'

'I was only joking. You know the thing I've learned from living in England among so many different races, is that among most women there is no racism. We can share so many experiences. By the way, did you pack sanitary towels?'

'Yes, I did,' Helen smiled. 'I didn't fancy trying to ask for them in Italian.'

'You see, that's exactly my point. All over the world, women bleed once a month. When women share a house, their periods often become synchronized. Women are designed to cooperate with each other. To form communities and binding ties of friendship. Men are completely different. They have aggression built into their genes; they compete rather than make genuine friendships.'

'But then Elliott doesn't really make friends with women. Most of her life seems to be spent chasing men. As for her talking loudly about her periods on the plane, I think the curse is a private matter.'

'I agree with you, but then Elliott's American and they are as incontinent with their emotions as a baby in nappies.' Marcia lit a cigarette and took in a big lungful of smoke.

'Yes,' Helen said, 'but Elliott's never had to grow up.

She's always had money. It's not like us after I left Paul. In those first few months, I was forced to rethink my life entirely. Still, I love Elliott, she's warm and she's funny and intelligent. Hopefully she'll make friends with us before the end of the trip.'

'So do I if we get to stay alive. It's a hell of a journey, and the Straits of Messina are really dangerous. It's narrow and the currents criss-cross like crazy. I've been poring over maps in the library.' Marcia sat down on her bunk.

'The bummer is that we will have to share the boat with a man. I was hoping to have a break from them. Still, we'll have to remember what Fats said, "Thought creates matter". I'm going to think hard about sailing this boat and visualize a really good master mariner to do it. There's a boat club I saw as we walked down the pontoons this morning. There's bound to be someone in there who can help us out. Even if we spend tomorrow learning the basics and leave a day late, it can't be all that difficult. I know some dreadful fools who go sailing.' Helen was thinking of Paul's friends who were yachting yuppies.

'So do I,' said Marcia grimly, 'and they're all dead . . . What shall we have for dinner besides the smoked salmon and champagne? Shall we go into the village and get a real Italian takeaway pizza?'

'You're on.' Helen's face was flushed with joy.

The blue pontoons swayed as they walked across them towards the boat club. Helen felt as if her heart would burst with the beauty of her surroundings. All round her, hundreds of different types of boats were moored. Seagulls filled the air with their haunting, well-remembered cries. Italian seagulls seemed to be more noisy and aggressive than the sedate seagulls she remembered from her early childhood.

There was a buzz and a chatter of people leaning on the sea-walls. 'Italians don't half stare,' Marcia remarked as they made their way towards the little bridge that took them from the world of the sea to dry land.

Initially, Helen didn't want to leave her new, watery world. 'Yes, they do stare, but it doesn't feel as if they don't like us. In Spain they glare at you. Their eyes are sombre and they seldom smile. Here, everyone is smiling.'

'*Ciao bella!*'

Helen blushed. 'That man just said we were beautiful.'

'I don't think he was talking to me,' Marcia smiled. 'I bet they think I'm some sort of freak. I can't see one other face that isn't brown with brown hair and brown eyes. Except for what looks like German tourists – they're not motheaten enough to be English. Wow, I'm an oddity. This must be what my mum and dad felt like growing up in Bristol.'

'Come, let's go to the clubhouse and hope it has a telephone. I need to tell Fats that we're safe. I hope somebody there can speak English.'

'Don't you want to telephone Charlie?'

'I do but I don't want this trip to be haunted by regret that I'm not with him. Before I get involved with any other man again, I want to make sure I know who I am first. I don't ever want to lose myself in a man again. If you don't have a very strong sense of self, that is what happens to women. I've got to make like an onion. I need to grow lots of skins so that I can never be stripped bare again.'

'I know what you mean, though I haven't grown like an onion, more like a parsnip!' Marcia laughed. They'd reached the worn step of the clubhouse and Helen wondered, looking down at the indentations in the step, how many pairs of shoes had stepped into this beautiful, mellow building?

The marina lay in the sunlight, giving off a rich and peaceful air. The clubhouse was painted a honey shade and was shuttered with green shutters. She glanced upwards, and saw a man with a beaky nose staring down at her from the first-floor window.

He waved a folded hand at her. She laughed. How could you take a nation seriously that flapped a right hand in greeting like a child? But then in the few hours she'd been here she'd realized that that was precisely the quality that she so liked about Italians. They waved their hands in greetings and they stared in an uninhibited fashion, like children.

They walked through the door into the main room of the boat club. On the wall Helen saw a telephone. There was a bar in the far left-hand corner, and a big square television set showing weather charts. All around the room were framed pictures of boats with huge sails unfurled or billowing out and racing. Gold and silver trophies sat on a long table against the right-hand wall.

The door to the office was open. 'I need to make a telephone call,' Helen said loudly and clearly. Her heart was thumping. Would he understand her?

The man smiled and stood up. '*Certo*,' he said. He pulled out a phone card from his pocket and pointed at it. 'You need this,' he said. '*Cartoleria*,' he pointed down the road.

'OK.' Helen pulled out her Collins dictionary and looked up the word '*cartoleria*'. 'Ah,' she said, 'no problem, it means a stationer's shop.' She looked at the man and put out her hand. 'My name is Helen Beckett and this is my friend Marcia. We have come to collect the boat called *Carnevale* to take her down to Greece. Are you expecting us?'

'My name,' the man began awkwardly, 'is Roberto. *Mi scusi*, I have *poco poco* English.'

Helen laughed. 'Well, it's better than my Italian.' Roberto went back to his desk and sat down. He shuffled through some papers. 'Here,' he said, and handed Helen a sheaf of documents. 'You have a *marinaio*?'

'We thought we did,' Helen said ruefully, 'but no, we don't. We'll need to hire somebody here. Do you have any *donna marinaio?*' She looked hopefully at Roberto. '*Non,*' he shook his head. He smiled at her. How come English men had such dreadfully bad teeth and the Italians seemed to have wonderfully white teeth?

'So is it possible for us to hire a captain here?' she asked timidly. 'You know somebody to . . .' she made furious gestures of furling sails and then she mimicked pulling in a rope. 'I'll bloody well have to dance the hornpipe if he doesn't cotton on,' she grumbled to Marcia.

'Carry on, Helen. You're doing a wonderful job: he knows now that we're both barking mad.'

'Ah,' Roberto exclaimed as the penny dropped, '*un capitano?*'

Helen nodded furiously. '*Sì sì,*' she said, 'and not too *vecchio.*'

'He'd better be ancient or Elliott will nobble him,' Marcia grinned. Now it looked as if they were going to get a captain, Marcia felt she could relax. Sometimes between the innocence of Helen and the lecherousness of Elliott, she felt squeezed like a lemon. 'Thinking about lemons, Helen, I fancy a gin and tonic. How about you?'

'How decadent. Oh, what the hell, it's our holiday. You order the drinks. I'll restrain myself from running behind the bar and go and get the telephone cards.'

'OK.' Marcia picked up a newspaper. 'Can't understand a bloody word.' She settled down on a chair with a cigarette. 'Don't get lost,' she advised. Helen smiled.

Walking along the sunlit street, Helen didn't feel at all lost. She was surprised to feel as if she'd always lived in this little village. Soon she came across a shop that had a rack of postcards outside. She gazed at them for a moment and then she picked out a postcard of the marina for Charlie. She wandered into the shop and held out the postcard. She smiled and said 'Cart, *per telefono*,' she hoped the words made sense to the man behind the counter.

He glanced at her, then bent his head and took out a stack of phone cards. '*Quante*?' he asked. Helen held up four fingers. '*Quattro*,' she said, blessing her old Latin teacher at school. She handed the man a five thousand lire note and put the change back in her little blue purse.

Back at the clubhouse, pushing the phone card into the telephone on the wall, she waited for Fats to answer. She noticed that the Italian telephone rang very musically, as opposed to the harsh tones in England.

'I can hear you, Helen.' Fats's voice was loud and cheerful. He boomed down the telephone line. 'How's it going?'

'Great, I love it here, Fats.'

'I knew you would, darling. Italy is a very special place. Elba is filled with magic and mystery. Did you know that when they grounded Napoleon there they let him keep his court and his elephants. Can you imagine the little town with elephants strolling round? He was also allowed to keep his army. But he was like a caged bird.'

'Fats, are you OK?'

'Of course, I'm fine, but I'm missing you all like crazy. How are the boys?'

'Fine.' Helen didn't tell Fats that Elliott had been lying. She didn't want him to worry about them. He had enough on his plate with all his teenagers. 'Has Cricket picked up a girl yet?' She could hear him chuckling down the other end of the phone. She wished he was here so she could hug him. He was so warm and so huggable. 'I was young once myself, remember?'

'You still are, idiot. I'm just about to drink my first gin and tonic of the holidays. We're off to get a big pizza for supper and then open the champagne and drink to the trip to Greece. Fats? Are you sure you're OK?'

'Get on with you. I'm fine. You go off and have an exciting adventure.'

'Here's to us and our journey.' Helen raised her glass of gin and tonic and clinked glasses with Marcia.

'Bottoms up,' Marcia said, 'and I don't mean Elliott's.' They both giggled.

Chapter Forty-five

Marcia and Helen stood looking up at their captain. He had a paunch but not much of one. He had a pair of moist, spaniel-like brown eyes and a beard. His hair was curly. He smiled. 'I now speak English,' he said. He bent over Helen's hand and kissed it.

'Why doesn't he kiss my hand?' Marcia was jealous.

'Because you're not wearing a wedding ring. In Italy the men only kiss married women's hands.'

'Hmmf . . . rum lot these Eyties.'

'Come on, Marcia, jealousy won't get you anywhere. Let's concentrate on asking him about the trip.'

'My name is Ricardo. I live in Marchiana Marina. My address is 343 Centro Mercato.'

'Well, well. Who taught you English?' Marcia was smiling. Ricardo had delivered his name and address so earnestly.

'Very good teacher.' Ricardo made a huge circle above his head. 'Very fat English woman. Very fat,' he said with evident satisfaction.

'Oh dear,' Helen said, 'I hope he's not going to go on about being fat. He's going to see me in my bathing suit. At the moment all my wrinkles are pale green. As for Elliott, did she show you what she laughingly calls her bathing suit?'

'Don't, I can imagine.'

'We go to the boat,' Ricardo said. He tucked Helen's arm under his and they led the way down to the pontoon. Helen looked at him sideways. She was wary and uncertain. He reminded her of Fats and that comforted her. She needed a friend.

As they approached the boat, Helen could see Elliott sitting in the cockpit. She had on a minuscule bikini. The top half barely concealed her nipples. A thong ran between her legs; she was already a warm dark brown. For a moment Helen felt an unusual pang of jealousy. She wished she still had the body of a young woman. Now she bagged and sagged. She sighed.

Ricardo's face lit up and his eyes shone. He was gazing at Elliott as if he had his nose pressed to the window of an ice-cream shop.

'Hi folks,' Elliott screamed, 'I got a book. Who's that?' she pointed at Ricardo.

'It's our new captain. He's coming with us to Greece, and you're paying, Elliott.'

'Oh, OK.' Elliott took the news quite cheerfully. 'Did you get the pizzas? I'm starving.'

'Oh shit.' Marcia put her hand to her mouth. 'We forgot. We got stuck into a gin and tonic and then Ricardo arrived. Toby, could you and Junior run back into the village and pick up two big ones?'

'Sure thing.'

Marcia took a fistful of money out of her bag. 'I have no idea how much this money is. I can't count the bloody stuff, but that should be enough.'

'Wait on, everybody, we'll be back in a minute.' Both boys tore off the boat and ran up the pontoons. The pontoons bounced up and down in protest.

'Hi Ricardo.' Elliott stood up and then bent over the side of the boat and put out her hand. Ricardo was afforded an excellent view of her nipples. Ricardo shook her hand and then swarmed up the gangplank. He kicked off his shoes and stood looking down at Helen who was still on the jetty. Standing in his bare feet, he looked so at home on the boat that Helen wondered if he'd not been born on her. '*Vieni*,' he said, stretching out a hand to her. Helen, who was unsure of the ladder leading up to the boat, took his hand gratefully. It was a kind, warm hand. Not like Paul's narrow, cold hand. She slowly inched up the ladder. Marcia had no such problems. 'You'll get used to it,' she advised.

Elliott stood, arms akimbo, running her eyes up and down Ricardo's body. 'Where did you find him?' she inquired.

'He's coming with us to Greece, thanks to your porkers, Elliott,' Marcia said. 'Leave him alone.'

'Why should I? Hi, honey,' Elliott said, dropping her voice several octaves. 'My name is Elliott. I'm *soooo* pleased to meet you.'

Ricardo's nose wrinkled. He stared at Elliott as though bewitched. 'That's it, then, we won't have any peace until Elliott's bonked him.'

Marcia started to climb down the ladder. 'Come on, Helen, let's leave Elliott to fascinate the captain and get ready for the pizza.' At the word 'pizza', Ricardo looked hopeful.

'Pasta?' he inquired.

'*Certo*,' Helen said, proud of her new word.

Ricardo couldn't believe his luck: three women, one with amazing tits. He liked women's breasts. He shared the common Italian's problem that there just weren't enough of them to go round.

The boys arrived back with two big multi-coloured wheels of pizza. Ricardo stopped thinking about Elliott's tits and drew himself up. 'I cook pasta for you,' he said. Helen loved the way he rolled as he walked. It was as though he was already at sea.

'OK,' she said.

He hauled himself into the cabin and then dropped to the floor. 'There's the cooker over there,' Helen pointed to the corner of the cabin.

'I know this boat,' Ricardo said. 'Good boat, very good boat, sail very well.' He busied himself with the pots and the pans. He opened the fridge. 'Here, I make *sugo* for you.' He smiled up at the three women who were gazing down at him from the deck. 'My mother's *sugo*,' he said proudly. '*Fatto a mano in casa*.'

'Shit,' Elliott said loudly. 'Another mother-damaged man.'

'Shut up, Elliott,' Marcia said. 'At least he can cook.'

'Yes,' Helen said with a sigh. 'Now let's sit down and relax.' She sat on the bench beside Toby and he put his arm around her.

'Mum, if you don't give me a bit of pizza now, I'm going to bite your shoulder. I'm starving.'

'Since when were you not starving, darling?'

'Since all my life.'

Ricardo appeared again with a long plank of wood. He tied a bit of string to another bit of string.

'Hey presto,' Marcia said admiringly. 'The man is of some use.'

Within minutes he had a pot of water boiling loudly on the stove. Why does Italian water seem to boil so much more loudly than English water? Helen cocked her head to one side; maybe it was the acoustics in the cabin, but the water seemed to roar with a good-natured Italian roar.

Ricardo passed the two enormous wheels of pizza up to Marcia. '*Per primo, la pasta et poi la pizza*,' he said firmly to Toby.

'Huh?' Toby reached for the pizza.

'*Di firma firma*.' Ricardo smacked Toby's hand. He pulled the two pizzas out of Marcia's hands and stomped down the ladder.

'Well, you've upset the captain, Toby,' Helen said, looking mystified.

'I had an Italian lover once,' Elliott informed the starving passengers. 'He said if I put vegetables on the same plate as his meat he'd throw up.'

'What happened?' Cricket asked.

'I did and he did. The Italians are very funny about their food. It's got to be just like their mom cooks it. I threw him out. I got tired of pasta in all my shelves and my fridge stuffed full of dead bunnies gazing back at my hangover with their dead eyes. Ugh.' Elliott shuddered at the memory.

Ricardo hung out of the hatch, a plate of pasta steaming in his hands. 'In Italy,' he said, 'first plate pasta, secondo *insalata* and *poi la carne*.' He nimbly extracted himself from the hatch and then sat down beside Toby. '*Mangiamo*,' he said.

Toby tried to spin the pasta round his fork but made his usual mess. Ricardo had no such problems. Round the table the others struggled, except for Elliott.

'My lover said that we can never eat pasta like an Italian because they are born with a special gene. As far as he was concerned, all Italians were better at making wine, food and love than anyone else in the world.'

'Was that true?' Marcia inquired.

'Nah, English men are the best in bed.'

They finished the meal almost in silence. The sea air had given them all enormous appetites.

When Ricardo was back in the cabin supervising the washing up after the meal, Marcia lit her cigarette.

'I think we're going to hear rather a lot of the "*non è possibile*", lark. Still, once we get the hang of the boat, we can retire him. I don't fancy being told what to do by a man. It's been far too long for me to take orders again. He's bossy.'

'All Italians are bossy.' Elliott was stretched out in her favourite position on the deck. She rolled over. 'Come on, Toby, you can rub suntan oil on my back.'

Toby blushed. He got to his feet and climbed on to the deck beside her. He picked up the orange jar of suntan oil and began to smooth the lotion on to her back. He was kneeling beside her, hoping that she would not notice his erection. Toby felt her warm silken skin under his hands. He spent so much of his life aware of his body. He wished his dick didn't have an independent life of its own. Girls were so much luckier: what happened between their legs was their business and their business alone. Boys had to struggle with the embarrassment of having no control over their bodies.

He envied Cricket, who had an intimate and proud relationship with his dick. He was always fiddling with it or playing with it. Toby wished he could share Cricket's open enthusiasm. Now he cast a guilty glance at Cricket who was gazing at Elliott with unashamed lust. Cricket concentrated on the sounds of Ricardo putting the finishing touches to the now immaculate kitchen.

Elliott rolled over on to her back and stuck her hand out for the suntan lotion. She was now lying naked, except for her G-string.

'Elliott, you cover up.' There was a warning in Marcia's voice.

'Why?' Elliott opened her eyes. 'Why should I? I want to get my boobs brown.' She gazed down at her pink nipples. 'No stretchmarks yet, I'm happy to say.'

'Come on, Elliott, cover up.' Marcia was talking through gritted teeth.

Ricardo's face loomed through the hatch. He saw Elliott and beamed. 'Pretty lady,' he said. 'American women take their clothes off all the time?'

'As often as they can,' Elliott said, laughing. She sat up. 'OK, if you're going to get sniffy about it, I'll put on my T-shirt.' She slid a pale blue silk shirt over her head. There was a strained silence in the boat. Both boys shifted uncomfortably. Damn, Helen thought, if Elliott is going to act like a bitch on heat, life was going to be difficult. She put down her book on the table and ostentatiously began to read.

Ricardo looked as if he'd been cheated out of a binding promise. He sat down next to Helen. 'I go to Greece with you,' he said, wiping his mouth with an enormous handkerchief.

'Yes,' Helen agreed. 'We must have a captain with us. You can teach us and the boys to sail.'

'*Molto bene*,' Ricardo said amiably. 'I no like Grecia. I no like food. I buy pasta for the boat. But first I sleep. My cabin,' he said, pointing down to the small cabin under the cockpit.

'Well, at least he's not planning to bunk up with Elliott,' Marcia said. 'Not, of course, that you were thinking of offering.'

Elliott smiled her tiger smile. 'Of course not, cutie pie, but there's time.' She stretched out her long slim legs. She winked at Ricardo. He looked around and then realized the wink was for his benefit. Hurriedly he swung himself down the ladder and within a few minutes great rumbling snores could be heard from his cabin.

Toby belched loudly and Cricket laughed. Toby grinned at his mother. 'Sorry, Mum, it's too much pizza.' The only time he didn't think about sex was when he was thinking about pizza. Sometimes he thought about both at once, but it was better to separate the two otherwise he got a headache.

Chapter Forty-six

'I still don't believe we're here.' Helen smiled at Marcia. There were the familiar two small frown lines on Marcia's brow. Helen knew she was plotting to get rid of Ricardo.

'How can we possibly share the boat with a strange man?' she leaned forward and whispered to Helen.

'I don't know, Marcia, but it looks as if we'll have to.'

'Ricardo.' Helen leaned into the boat. Ricardo was washing his face in the kitchen sink. He'd probably leave hair all over the place like Paul did. 'Do you know who owns the boat?'

'I see 'im.' Ricardo was giving nothing away, and Helen watched with approval as he carefully washed out the sink. 'Is he a nice man?' Helen inquired.

'He is a woman, not a man.'

'Ah, the plot thickens.' Helen grinned at Marcia. 'We're not going to be embroiled in the slave trade after all.'

'We're not going to be so lucky.' Elliott ran her hands down her long, silky legs. 'No great big Arab lover is going to come galloping over the horizon and cart me off to his tent in the desert and have his wicked way with me.

'Just my luck; I'll have to make do with an Italian waiter and get sand up my bum. I have a feeling that Ricardo won't take too kindly to my moving a lover on to the boat, even if I am doing the paying.' Elliott was interrupted by Ricardo heaving himself out of the hatch.

'Why oh why do men make so much noise and commotion?' Helen wondered out loud.

This morning, three women and two boys had arrived quietly on the boat; now Ricardo had joined them the boat felt as if it were in the middle of World War Three.

Down below in the Stygian gloom of the cabin, Helen knew she must go to the loo. She waited for her eyes to recover from the bright sunlight on the deck. She wandered towards the bathroom and then stood dumbstruck yet again when she saw the monster in the lavatory. Heads, she corrected herself.

First of all she wondered if she would have to have a ladder to climb on top of it. But she really needed to pee, so she would have to get to grips with it. Gingerly she advanced into the tiny cabin. She closed the round door behind her and was relieved to find that the door had a lock. It was a sweet little door, if that's what you called a door on a boat. It was perfectly round, like a big porthole. She stood surveying the structure. Obviously, it was cantilevered so that it could rock with the boat. A sudden vision of getting caught short with a stomach bug in the middle of a storm and hanging on to the loo for grim death made her grimace. No, in a case like that, death would be infinitely preferable.

She could see two struts sticking out of the base of the loo. Obviously, these were to be climbed on. Laboriously she heaved her behind on to the loo seat. Above her was an open hatch. Looking up she could see the shadow of the boom and a bit of white sail.

'This is the life,' she thought happily. She looked down at the lattice of wood that covered the bilges. She could see the sludge of dirty grey water. The water surged and chuckled to itself. 'Bloody tourists, land-lubbers,' it complained.

'You're supposed to be Italian,' she reminded the sludge. She grinned. 'Definitely going off my rocker,' she announced to the kidney-shaped washbasin. She could see her white face in the mirror of the dressing table that was built into the other wall.

The boys had already staked out their claim. Their

toothbrushes and toothpaste lay side by side on the third shelf. Cricket's hair lotion and eau-de-cologne sat next to Toby's Givenchy. Helen resolved to keep her washbag in her bunk. Both boys were dreadful raiders of both women. She had bought herself razors to shave her legs and under her arms. She didn't care what the harridans in the women's movement said. She, for one, liked the feel of smooth legs. She didn't fancy the great fuzzy arm-pits she'd seen in the village. The Italian woman obviously wouldn't agree with her.

When she emerged, Elliott was counting out change from her purse. They heard Ricardo and the boys laugh-ing on the deck. 'There's no way round this mess, is there, Elliott?'

'No,' Elliott grinned. 'Anyway, I'm glad. I'm not used to all-women jaunts. In fact, thinking about it, I don't have any women friends. Just my mom, and she's no friend. I'm just going off to the village to ring her, other-wise she'll be having a heart attack and asking Interpol to find me.' Elliott tucked her bag under her arm.

'You can buy telephone cards at the *cartoleria*. They also have cigarettes, stamps and postcards,' Helen offered. 'You're not going into the village in your T-shirt and bikini, are you Elliott?' Helen felt stupid and priggish, but even their little stroll to the clubhouse had told her that to dress like Elliott was dressed would only invite disapproval.

'Sure, why ever not? We're on holiday, aren't we?' Elliott stood with her hands on her hips looking at Helen. 'Come on, honey, lighten up will you?'

'We will lighten up, Elliott.' Marcia's voice was tight. 'But you must understand that you are in Italy now. The Italians don't walk round half dressed. I know it's OK in Texas, but it's very definitely not OK here.'

'Look, honey-child. You don't worry about me and I won't worry about you, OK? Otherwise this trip is goin''

to get a little tense. When I get tense I get really tense.'
Marcia could see a cold light in Elliott's electric blue
eyes. She swung herself up the ladder and walked off, her
blonde hair bobbing as she walked purposefully across
the blue pontoons leading to the boat club.

'Well, I guess the battle lines are drawn,' Helen said to
Marcia, pulling a face. 'I feel like an old mother hen
telling Elliott off. She makes me feel middle-aged and
unadventurous. Come to think of it, that is exactly what
I am. I've never taken the risks Elliott has. I've never been
to bed with any other men than Paul. Maybe I should
buy myself a sexy bikini, but then who'd look at me?'
She remembered the two blue varicose veins running from
behind both her knees. Her skin was scaly from where
she'd spent the winter in front of her fire.

'It's not your figure or your face that makes a woman
sexy, Helen. It's far more what's inside. Charlie thinks
you're beautiful and so do I.' Marcia smiled at Helen.
'Anyway, I think Elliott will settle down. She's not been
out of America. I don't mean that she hasn't travelled,
she has. But she's always travelled in that very American
way. In a bubble. Now that she's on her own with us, I
think she's going to be rather bewildered by Italy. In fact,
if she could, I think she'd admit she's rather frightened.
She's used to being surrounded by adoring men and
lovers. She said herself she has no girl friends. We at least
have each other.'

'We do,' Helen smiled back. 'And thank God for that,
Marcia. I don't know what I would have done without
you.'

There are so many kinds of love, Helen thought later
as she sat on deck waiting for Marcia to join her. The
love she felt for Marcia was a very new feeling. Women
hadn't made close friendships in the circles she'd moved
in in Swiss Cottage. They betrayed each other and spent
most of their lives competing with each other. She valued

her friendship with Marcia enormously, and she knew that her love was reciprocated. She heard Marcia laughing with Ricardo and the boys in the cabin. Marcia was such a strong, sure woman. Helen very much wished that one day she would be like that.

Chapter Forty-seven

Helen lay in her small bunk feeling perfectly enwombed. I don't think that's a real word, she told herself. In fact so much of her life was expended in her interior dialogue with herself, she often forgot to share her thoughts with anyone else. Maybe because she was shy of her thoughts. 'People who talk to themselves are usually considered mad,' was Paul's often dismissive reply when she tried to discuss her visions of the universe.

On a bad day, Paul's criticisms could begin in the morning and, like a movement of music, rise to a crescendo in the evening upon his return from work; finally he would end his hostile comments in bed where there would be a slight reprise of the day's complaints.

Now, with the boat rocking gently and intimately holding Helen in her metaphoric arms, she tired, full of wine and unaccustomed laughter, Helen felt close to tears again. She had no right to be this happy. A failure was what she was, and failures had no rights.

The next morning, as they forged along the sidewalk looking for a cup of coffee (and Helen very much hoping to find a decent loo), she noticed that she was anonymous in the eyes of the people passing by. The boys attracted fascinated stares. Toby, because he was tall and fair and the straight bridge of his nose had already caught the sun, Cricket, because his brown-black skin was such an unusual sight.

Both boys towered above the small residents of Elba. Marcia absolutely elegant in a scarlet wrap, her black hair piled on top of her head, swayed beside Elliott. Elliott, of course, was the centre of attention. Not only did she cause the village to stare, but also Ricardo's friends in the boat club. Elliott wore another bottom-flirting T-shirt, beneath which you could just catch a glimpse of her tanned buttocks. Helen was envious of Elliott's bottom. She thought hers was hideous: two little cushions of fat clinging to the top of her thighs. Lines descended down from the front of her thighs to her knees. She thought her thighs looked like ski slopes after a heavy day on the piste.

Ricardo walked beside her this morning. At one point he rolled his eyes sideways and gazed at her. He nodded his head, as if he understood some of her thought processes. Then, to her surprise, he tucked her arm under his own and walked her to the bar where they all sat down. Ricardo ordered coffee for everyone except Marcia, who wanted tea.

'Good heavens, Ricardo, you look as if you've been ordering English tea all your life.'

'English people I like,' he said, as though it were some sort of explanation. 'Americans I no like.'

'Hey, I'm American,' Elliott said.

'*Una donna eccezionale*,' Ricardo twinkled at her. Elliott sucked in her cheeks and leaned forward, as if to kiss Ricardo. How on earth did Elliott do it? Helen wondered. Every move must have been studied in the mirror.

Now in the bunk again, she let her mind drift over the day before. The breathless arrival. The nervousness of not catching the ferry from Piombino. The first sight of Elba. The little promontory where she imagined the tiny figure of Napoleon once stood so very long ago and gazed at the mainland of his beloved Europe.

Now she was to be exiled also. Exiled by her husband who had left her for another woman. Now she had put herself into exile from her flat in Shepherd's Bush, from the bar where she was safe and loved, and from Charlie who wanted to love her. From her best friend Fats. She was going away on an adventure to lay some ghosts.

Would her island be haunted by the ghost of Paul? Paul laughing, his head thrown back, drinking their once shared bottle of champagne? Last night, as Ricardo had expertly opened the bottle of champagne supplied by Elliott, there had only been a shade of a ghost. A glitter of the familiar cut-glass wine glasses they had been given by Paul's mother as a wedding present. Alas, they remained with Paul. One day, she promised herself, she would again own a whole set.

That night, still in Marciana Marina, the boys lay sprawled on the deck, listening to Ricardo, who had produced his guitar. He sang old Neapolitan love songs. Helen sat by the step-ladder and listened to the music. She dropped lumps of crusty bread into the sea and watched the flash of silver as the small fish turned on their bellies to take the crumbs in their mouths. Her nose was full of salt, her hair stringy to the touch. Her back was sore from the sun but she was limp with happiness and now the acknowledgment that happiness was an emotion that could be reborn reduced her to tears and she cried until she could cry no more.

Helen knew that she had a face that other people wanted to hurt. Too shy at school to defend herself, she was often pinched and slapped. Not because she was pretty like the other girls, but because she was clever. She tried to hide the effort she put into her work from the other girls but, try as she might, she always came out on top in the examinations. 'Snidy bitch,' the other girls would giggle. A barely repressed groan would greet the news that she was top in Latin, and first in History and English Literature. There was also the awful day when the school inspector asked her to recite a poem and she dragged herself from her seat and stood nervously recounting the 'Wreck of the Hesperus'. When she had finished and the rest of the class were stupefied with boredom, she had eagerly, encouraged by his kindly interest said: 'I can also recite the whole of "Hiawatha".'

'That will do, thank you, dear,' he'd said, smiling at her. 'She'll go far,' he'd predicted.

'I don't think so, sir,' was her teacher's wounding reply. 'She has absolutely no presence.' From that moment on, Helen didn't feel she existed. That was why she'd stuck with Paul. He knew he existed. He knew he was clever and talented. He'd been to university. He'd also passed out top in his examinations but, unlike Helen, he also knew that he had a real physical presence.

When she became pregnant with Toby, she often wondered if she'd give birth to a shadow like herself. It had been a tremendous relief when she'd first held him in her arms: not only was he all in one piece, but he also possessed fingers and toes in the right order, and was a big chunky baby. He did exist, as the noise he made when he screamed for her presence, told her.

'I am a person, I am real, I am alive,' she told herself as she drifted into a tearsodden sleep. How long will this agony go on, she wondered? What was left unsaid was that she was still a failure. Alive or dead. But at least she had found a loo.

Chapter Forty-eight

Helen was in the galley trying to open a jar of capers. The trouble is that I'm totally useless at most things. She felt an intense feeling of frustration. No wonder Paul yelled and screamed and banged his fist on the table. She couldn't even open a jar.

This morning they had stopped the boat for a swim in the sea. When she'd tried to climb back into the boat, she had found herself totally unable to lift herself out of the water. Ricardo had had to stretch out his big hand and haul her out of the sea like a sackful of rubbish.

'I'm sorry,' she apologized. 'I've got no muscles in my arms.' Nor now in my hands, she told herself, close to tears. Sometimes she felt she would never stop crying. Everything hurt her – even to see a dead moth. She felt as if layers and layers of skin had been stripped away from her body, and she was now naked and so raw that she couldn't even look into the butcher's shop in the marina. The pieces of beefsteak looked as she felt.

'Toby,' she yelled, 'could you come and help me?'

Within a minute, Toby was down beside her, towering over her. 'Mum, what are you so upset about?'

'Oh Toby, I don't know. I'm so useless at everything.'

'No you're not, Mum. You're the best cook in the world. I'm going back to join Elliott and Cricket in the water. She's drowning him.'

'Don't you think Elliott's a bit, well, you know what I mean, Toby?'

Toby laughed at his mother. 'You mean, does Elliott fancy Cricket like mad, don't you, Mum?'

'I'm not sure that I want to hear the answer.'

'The answer is yes, Mummy, and what are you going to do about it?'

'Nothing, I suppose, but Marcia will kill Elliott or both of them if she finds out.'

Toby shrugged. 'It's not as if Cricket hasn't shagged a lot of birds, Mum. And ones Elliott's age. He can take care of himself, you know.'

'I know that, Toby, but she is rather a lot older.'

'What's that got to do with it? Sex is sex.'

Helen gazed up at her son in surprise. 'Toby, where did you get that idea?'

'It's just a fact, Mum. Come on,' he said, trying to cheer her up, 'just because you choose to live like a nun that has none.' He watched her smile. That phrase was a shared joke between them. She had such a pretty smile, but for so long she had not smiled or really even laughed. Toby wondered if she would ever really smile again.

For himself, he was fiercely jealous of Cricket, but not ready to extend himself into a relationship with a girl that would at best be impermanent. He still fiercely missed Louise. It wasn't even the sex, he realized. It was far more their long, intimate talks. He knew everything there was to know about her and she him.

Toby felt guilty about leaving his mother struggling with the lunch while he dived back into the water. But he also felt a flash of resentment that he had had to take the full responsibility for her grief over his father's behaviour. He had had enough of his own to carry. Thinking about Louise made him swim harder. He reached out a hand to his much younger self. The self that had made love to Louise so long ago on those golden days on the sun-warmed heath. He was still so traumatized by losing her he never wanted to give his heart away again.

He could see Elliott's blonde head in the distance. She, upon seeing him, shrieked, 'The water's freezing my ovaries, but it's OK now I'm used to it.' She waved her arms at him but he set a course for the nearby beach. He wanted a few moments alone.

When he finally got there, he paused for breath and then ran up the beach, glad to find it empty. He could feel the hard round pebbles under his feet. He was wearing an old pair of plimsolls. He listened to the scrunch of the stones and he slid down small hillocks. There was a pronounced smell of dry seaweed, and the haunting call of the gulls looking for the left-overs from yesterday's picnickers.

He ran straight back into the water when he saw his mother waving at him to come back to the boat for lunch. The cold sea caused a searing pain in his testicles. Anxiously, he felt for them. He somehow felt he might never see either of them again.

'We're the only ones in the water,' Toby observed.

'Yeah, the only ones mad enough to go in.' Cricket ducked Elliott, who responded loudly. Toby looked up the beach, which was now splattered in little dark pools of black clothing – Italian mothers, aunts and grandmothers gazing implacably at the swimmers. Small children in formal clothing were clamped to their sides. Wrinkled hands petted and patted their small charges. They screamed in unison as their charges tried to get away and play by the swelling water.

'Wow, I wouldn't like to be an Italian child,' Elliott observed. 'Look at them all, like a nest of crows.'

'Yeah, but the woman in the pizzeria is really cool.' Toby was stung: this was his Italy and he didn't want it criticized. 'Italians love children. In England you'd never see the restaurants full of kids as you do here.'

'Sure, you don't, thank goodness. I don't like kids, and I don't want them around when I'm eating.'

'Are you sure you don't like children, Elliott?' Cricket was watching her carefully.

'Only in bed, idiot.' She pushed him under the water.

'Hey,' he said, coming back up for air. 'Hair-pulling is out, man.'

'Rules weren't made for women. Anyway, I'm not a man; maybe you hadn't noticed?' Elliott gave her shrieking laugh and chased Cricket with a fast crawl. As their noise receded towards the boat, Toby lay flat on the surface of the sea. He allowed the waves to tug and to pull him. At least, for a few minutes, he felt a moment of peace.

Helen and he were far away from sorrows they had both left behind them. Hopefully, this trip would restore some of the relationship they used to have when they lived together in Swiss Cottage. After the bombshell of his parents' separation, he was still confused by the emotions he felt for his mother.

All his emotions felt melded. On the one hand he felt guilty and protective, on the other he felt angry that he had had to play this role in her life. He was still young, and he shouldn't have to feel responsibility for his mother's happiness. Or, for that matter, for his father's abandonment of both of them and his weakness.

Or maybe his father had had to abandon both of them. Maybe they had been very boring company for him. His father liked crowds and lots of entertaining. Both Toby and his mother were home bodies. Now his dad was living like a middle-aged teenager, and that was embarrassing enough.

The sun was warm on his face. He rolled over and wondered what it would be like to just stop breathing? To drown. To exit from all feelings. Blindness, oblivion. Then he shook his head in the water. No, that was not what he wanted. Life inexorably moves on and he, Toby, would move it. Anyway, it was time for lunch, and he was ravenously hungry.

Chapter Forty-nine

'Elliott,' Marcia's voice was strained, 'do you have to make so much noise?'

'Aw come on, Marcia, lighten up.' Elliott was sitting back to back with Cricket. He was steering the boat. She was dangling her long legs over the stern. She was hauling up a bucket filled with sea water and pouring the bucket over Cricket and herself. Every time she upended the bucket over the both of them, she shrieked with laughter. 'Hey, Marcia, wanna change places? It's really cooling. Boy, it's a hot day.'

Marcia watched her son carefully. No, so far, she didn't think they'd made love. Why did it bother her so much? She was never bothered by the other women he took to bed, as long as they weren't in her house. Some of them had been older and others married.

Marcia tried to smile at Elliott. 'No thanks,' she said evenly. 'I'm going below to read,' she grinned at Helen. 'I'm in the middle of a fabulous bit about pirates in the Cayman Islands. Apparently, Blackbeard's treasure is still on The Brac island in one of the caves. Maybe, one day, when we've all learned to sail, we could go down there and find it.' She laughed cheerfully, a laugh that belied the fear she had of Elliott in her heart.

Once down in the cool cabin, she ran the water over the kitchen knife and then fell backwards against Elliott's bunk. The boat lurched forward again and she had to hang on to the sink. 'This sucks,' she said out loud. She was bruised by yesterday's sailing. Her fingernails were torn from pulling down the sails, and it didn't help that all Ricardo's instructions were in Italian, so her limited knowledge was of little use.

Helen joined her and grinned. 'Found your sea legs yet?' she asked.

'I'm finding my sea legs, Helen, but I'm ashamed of myself because Elliott makes me tense.'

'She makes everyone tense, Marcia. She's just a big kid. She enjoys playing with the boys. I know she's loud, but then most Texans are. I'm used to clients of Paul's who would come to dinner. My goodness, the noise! But they were all very generous, especially the men. I liked them all. No head games like his English clients. They weren't snobs. They loved England and the English. Anyway, I have a much more serious problem than Elliott.'

'What's that?' Marcia raised her eyebrows.

'Marcia, I'm constipated. I just can't use that awful machine. It's OK now while we're still learning and I can use the boat club loo, but what happens when we go to sea? What happens if it gets blocked? We can't ask Ricardo to unblock it.'

Marcia laughed. 'Well, to tell the truth I'm the same. By the time I've climbed up there and hung on for dear life, nothing happens. I think when I do go I'm going to shit cannonballs.'

'It's not fair, the boys are fine. Let's buy loads of fruit this evening. Ricardo says one more day and he's ready to push off for Greece. You know, I'm actually beginning to quite like him. In a way it's probably for the best that he is coming with us. Marciana Marina is such a cheerful, friendly place, I don't feel at all threatened here, but we don't know what it's going to be like down south.'

'Much the same, I guess.'

Helen sat down on Elliott's bunk. 'Ouch,' she said, 'there's a lump under the duvet.' She pulled out a bottle of Jack Daniels. 'Humf,' Helen frowned. 'I'd rather Elliott drank openly like we do.'

'So would I, but Elliott drinks far more than you realize, Helen. She's from a very different background and a different life style. She tends to drink from about ten o'clock in the morning. The thing about being on a boat is that there are no secrets, and I've watched her. She usually drinks vodka because there's no smell.'

'Oh great, that's all we need: Elliott the alcoholic.' Helen stood up and began to rinse out the lettuce. 'But then, Marcia, that might be the way she copes with her pain. I know I drink too much. After a bad day I hit the wine bottle. I've given up gin and tonics. They just depress the hell out of me and I get miserable. I know Paul was always at his worst on whisky. Boy, if he had several shots, I knew there'd be trouble to follow.'

'Cricket's dad blew his brains out on rum. Down on the island they mix it with coconut juice.' There was a reflective tone in Marcia's voice. A soft strain of remembering. When Marcia talked about her son's father, Helen realized how hurt Marcia still was after all these years.

'JA is so beautiful. I can't tell you or even describe the wildness of the mountains and then the sweeping hills going down to the sea. At night we'd dance on the beaches and then cook fish over the brush fires. I've never seen smiling faces like that again. Funny, so many black people, after a while in England, get this funny grey look to their skin. I can always tell the new arrivals: they still glow from the sun and the sea.'

'Here, I'll make the *panini* today.' Helen cut the thick Tuscan loaf with the bread knife. She draped the pale pink prosciutto in between the slices of the bread. Together they began to pass the food and wine up on to the deck, bracing themselves against the sides of the cabin, and hauling themselves on to the deck.

Elliott was lying on her back sunbathing on deck. 'Hey, I'll wash up with Cricket and Toby. Thank you, guys, I'm starving.'

Marcia realized that, having shared her annoyance with Helen, she felt less threatened by Elliott. 'That's OK, Elliott.' Marcia slid on to the bench.

Ricardo leaned into the belly of the boat and neatly hooked the table from behind the map desk. Helen watched him and marvelled at the uncomplicated way Ricardo moved about the ship. He wore only a voluminous canary yellow pair of swimming shorts. He was completely unconcerned about how he looked, and Helen envied him that certainty. Hopefully, during the trip, she could lose some of her paralysing shyness, her feeling of being dreadfully ugly. She knew that when she looked into mirrors she saw only the bad things about her face and her body. The wrinkles, the drooping lines about her mouth. The threads of grey in her hair.

'We eat,' Ricardo said, throwing himself down beside Cricket. 'Good boy,' he said, slapping Cricket on the back.

Marcia was pleased to see Cricket's face light up. He was looking at Ricardo with sheer delight. 'You're cool, man,' he said, grinning.

'Cool?' Ricardo's face wore a suspicious scowl.

'It means that Cricket likes you,' Toby explained. 'Like you're OK for an adult.'

Ricardo gave a belly chuckle. 'OK,' he said. 'This afternoon I show you the ropes.' Helen bit into her panini. The taste of the saltless bread went perfectly with the pink wisps of dried ham. On her plate she had half of a big round 'beefsteak' Tuscan tomato. She studied the moist, gelatinous seeds of the tomato. Yellow-green olive oil created thick little globules and puddles of colour over the bright red of the tomato. A dusting of black pepper and some shining white salt crystals completed the picture. How beautiful, she thought. How very beautiful to be here on a boat in the middle of the bluest sea she'd ever seen. Her body rocked with the boat as the engine pushed it through the waves. The sea was suddenly calm and silky.

That night, when they tied up, they were a tired but very happy group of people.

'Good boys.' Ricardo slapped Toby and Cricket on their shoulders. Cricket gave Ricardo a high five and then said, 'Ricardo, where do we go to hunt chicks?'

'I take you tonight, we go disco.' He moved his hips suggestively and winked at Toby. 'Ziggy-ziggy. You like ziggy-ziggy?' Although they hadn't heard this expression before it was quite clear that he was talking about sex.

'I rather think that the boys are tired,' Marcia said. 'We're leaving for Greece tomorrow and we don't even have a map yet.'

'Tomorrow.' Ricardo drew himself up and tucked his pasta belly into his shorts. 'Tomorrow we go to special shop.' He kissed his fingers. 'This shop have many map. But I take boys to disco. Tomorrow sleep when we go.' He waggled his hands in imitation of the boat flying through the water. 'Tonight we dance, we make love.'

'Hey,' Elliott interrupted, 'how about me? I wanna dance too.'

'Women stay home in Italy. Men go out together. You go to restaurant with your friends. We go to the disco.'

'Boy, I think that idea sucks out loud.' Elliott was pouting. 'Please, Ricardo, take me dancing?' She leaned forward and her breasts dangled just above Ricardo's nose.

He stood up and motioned to Toby to take the steering wheel. 'No,' he said, shaking his head.

'Shoot.' Elliott was sitting in the restaurant in the corner of the main square. She picked at her squid and octopus salad. 'What a bum steer. The boys are going dancing all night and we're going to sit on our bunks like virgins. Well, I don't intend to spend this trip celibate.'

'No one said you had to, Elliott. You can find a man

if you put your mind to it.' Marcia sat back with her glass of white wine. She felt a warm glow of contentment. If Ricardo was going to drag the boys off every night to the disco, that would keep Cricket busy and away from Elliott.

'I don't want to get involved with a man.' Helen twirled her linguine around her fork. 'I want to practise eating pasta properly. I want to see dolphins, and above all I want to find my peace. That bit of me that went missing so many years ago.

'You know, Marcia, I haven't felt this happy since I was a little girl in my sail-boat classes in Sussex. Which reminds me, I must send my mum and dad a postcard. They'll be tickled pink. I ought to organize Toby to send one to his father and to Laura.'

'No you don't, Miss Busybody. You let Toby decide if he wants to send a postcard to his father or not. Don't you interfere.'

'I guess you're right. I've always been so frightened of Paul. If we were at my parents' place and Toby didn't telephone Paul every night, there'd be ructions.'

'Fuck him, Helen.' Elliott sounded much calmer after half a bottle of wine. 'Tell him to piss up a rope, if he can manage that. Hey, look over there,' she motioned with her chin, 'see that guy just come in? Hubba, hubba, ding, ding, baby, you've got everything,' she crooned into her white wine.

Marcia laughed. 'Go for it, Elliott,' she said.

Chapter Fifty

It was five o'clock in the morning. Helen had been unable
to sleep. She was amazed to discover that since she'd been
on the boat she'd missed having sex very much. Even
having sex with boring old Paul.

What was it about the boat that made her miss sex?
Was it the beautiful weather? The hot sun beating down
on her now browning body? The gentle rays of the sun
tickling her stomach and causing her thighs to relax their
clenched hold on her bruised sex? The absence of cruelty,
the sound of the crew's laughter? The slightly woozy
lunches where Paul could no longer chide her for having
an extra glass of wine? Yes, it was probably all those
things. A slow finding of her own boundaries. The
regrouping of her hopes and expectations. Nothing was
a big deal. There were no shouted commands to send her
scurrying across the house like a frightened mouse. A
topo, permanently tied to a string. Now she could relax,
though at first it had made her fearful.

She quietly climbed down from the bunk. She resolved
to go to the loo when all the others got up and went into
the village for morning breakfast. This was the one meal
they now allowed themselves to have out. But she must
go to the loo or bust. Marcia had already triumphed, but
then Marcia had been on boats before.

She crept down the middle of the boat and looked up
at the stars. They gazed benignly down at her. 'Come,'
they whispered, their voices crackling with static electricity, 'come and talk to us. Tell us about your life.'

'Not much to tell,' she whispered softly back. 'I have

314

Fats to thank for helping me to see that I am worth more than Paul thought I was. He made me realize that I don't have to measure myself against this little life. Rather that I must measure myself against eternity.'

'He is so right.' A big flashy star shot across the sky. 'Weeee,' it shrieked, 'I've always wanted to do that.'

'So have I, so have I.' Helen sat totally alone on deck. There were a few weary figures draped on the wall outside the clubhouse, but she sat contentedly listening to the boat heaving and groaning. She missed hearing Ricardo snoring in his bunk under her. She smiled. She never thought that she'd find a big rumbling male snore comforting. It was so much better than Paul's high whine of a snore. She chuckled and felt the boat moving up and down. Up and down. 'It's a good thing Charlie isn't here now.' She leaned over the side of the boat and talked to the dark moving water. 'Otherwise I'd be guilty of a serious charge of rape.' She grinned.

Just as she was curled up again in her bunk, she heard the boys arriving back with Ricardo. 'Shhhh,' she heard Ricardo whispering loudly. 'Your mothers are sleeping. Quiet please.'

From the giggling and the whispering, Helen surmised that the three of them were quite drunk. She lay, pretending to be asleep. Marcia who could sleep through anything didn't move.

Helen felt happy for Toby. This was just what he needed. A man to take him out, and Cricket for company, to get him away from her endless female companionship. Living alone with Toby she realized that a man in Toby's life was essential. Paul had always been rather a failure. He didn't take any exercise, except for using the rowing machine in his study which he forbade them to use.

He never played football or volleyball like so many other fathers. Toby had grown up with Paul largely absent, if not in body then in spirit. He was an unmanifested bad-tempered phantom in their lives, and now he was gone. A growing sense of freedom filled her days.

Ricardo's large bulk brushed past her bunk. He swung himself into the lavatory and peed loudly. 'Good heavens.' Helen tried not to blush in the dark cabin. Italian men seemed to live so loudly, and without the modesty practised by their English counterparts. Ricardo gave a loud belch and then climbed back out of the circular door and stumbled off to the back end of the boat which housed his cabin.

Soon the air was rent with enormous snores. Helen stretched, and then she sank back into a light sleep. She awoke with a start. The snoring had stopped. Was he dead? Had he had a heart attack and died? Should she go and check? But then, if he opened one eye and saw her face hanging over him, he might think she was trying to make a pass at him.

To her relief, the snoring resumed, and she drifted off thinking that she must ask him to snore consistently; but then maybe he couldn't. Men, she thought, drowsily. Why do we bother?

Struggling into the waking day, Helen smiled at Marcia. Marcia lay in her bunk, her long elegant body draped over it like a black silk scarf. She was wearing red bikini bottoms and a yellow T-shirt. 'You'd think I'm too black to burn but I'm not,' she said, stroking her shoulders. 'Wow, I'm sore. Throw me the suntan lotion, will you? It's on the rack by your bunk.'

Helen threw the yellow labelled bottle. Marcia caught it neatly. A photograph fell out of the rack. Helen picked it up. She giggled. 'Look at this, Marcia.' It was a photograph of a very fat blonde with nothing on but a lot of hair.

Marcia stretched out a lazy hand. 'Will they ever grow up?'

'No, not while there's a whole lot of women who are willing to pose like that. She looks awful. Like a big fat cow. Look at those tits, Marcia.'

Marcia handed the picture back to Helen. 'Put it away,' she advised. 'If Cricket sees that he'll be a problem for weeks. Under his mattress he has the most disgusting magazines.'

'Does Toby know about that?'

'Of course, silly. Helen, all boys look at dirty magazines.'

'I guess so. I never did. I think it's so sad for women to take off all their clothes for a magazine. That sort of thing should be left for lovers.'

'That's because you're a normal woman and so am I. But you should know from Lace and Maisie that women like us are not the norm now. Thanks to all that porn, sex and violence exported from America, people need more and more excitement.'

'I hope the island will be an innocent place. I'm afraid I'm rather in need of innocence for a while. London has become so decadent and so frightening. I guess a childhood protected by my mother and my father is not necessarily a good recipe for life.'

'It makes you short on street cred, honey, but you're getting there. You're nothing like as naïve as when you first arrived in the Bush. I never thought you'd make it. But you have.' Marcia reached out and gave Helen's hand a squeeze.

'Well, I don't think I'm going to be able to shit this morning. This lot aren't going to get up until midday. Let's take our things and shower at the boat club. I'm looking forward to my coffee and a panini. Fancy eating pig for breakfast. Who would have thought it?' She smiled. That was her mother's voice talking.

Chapter Fifty-one

'I wonder,' Helen addressed the toilet-roll holder. 'No,' she reminded herself, 'not toilet, lavatory. But that didn't make sense. The thing I'm sitting on is a lavatory, so you must call toilet roll, lavatory paper. Oh, who the hell cares?' she added. Paul cares, she reminded herself. He had a special sneering voice which she had internalized after all those years of living with him.

'Without me, Helen, you'll never make it. I created you. When I first met you you were nothing. A little country mouse. You couldn't even speak English properly. You couldn't dress properly. I taught you everything, everything you know. I warn you, if you don't stay friends with me and let me advise you, you'll end up in the gutter.'

Even now, perched on the toilet in the boat club, she felt Paul was the thought police. He and all his friends seemed to have a fraternity, which included women, who all knew how the rest of the world should run. Helen had fallen foul of the fraternity. They wouldn't let her join their ball-game. She wasn't Quite One Of Us, Dear. She thought of them as the great bureaucracy that held her life and Toby's in check for all those years.

She caught sight of her brown face in the mirror. Her hair was streaked blonde in the sun. 'I'm far away from the thought police now,' she reminded the washbasin. 'Anyway, I never realized that sailing made you think so much about shitting. Here I am, as constipated as a chicken. Elliott never talks about anything else.' She laughed, sitting there in this strange toilet in Elba. The sun shone outside, in a green garden with ivy-leaved walls.

'Well?' Marcia was waiting in the main room of the

clubhouse. She was watching the television set which ran a continuous news service about the weather. 'All OK?' she asked.

Helen made a circular motion with her thumb and first finger. '*Tutt'è a posto.*' She took Marcia's hand and pulled her to the door. Towards the sunlight, the sea, and the harbour. 'We couldn't walk down Shepherd's Bush holding hands; everyone would think we were gay, wouldn't they?'

'I guess.' Marcia looked about her. 'I can't get over the way men kiss each other and walk around with their arms around each other. Nobody cares who or what you are. They stare at you, but it's not rude. It's more that they are inquisitive. Funny, I feel so odd being the only black person besides Junior. I do remember, as a child in Bristol, feeling an outsider. There were Jamaican kids, but no other African kids. I was so much blacker than everybody else. I had trouble with boyfriends. Children can be such racists too. Here it doesn't really matter. It's all so exotic anyway, if that makes sense.'

They rounded the corner and came into the main square which housed the cathedral. There they moved towards the restaurant they had made their own. 'Espresso e panini,' Helen said shyly to the waiter. He grinned at her. His long black eyelashes gave him the look of a shy faun. 'Certo,' he said. Marcia ordered a small coffee and *dolce*. 'You know the one with the thick yellow custard,' she said hopefully. She smiled when he understood. 'You know, I'm getting like Elliott. Just look at his bum. Italian men make the best sex objects, they're so beautiful. So different from the men in England.'

'Go on, Marcia, what's wrong with Charlie?' Helen stretched her arms above her head. 'I know what you mean, though. What with all this wine and the hot sun, to say nothing of the boat bobbing up and down, I feel really randy. I haven't felt like this since – well, since the first days of my marriage.' She was surprised by her own surprise and then there were no flashes in her life of the feeling of freedom.

Here she was sitting, without Toby, with her friend Marcia, about to put her lips into a frothy moustache of deep brown coffee. There was nobody around to insult or upset her. The square was quiet. A little brown dog on a gold leash trotted silently past the table. His owner tottered past, slightly ahead of the dog. She wore a black tight-fitting skirt, a matching jacket that hugged her pointed breasts, and a tall black hat made from shiny straw. 'Wow, Marcia, that's some fashion statement, and she's only going to the shops.'

'Yeah,' Marcia smiled. 'I'd rather be wearing my T-shirt and bikini bottoms and about to set sail for Greece any day, but only Elliott dares walk round town like that. You and I have our Marks and Spencer's best on because we're too shy.' The waiter carried out the coffees, expertly holding the two plates in one hand. 'I've never learned to do that yet at the bar, Marcia.'

'You will, honey, you will in time. If we ever get back there, that is. Do you think Ricardo knows what he's doing?'

'Yes, I do. Lots of the sailors at home were like he is. All mouth and trousers, talking about women all the time and partying all night long, but once they went sailing they stopped all the showing off and were excellent. I don't think we're going to see much of him and the boys after dinner when we come into port, though.'

'Good, it will keep Elliott away from Junior if Ricardo refuses to take her with him.'

'I wouldn't count on that, Marcia.'

Marcia bit into her big cornucopia of a *dolce*. 'Um,' she muttered, 'this even beats sex.'

Helen watched the soft pink of the early geraniums in the flowerbed in front of the restaurant. Beside them there was a big tub of basil, rosemary and thyme. In her mind she could hear the soft voices of the singers. 'Remember me to the one who lives there. She once was a true love of mine.'

She felt the pain again, sighed, and Marcia glanced at her. 'Still hurts, honey?'

'Yeah, but maybe it always does, Marcia. D'you ever get away from the fact that you once so loved a man that you had his child and shared silly little secrets? Told him you were afraid he'd die before you when you were in bed together at night. You had a special name for his willy and he called you a special name?'

'That happens to us all, Helen. But then men don't seem to share that terrible sense of failure when the relationship flies out of the window like a black crow. That's why I've given up on men. I don't want some irresponsible bastard sharing my life, Helen. I've been caught twice and that's enough.'

Helen looked down at her hands. She could see a couple of faded, barely brown spots. 'Liver spots, Marcia; already I've got thighs that look like loose elastic, and now liver spots. I'm going to hell in a hurry.'

'No you're not, fool woman. You're going to Greece, and we're going to have a blast.'

Helen smiled. 'Marcia?' she said, sipping her coffee. 'If Greek men are anything like Italian coffee, it should be fun.'

'Hot, brown and tasty, like Jamaican men. I do hope Greek men have more life than English men.'

'They have to, Marcia. It's that awful English climate that kills passion.' She gazed again at the geraniums. The worst of the pain was over. Yes, she did have pots and pots of geraniums in her old garden. Yes, she left behind her the roses, delphiniums, and usually by now she would have planted her tomatoes, zucchini and aubergines and all sorts of herbs.

But not in her Shepherd's Bush flat, though. No, the only vegetables came from the market, and the main herb to come through the door was illegal. Well, at least if they smoked at home they were safe. Better to be told straight by your son than to find out after some trouble occurred. If she hadn't known Marcia, she would have freaked out at the idea of Toby smoking dope. Marcia was a realist, though, and that was why she had such a good relationship with her son.

'Come on, Marcia, let's go back to the boat and practise hauling up the sails.'

'OK. Elliott will be hanging out of her bikini as usual.'

'Yeah, but she's not getting anywhere with Ricardo, Marcia.'

'It's not Ricardo that she's after, Helen.'

'I know that, but Cricket can look after himself. You know, in a funny way, I wonder if Elliott needs to be an adolescent again? Sort of to make up for all those years when she didn't have a childhood? Trapped with that awful mother of hers. A sort of nanny to the old bat. Abandoned by her father and co-opted into being her mother's best friend. I don't think one's child should ever be forced to be your best friend, do you?'

'I agree we're lucky, though I'm your best friend.'

'I know that but, even if I were alone, I'd want to feel Toby had his own circle of friends and didn't have to feel responsible for me.' Helen took out her purse. 'It's my turn to pay this morning.' She extracted a handful of notes. 'Goodness, what a bundle of notes, and then when you add it all up it comes to so little.'

'Oh, that *dolce* was wonderful, Helen. I feel like a walrus after eating that. I'll have to waddle to the boat.'

'Nothing that a brisk swim won't get rid of.' They walked, arm in arm, back to the boat.

322

Chapter Fifty-two

It was night, their last night before leaving very early in the morning for Greece. The first port of call was to be Riva di Traiano, Civitavecchia. 'It can't be more beautiful than Marciana Marina,' Helen sighed. 'I think we should just stay tied up here and spend our holiday lying about on the boat. The boys can go off with Ricardo every night to the disco, and we'll get peace and quiet from Elliott. I don't even know who she's bonking now. I've lost count and I don't care.' She made a face. 'You know, Marcia, it's such bliss to be manless. I rather think my equipment is going to go rusty, but I don't ever think there'll be a man full time in my life because I just don't think I could stand the fuss any more. Look at the disturbance Ricardo causes on board. Why can't men move quietly, like cats, like we women do?'

'Because men are much more like dogs. Haven't you noticed?'

'No, I suppose not. But you're right.' Helen sat quietly astern and Marcia climbed down the ladder to check on the boys who were washing up. She smiled. It was obviously Junior's turn to dry. All the pots and pans were flung higgledy-piggledy into the sink, and plates lay unwiped on the draining-board.

Several pots lay on Elliott's bunk, making damp patches on the sheets. Marcia hurriedly removed them. She was looking forward to sailing on the early morning tide. She stood with the dishtowel in her hand and remembered standing like this before. Sonny, Junior's father, had given her such a good time in those early days. Days before he took to the brew and the weed. But then,

323

she reminded herself, life for a man from JA in England was a contradiction. These were men from the sea. Real men, used to casting nets and fishing for food, or climbing in the beautiful blue-green mountains searching for fruits, then running down the hill to their pretty white gabled cottages with arms full of paw-paw.

She had been the one who had wanted to go back to England. She missed her parents. She wanted her child to have an English education. To go to the grammar as she had, where she'd received a first-class education. Even now she could speak French. She had studied Latin. She still remembered long passages of poetry. It was her watershed when she'd met Sonny and thrown away her whole future just for one long, wild love affair.

She changed the dishcloth, it was sopping wet. She poured herself another glass of wine. 'Ahhh, wine,' she murmured. 'Where would we poor abandoned women be without it?'

On deck, Helen sat gazing out at the endlessly twinking lights of the marina. She sighed and moved restlessly. There were more thoughts to be had about her manless future. Yes, she knew that for now she was better off, but she did not want to face the possibility that she would spend the rest of her life without a man to love. But love, and so few men knew this, also means responsibility. Without responsibility there could be no love. That was a lesson Paul failed to learn.

Toby would soon move off in the next few years. Helen knew that, unlike Marcia, she liked looking after a man full time. She liked waking up and thinking about what he might like for breakfast. Choosing his favourite supper, finding his most liked pudding in the market. Even now, she knew that she shopped not for Elliott and Marcia but for the boys and Ricardo. It wasn't that she preferred to feed the men because she loved them better. No, it was rather that she so enjoyed the pleasure on their faces when they tucked into their food.

Paul had been impossible to please. His wish for bland English food, cooked as his mother had cooked it, had made him a chore to feed. So far, Ricardo loved her cooking and said so loudly and often. He kissed the tips of his fingers and shouted, '*Brava*, 'Elen. *Sei bravissima; la donna dei miei sogni*.'

She rather doubted the last statement to be true. Ricardo seemed to have an enormous amount of donnas when he wasn't busy rolling his eyes and announcing that he was alone in the world. '*Solo*,' he would sigh. '*Sono solo*.' This was usually accompanied by a pitiful gesture with his hands.

'But what about all the birds you pull in the disco, Ricardo?' Cricket was always reduced to hysteria by Ricardo's pleas for sympathy. '*Non è* serious.' Ricardo's English was improving by leaps and bounds. That was more than Helen could say about her feeble attempts to speak Italian.

Toby said he was getting big on the love words. 'An awful lot of them, Mum.'

Helen smiled as she sat on the boat in the silence. The other boats around them had all been closed down, and their occupants had left to find meals in town.

They couldn't afford to eat out, except for Elliott, who had a series of men arriving to stand nervously at the end of the boat waiting for her to appear. When they arrived, they were usually greeted by Ricardo, who stood with his hands on his hips and a fierce look on his face. Usually he yelled at the poor, hapless men. Nobody could make out what he was saying, but he seemed to have appointed himself as father-in-chief to Elliott. 'Stop it, Ricardo,' Elliott implored him. 'You're frightening away my boyfriends.'

'I not trust Italian men. Italian men want only one thing. Ziggy-ziggy.'

'Ricardo,' Elliott interposed after one fearsome yelling match, 'hasn't it crossed your mind that American women might like *ziggy-ziggy* too?'

Helen laughed at the memory of the look on Ricardo's face. For a moment he looked stunned. A bit like a gorilla without his banana, and then Ricardo looked at Elliott and shrugged, 'Tourist woman,' he spat.

'No.' Elliott was furious. 'Not tourist woman. When will you guys realize that women are just like men. If men want ziggy-ziggy they go and find it. If I want ziggy-ziggy, I go find it too.'

'Women not like men.' Ricardo's voice was adamant.

'Have it your own way, buster, but get out of mine.' Elliott had waved a dismissive hand in Ricardo's face. After that incident, Ricardo had said nothing. Helen felt the rift between Ricardo and Elliott. He still teased her and made jokes, but he didn't hug and kiss her the way he did with everybody else.

With his warm, funny presence about, it was easier to feel loved and admired. Helen found the Italian men she met so far in the marina were all friendly. They patted and stroked Marcia's hair. The men in the boat club naturally kissed and passed a gentle arm around Helen's waist. She never felt threatened as she would in London. Now Toby and Cricket had taught the men to do high fives, and the little marina was loud with the boys running down the long road to the little town striking at willing hands. 'Cool, man,' could be heard all over the square. Helen felt herself loved and accepted here. Tonight was their last night, and she also knew she was nervous. It was one thing to fantasize about sailing to Greece, and quite another when you arrived and actually experienced the power of the sea.

'OK,' she told herself, 'truth time. I'm going to list the

things that frighten me. One: Elliott and I will fall out. Two: Elliott and Marcia will fall out. Three: Elliott will bonk Cricket and we'll all fall out.'

She realized after her catechism that all her fears were based around Elliott. Why did she feel that Elliott was a loose cannon? Probably because the rest of them all had contained relationships. They did not have the need to pick up strange, unknown people and bring them into this safe family circle. The boys and Ricardo danced the night away but came home alone. No girls lurked at the end of the boat. Marcia and Helen were not interested in discos. Yes, that was probably it, the fear that Elliott would attach herself to a totally unsuitable man and force his presence upon them all.

Was she afraid of the sea? Oddly enough she didn't think so. The sea was something she'd always loved and understood. She was always at home on or near it. To her the sea was like a big mother, which could either hold Helen gently to her breast, or storm and roar on the beaches like she did when Helen was a child.

Did the roughness of the sea make up for the placid loving household that she'd grown up in? In her childhood there had been no preparation for suffering, so when her world fell apart she had no defences. Paul had plenty of defences. His cruel mouth he had inherited from his mother. His bullying ways his father. He needed to plot and to plan and to harm her and destroy Toby because his son was closer to Helen than to him. It had been a sad moment for Helen when she realized this.

Sitting on the boat feeling drowsy, she forbade herself to think about Paul again. Now days went by and the sadness did not hit her. She was not going to spend tonight crying. Tonight was a night for deep sleep, and then she would get up in the early light of dawn and help Ricardo cast off. Nothing would get Elliott out of bed early, so she volunteered to do the night-shift when they sailed for several days.

'Goodnight, Marcia.' Helen kissed her soft cheek. 'Night, honey bunch, sleep well.' Marcia hugged Helen. Helen moved into the bathroom to clean her teeth. 'Well, after tomorrow,' she said addressing the lavatory, 'I'll have to use the beast.' She glared at the lavatory which was, for the moment at least, stationary. 'I'll just have to shit when I'm drunk,' she told the speckled mirror.

Chapter Fifty-three

During the night, the clouds had covered the normally smiling face of the sun. 'Well, at least we find out who can stomach bad weather,' Marcia said cheerfully as she stood swaying in the boat, trying to save the plates of bacon and eggs crashing on the floor.

'I don't think I'm a good sailor,' Elliott moaned from her bunk. 'I'm used to proper boats. Not a bucket like this one.'

'She's not a bucket,' Toby said fiercely. 'She's the most beautiful boat in the world. You're talking about gin palaces, Elliott; they're horrible and vulgar.'

'I'd rather be horrible and vulgar and not sick.' Elliott's voice was high and whining.

'Here, Elliott.' Cricket grabbed a sausage from his plate. He was perched on the double bunk by the ladder. He stood up and loomed over Elliott. 'Smell this, darling,' he said, laughing.

'Fuck you, Cricket.' Elliott sat bolt upright in her bunk, her blonde hair dishevelled.

'Chance would be a fine thing,' Cricket grinned down at her. He put the hot sausage into her hand and stared meaningfully down at her.

Elliott stared back at Cricket and there were tears in her eyes. 'You don't have to be mean to me, Cricket.'

He moved back to his bunk. 'Oh yes I do,' he muttered under his breath. Only Toby heard him and he looked at Cricket warningly.

'Problem?' Ricardo put his head around the door.

'No.' Marcia tried to smile at Ricardo. He'd been doing the last-minute chores on the boat. She was straining at

329

her ropes. Helen, who had been helping Ricardo, felt as if the boat were tired of being tied up and wanted to go off into the wind and pitch and toss and exercise herself against the pull and the sway of the wind and the water.

'She's ready to go, Ricardo. Do you think we can go out in this weather?'

'This is not weather,' Ricardo insisted. '*Carnevale* like a bird, go anywhere. Any weather. This is good boat. Best boat. My loff is this boat.'

'I can imagine,' Helen said. There was a crash as the boat hit the side of the dock. 'OK, boys, we're about to cast off. We need you both up on deck,' Helen yelled into the cabin. The boys shoved their plates into the sink and leapt up the ladder to join Ricardo on deck.

Helen followed Toby to the front of the boat. This was the beginning of her spiritual journey. She wanted to enjoy every last minute of the leaving. She'd heard Elliott screaming at Cricket and she was upset by it. Why, she wondered, was he so cross with Elliott? They had been such good friends, Elliott and the boys. Maybe they'd had a falling out. Elliott was very immature for a woman of her age. Maybe it was because she'd had no children. No need for that terrible responsibility that hit a woman the moment she'd given birth. Yourself and this tiny vulnerable bundle. That feeling overwhelmed Helen when she first held Toby. No need for all that tedious self-discipline that also came with having a child. Elliott had the freedom to pick up men and use them when she wanted sex. But then Helen didn't envy Elliott that part of her life. Elliott thought she used men, but she didn't. They used her, and if her descriptions were to be believed, not only did they use her but they didn't even bother to buy her dinner or to bring roses and chocolates. It was off with the clothes, into bed, bang, slam, and thank you, mam, and then they were gone. Oh no, there was nothing romantic or loving in Elliott's descriptions of her love life, or her mother's, come to think of it.

All thoughts of Elliott were cleared out of Helen's brain as she watched Ricardo's big, competent hands start to untie the various complex knots that had held the boat.

Cricket was standing by the anchor chain. The chain was wrapped around a stanchion and Cricket held the electric motor in his hand. He stared over the prow of the boat, gazing intently at the sea bed.

'Up anchor,' Ricardo shouted, and the sound of the anchor chain running up through the hole in the deck thrilled Helen. She'd never heard that amazingly musical sound until she came on this trip. She thought of it like the sound in an orchestra when the brass section was busy cleaning out its instruments. It was a wild, free sound. The sound of a boat with its precious human cargo about to leave the safety of land for the wide, sweeping embrace of the unknown, the uncharted.

For all Ricardo's protestations, they had neglected to take a map. Elliott took the news with a shrug, but Helen and Marcia realized Ricardo would only have the small computer with which to plot his path. Helen watched Toby pulling up the gangplank and tying it firmly in place. Beside the gangplank was a little basket for their shoes. Now Ricardo's big Chinese shoes, bright blue, lay under the two pairs of black Chinese shoes owned by the boys. Anything Ricardo did or had, the boys followed suit. Helen had bought the boys' shoes at the local co-op. Here the co-op was designer-communist. User-friendly socialism. Here, each according to his own, worked. Helen was glad to see that the local co-op had Dom Pérignon champagne. Along with the shoes for the boys, Helen had bought a pink pair for herself and a navy blue pair for Marcia. Then she'd bought a bottle of the Dom Pérignon. She took it proudly back to the ship. It was the first time she'd bought a bottle of Dom Pérignon by herself. The expensive wine buying had always been done by Paul. Well, tonight she'd drink a toast to herself and the others on the boat, and Paul could go fuck himself. Would she ever find her own lost self? she wondered.

She was interrupted by a loud roar. Ricardo leapt from behind the steering wheel and erupted on to the foredeck. He lumbered up to Cricket, yelling in incomprehensible Italian. He wrenched the electric gadget out of Cricket's hand. '*Eh, non fai così!*' he screamed. Cricket stood helplessly, drowning under the flow of words. His face was sullen and his shoulders shrunken.

Marcia came on deck and watched Ricardo through narrowed eyes. Helen watched Marcia carefully. Toby, meanwhile, had quietly taken Ricardo's place at the wheel and was holding the boat steady. Cricket had not been concentrating and following Ricardo's hand signals. He'd pulled up the chain too fast, so they had not swung out on the chain and cleared the other boats alongside. Ricardo was busy pushing the next boat out of the way. 'You,' he yelled at Marcia and Helen, 'quick.'

Marcia with Helen beside her, strained to push the yacht to safety. 'This is hard work.' Helen was laughing, but she could see that Marcia was still angry.

'Fucking git, yelling at my kid.' Marcia's face was rigid. 'Nobody yells at my boy.'

Once the boat was away and clear, Marcia sat with her arms folded by the wheel. Ricardo knew he was in trouble. Ricardo knew enough about women to feel the real anger in Marcia's stiff sitting position. He tried to look unconcerned – after all, what could she do, she was a thin stick of a woman – but then he thought of his mother. She too was a thin stick of a woman, but she could pack a punch like a bull-minder. He thought about the big white bulls that ran in the Maremma, in the south. Bovine country. He cast a quick look at Marcia.

'Ricardo,' she began sweetly, 'who is paying you for this trip?'

'Elliott,' he said. A big knot was forming in his stomach. 'I'm the boss,' he added, trying to keep his voice confident.

'Yes, you are the skipper and responsible for the boat and our safety, but I'm the boss of everything else. While we are on this boat, you do not raise your voice to anyone. Have you got that?' Marcia's voice was a sibilant whisper. Helen imagined she could see a whole nest of vipers slithering about, waiting to strike. If she could see vipers, just what could Ricardo see? Helen didn't know, but a very bright red flush was climbing up his neck and his knuckles on the wheel were white with fright.

'Sì, signora, sì,' he said meekly.

'I'm so glad we agree on that.' Marcia was smiling in triumph and the only sound to be heard was Elliott being sick.

Chapter Fifty-four

Helen slept like a child their first night out at sea. Every so often she would open her eyes as the knives and forks rattled in their wood-lined boxes. The plates, fortunately made of plastic, clattered and chattered to each other as the boat lurched from side to side.

Then there were huge bangs as wooden brooms fell to the floor, but the rocking of the boat was all that mattered to Helen. It seemed as if years of sorrow had fallen away. When she awoke the next morning she gazed at her bright eyes and fresh face in the bathroom mirror. 'The pain's gone,' she whispered. 'It's over.' She waited, breathless for a moment, and then she smiled at herself. 'Well, most of it's gone,' she said.

She returned to the kitchen. Galley, she reminded herself. Oh, why did the English have so many different words for so many activities? There was a tennis language, another for sailing, one for cooking. So many different words. English was such a huge language compared to Italian. Her Oxford English dictionary, which she carried with her wherever she went, was huge beside her Collins Italian dictionary. She ran up the ladder and gazed into Ricardo's exhausted face. 'Coffee you two?' She smiled at Toby. He too had been up all night.

Ricardo nodded and Toby grinned. On her way down, Helen poked Elliott's bottom. 'Come on, Elliott, get cracking. I'm making coffee for Ricardo and Toby. Do you want some?'

'Sure. At least I'm not feeling sick any more.' Elliott sat up.

'Beats discos, Elliott.' Helen raised one eyebrow.

'Does it hell!' Elliott laughed.

Helen realized why she liked Elliott so much. There was something immediate and honest about her. Helen found that quality in most Americans who came into the pub. Yes, they could be loud and vulgar, but many weren't. Just happy and carefree and very proud of their country. Not like the grim, sour-faced Londoners. 'Mustn't grumble,' Crinkly Hinkley always said every Monday morning, and then proceeded to grumble for the rest of the week.

Ricardo took his coffee with two sugars and no milk, Elliott with two sugars and milk. Cricket was still asleep, as he had taken the first watch with Ricardo. Marcia was reading in her bunk. 'Tea, darling?' Helen asked.

Marcia took off her reading glasses and leaned over the bunk. 'There's a different tone in your voice today, Helen. What is it? Has something happened?'

'Marcia, you'll never believe this. I slept so well last night. All through the storm. I'd just wake up and fall asleep. It is as if that dreadful pain has gone. You know, the one that makes you want to kill yourself to make it all stop. And I'm not scared all the time.'

'Yes, that's right. It takes half as many years again as you spent in the relationship to truly heal, but we're adventuring now. You're away from the telephone. He can't try and ring to resurrect old wounds and insecurities. You're free of him, and when you go back you'll wonder what you ever saw in him or why you were afraid of him. He'll be the silly little jerk he always was.' She settled back into her bunk. 'Tea would be lovely,' she said. 'Thanks.'

Now the wind had subsided. The boat was sailing in clear, calm water. *Carnevale* rode the waves as if she were a drop of water on the side of a very rare and beautiful tea-cup. Perhaps from the set owned by Catherine the Great in Russia. The Tsarina had a beautifully worked coffee set as well, which Helen had seen in a book.

Helen climbed carefully up the ladder carrying two cups of coffee. She hooked her arms over the bottom of the hatch. 'Coffee's up,' she said, grinning.

'*Cara*, 'Elen.' Ricardo beamed back at her, his tired eyes lighting up at the sight of the coffee.

Elliott was now sitting next to him. 'Thanks, honey.' Elliott reached for her cup. 'Funny thing, Italian coffee only tastes like Italian coffee in Italy. I forget how good it is. Pure heaven.'

During the morning they peered along the horizon looking for land. The water sparkled in the sunlight. 'Land!' Toby saw it first. Just a thin ribbon against the sky, but it was definitely land. Helen felt a surge of pleasure. She felt as she had as a child when her mother had taken her to see *Peter Pan* in Bournemouth. She wondered if a pirate ship might not glide up behind them and Captain Hook politely ask to board her boat.

The first port, Civitavecchia, was a blur in her mind. She seemed to have been caught up in a mass of instructions from Ricardo. They glided in and then moored the boat. Tying up consisted on Helen's part of running about, then letting down the big rubber spheres that stopped the boat hitting other boats or the dock.

She fell asleep that night exhausted. She'd taken the boys into town to get groceries and fresh drinking water. The three of them staggered back, loaded up with goodies. Then she and Marcia cooked a huge meal of fresh swordfish steaks with lemon juice and oil. Helen cooked baked bananas with white wine, brandy and brown sugar, then she poured a thick rich chocolate sauce over the concoction. 'My,' Elliott gasped, 'that's a lethal dessert. I'm going to be as fat as a pig if I go on eating your cooking.'

'Toby calls it Nun's killer pudding,' Helen laughed. She watched everyone eating and drinking happily. All tension between Elliott and Cricket seemed to have gone.

'Tomorrow we go to Nettuno.' Ricardo wiped his

mouth with his big red bandanna. Already he'd established his bucket, which was now filled to the brim with soapy water. In it swam his other pair of shorts and his only other T-shirt. Attached to the bars of the handrail hung a pair of shorts and a drying pair of underpants.

'I don't think I'm up for having my knickers billowing in the wind,' Helen said. 'I don't wear exotic underpants and bras like Elliott. I buy passion-killer pants from Marks and my bras would launch cannonballs. I don't feel secure if my enormous knickers don't come right up to my belly button. We wore those sort of knickers at school. I've put my knickers outside the hatch over the loo.' They were sitting on deck while Ricardo and the boys finished the washing-up.

Elliott had already gone into town. She'd flicked her wrist at Marcia who was smoking a cigarette. 'If I don't come back by the time you leave, call the police,' she said jokingly.

'Sure thing,' Marcia had replied. But Helen felt a bitter wind blowing somewhere in her brain. She shivered.

The journey to Nettuno was made memorable by an advance description of the glories of the lentils served there. All morning, as they sailed towards the little island, Ricardo was dribbling at the thought of the meal ahead. Elliott insisted that she buy everyone dinner. Helen was only too happy to comply.

To get into the little harbour, Ricardo had to turn sharply to starboard. Helen was glad he'd done it many times before. On the way to the island they passed what had been a prison island. Dusk was settling in, and the prison island seemed shrouded in pain and misery. How many human beings had been held there in bondage, humiliation and pain? How was it that not only did a man who was supposed to love you turn out to be a tormentor, but other men gathered together for so many thousands of years to treat other humans as animals. Even animals were not as cruel as the world of men. Helen shivered and wrapped her arms around herself. They pulled away and then she saw the lip of the harbour that was Nettuno. Docking was difficult, but by now they had had some experience.

There was an undignified scuffle as Elliott fought Cricket for the shower. 'Hey,' Marcia said, 'Cricket, ladies first.' She frowned.

'Elliott ain't no lady, Mum.' Cricket elbowed Elliott in the stomach and Elliott stamped on his foot. 'You bitch,' Cricket shouted, 'I'll get you back for that.' But Elliott was in the bathroom with the door firmly bolted. Cricket raced on deck. Cautiously he filled a bucket full of dirty water from the harbour and crept up to the open hatch. He drained the bucket over Elliott's shoulders. The scream of rage made him double up with laughter.

Later that night, they all sat at a table in the middle of a tiny square. They had to walk up flights of stairs. There were no cars, and there seemed to be no other tourists. But Ricardo was so right. Helen savoured the lentils. They came on big thick china plates, with a dribble of yellow-green olive oil in the centre of the tiny brown beans, topped with some coarse salt and very spicy black pepper. 'How simple,' Marcia said, 'and yet how wonderful.'

Helen ordered grilled stuffed squid. It was delicious and tender. Then all of them, stuffed with food and filled with wine, walked slowly down the steps to the waiting boat.

The boat was now home, and would be for a very long time. 'Tomorrow Ischia,' Ricardo announced before retiring to his cabin. 'Ischia very beautiful.' Helen fell asleep with his snores rending the night air.

Mid-morning, with Ricardo's instructions to look for a tall hill ringing in her ears, Helen sat on deck with an Italian book of directions. She loved the book, and found that she was probably better at finding their way in between the ports than the others. She had always loved geography at school, and drawing maps was a special pleasure for her, so now not only did she have the practical pleasure of living geography, but also the ancient history of Italy at her feet.

She'd left Nettuno almost sensing the spirits of the Roman troops who had carved out a bathing area under the rocks on the opposite side of the harbour. It had been a restless night for Ricardo because the anchor was dragging and he was up and down the ladder all night. Helen found herself thinking how odd it was for her still to be in bed and not trying to help him. When she offered, though, he waved his hand at her and took both boys instead. Helen was used all her married life to taking the whole responsibility for her family. If Toby cried in the night or was sick it was Helen who went to him.

Paul signed the cheques but Helen wrote the letters and posted them. If their bank manager wanted them to go to his house for a drink, the implied assumption was that she was only asked to drinks as an accessory to Paul, but if a loan was required for a car or a holiday, then it was Helen's turn to go and do the begging.

On the boat, however, things seemed different. Ricardo had very definite ideas of what women did and what men did. He really was not keen that the women touched his sails, but he bore with their practising their sailing skills with great fortitude. Much rolling of eyes at the boys, and huffing and puffing. However, inside the boat he left the cooking and cleaning to them. He did wash up, and he most certainly checked that the cabin was *a posto*, his version of shipshape. What he made Helen feel was that Ricardo in his role as a man would see that they were all kept safe. That was an unfamiliar feeling for Helen. A confusing feeling. She lay in bed feeling part puzzled by the comfort that the thought gave her, and part wondering if something hadn't gone so badly wrong between men and women that most men had abnegated their responsibility for women, but then she thought, look at women like Elliott: she took responsibility for no one but herself. Even her mother she regarded as a cashpoint.

Helen looked up and then shaded her eyes. Far away a little speck was growing slowly from the flat blue horizon. 'I think that's Ischia, Ricardo.' She pointed to the little nipple on the edge of the waves.

Soon the boys were running about the boat. The sails came down with a satisfying whump. The smell of the cloth hit Helen's nose. At first she'd been frightened for them when they ran about, but now she could see how sure-footed they'd become. She was so glad of their company. When they weren't needed, they flopped on the deck and fell asleep, with Cricket's boom box booming out Italian love songs. Watching them both she felt a lump in her throat. Once she had been young and carefree like that. Once she too would fling herself on the beach at home and sleep like a puppy.

Before the boat, sleep was a difficult and tenuous stranger in her life. Wine was the only thing that would blot out the hideous memories of her years as a married woman.

'Look,' Cricket screamed. He was jumping up and down in a frenzy. 'Look over there! Dolphins!' He pointed wildly and then Helen saw them. She had always dreamed about dolphins, read about them, studied them, and now they were here. A huge pod of them, jumping in the waves. Suddenly one dived under the boat and surfaced just behind her. If I died right now, she thought, I would die happy. Everyone's faces were glowing. There were roars of laughter and the boys hooted to the dolphins as they finally rolled away.

'Next time, Ricardo, do you think we could stop the boat and try and swim with the dolphins?' Elliott asked him.

'Yes, next time,' he promised. It mattered not to Ricardo how many times he saw the dolphins, each time touched his heart. Nothing made him happier, except perhaps to sit in his mother's kitchen with a steaming plate of pasta in front of him.

Helen watched as the little harbour at the base of the hill came into view. Each time they landed there was a fresh pleasure. Each port so far had been different. Before entering the port, Ricardo put down the ladder and Helen followed Elliott into the water. Does the state of marriage suck the life out of all women, she wondered? When she was suddenly on her own without Paul, she had been amazed at how frightened of everything she'd become. Where was the young girl who was shy and withdrawn but still capable of riding, swimming out in the bay in front of her house, or taking her boat into the capricious bay and battling happily and successfully with the elements?

She swam down under the water and then she gazed at the beautiful deep hull of the boat. *Carnevale* was carved out of wood, but her hull and the deep fin would keep her steady in the worst of storms. What a work of art the boat was. She breathed. Helen was wearing Ricardo's face-mask, and only the sound of the air going down the rubber tube disturbed her deep feeling of peace.

The sea below her seemed bottomless. There were different shades of blue and green in layers, with the rays of the sun cutting through the colours and stencilling them against the side of the boat. She could imagine big overhead, cumulus clouds above her prostrate body. She could see their mirror-image in the water. The feeling of happy aloneness came over her. She was not lonely any longer as she had been formerly. She was integrating a new feeling of aloneness within her soul.

This was an important part of healing, she told herself. Lying now on the skin of the water. Her ears were

341

immersed and she could hear no sound. What had been ripped and torn apart was now putting out little vulnerable pink tendrils of healing.

She felt hungry. There was a pulling tension in her stomach and the thought of the gentle pink of the prosciutto. A glass of white Chardonnay. A thick, saltless Tuscan loaf of bread. A rough scraping of garlic and then a pinch of salt over roughly chopped plum-red beefsteak tomatoes. Lovely, she decided, and hurried back to the boat to climb out and make lunch for them all.

Chapter Fifty-five

The hill which now looked like a proper mountain reared up out of the sea to greet the little boat bobbing so comfortably on the crest of the waves. As they ate in a contented silence, Helen wondered if she were now reaching a new stage in her life.

So far her life had been divided into two parts. Her early life with her mother and father which, with Marcia's help she now realized had left her sadly unprepared to deal with anything like the cruel and envious world outside their comfortable little house at the seaside; and then her life with Paul.

Only slowly as she experienced her new life day by day did she realize what an awful concentration camp she had made for herself. Yes, true, Paul had been the commandant and her tormentor, but she had to admit she had let him be. She had failed to fight back. Try as she might, she could not forget her guilt in allowing him to behave exactly as he pleased. Many a time she'd watched other warring couples fighting at the dinner tables in Swiss Cottage. Red in the face with wine, hurling abuse and insults. She too had, during the last terrible years, been reduced to screaming like a fishwife, but it was not in her temperament to behave this way and rows like that left her ill and shaking.

Her neighbours came to moan at her kitchen table, and she never moaned back. Loyalty was a word she learned from her mother and father. Never in all her life did she hear her mother and father shout insults at each other. Yes, there were times in bed when she could hear the sound of either of their voices rise in irritation, but they never let the sun go down on their anger. Her mother always apologized with her favourite cliché the next day. 'Dad and I make a cup of Horlicks before we go to bed and then we kiss each other better.'

Well there had been no kissing Paul better; he always refused to speak to her for days. And when he did decide to speak to her, he used Toby as his intercessor. That made Toby miserable. Now, looking at Toby, brown and healthy in the sun, stuffing his mouth with a big panino with prosciutto hanging out of it, she smiled at him. 'Happy?' she said.

'Ummm,' he replied, his eyes dancing with affection. 'Cricket says he hopes the girls are slack in Ischia.'

'Toby.' Helen found herself irritated. 'Have you heard of Aids?'

'Of course, Mum, you told me about it.' He grinned at Cricket. 'You're supposed to wrap up,' he said smugly. This silenced Helen. Firstly she didn't want to discuss Aids when she was eating, and secondly, she hadn't wanted to think of Toby sexually active. He'd only been thirteen when his father had decided to give Toby a packet of contraceptives. He'd patted him on the head and told Toby that he expected him to be a 'chip off the old block'. So Toby's débâcle with Louise had been inevitable. What could she expect?

She wondered idly why Paul and his friends spoke in such awful clichés. Most people did, she pondered, chewing slowly. Certainly her mother and father did. Helen knew that she irritated Paul because, like most men, he thought linearly. Helen's thinking was more like scattershot pellets that landed everywhere and then coalesced into an idea. That's why when Fats taught that 'thought creates matter', it made perfectly good sense to her. Words were multifaceted, and each word carried with it a plethora of meanings. Most people did not follow much of what Helen said.

That's why Paul got so angry. 'You're so stupid,' he'd shout.

Helen's quiet thinking was interrupted by the boat coming near enough to the jetty for the boys to rise and take their places. A little village nestled in the crook of the island's arm. She could see little dotted figures running about. She pretended her mind was a handheld camera and she zoomed her mind in and out of the scurrying people.

She laughed out loud at the delight of it all. 'Why you laugh?' Ricardo asked curiously.

'You wouldn't understand,' Helen said.

'I do.' Marcia picked up the plates. 'It's Helen's way of talking that first made me like her. She says things differently to everyone else.'

'I don't,' Elliott grumbled, 'I never understand what you're up to, Helen. Sometimes I think you're a witch.'

'Sure I am.' Helen grinned at Elliott's sombre face. 'But if I am, I'm a white witch. I've decided that when we get to Ischia, I'm going to get my hair cut short. I feel a whole new me is about to be born.'

'Better watch out,' Elliott said, 'you might wake up with a tail and horns.'

When they were coming into port, Helen stood behind Elliott, who was steering. Helen had the docking rope in her hand and was looking for the man on the pontoon who would catch it from her now-expert throw. 'What's the matter, Elliott?' she asked. 'You look so miserable this morning.'

'I am miserable. I watch you and Marcia with your boys and I feel I've missed out on a very important part of my life. I'll phone Philip as soon as I get in. He's good at dealing with the big mean depressions that steal over me from nowhere and drive me from shrink to shrink. Maybe if I'd got married young and had a bunch of kids I wouldn't have made such a mess of my life.'

They were now approaching the dock and Helen could see the small figure waiting for them. 'I don't think so, Elliott.' She wished Elliott hadn't begun this conversation when she wanted to concentrate on the rope. But then, it was so rare that Elliott opened up that she didn't want to lose the movement.

'I got married far too young,' Helen offered. 'I didn't know anything about anything. I just thought if I loved Paul and had a child by him, he'd love me back. Life's not like that unfortunately, darling. You're you, and you will find your way, just like I will. We'll all have a wonderful holiday and each of us will come back with some of the broken bits mended. I want to come back feeling as if the hole in my heart is like a perfectly darned sock. Do you know what you're looking for?'

'No, not really. I guess I just want an answer to why my dad ran off and left me with this awful dingbat of a mother.'

'Well,' Helen said, 'I'm going to lay some ghosts. To be somewhere Paul isn't, and where he can't get to me. He hated the idea of me cutting my hair short, and I've always wanted to do it, so that's what I'm going to do next.' She laughed, but the words tasted bitter in her mouth. Like sucking a lime.

She felt her shoulders tense. The black rope was in her hand. She felt the steel eyelet that would cleat them to the dock was watching her. Waiting for her to fail. Now she was within a few feet of the dock. Ricardo had taken over the wheel and was backing in, looking over his shoulder. The two boys were guiding the boat into her berth. Elliott and Marcia were standing by with steel-tipped boathooks to stave off the boats should they come too close. What a team we are, Helen thought. She rose on her tiptoes and then she threw the rope with a quick, deft movement. The man caught the rope and grinned at her. '*Ciao, bella*,' he said. Huh, Helen grinned with triumph.

Take that, you old frayed rope. She jumped on to the dock and looked at the others as they finished tying up. I could live like this all my life, she thought. Moving from port to port. Free to do as I pleased.

Ricardo joined her with the boys in tow. They were off to the ship's chandler for extra rope and cleats. They also needed new filters for the engine. Marcia wanted to buy a big sunhat and Elliott decided she needed a black lace body stocking. 'You aren't coming with me, Marcia?' Helen pleaded.

'Nah.' Elliott shoved Helen. 'Off you go. Go find a hairdresser by yourself. You're a big girl now. I need advice from Marcia. I want a real sexy outfit. One that takes a long time to get off.' Elliott wiggled provocatively.

'Oh Elliott, you're just saying all this to shock me, aren't you?'

Elliott feebly protested. 'Sure I do. You look so sweet when your eyes go big and you blush. American women don't blush any longer. We can handle our sexual freedom. It's you Brits that can't handle anything sexual.'

'Speak for yourself, Elliott. Black women never depend on their men. Men never mature, they're just tall children.'

'You two are just so cynical at times.' Helen felt hurt that she would have to go alone. Hurt and frightened.

'We're cynical, honey, with reason.' Marcia grabbed Elliott's hand and pulled her away.

Helen began walking, feeling a sense of puzzlement and fear. Here she was, alone in a new town. She could hear people burbling around her. All this noise and sound and none of it makes sense. Would she do the wrong thing? How do you ask for a haircut? Maybe she could mime it?

She continued to walk uphill. She noticed a definitely Moorish influence in the architecture. She felt a sweep of excitement. She put her head around the door of a shop

347

which had the sign of a wig over the door. '*Parrucchiere*', the sign read. 'That's not difficult,' Helen told herself. In English we say periwig or *peruke* from the French *perruque*. Those powdered wigs worn in the eighteenth century. She was now standing in the open doorway, overcome with shyness. Very polished, mostly plump ladies sat in a straight row having their hair done.

One was as fat above as she was below, and her squidgy little ankles were squashed into a tight pair of black court shoes. Her hair was rolled into big rollers and she had an enormous gash of red lipstick splashed on her lips. She rolled her eyes at Helen. '*Straniera*,' she whispered, loudly enough for the whole shop to hear.

Helen stood transfixed. '*Straniera*.' Surely that meant 'stranger'? She wanted to burst into tears, but she held them back. She turned on her heel and left the doorway, but when she continued up the hill, tears did indeed run down her cheeks.

Fortunately she was wearing her dark glasses and they comforted her. I will not run back to the boat. She reminded herself of how often the Italians had been kind to all of them in Marciana Marina. She wished for the protection of Ricardo, but then she knew she must learn to protect herself. She had let Paul do all the protecting. No, she had to learn to deal with spiteful women like that fat bitch in the chair. She pushed on.

Then, in a corner of a square, she saw a shop that said proudly, '*Parrucchiere per signore.*' Maybe they speak English in there, she thought hopefully.

She pushed open the glass door. The women sitting in the chairs were not the same sort of women as those in the last shop. No, these women clearly had less money. Their hands did not glisten with gold and diamonds. Their hair remained a glossy Italian blonde. Most of the women in the other shop had dyed, brassy blonde hair.

A young girl sat in the chair closest to the door. She

had waist-length dark hair. The young hairdresser was brushing out the lovely tresses. Helen stood for a moment watching them. Did she really want to cut her shoulder-length hair short? Then she nodded. I do. I need a different me, not just the same boring old Helen. A new, rejuvenated me.

'Does anyone speak English?' she asked hopefully.

'I speak a little English.' The woman who came forward was probably the owner of the shop. 'Wonderful.' Helen felt as if a lifebelt had been thrown to her. 'Yes, I go to stay with my friend in Stratford. I like Stratford but your food, *mama mia*.'

'Yes I know, I'm so sorry.' Then Helen shook herself. Why was she apologizing for something that was not her fault again? The owner motioned a young girl to take Helen to a basin to wash her hair.

With her neck comfortably tucked into the neck-rest, Helen closed her eyes and listened. What an odd country, she thought. All around her the women were talking about food. She heard the word pomodoro. She knew that was the word for tomato in Italy. The Italian words flew back and forward in the room. A light rushing sound, so different from listening to German tourists talking. In an English hairdresser's they would be more likely to talk about sex than food. Still, Italian was such a pretty language. She felt her shoulders relax.

Ricardo spoke to her slowly and carefully. By the end of the trip she was sure her Italian would be at least understandable. She didn't have Marcia's courage. Marcia floundered about, laughing uproariously as she described a man with blue ears instead of eyes. Marcia never minded making a fool of herself. Helen did, so she tended to say very little and just to listen.

Elliott made no attempt to learn Italian. 'Ziggy-ziggy will do just fine,' she grinned at Ricardo.

'I now make ziggy-ziggy with you,' Ricardo shot back.

'No way, baby,' Elliott smiled and winked. 'You're too old for me. I like my men young.'

Tonight they were all going out to a disco. Helen very much didn't want to go, but felt she would be such a downer if she didn't, so reluctantly she agreed. She would much rather sit on her bunk and read her books. She had never believed in the male idea that the mind and the body could be split like a walnut, in half; that the workings of the world could be described as mechanical; that the universe was an exact science. All this damaging thinking had been done by men centuries ago. They had been allowed to run amok. Matriarchy, with its deep under-standing of the mysteries of the universe, and the 'yin' energy that existed for women, was so much healthier for the world.

Helen knew she did not want to be part of any 'ism'. Politics bored her, but she had had enough sense and courage to pick herself up off the floor of life and take Toby out of what had become an unbearable situation. Behind her she had left the sisterhood in Swiss Cottage and their 'new' men, claws drawn to fight out the rest of their lives in their big middle-class homes.

Unlike around the Bush, the next day there'd be no black eyes or broken bones. Only broken hearts, torn to shreds with the violent words that poured out like a tor-rent of sewage after a few bottles of wine.

Her hair washed, she was led to a table. 'Short, please,' Helen told the hairdresser shyly. She made a cap out of her hands and fitted them around her head.

'You have such pretty eyes, signora,' the owner said, standing behind Helen's chair once the hair-cutting was finished. 'Your husband is a lucky man.'

Helen shook her head. She was delighted with the hair-cut. Now she could see her eyes. Usually she let her hair hang over her face to hide herself from the world. Her cheekbones looked dramatic and her eyes were huge. 'No,' she answered the owner, 'I'm alone.'

She felt a slight feeling of coldness where her hair had been. 'But thank you,' she said after paying the bill.

She sauntered down the road feeling the differences. She couldn't run her fingers through her hair any longer. She felt her body moving as she walked. She felt alive. Everything jiggling in the right places, she told herself happily. Then there was a loud wolf-whistle right behind her.

She swung around to see a gang of Italian youths lounging outside the cathedral. For a moment she felt angry. Wasn't that a sexist thing to do, she wondered? Well, even if it was, it made her feel good. Somebody else liked her new lifestyle. She waved her hand at the boys and smiled. 'Bella signora,' one of them shouted. She heard herself laugh out loud. A high, clear tone. She wondered if she should splash out and buy a new dress for the disco.

Chapter Fifty-six

Getting dressed, Helen felt like a young girl again. She hadn't danced in years. She always loved to dance. In her quiet house with her parents, there hadn't been much to dance about, but when she was older and they were out, she would put on the gramophone and dance with wild abandon. That's what she missed, she realized: wild abandon. Maybe that is what women had to give up if they devoted themselves to the needs and comforts of a man?

So many of her women acquaintances – for she'd had no close friends in her middle-class days – would be hushed and shushed by the men in their lives. It was rather as though they must crouch in the background and listen to the men talking about important things like politics. Well, Helen knew far more about politics than Paul ever did. He read nothing; he just slumped in front of the television. She shivered as she remembered those years, but now she was free.

She slipped the hot bright pink dress over her head. The straps were shoelaced in pink velvet. She did not wear a bra and she didn't need one either. She was proud of that fact.

There were the two fly-speckled mirrors in the bathroom. I must find out what the bathroom is called on an Italian ship. She knew it was called 'the heads' in English. She must ask Ricardo. So far she'd only learned the Italian word for sails. '*Vela*' was a sail, but she needed time to learn from Ricardo, and they had plenty of that ahead of them.

Later, after they had sauntered into the centre of the town to a small restaurant where they ate cheaply and magnificently, she finished her dinner with a glass of Vin Santo. Vin Santo, the waiter informed her, was not Italian but came from the island of Zante in Greece. She stored that bit of information away for her diary. The wine was local, thin but excellent. She felt relaxed and comforted. Toby was teasing Cricket about the local girls. 'They're not slack like the Norwegians and the Danes,' Cricket complained.

Helen felt a flash of anger. 'Why should you always describe a girl as slack because she goes to bed with you? What does that make you?'

'Lucky,' Cricket grinned.

'Oh Cricket, I give up.' Helen shook her head. 'Men!' she said.

'Italian men very good,' Ricardo joined in.

Elliott gazed coolly at Ricardo. 'Ever tried American women?' she inquired.

'Yes,' he said, and made a face. 'No good, talk too much.'

Cricket kicked Toby under the table. 'Yo, way to go, Ricardo.'

Toby frowned. He glared at Cricket. 'I don't see why you have to put Elliott down like that,' he said.

During the disco, Elliott came up to Cricket and asked him to dance. He slouched after her and then thought about Toby's remark. She danced well and her fluid body clung to his. 'Hey, this is the first time we've danced together, Cricket,' she said. 'Why has it taken so long?'

'Because you're too old for me, that's why.' He hated the look of hurt in her eager blue eyes. There was something so puppyish about Elliott.

Now Cricket was leaning against the wall outside the disco, drinking in the fresh scented air. He was holding a cigarette between his fingers and wishing it were weed. Where the hell do you find weed in a town like this? He wished he were home in the Bush where he could get stoned and high five down the road with his friends.

The Italian boys had no street cred. No bad attitude. No 'dis' for anybody. They seemed to follow their mothers and grandmothers round. Clumps of families. The sounds of piercing Italian screams. Families, all in black, fully dressed on the beach. Except for the girls, who wore almost nothing on the beach but two postage stamps and a thong between their well-tanned buttocks. Later, in the disco, if Cricket made a pass at the same girl, she declined very forcefully. Those girls weren't just gold-diggers, the gold had to be wedding rings. It all made Cricket's blood run cold.

'Italian girls are trouble, man,' he confided to the friendly wall that supported him. He took a deep breath and then walked back into the disco. Elliott had gone. He could not see her blonde head anywhere. He guessed she'd gone off to find a man. He was surprised at how much he minded. Yo, bitch, he heard a voice inside him shout, *behave*. There was little chance of that, and he knew it.

Helen was laughing, her cheeks damp with sweat. Ricardo was dancing energetically. 'I have not danced for a long time,' Helen said slowly so that he could understand.

'Good,' he beamed back at her, 'you dance good.'

Helen found she was really enjoying herself. Toby leapt past his mother dancing furiously by himself. How things have changed, Helen mused. She preferred the old days when a man held you close and you hoped he could smell your perfume. The male hand in the small of her back guiding her around the floor. Life was so full of sweet expectations in those days. The waiting for the telephone call. Nowadays, girls called Toby instead of the other way round. Flowers and chocolates were considered naff. 'Don't be so romantic, Mum,' Toby said. 'Girls would think I was a nerd if I gave them flowers and chocolates.'

When Helen waited up for Toby to come home it just made him cross, so she lay in bed and waited until she heard his hand on the door and then she fell asleep. She supposed there was no fumbling kiss in the car. It was all so very very innocent, and she was glad of it.

Ricardo was now doing an impassioned tango with a beautiful long-haired woman. As he leaned her back, her hair touched the ground. Helen stood by the bar watching the young people dancing, as if the movements were the only things sustaining their lives. Her heart was racing and she could feel the blood of excitement in her veins. One day she too would stand pressed close to a man that she loved. Or she hoped she would. Toby looked extremely happy, dancing and smiling at a pretty girl. Only Cricket leaned alone against a wall, his arms enfolding his body. A cigarette was clamped to his lips.

'Anything I can do?' Helen moved towards him.

'Nah, man, some women are whores, that's all there is to it.'

'Are you talking about Elliott?' Helen watched, surprised at the anger on Cricket's face. 'Cricket,' she said, leaning over and touching his arm, 'just because I'm years older than you, that doesn't necessarily mean I'm any wiser. You've had many relationships with girls and grown women. I've only had one relationship, so in one way you're light years ahead of me in understanding relationships. I can only tell you what I know about women like Elliott. She's actually a really nice human being but, like so many women, she's confused. She's grown up in a time when women were told that they could have it all. Money, men, sex, and power. Nobody can have it all, Cricket. Least of all men. They've been trying for centuries.

'I see life as a balance. If you want a particular thing, then there are certain consequences. You have to be willing to take the consequences of what you want. I wanted to get married and have children. I married Paul and then I had to take the consequences. It was my responsibility that I picked a man who was childish, weak and selfish. Nobody else's but mine. Does that make any kind of sense?' Helen realized that this was an odd conversation to be having in the middle of a disco. Maybe with so many people paired off, those like Cricket and herself who weren't in a couple needed this kind of conversation. Being not part of a couple was a bit like being left on a train track and watching the engine, the one thing you relied to pull you along life's tracks, disappear over the hill.

'Yeah, I guess it does make sense, Helen.' Cricket put his arm around her shoulders. 'If I ask you something, you promise you won't tell Mum?'

'As long as I don't think it's something that might damage you or her badly, you can trust me.'

'What do you think about Elliott and me?'

'Oh Cricket, I've been watching that relationship between the two of you for weeks now. Ever since you met, actually,' she sighed. 'What do I think? Well, I think you should both stop hurting each other for a start. You should promise to give yourselves time and space to really talk through your feelings for each other,' and then Helen smiled. 'If you both decide that you both have good things to give each other in a love affair, go for it, Cricket. Sometimes I think we learn some amazing things about ourselves in the most unlikely situations.'

'Thanks, Helen.' Cricket pulled her into his arms. 'Hey,' he said. 'Come on, let's show these dudes how to dance.'

Chapter Fifty-seven

Why, Helen wondered, must life be so difficult? The air between Elliott and Cricket was sulphurous. 'Oh God,' she prayed, 'please deal with all this tension.'

Docking the boat in Vibo Valentia was not easy. It was night. The rain was pockmarking the waves and flattening them, but the swell of the sea was heavy.

The boys were out in their oilskins with Ricardo, and Helen could hear him bellowing orders above the roar of the wind. She hoped Toby would be safe. Finally they were secured to the dock, but Helen felt that the boat clung perilously to her moorings. She felt her shudder as she hit the plastic bollards and Helen, who by now felt the little boat to be a very valued friend, felt a surge of compassion for her brave little craft.

'Come on, everybody,' Marcia finally said as she surveyed her sullen son, the tearful Elliott and the morose Toby, 'cheer up.'

Ricardo was muttering into his beard. Marcia now spoke enough Italian to catch the words '*donne*', '*barca*' and '*problemi*', and knew that Ricardo was yet again complaining that women on a boat were nothing but trouble.

'You stop that, Ricardo,' Marcia said sharply. 'Just remember that it was Noah's wife in the Bible that sailed the ark to safety. Noah couldn't sail for shit.'

'Eh?' Ricardo wrinkled up his long nose, rolled his eyes, and spread out his hands helplessly. He glanced sideways at Marcia as if he were about to say something. Then he thought better of it. This lady looked very dangerous to him. He'd never met a black woman before, let alone sailed with one, and she looked as if she could give a man plenty of trouble. He shrugged and backed down. Marcia released him from her gimlet stare.

'Why don't we all bundle up in the rain and go out for dinner together? Hey, have a night out. Eat pasta or pizza?'

'Great idea.' Helen jumped at the chance. 'Maybe I can find a hot shower and wash my hair? My head is itching from all that salt.'

Toby smiled at his mother's enthusiasm. 'I'm on, how about you, Cricket? It'll make a change from having to do the washing-up.'

'And from me having to clear up after both of you,' Marcia smiled brightly at Elliott. 'How about it, love?'

'OK, I'm in.' There wasn't the usual Elliott sparkle in her eyes. She looked like a beaten dog. Oh, why do women go to pieces when they get hurt? Marcia sighed inwardly. Men to her had always been expendable, rather like her old tights. If there was a man in her life, all right, but most of the time she couldn't care less.

Now she was hauling arse with two women who were rent apart by their relationships with men. She stood up in the now stuffy cabin and stretched. She felt the tension from the day beginning to ebb. She swung her arms down to touch the deck with her fingertips. She heard the bilges sloshing with water. 'Better pump out the bilges before we move tomorrow.'

'Sometimes I think Ricardo must think I'm mad, especially when I'm miming chicken breasts.' She made an enthusiastic pumping motion with her arms. 'Laugh? I nearly died.' This last remark made Helen giggle. It was one of Lace's phrases. When she and Maisie had done something terribly perverse, that's what they'd cry in unison.

'OK, I'm pulling on my slickers,' Elliott said, trying to sound enthusiastic. She hauled on her bright yellow pair of sailing trousers made from shiny pvc, and her hooded jacket. Once she was ready to leave, she looked so much like a forlorn child that Marcia hugged her. 'Choke up, chicken,' Marcia said.

'What?' Elliott looked startled.

'It's lingo for tell us what's on your mind.' Marcia suddenly realized that she very much did not want to know what was on Elliott's mind. It was Elliott's obsession with her son that was bothering her. 'Never mind,' she said quickly. 'Nothing a glass of red wine or two can't cure, eh Elliott?'

Everyone agreed and disagreed about the menu at the restaurant. The wind was blowing down the streets of the port. Helen felt clean and fresh after a very hot shower. As usual the shower and lavatory had been spotless. Now she felt the tension loosening from the muscles in her neck. She always found that she was frightened by other people's bad moods. She would slowly stiffen up and then a vice would clamp its bony fingers around her neck. Sometimes, when she was still married, she felt as if she also had a phantom knife sticking out of her back.

For a moment, there was an incredible dull ache, and then she sighed and the tensions leaked out through her fingers. Thank you, God, for wine, she thought.

Helen ordered a plate of tiny clams. Marcia joined her and Elliott and the others had pizzas the size of dinner plates. The smell of the oil and the vegetables on the pizzas tickled their nostrils. Helen listened as the boys teased Elliott. The trouble was, Marcia decided, watching Junior soften towards Elliott, that Elliott was such a child herself.

In some ways, Junior with all his street cred was a lot more sophisticated than Elliott. Elliott, blanketed by privilege and money, had nothing to grow up for, and therefore was a perpetual adolescent. A sense of the inevitability of their pairing off loomed in Marcia's mind. But tonight, sitting in the warm friendly restaurant where the tables were filled with Italians all happily leaning across and talking to each other over dinner – something that would never happen in England – Marcia felt that perhaps she could manage to come to terms with their relationship.

Ricardo was bent over his food and grumbling as usual. 'Too much belly,' he said, slapping himself playfully. 'I don't eat nothing. I don't drink nothing.' He sloshed some more red wine in his glass. By now Ricardo's protestations were part of the scenery.

'I think,' Toby said, 'if Ricardo tells his tummy that he's not eating and drinking, it will believe him and he'll just fade away.'

Ricardo continued to grumble. 'Your mother, she feeds me too much. I put on fifteen kilos.'

'Mustn't grumble, Ricardo, only the English are allowed to grumble. It's our national pastime. Italians scream and the English grumble.'

'No, he can't scream,' Helen said with feeling. 'It frightens me.'

'Yeah, but then Italians must have very low blood pressure. When my mom screams at me I get nose bleeds,' Elliott interjected.

'Does she scream at you often?' Cricket asked with interest.

'Yeah, all the time. That's why I came to Europe. Mom doesn't like Europe. She thinks Europeans don't wash and the food is lousy. Mom only eats fast food. You know, the stuff in white Styrofoam boxes. We have a freezer full of Lean Cuisine. I call it Lean Mean Cuisine because I starve on it, but then she's always on a diet. All American women are on diets. I even diet sometimes if I'm too bored to cook, and that's most of the time. Boy, I'm getting fat this trip, really gross. My buns are going to look like hamburgers.'

'Then don't bend down when I'm hungry.' Toby laughed at his own joke and the three of them forgot they'd been at odds with each other. After they'd finished eating and after several bottles of wine, Elliott challenged the boys to a race to the boat.

Chapter Fifty-eight

Helen awoke to the sound of Ricardo's grumbling voice. He wasn't actually grumbling, but it sounded like it. He was teaching the boys Italian. '*Gabinetto*,' he was saying.

'We say heads in English,' Toby said. Helen was pleased to hear just how much Italian Toby was learning.

She pushed her head through the hatch and checked Toby's face. She was reassured: he was tanned and healthy. The green London pallor had left his face. They were tied up to a brown pontoon in among a nest of boats in a crowded port. People were moving fast. Laughing and shouting at each other. The mood had changed now they were lower down south. Tuscan people, Helen decided, had strikingly beautiful faces. They sounded their aitches like a gasp at the back of the throat. 'Cho cho chola,' she heard them order.

The months of working at the bar made her quick and efficient. 'Cups of coffee and breakfast all round?'

'Better let Ricardo make coffee, Mum.' Toby was smiling. 'He says *stranieri* can't make Italian coffee properly.'

'OK,' Helen said cheerfully. Normally Toby's words would have hurt her, but nothing was going to faze her on this glorious morning. She went back down the ladder and remembered that she meant to buy a kettle. Italians didn't drink tea in teapots, neither did they have kettles. She looked around the cabin. All about her lay hand-fitted wooden panels. She loved her little bunk. She felt cradled and secure in it.

The boys teased her about her hot-water bottle, but Pooh Bear's lovely face reassured her. 'Tea?' she asked Marcia, who was reading an Oliver Sachs book.

'Sure . . . This book is so sad, Helen. It's about people with sleeping sickness who are intelligent but trapped in their bodies.'

'I know, I've read it. Some people don't even have sleeping sickness, they just spend their lives living in limbo. Eating, shitting, and fucking. That's even sadder.'

Helen prodded Elliott. 'Come on, Elliott, we have to go into town to buy food and wine.' One of Helen's great luxuries was that she could buy great big bottles of red and white wine. She always felt so triumphant when she came back, loaded down with white carrier bags filled with the best vegetables Italy had to offer. The joy of a bite out of a ripe, juicy, beefsteak tomato. The feel of the juice running off her chin delighted her. The saltiness of the anchovies picked out of big wooden barrels. These anchovies were big and hairy with bones. The salt was thick white crystals, not the mean grainy stuff she bought in Chiswick High Road. She wondered how she was ever going to settle back into what was laughingly called 'real life'?

She saw Fats's face in her mind's eye and then she knew she would be happy to be back. Rested and full of energy, she would ask the landlady's permission to paint the flat in lovely warm colours, then make cushions and hang curtains so that the little flat became a thing of joy. All this was due to the confidence the boat had given her.

It seemed to Helen, as she put some water into a brightly painted jug and put it on the stove, that this little boat had handed her more than just a holiday. It had given her back the will to live.

For many years her life had consisted merely of existing. Of loving Toby and doing the best for him. The rest of the days and nights with Paul had been like being in prison. She very much wanted to escape but she didn't know how. She knew now that she had learned how to escape, and that she would never be trapped by a man again.

The shock of how much she and Paul had ended up hating each other hit her from time to time. She wondered if that sense of shock would ever leave her. Love and affection had been replaced with a deep, venomous hatred on his part, and dismay and incredulity on hers. 'He changed, you didn't,' was Marcia's wise analysis of the situation.

Some days the panics and the shakes weren't too bad. In the latter years of her life with Paul she would often shake as if she had Bell's Palsy. He would stand there, his little reddened eyes glaring at her behind the mock sincerity of his smile.

At night she would bunch her pillows against him. Trying to keep him away from her. Kissing became revolting. She shook her head at the memories. She handed the coffees up through the hatch. She watched Ricardo as he made the coffee this morning. She saw that he filled the base to the brim with coffee and then patted it down with a teaspoon. Toby was right: he did make the best coffee in Italy.

'You OK, honey?' Marcia's gentle voice broke her reverie.

'Just ghosts,' Helen said, trying to smile.

'I don't think I'll ever get over Junior's dad.' Marcia's voice was sombre. 'But then he was fun when he was not drunk and violent. Paul is such a wimp and a bore. I had fun in the early days and then kaput.' Marcia waved her hands in the air.

'Today is just a difficult day, Marcia. I saw Gaylang in my dream and he reminded me that I hadn't been meditating. That always helps to reorientate me. I read the Bible every morning, particularly Ecclesiastes, it is so beautiful. It reminds me how timeless the whole world is.'

Marcia stood up and stretched. Helen cleared the cups and took them into the boat to wash. 'Elliott, are you coming with us into town?' she called.

'Sure, if you'll let me go shopping in a taxi; otherwise no way. It's too darned hot.'

'It's such a waste of money, Elliott,' Helen said.

'Yes, but it's not your money or your business. I like to spend money: it's just concrete energy as far as I'm concerned. If you have money you can move, if you haven't you're stuck and you don't have choices. Anyway, it's the old bitch's money. So I'll spend it. When the going gets tough, the tough go shopping. It's an old American saying.' Elliott effortlessly arose from her pile of pillows and duvets and walked stark naked to the lavatory. She looked so beautiful naked that neither Marcia nor Helen found it within themselves to object. Yes, she walked around nude in front of Ricardo and the boys, but then nudity was a normal condition for Elliott.

After the first few days, both the boys had accepted her nudity without batting an eyelid, but Ricardo was another matter. '*Madonna*,' he muttered as he hurried away. At least she didn't sunbathe in the nude. Ricardo made it plain that, as the skipper of the boat, he would be fined. To all intents and purposes, she might as well have been nude, though. Somehow the thongs made her look far more erotic than the innocence of a very bare beautiful body.

They all left the boat except for Ricardo. He didn't like to leave his boat in a strange port. He was much happier pottering about with his paintbrush and generally behaving like Ratty from *Wind in the Willows*. He busied himself coiling the tarry ropes in neat piles and generally pottering about. His looming presence added to the new-found peace and security she felt now that she was away from Paul.

Once out of the marina, after Elliott had held them up

by having a long talk with a big fat glossy ginger cat, they jumped into a taxi. Elliott climbed into the front seat. The driver was handsome in a swarthy way, and Marcia looked meaningfully at Helen. 'Gee, you've got a great little town here.'

'You Americana?' the taxi driver said, eyeing her expensive gold rings.

'Yeah.' Elliott's hair blew about her head in the wind. There were big palm trees; it felt so tropical that Elliott was reminded of Houston and for a moment was tearingly homesick. No, she told herself firmly, I'm not going to bonk this one. She also knew she was biding her time to take Cricket to bed with her. She would have to wait until they got to Greece and she could separate Cricket from his mother. Elliott wasn't so bothered by Marcia's jealousy any more. She sensed that Marcia had accepted the inevitable and now seemed indifferent. She knew if she had a love-affair with Cricket the one salient rule was that they must keep their affair a secret from Marcia. But Cricket would be discreet enough so no one need know, she comforted herself. Anyway, that was half the fun of a love-affair. The secrecy, the meaningful looks, the quick squeezes of hands and then the passion. The grand, breathtaking excitement of getting to know your lover. The endless talking. Hours of it. Elliott thought of how she talked with Philip. He always listened so carefully, his head a little forward. She missed him. 'I'll give Mom a ring and then Philip,' she said to Helen over her shoulder. 'Who are you going to ring?'

'Toby will have to speak to Paul, I suppose.'

'Yeah, I'd better talk to Dad, otherwise he'll be cross and cut my pocket money. When and if he remembers to pay it.' Toby's voice was bitter and a shadow crossed his face.

A little later, Toby was standing in a bar with his ear to the telephone. 'Mum,' he called, 'Dad wants to talk to you.'

Helen made a face. She didn't want to hear Paul's whiny voice. She didn't want her beautiful dream shattered by his aggressive behaviour. 'OK.' She took the receiver wearily. 'What do you want?' She tried and failed not to sound too defensive.

'Just wanted to know how you were doing?'

'I'm fine.'

There was a silence on the line, then, 'You do realize that you've kept Toby out of school and that's against the law, don't you?'

'So sue.' Helen felt truculent. 'Anyway, Paul, I don't want to talk to you, just fuck off.'

'How can you speak to me like that? After all these years. I've tried helping you, Helen, but you just wouldn't sort yourself out.'

'I don't need sorting out, Paul. You and your perverted friends can hang out together, Toby and I are fine.' She slammed down the receiver and wondered whether she was really upset. To her surprise, because she could hand her anger over to Paul, she felt good. 'Huh,' she said, rejoining the table, 'I told him to fuck off.'

'Great,' Elliott grinned. 'If more women told men to fuck off, the world would be a much better place.'

'Yeah, but men also have got to learn to stay away from bad women.' Cricket's voice was reflective. 'I'm thinking of getting a T-shirt designed that reads "Ditch the Bitch".'

Elliott laughed. 'You do that, Cricket.' She patted his shoulder affectionately. 'And we'll continue to live in our wicked world of women.'

Chapter Fifty-nine

It was when Helen was standing in the stern of the boat with her arm around Toby's waist that she felt the hairs on her arms rising.

Réggio di Calabria was a big port. The first really commercial port she'd seen. A massive sea-wall surrounded the city. As they came into port the waves were rising. Huge, rolling waves that tossed the boat and toyed with her.

Carnevale hung in the air and then gracefully, as gracefully as an Italian swallow flitting in the little Italian towns, she righted herself.

'You know, Toby, she is such a beautiful little boat, our *Carnevale*; she really is a celebration. I feel really peaceful, but this port feels so different from the others. So dark and disturbing. So far I have felt so centred. As if the whole of the rest of the world can go hang. We've no telephone to bother us. We've had nothing of "the real world" to frighten us. I sleep so well on the boat that I feel ten years younger.

'I wish I could live like this for ever. But I know it will all come to an end and we will be back in Hammersmith. Still, I have the bar and Maisie and Lace to gossip to. I wonder how they are and what they are doing?'

Helen looked up into Toby's face. She realized how much taller he had become, even in these short weeks. He was like a bamboo shoot, ever sprouting upwards. She remembered him so small and frail, raking her garden with such love. How her heart used to go out to him, for she was forbidden to help him. Paul sought to 'make a man out of him', by bullying Toby until he cried. That's all Paul knew how to do. Feminized by his mother, he created the worst of both worlds. A man's need to physically bully and terrorize was coupled with a woman's ability to spend his life plotting and holding grudges. She could see that Toby had had a tense night.

'A penny for them, Tobe?' she said.

Toby grinned at her. 'They are not worth a penny,' he said, but he smiled a little sad smile. 'I guess it's just that I don't know if Dad will ever get to respect me. I try to respect him and to remember that he's my Dad, but it's difficult to like him, he's such a shit. Now I'm perfectly happy, happier than I've ever been, and I think he's just jealous that we've got away from him. We're rebuilding our lives and he's stuck with poor Laura whom he bullies and mentally batters. At least he didn't physically beat you up.'

'Ah Toby, the terrible thing about it is I would have been better off with a black eye to show a judge. He nearly killed me with his bullying ways.'

'Never mind, Mum, he's gone and he won't be back. When I grow up and become a famous rock star, I'll buy our house back for you.'

'Oh no, Toby, I wouldn't want that. I wouldn't want to live again in a house whose walls heard my tears, my weeping and my wailing. You buy me a nice house in the country, and above all you must buy me a boat.

'When we say goodbye to *Carnevale* I shall be dreadfully upset. Marcia's got our tickets for our flight back from Cephalonia. There we say goodbye to Ricardo and he goes back to Elba.'

'I promise I'll buy you a beautiful boat just like *Carnevale*.' Toby hugged her. The boat swung around the corner and then, with Ricardo yelling like a brigand, they seemed to race for the shore. Everyone was clinging on to the rigging. Helen was glad they all had oilskins on. The waves hurled over the side of the boat. She felt as if the sea wanted to pull her out of the boat to rock her in its choppy bosom. She laughed; the wind whipped the sound of her laughter from her mouth and threw it high into the stratosphere.

Gaylang was in the fourth dimension, but he heard Helen's laugh. He loved her especially and took good care of her. Her healing was just now beginning.

Ricardo and the boys tied *Carnevale* up carefully. They remembered the night she had dragged her anchor, when the sea had been rough even in port. The boys, now expert, didn't have to be told what to do. They leapt like gazelles from the boat, pulling and tugging at the ropes. Réggio di Calabria, unlike the other ports, did not make them feel welcome. '*È pericoloso*,' 'It's dangerous', is what Ricardo said while they were coming in alongside.

'*Molto pericoloso*,' Elliott replied nervously, pulling up her tank top. She was wearing a pair of tight bum-hugging white jeans. No knickers, Helen noticed. There was no tell-tale panty line. Helen wondered if men checked details like that and then, catching a look of lust and longing on Cricket's face, she decided they did.

Helen went downstairs and scrambled around in her soft blue case which was sitting on the bottom of her bed. In that case lay her whole life for the weeks on the boat. The bag was heavy because Helen had brought with her a load of must-be-read books. She was now struggling with a sense of shame for having failed to read Proust.

The fifty pages it took for him to eat the madeleine and dip it in his coffee was fifty pages too long. She put the book down and picked up her science magazine. She was far more at home in the world of neural biology than in the work of a world-class neurotic, and happier with a world where she could browse among the myriad possibilities of the why and the wherefores. Molecular biology fascinated her. Now she had all the time in the world to read and didn't nod off by the fire as she did in Hammersmith, exhausted by running around the bar.

'Now, did I come down here to do something?' Helen felt empty-headed.

'I don't know, honey, but you sure are vague.' Marcia came down behind her.

'Ah, I know.' Helen felt vaguely foolish. So much of the time she simply spent in a reverie. The outside world was so difficult for her. Her inside world was so much more beautiful. From a few moments ago when they were docking, she had carried in her head a picture of a forest of masts. Réggio di Calabria was the biggest port she'd ever seen. Bigger than Calais or Dunkirk where Paul insisted on running about shopping to buy cheaper goods like alcohol. Whole dinner parties could be spent where their friends and Paul had intense discussions on how much they'd saved.

It was within those first years of marriage that Helen, bored to tears, learned to keep a polite smile on her face, look interested, but to treat these ghastly people as if they were simply wallpaper on her walls. She was in her interior world, tucked away with her thoughts. Or at least she imagined she was painting. 'Ah, I know what I wanted,' she exclaimed with relief. 'My body-belt. I don't want to go into Réggio di Calabria with a handbag.'

'You're quite right, it feels very dangerous, and if Elliott isn't careful she'll find some brigand who will carry her off over his shoulder. Those pants of hers leave nothing to the imagination.' Marcia was wearing a dress from the Bush. It was a Malayan batik dress. Cut low, but not indecorously. It was not Marcia's style to let it all hang out, Helen observed, not for the first time. There was something very sexually attractive in the way Marcia projected her sensuality. She withheld it and gently teased men. Helen knew glumly that she projected nothing at all.

Nothing at all. Such hollow sounding words. How can

you be a nothing? Easy, just grow up an only child. Live on the sands at the seaside. Live in your little mahogany rowing boat. Don't join in with the girls that giggle. Don't like boys very much because they are big, ugly, graceless creatures. Spend most of your life reading. Books are your boundaries. Jane Austen your only friend. Jo from *Little Women* your model and your mentor. Stubborn, boyish Jo. She marries a little round professor, and that is what Helen wished she had done. She would have liked a quiverful of children. All of them boys except one daughter. She so wished she'd had a daughter.

A girl to be her friend. Now she looked across at Marcia and smiled. 'You know, just this once I'm going to be totally irresponsible and take us all out to dinner. To the best restaurant in Réggio di Calabria. This is the sort of place that makes me want to take a risk.'

'Sure thing, sweetie-pie, I'd like to see you take risks. Who knows, you might find a lovely Latin lover?'

'No.' Helen shook her head. 'I think making love is too important to just pick up a man like Elliott does. In the beginning, Paul and I had good sex. It was wonderful.' Her eyes misted over dreamily. 'You know, describing good sex is so difficult because there is nothing to describe except rolling into the man you love, and that amazing moment when you both come back to earth and you find him still inside you. I wonder where we go to when we make love?'

'I don't know, Helen. You are so odd. Do you always analyse everything so much?'

'Yes, I do. I have a passion for knowing how people and things work. I'd love to have been a surgeon but my mother thought that was above my station. Being a secretary was a step up. My mum never worked. She didn't want to, but she was determined that I should have a career in case I married a rotter. How wise she was.' Helen wrapped the body-belt around her waist. 'Come on, let's break the news to the others that we're going to party tonight.' Marcia watched Helen's slim brown legs move lightly up the ladder. She was so beautiful when she was happy, and now she was happy most of the time.

'Two skins too few,' Marcia said as she followed her friend. 'She has to grow up. This is a big cruel world we live in and you have to be tough.' Marcia heaved a sigh of relief. She'd take care of her until Helen metaphorically took her finger out of her mouth.

Chapter Sixty

'Ugh.' Elliott was standing on deck with her head between her knees. The rest of the party were standing on the dock looking at her. Helen could smell the wonderful pungent smell of dried-out fishing pots and nets on the boats next to them. They were stacked up to the gunnels with fishing equipment, and the boats were painted bright shiny reds and blues.

'Come on, Elliott,' Marcia said impatiently, 'you're keeping us waiting as usual.'

'Sorry.' Elliott was rubbing hair mousse into her long blonde hair. She expertly scrunched it with both her hands. The grey expensive jar of mousse sat on the bench. 'I can't stand this stuff,' she said vehemently.

'Why not?' Toby asked innocently.

'Reminds me of spunk when a man comes all over your hair and it dries before you have time to wash it.' There was a moment of horrified silence. Toby went bright red. Only Ricardo was unaware and humming to himself.

'I can't believe you said that, Elliott.' Cricket stared at her. 'Do you do it to shock?'

'Nah, I don't care enough about people to worry about what they think, and it's true that it feels like spunk. Every woman knows it but won't say it because they're too busy trying to be liked by everyone.' She stood up; her hair was a mass of waved curls. 'Besides, most women won't talk about oral sex. Most of the women I know don't even like sex. My mom used to say, "Don't care was made to care." Well, not me.' She stood up and nimbly climbed the ladder which led off the boat. She collected her blue sneakers that were in the basket by the ladder. 'Let me hang on to you, Cricket, while I put these damn things on.'

Cricket looked into her deep blue eyes. He smiled at her. 'You care about what I think of you, don't you, Elliott?' She paused for a moment and stared thoughtfully at him.

'Yeah, Cricket, I think I do. Do I shock you?'

'No.' Cricket shook his head. 'You can't shock us Jamaicans. We've got a great sense of humour. We have attitude and style. It's the whites, the ice-creams, that are puritans. They can't dance or shake it like we can. Franz Fanon once said: "When the whites feel they have become too mechanized, they turn to men of colour and ask them for a little human sustenance." Don't you agree, Tobe?'

'I guess so.' Toby was very shaken by Elliott's remark. He was aware that Cricket probably wasn't fussed; he'd probably done it in a woman's hair. But Toby hadn't even considered the matter. Shit, he thought. Sex was a much more complicated thing than he'd first thought. He walked protectively by his mother. When they were in port he always did this. He watched men's eyes and then glared at them if they didn't look at his mother right. Cricket teased him. 'Lots of men fancy your mother. She should go for it.'

'My mother's not like that,' Toby answered crossly. They had already been to the shower rooms which were clean and sparkled.

'I feel so wonderful at this time of the evening,' Helen said happily. 'We're off to have a wonderful meal. We don't have a care in the world.' She could feel the sea wind blowing through her hair. She felt her body moving; her newly formed muscles. 'Everything jiggles just as it should,' she reminded herself, and then she grinned.

'*La Torre*,' Ricardo advised her. 'Very expensive,' he added, rubbing his fingers. He was right, but Helen decided the way to enjoy it was not to think about the price. After all, as Elliott said, if you had to ask the price then you probably couldn't afford it anyway.

The restaurant was very formal. They stood in the doorway feeling very self-conscious. Helen was glad that she had put on a dress, but the others were in jeans, and Elliott was in her painted on pants. The maître-d' moved towards the little party which was marooned among Armani suits and Yves St Laurent ties that dotted the room.

Beautiful bejewelled women with newly set hair sat gracefully in their seats. One woman, Helen noticed, had an enormous five-carat diamond on her married finger. It made her own poor little diamond engagement ring with its square-cut emerald look very small. She tucked her ring finger into the palm of her hand.

Only Ricardo seemed unfazed. He walked with his rolling gait behind the maître-d'. 'Good, good,' he crooned softly to himself. The others fanned out around him. He tucked his thick white napkin under his chin.

'Wow,' Cricket said grinning, 'smell that food.' Large plates of lagooned lobsters were passing by. Langoustine were stretched out as if they had fainted on the spot. They lay, pinkly swimming, in sauces of green parsley and garlic.

Helen felt her face flush with pleasure. Really, food was so sensual, she thought. The whole of Italy was a huge sensual turn-on. Maybe Elliott was right, at least she found in sex something that was fun and she could express her own sexuality whenever she felt like it. Elliott was also right that Helen was far too repressed ever to behave like that. Helen watched the men in the room light up like lightbulbs. Elliott grinned at each and every one of them, her pink tongue between her teeth.

The waiter immediately pressed huge menus into their hands. 'Ah,' Ricardo said. 'I 'ave *affettato*.' He gazed at the very hungry little crowd around him. '*Prosciutto*,' he said. "'Am very good in this province.' There was a mass nodding of heads.

After much arguing the ordering was done, and a great silence fell on the little group as they carefully used their unfamiliar metal knives and forks (they used plastic on the boat) to cut the different types of local meats into squares and put it in their mouths. 'Bit different from eating on the boat,' Cricket observed.

Helen smiled at him. 'I've almost forgotten how to use a proper knife and fork.' She lifted her glass of wine and appreciatively tasted the blood-red drink. 'It's really good,' she said, surprised at her own ability now to choose wine and to choose wine well. To her that had always been a man's domain.

Elliott's eyes were searching the room. Helen felt her heart stop beating. There was a huge man crouched at a table in the far corner of the restaurant. When they all raised their glasses for a toast, Helen's toast was 'God Bless the Queen', Ricardo said 'chin-chin' and looked so desperately pleased with himself that it made Marcia laugh. But Elliott's toast was to the man in the corner of the room. Helen felt the man's violence cut her like a knife. She had seen this sort of man in her bar. Crinkly Hinkley usually took them aside, bought them a drink, and then ushered them out of the bar, banned for good. Crinkly had taught Helen how to take care of herself in a rough situation. Never to acknowledge a violent man or woman, and to avoid all eye-contact. The man raised his glass in acknowledgement of Elliott's salute.

That's Elliott gone for the night, Helen thought. Cricket looked impassive, but Helen knew he was hurting.

'Darling,' Helen put her hand on Cricket's shoulder, 'want some pudding? Look at that dessert trolley, isn't it beautiful?'

She felt Cricket relax under her touch. 'Yes, it is.' He sounded like an enthusiastic boy again. 'Oh boy, what are those fab round chocolate things?' he asked.

'Profiteroles,' Ricardo said, smiling at Cricket. He kissed the tips of his fingers and stuck his forefinger into his cheek. 'Very good,' he said.

Yet again, Helen was overjoyed at this very Italian way of expressing pleasure in food. The English just don't have approving gestures like that, she thought. We don't enjoy our food or our sex like the Italians do.

Helen felt herself relax. Cricket too was smiling again. The young are really so resilient these days, she thought. She was never like that. Her world was hidden, so obscure that she didn't ever think she'd find anybody to understand her. Maybe she understood too much? She could oversee what was happening. Instead, most people just saw one frame after another in the cine film of their lives. They could see the past, the present and the future, but they could not see the consequences of their past behaviour, both good and bad, embedded in the soil of the past.

At that moment, sitting contentedly in her chair, she felt all was well. She watched a very beautiful woman sway past Ricardo's chair. She bent to his ear and her expensive perfume assailed the table. 'No,' Ricardo grunted. 'I am the skipper. I stay with my boat.' The woman walked on, her shoulders sagging at the rejection.

'But her husband's over there,' Toby said, shocked.

'Italy,' Ricardo said. 'Italy is different. Italian woman like men. They make ziggy-ziggy but,' he frowned, 'I am captain and I stay with my ship.'

Marcia leaned forward with a slightly tiddly smile on her face. 'Yes, Ricardo, you are the captain, but who is the boss?'

'You are,' Ricardo said quickly. Marcia leaned back and twinkled at him. For a moment he froze like a stoat facing a mongoose, but then he smiled. A big, warm, generous smile. 'I don't mind you are boss.' He shrugged.

In the days they'd been together, he'd very much come to respect Marcia's quiet, unassuming command of herself and of the others. He particularly liked the way she took care of Helen. And, he said to himself, that woman needed caring for.

As they left the restaurant Elliott walked to the table where the man sat. He'd spent all evening staring at her. She was pulled by his hypnotic eyes. As she reached his table, he pulled an almost black rose from the silver vase on his table. 'Mind the thorns,' he said. Elliott took the dangerous rose from his hands, the backs of which were matted with hair. Elliott waved at the others.

'Later,' she said casually.

Helen shook her head. The lights about the man's head were black and purple. She said nothing to anyone, but she could tell Marcia was troubled too. 'I hope Elliott's all right,' Helen said as they put out the lights over their bunkbeds in order to go to sleep.

'So do I,' Marcia said. 'All we can do is pray.'

A silence descended over the boat, except for the sound of Ricardo's snoring which brought peace and sanity to Helen's soul. The boat began its familiar rocking, sending Helen to sleep in her safe, warm timbers.

Chapter Sixty-one

Elliott always enjoyed these first few minutes with a new man. The men she'd picked up in Italy so far had been fun, but all three were young and still living at home, so making love had been under rowing boats on the beach. She enjoyed the love-making, but the sand up her buns bit annoyed her.

She stretched out her legs and watched the man shift his gaze to her long slim legs. She crossed her ankles and studied her pink painted toenails. 'What is your name?' he said in a wonderful, flawless English accent. Somehow an Italian speaking such perfect plummy English was very sexy.

When she was in London with her lover, she listened to the chipped cut-glass English accent and she found it irritating. 'My name is Lilac and,' she gazed down modestly at her folded hands, 'I won't tell you the rest until I know you better.'

'My name is Raymond and I also shall not tell you the rest.'

Elliott looked at him rather sharply. There was something odd about his eyes. They were brown but they looked like currant buns that had been glazed with too much sugar-water. It made him look as if he were living in a deep inner world and just gazing impassively at the real world from behind a dark space.

'What are you doing with that strange crowd of people?' he asked. There was no curiosity in his voice. There was also no lilt in his voice. It might have come out of a Dalek's chest.

Elliott shifted uncomfortably in her chair. She wondered for a moment if she should just get up and go. Run into the night air and back to the boat. To the warmth and friendship she knew she would find there.

Her mother's voice was in her ear, 'Always try to please men, honey. Don't make a show of yourself or men won't like you, and then where would you be?' This was the advice she had resented for years but now, in front of this much older and sophisticated man, she felt she had to please him. Besides, he was the sort of man she hoped resembled her father who was somewhere in Greece.

He leaned back and crooked an elegant finger for the bill. He put a hand on her shoulder; for a moment Elliott wanted to sob. Where was that male hand that should have guided her as a child? Her shoulder had been empty for a father's touch. She felt a deep well of gratitude beginning to form in her heart.

As they walked down the stairs of the restaurant, she put her hand in his. His hand was dry and scaly. Under the phosphorescent light his nose dipped sharply into his chin. Elliott felt a thin vein of fear. It pulsed with green blood. He walked in measured silence towards a row of cars. He put out his hand and the car doors clicked open and the headlights went on. She could see he owned a big black sleek Mercedes car.

'Get in, my dear,' he said and smiled.

Elliott felt reassured. 'Where are we going?' she asked. She looked at him sideways as he climbed into the driving seat.

'Let's just say, to my home. The rest you really don't need to know. After all, I imagine looking at the Italian man you were with, you are from a boat and will be moving on tomorrow. Ships in the night. How romantic, dear, don't you think?'

'Very.' Elliott tried to keep her voice light. She felt out of control. Alone with this very big man in a luxurious car sliding through the streets of Réggio di Calabria, she looked out of the car window at the flotsam and jetsam that lounged around the streets. Big crowds of boys in black bomber jackets astride their motorbikes, some with girls with dirty dyed blonde hair clinging to the bomber jackets. Lovers ensconced in each other's arms, sucking each other dry with sexual passion. Elliott wished she was with a simple, easy-going young man with a Harley Davidson of his own. A happy impersonal fuck and then back to the boat. A quick shower under the big rose of the shower in the now much loved *gabinetto*. But that was not what was happening. They were driving up a steep hill. At the top, in the beam of the headlights, she could see a very big house. The car slid to a halt.

'We're home, beautiful Lilac,' he said, and leaned over her. He kissed her, his tongue darting in and out of her mouth like a viper's.

Elliott shuddered. 'Maybe I ought to go home, back to the boat,' she said, her voice quivering with unease.

'I don't think so,' he said. 'I think we should have some fun.' The tone of his voice didn't sound as though it would really be her kind of fun. Elliott then felt a perverse surge of interest. Just what kind of fun was he talking about? She had to find out.

There was still a long way to go to the mansion on the hill looming above them. The car, silently purring like a big cat, nosed its way up a very steep hill. Up and up they climbed. By the dashboard light, Elliott could see the thin high profile of this man. She leaned back in the luxurious seat and wondered how many other women had sat there before her. Usually she would flip open the flap of the dashboard drawer and rummage around in a stranger's car, just as she did when she was in the house of a lover. The contents of their medicine chests soon gave them away. Often there were rows of ointments for haemorrhoids, bad-breath remedies and, if he were married, his wife's tights would be hanging wetly from the shower rail.

But this time she didn't dare stretch out her hand. She put her head back in the soft leather cushion of her chair, and tried to remember her yoga breathing. Seven breaths in. Breathe deeply from the stomach, hold it for seven counts and then let it slowly out.

Thank God for those years spent squatting on the floor with her old flame Roger. He had been the wildest, freakiest hippy of the whole gang that had hung round Houston. He looked bad and dangerous. He was as big as the man that was sitting beside her. But he was a very gentle giant and, in his arms, Elliott learned real sexual pleasure. Sensual, soft love-making that was unusual in American men. She stole another look at Raymond. 'Are we nearly there?' she said. She was aware that her voice sounded frightened and childish.

As she spoke, he stretched out his hand and a massive pair of gates opened silently. The car crunched up the drive. She could see the vague outlines of what looked like olive trees lining the drive. The car turned into the basement of a very big house. There were no lights on in the house. No sign of human life. Just stillness and silence. The car glided into a big double garage. The walls were whitewashed. The floor was tiled with terracotta tiles. The car came to a halt. 'You can get out now,' Raymond said. As he opened the door to the house he switched off the lights in the garage. He took her by the hand. 'Follow me,' he said.

He led her down a dark corridor and then opened a big door and switched on the light. For a moment Elliott blinked in disbelief at what she saw. There was a cord with an electric lightbulb dangling from the ceiling. Under it was a hospital bed with leg-irons. On a three-legged chair lay a long black whip, its tasselled end resting lightly on the floor. There was also a bucket with a cloth in it, and from the wall hung two long iron chains with restraining cufflinks.

'I don't believe this.' Elliott felt a terrible fear rising inside her.

'Well, you'd better believe it.' Raymond's face had now changed. His eyes were glistening and he had a strange feral grin on his face. 'Get your clothes off,' he ordered.

Elliott turned to run but he got to the door before her and locked it. 'Take your punishment like a good girl,' he said, tearing off her shirt. He picked up the whip. 'Take off your slacks.'

Trembling and now crying, Elliott obeyed.

'Bend over and touch your toes,' he said. As she bent over, he hit her once, hard, with the whip.

'Please don't!' Elliott screamed. 'Please don't hurt me,' she begged. She felt a warm trickle of what she knew must be blood running down her legs.

From then on she was beyond pain and beyond reason. Fear blotted out everything. She felt him roll her on to the hospital bed. She felt him tearing into her, forcing her knees to her chin. 'Help me oh God,' she heard herself praying loudly.

'He can't help you now,' Raymond boasted. 'Bleed, you bitch,' he screamed. 'I like the smell of blood.'

Eventually, when she became unconscious, he roughly threw the contents of a bucket of water over her. He picked up her clothes with one hand and slung her over his shoulder. Elliott came to as he deposited her in the car.

He opened the doors of the garage and drove out in the early dawn of the day. Elliott, slumped in the car, could only say, 'Why, Raymond, why?'

'Because you're a whore and you needed to be taught a lesson. I'm good at teaching women lessons. Just a bit of fun really, nothing to it.'

Elliott pushed her hair off her forehead with a bloodstained hand. She was so glad to be alive. So glad that he hadn't killed her that she felt almost grateful. He saved her life. She shook her head wearily. 'Where are you taking me?' she asked.

'To the dock to join your friends. Do tell them we had fun, won't you?'

At the gates he stopped the car and roughly pushed her out. She lay on the dock in a curled fetal position. He threw a hundred thousand lire at her and then he laughed. Elliott thought she would never forget his laugh. The odd thing about it was that it was a high-pitched, hysterical woman's laugh.

'I enjoy being cruel to women when they're at their most vulnerable,' were his last words to Elliott as he drove away.

She climbed to her feet, aware that he'd also thrown her shirt and her trousers at her. She looked down at her body. She still felt no pain. Only an urgent desire to get to Helen and Marcia. To feel their arms about her. She looked down at her bloodstained body. She started to walk.

Chapter Sixty-two

During the night, Helen awoke with a start. She felt as if a hand had reached out and plucked a vertebra out of her spine. The phantom pain was excruciating. She sat up and put on her little pencil-slim reading light. The time was one o'clock. She smiled at the familiar face of her watch. It was a twenty-first birthday gift from her mother and father.

She felt a chill of premonition. Was Elliott all right? Helen hadn't at all liked the look of the man she was presumably spending the night with. His face emanated darkness. There was no salvation in his face. Helen hoped she was wrong. He frightened and disturbed her. She reached for her science magazine.

Now, with virtual reality, it was possible to map the brain thinking. This fascinated her. She looked at the diagrams of brains emitting red flashes of light as the electrified neurons flashed and signalled. Soon it will be possible to make soft computers. Already scientists had dishes full of synthetic cells breeding at a fast rate. Helen pored over her magazine.

One day we will find that love is a real entity, she thought. Helen had always believed in this. The love she had given Paul had not been wasted. That bright clear glowing light which is what love is will go on existing in the universe. Go back to the source of all intelligence. To the maker of all things.

She fell asleep with the little red light still shining on her face, and the magazine nestled by her side. She was disturbed by the sound of feet, not walking but limping down the dock. She got out of her bunk and flew to the ladder. She knew without knowing that it was Elliott and she was in terrible trouble.

Helen put her head out of the hatch. She stared, her mouth hanging open in shock. 'Elliott,' she said, trying not to scream, 'what happened?' She tried to whisper so as not to wake the others. Elliott's bloodstained face stared back at her.

'He was a crazy, Helen, he battered me. He whipped me.' Elliott was holding on to the boat. 'I wish I were dead,' she sobbed.

Marcia appeared. Helen heard her say, 'Wake up, Junior, it's Elliott. She's been badly hurt.' Cricket, followed by Toby, came out on to the deck. Ricardo joined them. All three of them gasped in horror.

'That bastard,' Cricket said through his teeth. In one bound he was on the dock. He cradled Elliott in his arms as if she were a baby.

'Thanks, Cricket,' Elliott said. Gone was the big happy confident woman from Houston. In his arms Cricket held a frightened, beaten child. His eyes filled with tears. He struggled to keep his face composed.

'Why did he do this to me?' Elliott looked at Marcia. She knew Marcia would know the answer. Marcia knew everything there was to know about men.

'He was probably sexually abused by his mother, honey. Those men hate women. Usually they're impotent. Sometimes they suffer from retarded ejaculation which means they never acknowledge they have a problem, but blame women instead.'

'I'm not a wicked woman, am I, Marcia?' Elliott's voice was pleading.

'We're all wicked women to those men. We all have to be punished in their sick, warped little minds. Don't you worry, Elliott. Let's get you into your bunk and clean you up. I'll give you some painkillers and wash off your back and put some cream on the cuts and then I'll clean your face.'

This was not the first time Marcia had cleaned up a battered woman. Often Lace would bring her one of her friends who'd made an assignation with just such a man. Then, of course, there had been her own face when Cricket's father had too much to drink. But this was no time to discuss this subject with Elliott. For now she was in shock and the pain had not yet hit her, but by tomorrow she would feel the full effects of the beating.

'What's that bastard's name, Elliott? Toby and I will go and do him over.' Cricket's hands were clenching and unclenching.

'I only know his name was Raymond. He wouldn't tell me his surname.'

'OK, then. Where does he live?'

'I don't know, Cricket. We were in the car and there were no lights in the house; only this one electric lightbulb in that awful room.'

Cricket laid Elliott gently on her bunk. Her mouth was kissed with blood from the whip across her face. He stood looking down at her and then he said quietly: 'You know, Elliott, I love you.'

'I know,' Elliott whispered back. Their words were unheard by the others. Helen was on deck hanging out the washing. She was so upset she had to do something ordinary to stop herself shaking. Marcia was getting water from the *gabinetto* and Toby and Ricardo were making coffee.

'I know,' Elliott said again, but then she sighed gently. 'But I'm not worth loving, Cricket. I'm a wicked woman, remember?'

'You're nothing of the sort,' Cricket said. He bent down and kissed her on the forehead. 'Come on, Toby and Ricardo, let's get out of here while Mum tends to Elliott.'

Marcia handed Elliott four pills. 'You're going to need

these,' she said, her voice dark with sympathy. Helen handed Elliott a mug of hot coffee.

'You've been here before, haven't you, Marcia?' Helen stared at her friend.

'Yeah.' Marcia nodded her head. 'Junior's dad used to batter me senseless. He wasn't impotent, but he'd had an awful childhood. His grandmother was a cruel, evil woman and he never forgave her. That's why in the end I left. I didn't want Junior to grow up around a man who disrespected women. The problem these days is that women don't make men respect them. They drink with men, they swear like men, and then they wonder why they are not respected. All men are animals at heart.'

Marcia carefully washed the blood from Elliott's back. For now the mark of the whip had left pink, swollen tracks across her back, but within days those marks would be all colours of the rainbow. 'The bruises will fade, Elliott. Bones mend, but what it does to your heart is another matter.'

Elliott nodded. Both women watched as she drank her coffee. Then she sighed, handed her cup back to Helen, and her eyes closed. Elliott was asleep.

'Shock,' Marcia said. 'Thank goodness I have some sleeping pills with me. I'll need to keep her sedated for several days.' Marcia went on deck to look for Ricardo. She needed to give him a list for the chemist. Bandages, creams and cotton wool.

'*Bastardo*,' Ricardo said as she handed him the list and carefully explained its content. He shook his head in disbelief. '*Povera bambina*,' he added, his dark brown eyes filling with tears.

Chapter Sixty-three

'Why didn't you cry, Marcia? I was so upset I could have done the washing with my tears alone. How could a man do a thing like that to a woman?' Helen was sitting in the cockpit of the boat after dinner. They were at sea again.

'Because those impotent men are bastards. She's really lucky he didn't kill her. The only thing that saved her life is that he knew she couldn't find him to report him to the police. Even though the police are unlikely to do anything anyway. He probably chose that restaurant because he liked to choose rich women to humiliate. That, or he was searching for a woman who resembled his hated mother.'

Cricket was in the cabin holding Elliott by the hand. At intervals Helen could hear Elliott awake and moan or just cry piteously. It made Helen wince.

Now, as Helen sat on deck and watched the boat glide through the night waves, she shook her head. 'Funny, you know, I'm frightened of men. They're all so unpredictable,' she told Marcia.

'I'm frightened of no man, but the thought of Junior's dad still makes my hand shake. I didn't cry, Helen, because Maisie and I are used to emergencies. We women in the Bush help each other out. I've had friends with broken noses, bust arms.' There was a weariness in Marcia's voice that surprised Helen.

'Have men always been the same?' Helen wondered out loud.

'Yes,' Marcia replied. 'Whenever men get too much power they become animals. Whenever women don't expect good manners. Make them open car doors and offer us seats on the bus, or they become uncivilized inhabitants of a human jungle. Of course, what your husband did in a pinstriped suit was to batter you with words, and that's the only difference between Junior's dad and Paul. Junior's dad used his fists and Paul used words. I was better off because I could see what was happening but you had nothing to go on and nobody to see what he was doing.'

There was a silence broken only by Freddie Mercury singing his heart out. Helen loved Freddie Mercury's voice; she also had an unrequited love-affair with the lead guitarist of 'The Clash'. His broken-bottle voice seared into her soul. The agonized raw sound comforted her when she was having a bad day. He expressed her own raw feelings. Toby, lying under the boom, was nodding his head in time to the music. He had a pencil and paper and was writing a new song. 'It's for you, Mum,' he said shyly that evening. 'It's called "Almost There", and we are.' He gave her a hug. When Toby was upset he always retreated to his music, and Elliott's sobbing raked everyone's feelings.

At the prow of the ship, Ricardo sat silently meditating upon the sea. At sea he was a quiet man. A man content with the tiny world of a small ship afloat in the magnificence of the Mediterranean.

'You know, I always thought of the sea as my real mother and father.' Helen put her feet on the opposite bench and put her chin on her knees. 'When things were awful after Toby was born, I'd go home nearly every weekend and walk along the beach and cry and sing to the sea. Then, after telling the sea my problems, I was ready to go home and to cope. I couldn't really tell my mother and father about Paul. They wouldn't understand. I think parents who have a marvellous marriage can be a handicap because they don't understand anything but their own happy reality. If I tried to explain that I wasn't allowed to boil an egg or cook chicken liver pâté, they would just think I was nuts. They never screamed and threw tantrums like Paul did, and they couldn't imagine what my life was like. He was always such a perfect caring husband in their sight.'

'Yeah, maybe that's true, because I had marvellous parents, but the only problem was that they accepted racial prejudice as part of life and I didn't. I was a kid with a bad attitude and I fought back.' Marcia watched as Elliott awoke again and her long arms twined around Cricket's neck and she pulled him down on her bed so he could lie close to her. She lay there so bruised and broken that Marcia didn't have the heart to complain.

'I don't really think I can object to Cricket being with Elliott. She is still such a child.'

Helen smiled in the dark. 'I'm glad you're taking it this way. I think the two of them can help each other. After all, they have both been abandoned by a parent, so they can help each other to feel less abandoned. There isn't a malicious bone in Elliott's body. She won't hurt him and he won't hurt her. Not like my poor Toby over his lost and first love Louise. Still, he's getting over it. I've noticed him looking at several pretty girls in the ports.'

As they chugged through the day, Cricket sat on Elliott's bunk holding her gently in his arms. Helen and Marcia took food to them and Cricket gently pushed mashed potatoes into her broken mouth. Sometimes Toby joined them when he wasn't piloting the boat while Ricardo caught up on a lost night's sleep. Technically, neither Toby nor Cricket should have been piloting, so Toby kept a wary eye out to sea for the police boat.

This morning Ricardo had tried to apologize on behalf of Italian men. 'Italian men not like that man,' he said, trying not to look at Elliott's face.

'Don't worry,' Marcia comforted him, 'there's bastards in every country. American men are the worst.'

'Why do you think that is, Marcia?' Helen was puzzled.

'Partly because American women are the most aggress- ive women on this earth and their men are frightened wimps, and partly because there are now generations of men that have done nothing ever since they were little boys except watch women being beaten, raped, murdered and cut up with knives. They have lived in a twisted world where all forms of films, newspapers and comics glorify violence against women. They learn from pornography and sadism to get a sexual high, so sex for them is a brutal and violent affair. Anything else, any attempt at love or tenderness is a turn-off and makes them impotent. Also, they are so dependent on their women to make the smallest decisions in their lives, that they need them, but at the same time they hate women because of this depen- dence. But then I know some really great American women, and Elliott is one of them.'

'That's so sad. Also, since we've adopted American ideas and habits, England has become a lot less safe for women.' Helen was sitting on her bunk with her legs dangling down to the floor. For the rest of the afternoon she lay on her bed reading her new magazine on astron- omy, revelling in the spare time she now had. This night there was to be an eclipse of the moon, and Helen was pleased they would be in port before the actual moment of the eclipse. Still, the eclipse of the moon bothered her. The moon was the mother of the earth. The female spirit that was so much more powerful than the male sun. She obscurely felt a shiver of apprehension. With the moon in eclipse, the male yang would overcome the female yin, and that was always dangerous.

She wondered if that was what had happened a few nights ago to Elliott. Had Elliott been more self-aware, maybe she would have shied away from that awful man. But then she reminded herself that Gaylang had taught that there was no such thing as an accident. No pain, no gain. It was now up to Marcia and Helen herself to help Elliott learn from that brutal experience.

Helen lay on her back and brought to the screen of her mind all the different things she had noticed since she'd been in Italy. How Italians carried their babies in front of them on their hands. One hand under the child's bottom and the other protectively wrapped around its body. They carried their children with the same veneration an Italian priest carried the monstrance containing the consecrated host.

Helen had always carried Toby English style. Astride on her right hip with her right hand clutching his thin little leg. She'd had to carry Toby until he was three, and she thought that now her right arm was longer than her left. She smiled at the tender memory.

Then she wondered if the way she carried Toby was indeed English, or had the memsahibs learned to carry their children the way that all African and Asian women carried their babies? Certainly in English middle-class Victorian houses, mothers never picked up their children, but once the great sun fell over the British Raj, women in their hundreds came home and suddenly had to learn to cook, clean and take care of their children.

She noticed how Italian women lived for their looks. They even carried around designer carrier bags to go with their tiny designer dogs that always seemed to strain at right angles to their long spiky heels. Compared to those women, Helen felt as flat and uninteresting as the pancakes she never quite made right.

Last night she'd cooked coconut fish for supper, and everyone – even Ricardo, which surprised her – said how much they liked the dish.

Used to so much tongue-lashing from Paul about her cooking, she was still unsure they were telling the truth. She looked at Marcia questioningly. 'No, it really is good, Helen. I wouldn't lie to you, honestly.'

Lying below in her bunk, Elliott sent Cricket to help with the docking procedure. She didn't know which part of her hurt most. She was just a mass of violent aches and pains. What shocked her about the whole experience was that she had felt that appalling feeling of gratitude because he hadn't killed her. What on earth was that about, she wondered?

On deck, Ricardo reminded everybody that there was no water or electricity in this half-finished port, so to go slowly. They were well stocked-up with everything, but he was worried. The next leg to Cephalonia was a long leg, and they were sailing without a map. He smiled: if they did run out, which was unlikely, Elliott was all right with her now less than thirty-six bottles of wine under her bunk and some spare champagne.

The boat pulled into the ghostly haven. They docked in the clear blue water. The sun was beating on the big white stones that formed the harbour. After they docked, Helen got off the boat with Marcia to stretch her legs. Cricket stayed to look after Elliott, and Ricardo and Toby went off to find a fishing boat from which to buy fresh fish.

Walking alongside Marcia, Helen felt ineffably happy. Nothing she could actually put her finger on, but just a sentient feeling that all was right with the world today. Of course, she regretted what had happened to poor Elliott, but still she was safe back with them, and hopefully after this awful event she would think twice about going off with strange men. Helen felt a stab of virtue, and then she made a face. She'd gone off with moody violent Paul, hadn't she? Who was she to patronize Elliott?

Chapter Sixty-four

At about eleven o'clock, they were all sitting on the boat watching the moon. It was glowing so brightly that it lit the trestle-table where they ate at night, making Helen's candles superfluous.

Elliott sat between Ricardo and Cricket, gently settled on cushions because she so much wanted to see the eclipse. They all tried not to show their distress at the huge swollen eyelids where her attacker had punched her, and her bruised mouth. Marcia and Helen were aware of the state of her back and the bite marks on her breasts. Those, she said, were the most painful. But for now she tried to smile and she sipped her wine through a straw, wincing when it stung her lips. 'It helps take away the pain,' she said, her voice still hoarse from screaming.

The shadow crept stealthily across the moon. It seemed to Helen that the male darkness was covering the female light of the moon. She hoped that elsewhere, under cover of this unnatural darkness, men were not continuing to beat and batter women everywhere. She wondered if, when the moon was full, some people, feeling the effect of the pull and power of the moon, went mad. Lunatic. She knew that mental hospital admissions rose the night of the full moon. Then there was that awful moment when the moon was swallowed up by the shadow, and the breathless wait for that first sliver of gold as the moon shyly represented herself to her waiting audience.

The next morning they lay at anchor. Ricardo's sighs reminded Helen of a full-blown sirocco. They began deep in his stomach, climbed up his pasta paunch and then whistled out of his mouth at an alarming rate. Helen teased him and said he could blow away mountains.

As much as Ricardo disapproved of Elliott's behaviour with men, he felt very sorry for her. Gone was the big act, the showing off and the girlish giggling with the boys. Instead she slept most of the time, curled up under the duvet. If she were not sleeping, she was talking intensely with Cricket.

Helen was thrilled with the two extra days in this wild and desolate place. She spent the early part of the morning in her swimsuit and wrap, sitting on the sea-wall drawing. There, alone with the blue of the water and the sky, she whiled away hours as her pencil flew across the paper.

At eleven Marcia arrived with a long cold drink of iced water, and together they would find the tiny beach at the end of the derelict wall and enter the water.

Marcia swam as if she'd been in the water all her life. 'You've no idea how much I've missed this sea,' she said. 'Jamaica is still a magical dream to me. I loved it there. One day I want to take Junior back and live there among the coconuts and the guava bushes. I want Junior to know his big family. They all still live in Montego Bay. Most of them are doing well. He has one old uncle who knows the whole history of the island. How his forefathers came to Jamaica as prisoners from Scotland. How the white people were just as enslaved as the black.

'Some of the cousins are white with blue eyes and blond hair. Junior is not taught the truth of our history in his school. They were force-fed nonsense when those liberal bastards chased out our old teachers. I remember Miss Kingston, the maths teacher. She was brilliant. Cricket was doing so well in his maths class and then they got this present idiot. Goodness knows where they found him. He can't teach anybody anything.'

'Don't I know that. I remember the first day that Toby bought home Mao's *Little Red Book* and said, "Mum, what is all this shit? I'm supposed to tell on you?"'

'Ace,' Marcia said in disgust. 'It's the thought police again. Come on, we're having a break from the likes of them.' They hauled themselves out of the water.

'Come on, Helen, I'll race you to the boat.'

'I don't stand a chance, Marcia: you run like a cheetah.' Once back in the boat, Helen went downstairs to prepare the pasta. It didn't matter what else went wrong in the universe, Ricardo had to have his pasta at one o'clock, otherwise he'd be sucking Rennies for the rest of the day.

Italian men, he explained, had to have their trousers properly ironed and the pasta on the table like Mamma made it. To make sure that Helen and Marcia were up to making Mamma's pasta, he supervised them the first time.

'No, no, too much oil,' he said to Marcia.

Helen's also failed the taste test. 'Not oil in water,' he said, throwing out her pot of boiling water.

'But my book –' She tried to object.

'Book written by *stranieri*,' he spat out the words. 'No good *stranieri* write books about Italian food. Only Italians cook Italian food.' He salted the boiling water with what seemed to Helen sufficient salt to give them all high blood pressure for the rest of the trip. Still, she did admit both his sauce and his pasta were delicious.

Helen sniffed the sauce. Tuscan olive oil was the best in the world. She had marvellously smelly lumps of well-grated parmesan cheese. There were craters and hollows in it where they had all grated the cheese. The sauce had that thick rich oily smell with a whiff of garlic. 'What am I going to do when we run out of all this lovely Italian food?' she asked Elliott who was propped up against her pillows.

'I guess we get to eat Greek food. It isn't nearly as good, but the grilled lamb is OK, and the yoghurt. My ex went to Greece a lot. He says you're either a Hyperborean, in which case you love Greece for the rest of your life, or you're not and hate the place.'

'What on earth is a Hyperborean?' Helen asked, amused.

'They are supposed to be the lost tribe of Israel: Jews who were the thirteenth tribe.'

'Where did you learn all that, Elliott?'

'I learned it from a lover years ago.' Helen noticed that there was no longer a sexual innuendo in any of Elliott's remarks. It felt as if a light had gone out inside her big blue eyes. Now Fear sat naked in Elliott's eyes.

'You'll go in time.' Helen addressed the old hag internally.

'I'm here for good,' the old woman leered back.

'Oh no you're not. You lived with me long enough; I'll kick you out,' Helen answered firmly.

Elliott blinked and the hag was gone.

Later that night, Elliott gingerly joined them on deck again. The bruises now looked worse instead of better. They were now hideous splotches of yellow and purple. Both eyes were still swollen and puffy, but at least she knew that her sight had been saved. They had all been silently worried about that. 'I ought to have gone to a doctor,' she said as she sipped some white wine through her straw, 'but all I could think of was that I had to get out of there.' She shivered. 'Réggio di Calabria is such a violent place, full of such violent people.'

'Maybe,' Marcia said slowly, 'you attract violent people? Have you thought about this? I've noticed in the dance centre that violent and disturbed people who join us thinking that they want to be dancers know just whom to approach to make dangerous relationships. I've done it once.' She winced as she saw the look on Junior's face. He'd seen her crying and beaten. He knew the force of his father's fist from when he'd tried ineffectually to protect his mother.

Sorry, Junior, I know this hurts, but I must help Elliott, she said silently. 'It's as if a person who has been abused in childhood gives off a special pheromone.'

'What's a pheromone?' Elliott's eyes were sparkling with interest.

'It's a special smell. Say, for example, a moth lets out a mating pheromone, all other male moths can smell her for hundreds of miles.'

'Wow, that's for real?' Elliott said in her valley girl voice. 'Smell me. What do I smell of?' She wrinkled her nose.

Ricardo relaxed and smiled into his beard. The American was back. She was smiling and Ricardo found it very difficult to look at her. His father would not have dared to lift his hand to his mother. She was only four foot nine, but *madonna*, what a wallop she used to give him with her cast-iron frying-pan if he came home too late after playing cards with his friends. Or if he dared come home drunk.

Cricket wrinkled his nose and snuffled her neck. 'You smell of honey and garlic,' he said.

'No, I don't. I smell of Opium, one of the most expensive perfumes in the world. Really, Cricket, you're such an asshole.'

'I know,' Cricket said cheerfully. 'We need to get out of here. There aren't any discos and no girls,' he said, teasing Elliott.

'That's my problem, you know,' Elliott said mournfully, 'I don't know if I'm a boy or a girl. You know, I dressed as a boy until I was fourteen.'

'You still dress as a boy, Elliott.' Toby was grinning.

'Shut your face,' was her amiable reply.

Chapter Sixty-five

Helen awoke with a start. She was being roughly thrown about in her bunk. She sat up, grabbing both sides of the rails. She looked around anxiously for Toby. He must be on deck, she decided.

Marcia came struggling through the bathroom door holding on to anything she could find. 'I'm afraid we're in a terrible storm,' she said weakly. 'I'm scared, Helen.'

'Don't be. I love storms, and *Carnevale* is a beautiful boat. Think of it as water-skiing, only on a boat.'

'I wish I could.' Marcia turned swiftly and Helen could hear her being sick in the lavatory. She got gingerly out of bed and made her way towards Elliott's bed. Elliott was still asleep. Marcia came out of the lavatory and made her way to where Helen was standing. Just at that moment, the boat lurched profoundly. There was a flood of bilge-water.

'Damn,' Helen swore. 'I should have pumped the bilges. I forgot.' Just as she said this, the door of the cupboard over the sink flew open, and all the bags of pasta fell on to the floor. There was another loud crash as all the china shifted in the other cabinet. The china was safe, as the boat had been constructed by a master engineer: all the cupboards were fitted out with special racks to hold the plates, and with holes for the glasses.

'Sod it.' Helen swore again as the pasta split asunder and strewed the floor with various shell-shaped pastas. 'You'd be better on deck, Marcia, the sea air will help your sickness.'

Helen tucked Elliott's blanket more securely around her. 'There,' she said with motherly satisfaction. 'She's still knocked out by sleeping pills, poor love.'

Marcia watched Helen's gesture of affection. How women took care of other women. A man only takes care of the woman he's screwing, she thought. And not always even then. She remembered how little Paul did for her and the sulks that accompanied any effort to get him to do any work around the house.

'Come on, Marcia,' Helen beamed, 'let's see if the boys need coffee.' Helen scrunched her way over the pasta in her bare feet. 'Ugh, this is unpleasant,' she said.

Once she had struggled her way to the top of the ladder, she gingerly slid into the corner of the cockpit. Marcia joined her on the other side. Ricardo was crouched down low over the wheel. Both boys were on deck, desperately trying to take down the mainsail. The big sail flapped and snapped like a starting gun in the wind. There was no sign of the lazy motion that had been its habit in the bright blue sailing days.

'Dear God, take care of all of us, but especially Toby,' she prayed. For a moment she felt a warm hand on her shoulder and a warm sense of certainty stole over her. God had heard her prayer and they would be all right. 'Coffee?' she asked.

Ricardo nodded, his eyes rimmed with red from lack of sleep and the sea-spray. Coffee was all Helen could do to help him. He needed all his concentration to deal with the force of the wind.

She guessed that the wind was about seven knots. That wasn't really the problem. The waves had an enormous swell. She sat down again for a moment, in awe at the size of the waves, which lifted the little boat high on their crests and then let her slide as if coming down a giant mountain of water. Each successive wave seemed taller than anything Helen had ever imagined. How could water get to that height? She didn't know, but the water threatened to engulf them. Ricardo read the waves like a genius.

If ever they had doubted him as a man, Helen knew he was a master sailor.

She smiled at Marcia. 'Who's boss now?' she said.

Marcia, white in the face, pointed at Ricardo. 'And if he gets us out of this one, he can be the boss for ever.'

'Don't tell him that, idiot, it'll go right to his head. I'll go down below and make the coffee.'

Milk and two sugars for Ricardo. White with three sugars for Marcia. The boys drank their coffee black with two sugars, she reminded herself. Her back wedged against the food cupboard that formed the end of Elliott's bunk, she worked at getting the kettle to boil. The stove swung crazily, but it was a good stove and well cantilevered. Shitting in this storm, Helen realized, was not going to be much fun. Funny how much time and thought had to be given to bodily functions on a boat, when at home she took it all for granted.

Much to Helen's surprise, she was not the least bit afraid. She, who was afraid of everything. Ricardo was an excellent sailor. The boat had a very deep hull and nothing much was going to happen to them. There would be a lot of clearing up to do after they had docked, but she was well used to that now.

She carefully made her way back up the ladder with a steaming cup of coffee. 'Here you are,' she said cheerfully. The boys by now had the sails down and were struggling with the ropes. 'This is fun, Mum,' Toby shouted.

'I know,' she yelled back. Toby always shared her great love of awful weather. While Paul sulked in the house, both of them had donned big boots and macs and squelched across Hampstead Heath in the driving rain to come back home pink and refreshed.

Now she felt the excitement rising. The boys came sliding down the deck to crash at her feet. Toby's eyes were sparkling, so were Cricket's. She saw Elliott's hands clutching the top rung of the ladder.

'Wow,' Elliott said, her black and blue face making her look like a tiny panda. 'What a storm! Help me out, Cricket.'

Cricket leaned forward and very gently lifted her out of the cabin and put her beside him.

Ricardo, tired as he was, caught the look of love and affection between them. Gone for good he hoped was the tough-talking American act. Elliott seemed to have changed from a golden aggressive valley girl to a sweet-natured child. Ricardo much preferred the Elliott of the here and now. He drained his coffee and handed the cup back to Helen. 'You not afraid?' he said, his eyebrows raised like the crests of the waves.

'No, Ricardo. I learned long ago that I was frightened of everything but afraid of nothing. I will always persevere. That's what living on my own with Toby has taught me. This journey is my healing. Gaylang told me before I left London that I would get back my sense of humour. I lost it living with a man who was so neurotic that he drained me dry.' She spoke slowly and clearly and she knew that Ricardo could understand.

He grunted. 'Women can also be bad,' he said with feeling.

'Yes, there are bad women, but a man can always go away to another house. Men have money, women don't. We don't have the options men have.'

'My dad did a bunk, left me with my crazy mom,' Elliott sighed. 'I guess I'd better ring her when I get ashore. If we get ashore . . .' She amended her sentence as another huge wave crashed over the boat.

'We go back to Roccella Iónica.' Ricardo made his decision.

'Yes, I think that's wise,' Helen agreed. The visibility was terrible. Fog was settling in. Ricardo swung the tiller with care and *Carnevale* almost turned on her side.

Helen felt her hair touch the water. 'Hold tight,' she screamed with joy.

The boat righted herself, gave a little shake, and settled down with the wind behind her to go back to the ghostly half-finished port.

'Great,' Elliott said with satisfaction, 'I don't get to call Mom.'

Chapter Sixty-six

They sat exhausted in the cabin of the boat, the boys on Elliott's bunk, which was supposed to be used as an indoor dining area, but was so loaded with Elliott's possessions that it was not worth using it. Anyway, they were all too tired to do much but sit and watch their wet clothes steam in the heat of the closed-off cabin.

The cabin smelled of wet-legged jeans, of salty flakes of crystal in the hair. The boat was docked with difficulty, and Ricardo was already fast asleep in his cabin, his snores shaking the boat.

Helen felt her hair, sticky and spiky from the sea-spray. She grinned at the assembled group. 'Nowhere to go out and eat tonight?' she said.

'I'm too tired to even think of food,' Marcia yawned. 'I've never been so scared in my life. I really did see all my life passing before my eyes. Whew, I saw some things I rather wish I'd forgotten.'

'What sort of things?' Helen was curious. The fact that for once since she'd known Marcia it was Marcia who was afraid delighted her. She felt a little stalagmite beginning to grow in the cave that had been where her heart was housed.

'Oh, just a bastard of a man I blotted out of my consciousness.'

'Gaylang said we shouldn't forget our past.' Toby smiled at Marcia.

'You're not a big man yet, and you haven't got as much to hide away from. Sure, we all remember what we've done, right and wrong, but sometimes,' she shook her head, 'a woman could sink under the memories of her foolishness. It was a long time ago, but just a few hours ago it came back like a haunting.'

'I think the idea of remembering always includes trying to clean out your attics and cupboards,' Helen said. 'I think there are four dimensions of time, not three. There's the past where we sow the seeds of the problems that are facing us. Then there is the present, where we can change things if we want to. There's a foreseeable future where we can be rewarded for past good or bad behaviour, and then there's the "future future" where we accept the consequences of our past actions. For example I suffer now in the future future for choosing to marry Paul.'

'Yeah,' Toby agreed, 'but at least now we've seen the kids in Italy who don't all drink and do drugs. Cricket calls them retards, but I think that's unfair. They have a much better future to look forward to than most English kids. Here they all learn at least three languages. The girls aren't cheap and the boys respect them for it. Mostly kids my age drink Coca-cola. When we go back I'm giving up dope. Hopefully in the future future that I can't see yet I'll be a successful singer and buy Mum a boat like this.' He smiled at Helen and she melted. Toby had such a tender quality about him.

Now, sitting in the boat, Toby knew it was going to be difficult to give up weed, but he'd never even tried crack or coke. Cricket told him that he'd got hooked on both for several years, and Toby didn't want to go down that road. It wasn't cool to do drugs any more. Music was too important to him. Besides, he wanted to take care of his mother. She was so little and so vulnerable. All those years she'd been so terribly bullied, and it had taken its toll on her. But now, watching her sitting happily on her bunk talking to Elliott who was leaning against the sink smoking, he was glad they both so enjoyed the storm.

During his life with his mother, he'd noticed that, even though she was easily intimidated by men or bossy women, when the chips were down – and they had been when they'd first got to Shepherd's Bush – she had an enormous amount of courage.

His father whined and cried. He emotionally blackmailed both of them, but his mother played no head games like his father. Life was straight down the middle for her. His early days of resentment and anger that she had taken him away from his well-regulated way of life had now dissolved completely.

He had asked God to rescue him from Shepherd's Bush when he first arrived. Now he would beg God never to let him become immersed in the middle-class way of life that he now perceived as a sick and vicious trap.

His past life had been a waste of his time, both emotionally and musically. The endless rounds of talking about sex. Sneaking behind your parents' back, drinking illicitly. Intense talks with Louise. Yes, even Louise was tainted with an itch to aspire. All of it a waste of time.

Time, Fats had taught him, was elastic. Time was a human conceit. As if you could measure the waves of oscillating neurons and electrons. No, you couldn't. Each human being and all things in the heavens and on the earth oscillated at their own speed. Some people like Cricket went into super orbit when excited. Cricket was a human dynamo. Toby knew he himself oscillated much more slowly. His time function was also slower.

Helen and Marcia finished cleaning up the floor and then Helen got ready to cook the pasta. Ricardo had taught her well. No longer did she fling the prosciutto into the salad bowl and crumble blue cheese into it. 'I get sick,' Ricardo said, gazing sadly at her proud handiwork. 'Don't like English or American food,' he added as an afterthought. Now Helen realized that Ricardo, like most

Italians, lived for his stomach. Not, of course, that he'd ever agree to eat a meal without grumbling about his weight.

Tonight she knew everybody would be hungry because lunch was an impossibility in the storm. She'd managed to make sandwiches but that was all.

Elliott was sitting cross-legged on her bunk. 'Do you know,' she said, 'that men fart thirteen times to our eight?'

Helen turned from the stove, her red ladle in her hand. 'No, I didn't know that. How did I manage to live without that knowledge? Really, Elliott, you must be getting better.'

'I am and I even feel horny again. I thought it would be gone for good, but no, it's still there, thank goodness.'

She sounded so relieved that Helen found herself laughing. 'I thought you'd learned your lessons at last, Elliott?'

'I have, but picking up strange men was such fun.'

'Not men like the last one.' Marcia's voice was clouded. 'When you get pushed over that line of fear and pain, you can get your head in an awful mess. Do you remember asking me why you felt grateful to him? Well, I didn't explain then because you were too shocked to understand, but a battered woman gets so deeply into a man's madness that she actually starts to feel grateful when he stops beating her. Then she's really in trouble. A woman can mistake the intensity of a dangerous neurotic for passion. I know because I've been there.'

'So have I.' Helen made a face. 'Then when can you trust a man?'

'You don't.' Marcia's voice was like the north sea. Cold and unrelenting. 'I've learned never to trust the bastards. By all means take a lover, but don't let him into your house or your heart or he'll loot your house and break your heart.'

'Aw gee, that sounds bad, Marcia. I want somebody for hugs and kisses.'

'Sure, have your love and kisses, but keep your distance. There's a war on, honey. A war between men and women. Men have kissed us, beaten us, raped us for centuries, and what did we fight for? We fought for the vote. What we didn't do, though we are now doing it a little too late, is to fight men on their own territory. To become women judges, lawyers and accountants, and to discriminate in favour of ourselves.

'For far too long women have fought and competed with other women. Felt weakly that they did not exist without a man in their lives. Cooked, ironed, cleaned, polished. Serviced a man's prick.' Words came tumbling out of Marcia's mouth.

Ricardo stumbled into the cabin. His bulk seemed to fill the whole place. 'Hungry,' he said, pointing at his mouth.

'You see what I mean.' Marcia stuck her finger up at him. 'Fuck off, you cretin,' she screamed at his rapidly retreating back.

'Poor Ricardo, Marcia.' Helen was laughing.

'Well, he deserved it. What does he think we are? His servants?' Marcia lit a cigarette and puffed angrily.

'Yes, but he sails the boat and he does offer to cook and he often gives me a hand cleaning up too!'

'He's a man, he's the enemy.' Marcia slumped on to her bunk.

'You relax, Marcia. I'll make dinner. I love cooking now that I can cook what I want and when I feel like it. I feel I've been in prison now for so long I've heard no birds singing.'

As Helen boiled the water in the big red saucepan that she reserved for pasta, she remembered the big house in Swiss Cottage. The French doors that opened in the summer on to the patio. The sound of the telephones ringing in the other houses around her. The telephone, the saviour of so many women's lives. The next-door phone sounded different to hers. The bell was higher. Who was her next-door neighbour ringing? Was she crying down the telephone? Sobbing in fear, or was it loneliness? Both, probably. The world was full of women and children battered by cruel men.

The world was also full of women like herself, with their accounts at Fortnums and Harrods, dying from the cruelty and violence of men. The difference was that the women who lived on welfare had nothing to lose but their possessions. Once they got away they had social workers to help rehouse them. Refuges to take care of them. But women like Helen, and she was guilty of doing it, had to take their children away from their private schools and make them face untold hardship. She knew other women who didn't dare try to get away. They had husbands who could wave chequebooks at social workers and lawyers. They were rich enough to stalk their wives like pheasants and take custody of the children. Those mothers would never see their children again. After all, many of the judges were old schoolfriends. A nod to the judge and tap to the side of the head: sorry, old boy, she's a little mad. Drink, d'you know? Everything understood. 'Nuff said.

Fortunately, Paul was a wimp and his stalking was not dangerous. And he was terrified of Marcia. Marcia's screaming-fits only made Helen laugh now that she was used to them. Other people took them terribly seriously, but not Helen.

She dropped the pasta into the boiling water. She had salted it first, the way Ricardo had shown her. Then she made plates of mozzarella and sliced tomatoes. Safe behind the sea-wall the boat was rocking but not dangerously so.

The wine she opened was her favourite, Rosso di

Montalcino 1994. The bottle came from a place called Buonconvento and the winery was called Altisina. 'I wonder where that is?' she said to Marcia.

Marcia was still lying on her bunk with her arm under her head. Her cigarette stuck straight up in the air. 'I don't know and I don't care.' She was still angry.

'Here, I'll pour you a glass of wine, Marcia,' Helen said diplomatically. Helen passed Marcia a glass.

'It would take a whole winery to put me in a good mood,' Marcia said crossly. 'Fuck men.'

'Amen,' said Elliott with a sigh. Helen was glad that both boys were attached to their Walkmans on their bunks and were unable to hear the attack.

Helen went off to rescue a very frightened Ricardo. 'Don't worry,' she said, looking at his sad face. 'In England we say, "Her bark is worse than her bite."'

At the word 'bite', Ricardo jumped. 'Bite too?' he said.

Helen laughed. 'No, Ricardo, come and eat. I promise Marcia won't bite you.' She was chuckling all the way back to the stove.

Chapter Sixty-seven

Marcia's mood was considerably lightened as they all breakfasted on deck next morning. Helen sighed with relief. Marcia, when she was angry, rather frightened people. But sitting with the sun beating on her face, with a clear blue sky above her, she realized that much of the problem was not Marcia's anger but their reaction to it.

The warp and the woof of the tapestry that had been her life had allowed her to play only a masochistic role. Not a role she had chosen, but one she adopted as the only role she knew women could take.

Her mother hadn't helped. It was an unwitting lesson, but all the same one that had gone deep. 'Daddy wouldn't like me to drive.' Helen had never really questioned that statement.

Daddy always drove the family car. A little round-nosed bluebottle of a Rover. Certainly the car was his most prized possession. Her mother used to joke that he loved his car more than he did his wife. He spent all Sunday morning after church cleaning the car until it gleamed bleakly under his loving yellow chamois leather.

All these years later, sitting on the boat sipping coffee and munching on a piece of olive bread, she remembered those honeyed days as if they were etched in gold upon a silver screen. Only now she was beginning to think that her early days in the safe bosom of her family had maybe contributed to her inability to form relationships with boys.

True, she had always told herself that she didn't need boys. She was clever, her mother told her. She would go far. Marry above her station in life. The obedient little girl in white ankle socks at the age of eighteen had nothing to measure those subliminal messages by. On board *Carnevale*, they had a small computer that perched proudly on the top of the chart desk. Try as she could, Helen couldn't understand it. Both boys with their hideous male ability to make sense out of all things linear played for hours with the machine. 'Beats Nintendo', Toby said proudly as he charted their way to Réggio di Calabria and Elliott's near death.

Thinking about Elliott's brush with death, Helen thought it odd that Elliott should feel gratitude to her attacker. Helen wondered if women were programmed like beaten dogs, to lick the hand of violence? They cringe in the hope that the frown might turn into a smile. Roll over and offer sex, anything the aggressor wished to take from the prone weeping body, and then to love the hand that held the whip?

'I guess the world is full of violent men,' she said out loud, and then she looked at Marcia, startled out of her inner world.

'Yeah, but then the world is full of wicked women as well. You have to learn to fight back early, Helen.'

'I guess I didn't. I just dreamed my way through until I met Paul. Well, I learned my lesson the hard way. I shan't do that again.'

'Do what?' Elliott appeared at the hatch. Her bruises were now smeared all over her face in an ugly omelette of browns and yellows. 'I never say never because that's when I get into trouble.' She grinned at Cricket and Toby who were prone on the deck under the mainsail. Both were chewing on very old pizza. Roccella Iónica had no electricity, so the fridge refused to work.

The storm washed clean the thick sea-walls that surrounded the derelict port. Helen imagined a giant squatting on the beach and making the port his project, building his own castle in the sand, and then abandoning his project and returning to his extra-terrestrial existence. Time to clear the table and fold it reverently with its long legs behind the chart table. She knew how to do this now without pinching her fingers. Ruefully she felt the top of her head where she repeatedly forgot to duck before climbing out of the hatch. The penalty for carelessness was a flash of red and yellow stars, and then a lump as big as a hen's egg. So far she had collected three of those.

She looked down at her fingers, pinched from the table. Her legs were now brown but her heels were assuming a thick sole of their own. No need for shoes. She wondered what it would feel like when she had to reclamp her feet into shoes in Greece?

Still, if she'd learned anything so far, she'd learned that she was not afraid of the storm. She had exulted in the wind and the waves. She was also learning from Gaylang that his advice about staying awake pertained to a boat. Asleep, and you paid the penalty of pain. She grinned as she carried down the plates and listened to the now familiar sounds of Ricardo and the boys making ready to cast off.

She heard Elliott's light feet on the deck and she smiled as she turned on the water. Casting off was always such an adventure. She would continue to learn to sail. Before she had no notion of just how much there was to learn on an ocean racer. She'd been spiritually fast asleep and for so long. The thought appalled her. How could she have been so frantically silly? All those wasted years. She shrugged as she scrubbed the thick Tuscan olive oil off the plates. Easy really, like almost all the other women she'd known, dance for your daddy was the silent, subliminal message that was given to every girl. The request was not made by the father, even though he loved to watch his daughter in her pretty little dresses dance around the room to enchant him. No, the fault lay with her mother, who whispered into Helen's shell-like ear, 'Dance for your daddy!' Helen finished the last words in the song, 'My little one.'

The boat heeled over as they left the dock. This was almost Helen's favourite moment. Now, she felt physically part of the boat. But then, she reminded herself, nobody owns a boat. A boat is like a woman should be. Men can tie her to a jetty, or chain her to a wall, but the boat will throw off her chains and untie her knots when she wishes. Off she goes to her rendezvous with her lover, the sea, his gold crown flashing in his thick grey locks. His eyes are eternally blue and his cloak spun from the gold coins from the bottom of the sea. In his hand he carries a conch-shell and he blows down the long pink corridor of the shell and she comes to him. A bride wrapped in her white sails. Or sometimes she chooses to come under her beautiful blue spinnaker.

Helen stood swaying with her arm around Marcia's waist. The boat nosed her way around the corner and then gybed with excitement. Ricardo steadied her but grinned. He too could feel the boat's excitement as she made her way to the open sea. '*Cara*,' he said lovingly, and then he stroked the ship's wheel as if encouraging a lover. '*Bella, bella barca*,' he whispered. Then he frowned and squinted at Helen. 'Bah,' he said, unwilling to be caught out in a moment of sentimentality.

Marcia smiled, her anger forgotten. Washed clean away in the summer's wind. 'She's great,' she agreed.

Ricardo acknowledged the apology and he grunted a reply. '*Ma*,' was what he needed to say.

Chapter Sixty-eight

'To Cephalonia,' Helen said, peering down the binoculars. She could see a fine line of rain on the horizon. The sun still shone but there were long chains of water riding the beams. 'Ricardo,' she said, 'it's going to rain.'

'No problem,' Ricardo shrugged. By now Helen was no longer worried about anything. Ricardo was very much a man in that he forgot almost everything. They all trotted after him, rescuing glasses, his cigarettes and finding ashtrays, but when he was sailing there was no finer sailor in Italy. Helen knew that, and that was why she was so safe and happy. 'You know, Marcia,' she turned to Marcia who was sitting on the bench with her arms around her knees, 'we both didn't want him on the boat and we were wrong.'

Marcia smiled and nodded in agreement. She didn't have to speak; they knew each other so well that words were unnecessary. Helen often thought that women had a whole other side of their brain locked off from men.

Here in Italy, where men could hug and kiss each other without restraint, she didn't feel the anger between the sexes. Ricardo was an immense character. He hugged and kissed anyone who took his fancy. He pinched the round-cheeked children and wolf-whistled at any woman who rolled her buttocks at him.

'Lawks a mercy, Ricardo, you'd be locked up in jail by the sisterhood if you came to Houston.' Elliott thought she ought to protest but usually collapsed in helpless giggles.

The one time none of them laughed was when they were walking across a road in Ischia. On the side of the road lay a dead cat and, crouched over it, the owner. Ricardo immediately put his big hand on the woman's shoulder. '*Vada*,' he said kindly but firmly. '*Vada a casa*.' He gave the sobbing woman a gentle push and she fled. The cat had obviously just given birth, her nipples were swollen with milk. She lay with her mouth open in a pool of blood. Helen winced and her heart went out to the woman. She too had lost a cat to a careless driver when she was a child.

The memory resurfaced as she stood on the deck and watched the rain approaching. Her cat had been still warm when she was called by the next-door neighbours. Her parents were out and the neighbours were keeping an eye on her. She had been playing with her dolls in the garden.

Her cat lay stretched out on the road in front of her garden. Helen remembered her cry of sorrow. She remembered the feeling of the tarmac on her knees, the small stones and the grit that dug into her thin, bony legs. But most of all the silence around the cat. The absence of life. The cat's failure to rise with her tail straight in the air to follow Helen like a dog.

The rain reached the boat. The weight of it smoothed the waves to an oily swell like the gentle hand of the mother, smoothing the forehead of her child, the sea. 'Nettuno, Ischia, Vibo Valentia Marina, Réggio di Calabria, Roccella Iónica,' she recited the places and the ports that she now knew like a mantra. A way of warding off the awful memory of her dead cat. Then she shook herself and the memory was gone.

Ricardo leaned into the boat to grab his oilskins and Helen went down into the boat to get ready to cook the supper. Two days at sea. Two days to lie on her bunk or on deck and to sort out her memories. She blessed the boat for giving her the time and the space to try to address the question of who she really was.

There needed to be a new Helen. A Helen that wasn't dependent on any man. A woman of valour and courage. That takes some doing, she told herself as she boiled the water for the pasta. Above deck she could hear the boys noisily teasing Ricardo about his women. She smiled.

Later that night, Elliott opened her eyes with a start. No, she wasn't back in that terrible room. Every night she hallucinated that she was in that room with that eerie man. Yet again she felt a sticky feeling of gratitude swamp her brain. This feeling troubled her deeply. Where had the gratitude come from?

She slid quietly out of her bunk and tiptoed past the bunk by the ladder. Good, she thought. Toby was asleep and Cricket was up on deck. Maybe he could reassure her.

She raised her head above the hatch. It was a clear, warm night. The boat rocked gently. Cricket was sitting behind the wheel. She could see his teeth gleaming in the light of the stars. Tonight the moon was benign. She pulled herself through the hatch and slid on to the bench beside Cricket.

'I know your mother tried to explain this feeling of gratitude that's giving me such nightmares, but I just can't come to terms with it. I guess I must be mad or something.' She curled into the crook of his arm. 'When that man dumped me on the road outside the dock, I had this strange sensation. Sort of, like I explained to your mother, I was grateful he hadn't killed me. I have no idea where this feeling came from. I have these terrible dreams every night that I'm back in that room and I'm kissing his hands after he finishes beating me because I'm not dead. Weird, isn't it?'

Cricket was silent for a moment. 'I don't know, Elliott. Emotions do mess up the brain. I was once with a woman I was mad about. So much so that I was frightened of her. We met one day at one of my gigs. She came up and it was like "zap", two electric wires touching. There was no question as far as I was concerned. We were no good at all for each other,' he sighed. 'In fact it was the worst year of my life. I felt as if I was possessed.'

'Yeah, that's what it is like, being possessed.'

Elliott was excited; she was getting somewhere. 'I knew when I saw him that he was dangerous, but instead of getting out I went for it. For the danger and the excitement. Living on the boat with everybody so straight, I missed the excitement and the sense of adventure I had at home. Sure, I had some bum men in my life, but never anything like that. He's the sort of guy you imagine making porno movies.'

'Yes, but think about this. There wouldn't be any porno movies if people like him didn't exist.'

'Do you really think that some women get turned on by what he does to them?'

'Oh, Elliott, you are hopelessly naïve. Of course some women get off on that sort of thing. I've had women ask me for rough sex. Men are just a lot more honest about their needs. Of course, if men want rough sex, they're seen as macho, but if a woman admits she has violent sexual needs, she's immediately called a whore.'

Elliott was silent for a moment. She gazed at Cricket with her big blue eyes. She could feel the heat of his body. He smelt clean and sweet, like hair cream. 'What about us?' she said shyly.

Cricket leaned forward and kissed her gently on her bruised mouth. 'What about us?' he whispered.

'Are we going to be an item?' Elliott grinned. Her gamine twinkle was back.

'Sure we are, and we have been for some time. Haven't you noticed?'

'Yeah.' Elliott gave a slow sigh of satisfaction. 'Yeah, sure I noticed, but I didn't know if you had.'

'Elliott, everybody's noticed, even my mother, so

we'd better be careful. We'll take it carefully, OK?'

'OK. I'm going back to bed.' Elliott raced forward and rubbed her cheek against Cricket's face. '*Mmmmmm*,' she said, 'you smell so nice.'

She slipped away down the ladder. 'Cricket loves me,' she whispered into her duvet. The thrill of the information made her heart pound. 'Cradle-snatching,' she heard her mother's angry voice. 'Fuck off,' she said, and turned over and immediately fell asleep.

Chapter Sixty-nine

Elliott opened her eyes and checked her Tag Heuer watch. She felt the boat rolling and she hugged her secret love for Cricket to her heart. She gazed at the watch: it had been a present from a German lover, who had been methodical in bed and had disliked her big jazzy Swatch watch. 'You're too old to wear a watch like that,' he had said the first morning after they had gone to bed together.

Now, after last night, Elliott wondered if she could retrieve her gaudy watch from her jewellery bag which was crammed under her bunk along with her supply of wine and brandy?

She peeked at Marcia who was standing by the sink discussing the day's menu with Helen. How those women could go on about food. She fantasized about the possibility of a fast-food place. Maybe they could request that two dolphins in harness tow a plate of Big Macs to the boat. What she would give just for a mouthful of Big Mac, french fries and mayo on the side. She felt her mouth filling with saliva. Nah, it was going to be another day of oily Italian food again. Helen and Marcia were besotted by the stuff.

Elliott fluttered her eyelashes at Marcia. Marcia's profile was always rather threatening to Elliott. Marcia had such a pure face. A long nose, and eyes that swept upwards. Then there was her broad mouth. A generous mouth, but it also carried danger in the curve of the upper lip. When Marcia was angry with Elliott, her top lip flattened out.

Elliott could see that today she was not in trouble. Mostly because Marcia did not know of her night-time tryst with her son. Somehow, Elliott felt sure that, had she known, her top lip would have been good and flat this morning.

'I do hope we can get mortadella in Greece.' Helen pulled out several large round pieces of the pink, fat-marbled meat. '*Mmm,*' she said, 'they look like big pink bedspreads.' Helen laid the sheets on a plate. 'Can you make a tomato and mozzarella salad, Marcia?'

'Sure.' Marcia began cutting through the chalk-white cheese.

Elliott lay thinking. These women don't live, she thought. But then they had men in their lives that gave them their children. So much of their time was now spent in servicing those boys. The boys were grown up now, but Marcia still did Cricket's washing. They expected the boys to wash the dishes, but then they cleaned up the resulting mess with great good humour. Her mother would have screamed the place down.

I guess I wasn't mothered like that. The thought created a pang of hurt. No American moms had stayed at home for the last twenty-five years. Elliott's mother didn't believe in cooking or doing housework. Her apartment was always in a terrible mess. Most of the clothes in her mother's apartment were dumped on the floor or pushed into cupboards. When she was much smaller, Elliott had had to help pick up the greying underpants and worn brassières and hide them from the various 'uncles' that visited her mother. 'Uncles' was a euphemism from her early childhood describing the various men that haunted her mother's vast apartment. Many of them invading her bath-times as there was no lock on the bathroom door; some had squeezed her breasts or tickled her between her legs.

Men, she had learned very early on in life, were untrustworthy bastards. Give them a moment of lecherous squeezing and a quick knee between her young adolescent legs, and then she silently held out her hand. Her message was unmistakable. 'Pay, baby, pay.'

Very soon she had a bank account which she kept in a Safeway carrier bag under her mattress. No, of course it wasn't a real bank account: it was her revenge fund. Men, in Elliott's life, would always be made to pay for their sins. Now she was involved with Cricket: he could hardly be counted as a bastard of a man. He was still a boy. Yes, she knew that he'd been to bed with plenty of women. Still, he didn't use women the way she was used to men using women. He still had a bloom of innocence about him, as if the beddings had been a mutually enjoyable event. This is what so attracted her to Cricket.

What she really wanted from Cricket was not just sex for once. And particularly now when she still felt violated and vulnerable. What she really wanted was to have fun. To play. Not to be responsible for any heavy major feelings. To be free and wild in Greece, a country that she loved. The Greeks, she felt, were a people carved out of the hillsides that surrounded them. At first she felt they had heavy disapproving faces. The Greek people, when she got to know them, smiled at her and it was as if the sun had forced its way through the clouds.

The Italians had much sunnier dispositions, but their emotions were so much more shallow compared to her Greek friends. Italians only had real relationships within the family. '*Conoscente*' was the Italian word for acquaintance. True friendship was a Greek construct. If given, it was a relationship for life and could only be broken over a matter of honour.

Elliott lay motionless. This is how she had to lie for hours as a child while her mother entertained her men. Elliott wasn't wanted. She was pushed out of sight, and if she rebelled and got out of bed or made a sound she was locked in her mother's black hellhole of a broom cupboard.

424

One of her rebellions was to tiptoe out to her mother's fridge and take a mouthful of black caviar with a spoon and taste the fishy popping balls. If she got caught, her mother beat her, but by now her pain level was so high she didn't feel much. Anyway, her mother didn't really like the stuff. She just kept it in the fridge to impress her men friends.

Her mother had no women friends. Women didn't interest her, only men. Maybe, Elliott often surmised, it was the shock of being dumped by her father that made her mother collect male scalps like a demented Indian chief. Maybe not; maybe the men were her way of avoiding ever being alone for a moment. This is why this boat trip was such a good idea. Absolute absence of mother, and now the possibility of a lover. Elliott got out of bed and bent down to touch her toes. Good, she was still supple enough to touch the deck. She felt the good feeling of her spine stretching out.

'So you've decided to join the land of the living? My, Elliott, that was a long sleep.'

'Yeah, I was tired and I sleep so well on this boat.' Elliott's voice was demure. What a bitch you are, she told herself. But then it was lovely to have someone to love and to kiss. The price you pay, the price you pay. She could hear the warning bells in her head like an angelus. OK, OK, her little troubled child answered, I'll worry about that tomorrow; tomorrow's another day. Elliott brushed past Marcia on her way to the john. How like his mother Cricket looked at times, she observed. She pushed open the round door and then grinned at her cracked image in the mirror. 'Shit, those bruises are hanging around for ever,' she swore at the mirror. She cleaned her teeth and, for the first time since the dreadful event, her mouth didn't sting from the toothpaste.

'It's such a relief to get away from the world of men.' Helen pulled the coffee off the stove. The smell wafted around the boat. The boat now smelt of her cooking. 'You know, it's so odd how my cooking smells so different to yours, Marcia. I use less garlic than you do and my cooking smells more of fresh parsley and cucumber and tomatoes. When you cook on the boat she smells of your garlic cloves and of spices like chilli and turmeric.'

'Poor old Ricardo, I wonder if he minds his boat smelling like a Far Eastern bazaar?'

'I shouldn't think so. I'll take his coffee up and ask him.' Helen could now run up the ladder without spilling a drop of coffee. Another milestone, as Paul had always hated her clumsiness. 'Do you mind the smell of our cooking in the boat, Ricardo?' she said slowly and carefully.

Ricardo stared at her and she watched as he processed the words through his head. 'No,' he said, his hands firmly guiding the boat into the far distance of nowhere. The clouds were still low and heavy and Helen could feel his caution after the storm. 'I like all food,' he beamed. Then he remembered, 'Except Greek food,' he scowled. 'Not Elliott's food,' he shuddered.

'Hey, why don't you like my food, Ricardo?' Elliott came up the ladder. 'Why not my food?' Helen was amazed that Elliott was almost in tears.

'Don't you remember, Elliott?' Cricket leaned forward from the deck. 'You put french fries and peas on his plate with an omelette. Italians can't eat food mixed up like that; they get sick to their stomachs.'

'Neurotic bastards, all of them. Italian men are just animals,' she hissed at Ricardo, whose eyebrows and hands shot up at the same time.

'What did she say?' he inquired of Cricket.

'Nothing. She's just upset, Ricardo. Come on, Elliott, we'll go for'ard and you can tell me why you are so upset.' Cricket took her arm and led her gently to the front of the boat. He motioned for her to sit down beside him.

The prow of the boat was dipping and plunging. The

waves brushed the bottom of Elliott's feet. 'Oh, it's nothing really, Cricket,' she said, wrinkling her nose. She enjoyed the muscular feel of his thigh. 'I guess I get real uptight when I feel I'm being criticized. My mom was the worst for that.

'I know I'm not much good in the kitchen. Philip used to yell at me when he came home from work, but then he had a mom that stayed home. He used to come home from school and put his head round the door and say "Who's there?", and his mom would go to the kitchen to make him his snack. It wasn't ever like that for me. I'd let myself into the apartment and there would be this big huge silence. I was five when I first went to school all day.

'My mom would be at some hobby or other. She didn't have to work like so many women did, but she wouldn't stay home, so I'd come in, get a glass of milk from the refrigerator, and then go put the TV on and watch "The Flintstones". Or anything to break the silence. It was always real scary and I never opened the door, even when I knew it was one of Mom's friends.'

Elliott felt tears flowing down her face. Shit, she thought, I'm being a real party pooper.

Cricket put his arm around her shoulders. 'I'm sorry about your hard life. I know Toby and I were lucky. Both of us had mothers who were home for us. Sure it was difficult for my mum, she had to race to the dance centre after taking me to school and then do the shopping in her lunch-hour. She used to take me home when I'd finished school and then we had a babysitter to look after me until I was old enough to be on my own in the evenings. My poor mum was always so tired. She had big black rings under her eyes. That's why I have promised myself that when I make it big in the pop world, I'll buy her anything she wants. She's a fabulous mum.'

'Yeah, you're so lucky, so is Toby.'

Cricket hugged her and then bent down and lightly kissed away her tears. 'Elliott, maybe you can't cook, but that's not the end of the world. You're beautiful and you're good fun and,' he bent down close to her ear, 'I love you, Elliott, really I do.' Now he'd said the words he'd been practising all night, he awaited her reply.

For a moment she was silent and then she hung her head. 'I love you too, Cricket, but gee, you're so young.'

'Ahh, that's a load of crap. People love each other because they just do: you can't make laws about love. Look at Romeo and Juliet. It's a magic thing. Two people meet and then *wham*.' He clapped his hands.

'Sure thing. I agree. But your mom's not going to be happy about any of this.'

Cricket shrugged. 'But it's my life now and she'll have to get used to that. And she *will* get used to it.'

Elliott looked up at Cricket, her eyes wide with amazement at his certainty. 'I hope so,' she whispered. 'I very much hope so.' She didn't believe a word she said.

Chapter Seventy

'I don't care, Helen, I really can't help it, I'm as jealous as hell – and anyway, Junior's for too young. Hell, he's not just a minor, he's my son, and I don't want that bitch to have him.'

'I can see that, Marcia, but don't you think that if you tear them apart, it will make the whole thing so much more attractive for them. I don't know much about love in real life, but in literature star-crossed lovers abound. Dante and his Beatrice, Abelard and Héloïse. The list is endless.'

'I couldn't tear them apart on this boat even if I wanted to, Helen. I can't just waft Elliott back to Houston, much as I'd like to.' The lines around Marcia's mouth and nose were deep. Her mouth turned down in disapproval.

'I know, Marcia.' Helen put her arms around Marcia's slender shoulders. 'I know how much you fought to take care of Cricket, but he's old enough to make his own decisions. It's not as if he were an innocent like Toby. If she had picked Toby, and Toby was Cricket's age and was as mature as he is, I don't think I would have stood in their way. At some point you pour everything you've got into your children and then you just have to trust them. Hope that all the love and the caring will bear fruit.

'Years ago I read an article by Anna Freud. She said that your teenage children have to tear themselves away from their parents. She also said you, as an adult, cannot "give" your children freedom. If you don't let them pull away, however uncomfortable the pulling away might be for you at the time, they will never mature, never be truly free.

'I think that's very true of Paul. His mother always kept a tight leash on him. He was ruled by her need for him and his guilt if he didn't telephone her every day. I lived for all those years with a man whose balls belonged to his mother.

'I do worry sometimes because I'm alone with Toby so much but he has Cricket and his band and his friendship with Fats, so he's not surrounded by females all the time. When we were in Swiss Cottage, I saw so many women form symbiotically incestuous relationships with their children, it frightened me. I saw boys flirting with their mothers and their mothers flirting back. With the men out of the house all day, never coming home until late at night, I suppose the women had no other company. Still, I found it difficult to watch women I knew with their arms draped around their sons walking like lovers down the streets.

'I didn't ever think it was normal for mothers to kiss their sons on the lips, or fathers to kiss their daughters like that, come to think of it. For a time Toby was puzzled. "Why," he asked, "don't you kiss me like Peter's mother kisses him?"

'I said, "Because you don't kiss your mother on the mouth, only the girl you are in love with." Anyway, my feeling is that Cricket wants this relationship and you'll just have to keep your cool.'

'My feeling is that you're right and I'm a jealous old fool. Do you get jealous, Helen?'

'Actually, oddly enough, no. I thought I'd be jealous when I found out about Laura, but by then I couldn't really care who took Paul off my hands. I just knew that it would be a matter of time and then he'd move on. What did frighten me, though, was the violence during the time we were separating.'

She drew a deep breath and Marcia noticed that Helen's face had grown whiter. 'I knew he was a hypochondriac,' she continued, 'and that he whined a lot, but not that he could be so physically threatening. I'd never seen him throw such screaming tantrums before. He must have been keeping himself in check for all those years.' Her voice trailed off in puzzled surprise.

'Don't, honey. Forget I asked. I didn't mean to rake up old memories. He's gone for good now, Helen. You can go ahead with the rest of your life.'

'Yes, I can,' Helen said reflectively, 'but part of me will always be afraid of all men. How do you ever learn to trust again?'

'The answer is you don't.' Marcia's voice was bitter. 'When that happens to a woman – and it happens to most women – what you do is keep a bit of yourself out of the relationship. Rather like knowing you have a liferaft, and then if you see the signs in another man, you get out quick.'

Helen could hear Elliott's deep throaty laugh on deck. She smiled. 'Really, Marcia, I think they'll be quite good for each other. You haven't really got anything to worry about.'

'I know that really,' she sighed. 'I guess I just don't want to lose Cricket yet. He's so young, I don't want him running off to Houston.'

'I don't think that will happen, Marcia. He's too bent on making it with the band. They're just about to happen now after all the work they've put in. I think they'll have a fling and then become the best of friends. Anyway, how should I know? I haven't any experience at all.'

Marcia smiled. 'Thanks, Helen, I don't know what I'd do without you.'

'You'd have to do all the cooking yourself, that's what you'd have to do. Golly, cooking for three men takes up all our time. By tomorrow morning we should be in Greece. I really can't wait, I've spent so many years waiting to get to Greece. I can't believe it's really happening.'

Later that night, Elliott awoke as she had planned. 'Good,' she thought, checking the end bunk. Cricket must be on deck. She gingerly climbed the ladder, listening to Ricardo's muffled roars in his cabin under the hatch. It wasn't Ricardo she was worried about, it was Marcia and only Marcia. She knew Helen would turn a blind eye. Helen was much gentler and calmer than Marcia.

She hurried on to the deck and then climbed carefully over the rigging and sat down quietly next to Cricket's sleeping form. How young he looked in the moonlight, she thought, and how beautiful. He lay fast asleep, one arm bent over his forehead, throwing his mouth and nose in dark shadow. His body lay flat and defenceless.

Only the truly young can lie like that, she thought, watching him keenly. Sensing the presence of another, Cricket opened his eyes. For a moment all he saw was a shadow sitting beside him. He was staring straight up at the moon. Then he recognized Elliott. 'Hi,' he said quietly. 'Can't you sleep?'

'No, I just wanted to talk a bit more about us, Cricket.' She grinned. 'Not that I'm about to seduce you or anyone else for a long time; those nightmares won't go away for a long time.'

Cricket rolled over on his side. 'Here,' he said, indicating a place beside him. 'Just lie down beside me and we can watch the stars. There's an epic shooting star up there.' They lay quietly watching the skies.

'Bit like downtown Houston on a Saturday night,' Elliott remarked. 'I wonder if stars party like we do?'

'Sure thing, Orion discos every night. He's my favourite macho guy.'

'I like Venus,' Elliott giggled, 'but then I would, I guess.'

Cricket hoisted himself up on his left elbow and loomed over Elliott. He bent his head and very tenderly kissed her. Elliott realized that it was his capacity for tenderness that so attracted her to him. He had a quiet confidence

432

and way of handling himself that only good mothering could achieve.

Well, she thought as she lay under his gentle caresses, at least Marcia had created a whole man in her son. It was more than she could say for most American mothers. They devoured their sons. Finally, with the sun rising above the rim of the ocean they both fell asleep beside one another. Toby, at the helm, watched over them.

Chapter Seventy-one

Ricardo cursed the wine from the night before. He always meant to have a glass or two, but his hand had an unconscious life of its own and it had sneakily filled his wine glass far too many times.

He also cursed the two women. The black one frightened him at times but she could cook. The English one, so shy and withdrawn, also cooked well. Between the two of them his pasta belly was on talking terms with his knees. He gave a groan and then a grunt, shook his head and went to relieve Toby at the tiller.

'*Mamma mia*,' he said, his voice floating in the wind. Then he saw Cricket asleep with Elliott cradled in his arms. '*Madonna buona*,' he said, his eyebrows running up the well-worn track to his receding hairline. 'What would the black one make of that?' He very much hoped he wouldn't be around when she found out. He motioned Toby to wake them both up with an urgent flapping of both hands.

He knew that '*stranieri*' had funny ways with them. Mostly he saw them ill-dressed in market squares, drunk and loud. The American woman never stopped talking. She talked from the moment she opened her eyes until she shut them. The only time she was quiet was when she had her Walkman stuffed into her ears, and even then she bounced and giggled to the music.

Americans seemed to need noise, lots of it. Also, she chewed gum all the time. He hated the way her jaws worked rhythmically up and down, and then, of course, there were the big pink bubbles which she popped at the table. He also hated the rubbery pink smell of the chewing gum. The crack of the bubble made him jump.

Come to think of it, this whole trip made him nervous. He was used to the boys now. After all, the boys were soon to be men, and men the world over understood each other. In any port he arrived in, after an initial greeting, men stood by men pissing in the same urinals. But women: now, there's another thing. Marcia was not a bit like Helen, who wasn't anything like Elliott. Now, with Cricket obviously in love with Elliott, a *disastro* was staring Ricardo right in the face. And on his own ship! The black *strega*, the witch, would be beside herself.

'*Vai vai*,' Ricardo said as Cricket walked back to the cockpit, followed by Elliott who was laughing at Ricardo's alarm. 'Don't let your mamma find out about this.' He waved a shaking finger at Cricket.

'My, your English is improving, Ricardo,' Cricket said amiably.

Ricardo felt his balls contract with fear. This reminded him of the first time his mother had caught him in the house with a girl. His mother had taken her broom to the both of them. '. . . And in my house. You don't bring your prostitutes in my house!' she had screamed. Later on his mother had grudgingly agreed that he could practise on 'tourist women', but when he did marry he must marry an Italian virgin to provide her with grandchildren.

Sitting down at the helm, still shaking with fear, he remembered his mother. She was a holy terror. She still ran his house with a rod of iron. She had a look in her eye that could boil a spaghetti pot without a fire. He'd left his sweet virginal wife many years ago. Sometimes he regretted that there had been no grandchild, but still he had many 'wives'. He liked getting married. The *festa* and all the fun. Sex was always so good when he was engaged to be married. Once married he moved off because there was no excitement left. No anticipation. Love-making became a chore and the *sugo* soon tasted the same. He could just about manage with less sex, but tasteless *sugo* – not possible.

Yes, life at sea meant that he got to exotic places. Now he realized that he envied Cricket. He was jealous of his youth. A boy with a woman in his arms? Women used to be mad for him, he reminded himself. All women. Women were still mad for him, he told himself firmly.

'Where are we?' Elliott was back on deck again.

'I don't know,' he said shortly. He leaned into the cabin. 'Coffee,' he yelled down the hatch.

Helen glanced at Marcia. 'Somebody's not in a good mood,' she observed.

'Get it yourself,' Marcia screamed back.

'*È così*,' Ricardo said wearily as he slid down the ladder. 'A man has to make his own coffee.' He pointed dramatically at his red T-shirted chest. 'Me skipper,' he barked.

'Me Boss,' but he could see that Marcia was smiling. 'Coffee?' he wheedled, returning her smile.

'*Prego*,' Marcia replied.

Helen watched Ricardo. Italian men knew how to manipulate women. I bet he had a heavy Italian mum. The idea of Ricardo being chased around a kitchen by a tiny termagant amused Helen.

She sat comfortably on her bunk and then realized that Elliott wasn't asleep in hers. Normally Elliott slept until midday. That meant that she must have been on deck during the night with Cricket. She looked across the cabin at Marcia who was making Ricardo's coffee.

Helen could feel no irritation in her friend's face or body. After Ricardo had made some computations on the computer and gone back on deck, Helen addressed the problem. 'Do you think Elliott spent the night with Cricket, Marcia?'

'I know she did. I woke up and heard them laughing.'

'How do you feel about that?'

'Pissed off, but I think you're right, it's far better to let them get on with it than to make it into an exciting big drama. Elliott is still a little kid in many ways, and she needs to grow up. I think I'm more shocked than anything else. You know how we worry about our kids. That they don't get Aids, or syphilis. There's an awful lot of horrible terminal sexual diseases about, not just Aids. I knew a man who had NSU, non-specific urethritis. He got it from his last woman and his balls ached all the time. He fancied me, but I couldn't fancy a man with aching balls.'

Helen relaxed. Things were going to work out all right.

Breakfast was spent taking turns in gazing out to sea. Sometimes Helen thought she saw land looming out of the white-clouded horizon. 'Are you sure you know where we are, Ricardo?'

'Maybe Greece,' he said, and then he sighed his theatrical sigh. 'Or maybe Turkey,' he shrugged.

Helen loved it when he shrugged. The movement began at his knees and climbed up his body until it reached his shoulders, which then lifted themselves up to his ears. All the weight of Italy sat on those raised shoulders. All the debt, all the taxes and the wicked women were there. Then Ricardo let the shrug go and emerged a re-energized man. A man ready to take on the world again. Helen smiled at him. 'Turkey would be a surprise,' she said.

'Turkey very good. I 'ave wife in Turkey.'

'Ricardo, how many wives have you?' Helen frowned.

'Many, many wives. I am good Catholic. *Sposo* my wives.'

Helen heard herself laughing. She was amazed at the sound. Soon they were all laughing helplessly and Ricardo was looking askance. Then he muttered to himself and went to the prow of the ship. 'Land,' he sang out. 'See,' Ricardo was dancing up and down on deck in his bare feet.

'Land.' What a beautiful sound. Helen shouted along-side Ricardo. Yes, indeed it was land. She could just see a whitewashed house on the edge of the dock. Just a speck of a house, but it was land and hopefully they were in Greece or maybe Turkey? It didn't really matter: they were there.

Chapter Seventy-two

Elliott and Cricket were the first off the boat. They dived in simultaneously. Toby watched their bodies arch as they both jackknifed into the sea. He felt a sudden sense of bitterness. Why did women always louse things up? He had so much looked forward to being in Greece with Cricket.

Now, of course, Cricket would take Elliott dancing. They would sit under the moon together, gazing into each other's eyes, and all that stuff. It felt like a long time since Toby had even looked at girls. Some of the girls in the ports had been pretty, but they had failed to catch Toby's attention for very long. He had huge erotic dreams about making love to a girl, but the body never had a face to it.

Louise was still too painful a thought to even try to remember the gentle, tender, loving moments they had shared with each other. No, he'd rather stay alone. That kind of pain was enough to put him off for life.

What Louise had taught him was that loving hurt, was plain old agony. He'd also watched his mother suffer for all those years with his father. Trying to love his weak, delinquent father and failing, and then Louise. He'd decided he'd give it all a miss.

He could see Cricket's long golden body striding up the white powdery sand. He was followed by Elliott, who ran lightly up the beach to reach him. They didn't touch, aware of the people on the boat, but only Helen and Toby were actually watching. Toby felt as if they enveloped each other in a golden glow.

'Come on, Tobe.' Helen put her arm around her son.

'Let's swim off the boat together.' Toby shot his mother a grateful look of thanks. She understood him. Would he ever find a woman like his mother? One who could read his mind and cook like a dream? Louise could read his mind. She didn't cook on purpose. 'None of my girl friends will cook for a man,' she often said scornfully. Especially, Toby noticed, after she'd eaten at his house in Swiss Cottage.

'I'm glad my mum cooks,' he defended Helen hotly. 'Yeah, but she can't be that good in bed if your dad's running off with other women.' That was the only time Toby wanted to hit Louise. She knew that he would never raise his voice or his fist to her. He explained that he was incapable of hitting a woman. Indeed, when he first explained this to her, he couldn't ever imagine causing a woman hurt. After months with Louise, he could begin to imagine an act of violence.

Nothing was very specific with her, but she did taunt him. Called him a wimp and told him he was weak. She knew how to hurt him and to twist the sword. It took a long time for Toby to realize that she was jealous of Helen. 'Your mum doesn't come from a posh family like your dad. Why did he marry her?'

'Because he loved her,' Toby replied firmly. And he did have happy memories of when he was younger and his father and mother took him for walks in Kensington Gardens. He remembered the swings and the slides in the park. He remembered them talking and laughing and then he remembered first the laughing stopped and then the talking. In the later years there were walks and holidays but a lot of silence. Two people alone in a bubble of hurt and pain.

Now Toby was in his own lonely bubble, and it felt as if he'd be there for life. 'OK, Mum,' he said, and he smiled at her, 'I'll race you.'

There was no hope of Helen keeping up with Toby.

Now he had developed powerful muscles pulling on the ropes and dismantling the sails. She swam strongly but slowly to the beach. The sand was silver-white below her and she could watch her shadow as she swam. The sun was high in the sky. As she got into the shallows close to the shore, she saw a little multi-coloured fish in the water. She got to her feet and sighed a deep sigh of satisfaction.

Happiness was now such a strange feeling. She was almost frightened of it. Happiness could be taken away from her again. She had been a very happy woman once, a long time ago. A page-yellowingly long time ago. She took another deep breath. 'Toby,' she said wonderingly, 'Greece smells so different to Italy. It's a clean, pine-scented smell. Not like the hairy underarm and garlic breath we smelt in Southern Tuscany.'

'Oh, Mum, stop it. I thought Southern Tuscany smelt of pizza and olive oil. You make it sound so awful.'

'In a way it is, Toby. The people were poor and the dogs were thin and starving. I was frightened down there at the feelings of violence and envy. The people Ricardo talked to were nice, but I bet those men beat their women. I saw women hitting their children in the face. The people were suffering so much. It's not at all like Elba where the people are happy and well fed.'

She walked on to the beach, watching the patterns made by the sand as she displaced the precious stuff. A tiny, grey-headed pigeon plummeted at her feet. It looked at her out of its round shiny eye. It had a plume and a bright yellow beak. Toby went on up the beach to join Elliott and Cricket.

'Hello, little bird, are you lost?' Helen asked. The bird shook its head and was immediately joined by his mate. Helen sighed again. Why was the whole world in such a hurry to couple up? She'd tried being one half of a couple and it hadn't suited her. She was much better off on her own. She liked the fact that she could make all her decisions herself. Buy what she wanted. She could see the bright yellow dinghy coming to the beach with Marcia sitting regally on the broad rim of the craft. Helen smiled. Marcia enjoyed making Ricardo ferry her about in the dinghy, so she'd obviously bullied him into bringing her ashore. As much as Ricardo grumbled, he was too frightened of Marcia not to do as he was told.

When they landed, he gallantly handed Marcia off the rubber boat. He bowed low, his peaked cap in his hand. 'Thank you, my man,' Marcia said with a flash of teeth. She hugged Helen. 'We made it, babe.' She let out a wild war whoop. 'My dad taught me that. Our tribe in Africa was one of the bloodiest. We were taking slaves long before the silly English ever thought about it.'

Helen followed Marcia's back as she strode along the beach. 'No one ever told me that in our history lessons.' Helen was puzzled. 'All those years people bleated on about the bastard English inventing slavery?' Helen had tried to argue with her history teacher but to no avail. 'What about the Egyptians?' she had argued. Her history teacher had firmly ignored her. He'd had a fearsome moustache that quivered with rage, so Helen had given up.

The next stop after this break on the beach would be to go further down the huge Cephalonian coastline and turn the corner into the port, but for now they were content just to potter.

Chapter Seventy-three

The channel into the port at Cephalonia was long and shallow in parts. They all hung over the sides of the boat to help Ricardo avoid the dangerous rocks under the water. Upon one very big pointed rock that just jutted out of the water there was a large float. Others just had plastic bottles tied to them. This was not a bit like the efficient buoys along the Italian coast.

As they turned the corner and prepared to dock, Helen was thrilled to see a huge ocean liner of a boat docked alongside the wharf. She was flying an Australian flag. But Helen knew that she much preferred their boat. She had such a strong heart beating in her hull. The huge boat was just a floating hotel.

Ricardo had instructed Helen to go into the police station with him to register his papers. He was out of cigarettes and announced that for him it was no problem. Marcia shared her last two cigarettes with him. She too was anxious to buy cigarettes.

'We go first to the shop to buy cigarettes,' Ricardo pronounced as they were tying up. 'No you don't,' Elliott said. 'The Greek police are very fierce and they'll shoot you if you don't comply with their rules and regulations.'

That piece of information made Ricardo frightened. 'Ma,' he exclaimed, and then for good measure, 'bah.' It made Helen giggle.

'Listen,' Marcia said, 'I'll run to the tobacconist over here,' she said, pointing across the busy road, 'then I'll come back and find you in the police station, OK?'

'Huh,' was Ricardo's ungracious reply, but Helen knew him well enough now to know that he wasn't being simply rude, he was just too macho to admit he was scared.

Helen had to admit that the police station was no picnic. It didn't help Ricardo's mood to find all the police officers smoking. '*Madonna buona*,' he said, crossing himself. 'Marcia, *dov'é* Marcia?'

'She's coming.' Helen tried to soothe him as they seemed to trot from one endless desk to another. Finally, Marcia arrived, and Ricardo lit up and smiled for the first time since he'd heard Elliott's threatening remark. They got out of the police station sweating in the heat and unimpressed with Greek customs authorities. Once back at the boat they got ready to leave. They wanted to find a taxi to take them out of the city and up to a café in the mountains.

'Pah.' Ricardo spat out his coffee in an enormous explosion that sent the hot liquid all over Elliott's white dress. 'Hey, Ricardo, that's gross,' was all that Elliott said.

'That coffee for motor car,' he said, unrepentant. Helen found the sandy taste of the powdered coffee very different from Italian coffee, but she rather liked the nutty flavour of it.

'We're in Greece now, Ricardo,' she said. 'You'll have to get used to Greek food.'

'Then he's going to starve,' Elliott said, smiling at him. 'Apart from the roast lamb and the yoghurt, Greece is a nightmare for Italians. When my Italian friends leave Houston to visit practically anywhere but Italy, they take all their pasta and meats with them.' Helen watched Elliott, sitting so prettily and self-confidently beside Cricket. She had a letter from her mother that had been left in the police station. They were all sheltering from the sweltering heat under a trailing vine. It was too early for the grapes to be anything other than tight little green nodules. Pale green ringlets of suckers stretched and swayed in the wind.

'It's the blue,' Helen said, staring wide-eyed out at the sea and the sky. 'I can't explain why it's different to the Italian blues of the skies and the sea. Somehow I feel it's gentler. What do you think, Marcia?'

'I think if I don't get up to the bar and get myself a glass of water, I'm going to get very ungentle. Come on, Toby, you telephone your dad and I'll get my water.' She pulled a reluctant Toby to his feet.

'Do I have to?' He glanced at Marcia's face. 'OK, OK,' he said. 'I'm coming.' She marched him into the depth of the dark, cool taverna.

The counter looked as if it had been hewed out of a tree before the beginning of time. A cheerful red-faced woman stood smiling behind it. She was wearing a bright red-checked pinafore.

'Could I have some change for the telephone and a glass of water?' Marcia was speaking slowly and very loudly in an effort to get the woman to understand.

'Sure thing,' the woman said in a marked American accent.

'You speak English,' Marcia said with surprise.

'Yeah, my father was an American soldier. After the war he stayed here and I married a Greek. He's dead now.'

'Oh, I'm sorry.' Marcia felt a pang of sympathy for this woman.

'Don't be. He beat me within an inch of my life.'

Marcia shook her head. 'It happens everywhere. Is there much wife-beating here?'

'Sure, and the men think they're entitled to do it.'

'Here, even in this paradise?'

'Yes, even here. We women do most of the work in Greece. I run the taverna, cook, wash all the family things. Feed the chickens, collect the eggs. But at least now I live in peace.'

Toby came to the bar. 'May I use your telephone please?' he asked.

'It's over there,' the woman replied, pointing to an old-fashioned telephone fastened to the wall. 'Where have you come from?' she asked.

'From Elba. We've brought a boat down for a charter in Ithaca. We'll hand her over and then fly back to London. Do you serve lunch here? We're all starving after two days at sea.'

'Sure, come with me and take a look in the pots.' The two women moved into the kitchen. Marcia briefly put a hand on Toby's shoulder. He was talking to his father. 'I know that, Dad, I've got my books on board, but we've been at sea for the last two days and I have to help Ricardo sail.' Toby said the last sentence with such pride.

'That's all very well, Toby, but you can't sail a boat for the rest of your life, can you?'

Toby felt his new-found self-confidence beginning to leak away. How did his father manage to neutralize any confidence he ever had? 'OK, Dad, I've got to go to lunch now. Bye,' he said, and winced as he put the telephone down. At least that horrid chore was over for the next few days.

He wandered into the kitchen, his nose twitching furiously. The food smelt wonderful. Whatever Elliott said about food in Greece, she was wrong about this taverna.

Marcia was hanging over a big square tray of macaroni. The macaroni was soft, creamy white and had a brown baked cheese crust. Next to it was a pan of roasted meat. 'Is that Greek lamb?' Toby asked.

'Yup, and here's some octopus and squid. I caught those at six o'clock this morning.'

'I'll have that,' Marcia said, smiling delightedly. 'I'll send the others in so they can choose.'

The woman dumped a big spoonful on to a thick white china soup-plate. 'My name is Theresa,' she said.

'I'm Marcia and this is my friend's son Toby.'

'I hate the idea of eating lamb but it smells so delicious

446

I'll have that.' He pointed to a pan filled with small pieces of lamb, sprigs of rosemary and fat slices of garlic.

They carried their plates back to the terrace and were greeted by a chorus of reproof. 'Why didn't you call us?' Elliott demanded.

'Because we wanted to take the best for ourselves.' Toby tried to keep his voice light, but Helen could see he was upset.

'How's your dad?' Cricket asked.

'Oh, just the same. It's really a waste of time trying to talk to him. He just can't get on to the same wavelength. He's way out of time. He's still in a sort of sixties wavelength. He thinks he's all hip but he wants me to have a degree. Anyway, I don't want to think about him. I just want to wolf down this great food.'

Marcia sat down purring to herself as she tasted the octopus and the squid. 'Like to try a bit, Toby? It's really fresh.' She picked up a small piece of squid and held it out to him.

'Wow, that's great. Normally I don't much like things like that but it's so tender. Usually it tastes like rubber.'

'We can go looking for squid and small octopus in the rocks after lunch at the port. I expect we'll anchor for the next two days in port. Ricardo needs a good night's sleep after being at sea for the last few days, and tomorrow we need to find filters for the boat.' She was interrupted by the arrival of the others.

'I was so hungry I forgot to read the letter from my mother,' Elliott said after she'd eaten a few mouthfuls.

'It seems like your mother follows you round, as if she has a magic eye,' Cricket said.

'Yeah, she used to tell me that when I was a kid. She said she was a videocamera and could see whatever I did. No, this time it's legit. I gave her our itinerary. Without it she'd go mad.' Elliott opened the letter. She read the first page. 'Ugh, Mom says Dad has written to me. Of

447

course, the bitch reads my letters. She telephoned and told him we were down here.' Elliott looked up at Helen. 'Gee, I'm scared, Helen.' She held the second page in her hand. Helen could see the handwriting. It was big and flowing. This was her father's letter, enclosed by Elliott's mother. It was a confident man's hand; obviously he knew what he wanted out of life.

'My darling daughter . . .' Elliott's eyes filled with tears. 'I never thought I'd read those words in my life,' she whispered to herself. She looked up. Tears were rolling down her cheeks. 'I guess I'll just go for a walk and finish the letter by myself.'

'Do you want me to come with you?' Cricket asked. He put his hand on her shoulder.

'No thanks, just don't let Toby eat my calamari.' She attempted a laugh but failed. The wound was too deep.

She walked off the veranda that surrounded the taverna and wandered into the pine trees. There was a moment of silence. 'Her father?' Ricardo said, puzzled.

'Yes,' Marcia said slowly. 'Her father Babo è *andato via*. Went away.' Marcia made a leaving motion with her hand.

'Ah *poverina*.' Ricardo heaved a sigh. He shook his head and went back to eating. 'This Italian food good,' he said.

Helen made a face at Marcia. 'Well, we all know where Ricardo's emotions lie,' she said, but she didn't laugh; her heart went out to Elliott.

Later, when they were back on the boat, Marcia was climbing around the rocks looking for octopus. She saw Elliott walking slowly towards her. She straightened out her aching back and rather wished she'd brought her sunhat with her. 'OK, Elliott?' she called, waving her arms above her head.

'Yeah, I'm coming.' Elliott joined Marcia. 'Where are the others?' she asked.

'They're all on the boat, sleeping off lunch. That retsina is lethal. I didn't drink any of it, but poor Ricardo practically fell face-first into his food. Anyway, are you feeling any calmer? It must be a hell of a shock to hear from your father after all this time.'

'You know, in a funny way I've been expecting this. He says he feels like a bastard leaving me with my mom, but it's the only way he could have survived. He says if he'd stayed with her the fighting would have been awful for me. He's right. Mom's violent enough with me, though now it's mostly verbal violence, but she's a demon with any man she's with. I guess some men find violence in women exciting. I know I gave Philip a hard time. But you know, Marcia, the difficulty is that I just didn't know any other way of behaving.

'My mom taught me that if I wanted something I should just go for it. That's what she always did. So when I got married to Philip I didn't have any rules. There he was, that very English gentleman who didn't even know how to fart without dying of embarrassment. He was so modest I never thought I'd see the day he'd walk around naked in the apartment. I dunno,' Elliott put her hand to her head, 'I'm so confused. Anyway, Dad's in Rhodes, and says if I want to see him he's quite willing to meet me anywhere I choose. I guess I'd feel safer seeing him in the Savoy in London. This way Mom doesn't get to mess us up again. But I think for once in my life I'll wait for a few days before deciding. I'm not going to jump in feet first which is my usual mistake.'

'You do that.' Marcia was crouched over a small shallow dip in the rock. 'See,' she said. She poked her stick under a piece of rock. The rock turned over and a very tiny octopus raised its arms in warning. 'I'm not going to hurt you, little fellow,' Marcia said gently. Elliott watched her normally fierce face soften. 'Here, baby.' Marcia stretched out her hand.

'I'm going to run back to the boat,' Elliott said.

Marcia watched her tear down towards the harbour. 'I hope my boy can help her,' then she smiled. For now jealousy was held at bay by her opposite sister, pity.

Chapter Seventy-four

Elliott had been crying for what seemed like a very long time. She lay on her stomach in the sand. She felt the grit in her mouth and the tearstained ridges of sand under her face.

Beside her, Cricket sat with a consoling hand on her back. Occasionally he gave her back a supportive rub, but he knew not to interrupt. He too had lost a father. He too had been abandoned. He knew the deep sense of loss. Unlike Toby, at least the break had been clean. He had good memories of his father, unlike Toby who had to deal with an almost weekly dose of rejection.

Still, this woman weeping in the sand captured his heart like no other girl or woman in his life so far. What was it, he questioned himself as he sat beside her?

It certainly contained a good deal of lust. She was so golden and so beautiful. So often the young girls he went out with bored him. Their uncertainty, their possessiveness. The subtexts between himself and the girl he was with. Would he love the girl for ever? Who could say? Would he father her unborn child? Would he settle down? After a few months, would he love her enough to marry her? All women, in Cricket's experience, except for this one – whatever their protestations underneath all the lies and prevarications – eventually wanted to settle down. If not with a man, then with another woman.

Most women had a terrifying biological urge to nest. He, like a cuckoo, was willing to invade the nest but not to stay. With Elliott he did not feel that she had any gossamer strings attached to her wish to be with him.

He knew that she intended to go to Houston without

him. He believed that she just wanted to have a glorious fling on a boat with him, and he blessed the day she answered the advertisement for this trip. Secretly Cricket thought that Elliott was still in love with her ex-husband Philip.

Now, as her sobs subsided, he rolled her into his arms and held her. 'I'm sorry,' was all he could say.

'I didn't know he hurt me so much.' Elliott's eyes were swollen.

Cricket took the edge of his T-shirt and gently wiped her eyes. 'Blow,' he said as he put the end of the T-shirt on her little button nose.

'You're treating me like a child,' she said after obediently obeying him.

'When someone is hurt so deeply, you feel like a child. A hurt like that goes so way back and so deep down that nothing can fill that hole. I know it. I've tried drink, drugs, sex, but nothing can take away the fact you had a dad or a mum who deserted you. Some kids I know die from it. They never get over the damage. I've known two boys who have committed suicide from the pain. I'd never do that because I'd leave my mum alone in the world.'

Elliott looked up at his half-man half-boy face and she smiled. It was a weak tremor of a smile that only involved half her mouth. At times, Cricket was so very mature in his thinking, and then at times he was a seventeen-year-old boy.

He had comforted her in a way that she'd never been comforted before. Certainly, girl friends could put their arms around her, but there was a strength in Cricket. A willingness to take her as she was. No attempt to mould her into anything else. It was not only comforting, it was also deeply tender.

Yes, she thought, it is the tenderness that he can display to me that makes me want to love him back. She also knew that this tenderness of his was learned from his mother, Marcia. And that Marcia would always be the first woman in his life.

On the boat, Marcia was quiet. 'Cricket's gone to comfort Elliott,' Helen observed, trying to break the oppressive silence. The boat rocked slightly in the sea. The afternoon sun beat down on the deck where Ricardo lay on his sleeping bag snoring.

'I wish I could sleep in the afternoon like Ricardo.' Marcia tried to deflect the conversation.

'Are you OK about them now?' Helen was relentless.

'I can't not be, Helen,' Marcia sighed. 'Of course I'm not happy. What woman would be? She's so much older than he is; but when she looked at her father's handwriting, my heart just broke for her. We are two lucky women. We both had loving parents and she really has had nothing in life but sorrow. In spite of it all, she's such a nice kid. I can't get too worked up any more over the age difference.'

'Good, I'm glad, because I think they'll be friends as they are now, then lovers, and then hopefully they'll be friends again. I know that sounds trashy and romantic, but I can't help it. I think falling in love and being in love is just wonderful. When I was a teenager I just loved Paul Newman. He was such a manly man and he had such a sweet, tender smile. That's what I want in my life from a man: tenderness. I've had none of that from Paul.'

'It's very hard for a man to show tenderness. It's not taught to them when they are small. In Bristol the boys were all taught to fight by their dads, and to stick up for themselves, and the little girls were given little kittens to take care of. I had my little black kitten called Lucy.' Marcia smiled gently at the memory. 'She was my first love, and when she died twenty years later, I thought I'd die with her. She was blind and deaf and I had to carry her everywhere for six months. She was incontinent, and other people asked why I did not have her put to sleep.

Other people,' Marcia snorted in contempt. 'As long as she could purr, I knew she wasn't in any pain. I held her every evening in front of my fire. She died in May and I had a fire for her, even then when the weather was baking. She gave me twenty years of her fierce life. She bit my guests and hated everybody. I loved that cat with such a deep love. So did Cricket. He was lost without her for a long time.' Marcia's eyes were full of tears. 'I've always preferred children and animals to men.' She got up and stretched. 'OK, sweetie pie, what's for dinner? We can't afford to eat out again for a while.'

'How about big tuna steaks with Tuscan white beans? I'll drizzle Greek olive oil over it with garlic and black pepper. I've put away the last two bottles of Italian olive oil to take back to London. I'll keep them on the edge of the kitchen window and never touch them, because I want to look at the beautiful colours and dream about our wonderful adventures. Before I get supper ready, I'm going off for a swim, and then I'm going to see if there is any Greek wild thyme in the shops.'

Marcia sat down on her bunk again and reached for her book. Helen was relieved that Marcia had not offered to join her. She wanted to swim to the shore alone. She wanted to walk in silence in the streets that criss-crossed the town, and feel the Greek wind which seemed so much gentler than the Italian wind.

She climbed carefully down the ladder of the boat. Its rungs hurt her slippered feet. She felt silly that she'd had to be hauled out of the water like a sack of potatoes. Why couldn't she have muscles in her arms like Elliott and Marcia? All she had were peapods, and she had to ask for help even to open a can of corn. 'I'm a wimp,' she told herself as she greeted the Greek inhabitants of the town.

She wandered on through the town and then out into some scrub land. She took another path, leading to nowhere, as far as she was concerned. She wanted to have an adventure. It might be childish, she chided herself, but it made her feel more confident. She had felt a little nervous. What might she find? Nothing bad here. She continued to climb, the sun hot on her back and the perspiration dripping down her nose. Horses sweat, men perspire and ladies glow. Her mother's little homily was wrong. She was sweating. Her T-shirt stuck to her back and mosquitoes and gnats dive-bombed her. She wished she'd brought some water with her. Her mouth was dry. She paused under a tree and then looked up to bless the cool shade. Then she smiled. Above her were the small beginnings of figs. Little tiny hard buds of green. 'How wonderful,' she said out loud.

Then she heard the sound of running water. She searched around the tree and she saw an outcrop of rocks. Quietly she moved towards the rocks. Lizards scuttled as she moved and she laughed. A field mouse, casting an indignant look over its shoulder, scuttled away.

At the base of the rock there was a loud trickle of water. Bending over, with her palm hollowed, Helen gathered the clear water and put it to her lips. She closed her eyes so as to savour this magic moment of moments. Then she swallowed the water.

For a moment she paused. She had never tasted water like this before. It had a clean, crisp taste. Like she imagined water collected off freshly picked lettuce would taste. 'Wonderful,' she said to the little stream. 'I'll be back with the boys and with lots and lots of bottles. We will carry you back to the boat and we'll drink to your good health every night.'

The stream continued to gurgle, mindful of Helen's promise. Helen turned and, on the way down the hill, she picked yellow and pink wild flowers. She put a stem in her hair. She collected some of the wild sage and thyme in a sweet-smelling bundle. She was happy now, really happy. This was the first time she'd been on holiday without Paul, and she had laid his ghost. He was not here in her forest. He was gone. His ghost vanished.

Chapter Seventy-five

They had to move the boat to the other end of the dock to fill the fuel tank, and collect fresh water for the shower. Helen, perched on the prow of the boat, gazed down to help supervise the lifting of the anchor. The electric gismo that usually lifted the anchor was broken, so it would have to be winched up by hand. That was Cricket's job; she just had to see that the anchor was not fouled up by anybody else's line.

She remembered with amusement an incident in one of the ports, when a huge gin palace had come in flying an American flag. The ship had swung its beam and dropped anchor, but the anchor had dragged and caught up several other lines. For a horrifying moment, boat-owners found themselves being torn from their berths. The ship, monolithically cut off from the real world, seemed to be oblivious to the boat-owners' fate. Helen could see a fleet of Filipino servants, running antlike up and down the decks, and then beginning the long negotiations to untie the huge, horrifying cat's-cradle of anchor chains.

The anchor up, Helen felt a surge of elation. Secure now in what she was doing, she had lost her trembling fear that she might fail. She could now add sailing, real sailing, to her list of accomplishments. For so long she had envied the other women she knew in those long-gone middle-class days. They had come from families where sailing, skiing, riding and show-jumping were a natural part of family life.

Helen did not resent their lifestyle; she just wished she could share in their superior air of confidence. Toby could play tennis but he was unenthusiastic about horse-riding.

There was no easy answer for Helen and her life in England. There simply seemed to be a ladder, on the top two rungs of which stood the rich and well-educated. Then, steadily down the rungs, as if descending into a Gothic painting of hell, came everybody else.

Helen felt Marcia, with her African heritage and her life in Jamaica, was in some ways better off than she was. Marcia, by virtue of her time in the West Indies, was naturally an excellent swimmer, rode horses, and knew an enormous amount about plants and animals. Her plant-boxes outside her windows were stuffed with rows of herbs and salads. 'If I can't eat it, I don't grow it,' she joked. What bound their friendship together was that both women were determined that their boys should have far wider choices than they had now.

Marcia was also standing on deck looking at the terrain. This part of Cephalonia was bleak and inhospitable. Long grey strips and jagged unwelcoming mountains. So different from Italy and the soft, gentle English countryside. Marcia shivered. Here, long-dead Greek heroes strode. Colossal giants heaved boulders into the sea. Here Marcia felt very small and vulnerable. One mistake out there in those straits and the boat could lose her bottom and they their lives.

At least the sea was warm, Marcia reminded herself. But the thought of having to jump and leave behind her precious possessions appalled her. Also, feeling vulnerable made Marcia uncomfortable.

Slowly they motored to the sea-wall and tied up. Ricardo suggested that they should be flying the Greek flag by now. Helen made that her job. Toby was on the wall pulling the hose and handing it down to Cricket, who unscrewed the lid to the tank on the boat. Helen pulled the Greek flag out from the map desk and ran upstairs with it. She tied the flag on to the rope and then ran it up. It fluttered, full of hope and promise.

'Oh, oh,' Marcia said. A car stuffed full of heavily armed policemen came to a screeching halt. '*Carabiniere*,' Ricardo muttered uneasily. They certainly looked unwelcoming.

'Probably thinks because there's two blacks on board we're drug-smugglers.'

The men came and stood without saying a word. They watched the boys finishing filling the tanks and then Cricket grinned at them. 'All done,' he said, and smiled again.

One of the men came up to Cricket and put his face close to Cricket's face. 'You black man?' he said wonderingly.

'Yes,' Cricket agreed, 'and my mother is a black woman.' He pointed at Marcia. She too smiled and waved.

That broke the ice. The men relaxed. One of them offered Cricket a cigarette. 'Where you live?' he was asked.

'My father is from Jamaica,' he explained, 'and my mother is from Africa.' They all nodded at the word Africa. They left shouting happy goodbyes.

Cricket looked at his mother who was still smiling. 'You know, Mum, I'm so used to racial prejudice in England that I expect it everywhere. They weren't offering aggro, they just hadn't seen black people before.'

'Well, I think you can expect racism everywhere. So much of that is fear of the unknown; but then Greece and Italy are used to thousands of years of strangers living in their lands, so they are less xenophobic than an insular and insulated island like England. I find it refreshing this trip that nobody has spat at me or muttered racial slurs under their breath, and I haven't had to worry about you getting beaten up in discos or punched out on the way home. I've been able to sleep better for it.'

That was not strictly true. Marcia pretended that

nothing was amiss, but Helen knew she was still having a struggle to accept her son's relationship, even though they both glowed with love and laughter.

Elliott tried very hard to be circumspect. For her, this was a matter of real tension. As they brought the boat back to its berth, she could feel her feet tingling to take off with Cricket for 'a swim'. In the early hours of this morning, she had crept out of her bunk yet again. But instead of merely hugging and kissing, they had been so carried away that they spontaneously made love.

Nothing had been agreed about love-making. Most of the conversations were 'what if' conversations. What if Marcia found out? That flattened out into a general agreement that it was impossible to keep secrets on a boat this size.

Elliott would be in London to see her father, and they had agreed that it was then, away from Marcia, that they would feel free to make love; but it was too late. They both lay in the dark, hugging each other.

What had come as a surprise for Elliott was that, as they moved together so softly and gently, she had experienced such a profound moment of sexual joy, and for once she was speechless. 'Hey,' she whispered into Cricket's ear, 'was that fabulous for you too?'

'Sure,' he whispered back, but he did not seem to be as greatly moved by the experience as she had been. This moment answered Elliott's real concern, which was that after the attack she had sustained she would find making love an impossibility. She was grateful to Cricket that this was not so. But then for both of them sex was such a pleasure, unlike for so many men she'd had who were afraid of normal love-making and struggled with their fear.

Cricket treated sex just as he ate his food, with great relish and without fuss. Love-making, Elliott thought as she lay in Cricket's arms, should be like licking a spoon full of honey. Or that first moment when you put a choice piece of pink smoked salmon in your mouth. Food and sex were indistinguishable pleasures; there was no possibility of having one without the other. Men who had no interest in food usually made bad lovers, but then there was Ricardo's rule about women and their *sugo*.

Elliott smiled in the dark and resolved to ask Helen to teach her to cook. It was time she learned not only to cook but to enjoy her apartment. Having spent these weeks with two women who enjoyed their homes and had turned the boat into a palace, Elliott felt she too would like to put down feminine roots in her own life. Cricket for her was not a permanent lover but a permanent memory, and hopefully a friendship that was, for once in Elliott's life, not a perverse relationship.

Now, with evening stealing over the town, little lights were twinkling along the dock and over the cafés and restaurants along the sea-front. Marcia felt the town and the surrounding mountains were much less threatening now that the shoulders of the mountains were swathed in the death-throes of sundown.

They were all leaving the boat to go their various ways. Cricket and Elliott were the first off the boat. Ricardo saw Elliott put her arm around Cricket's waist. A shock flooded through his stomach. He gazed anxiously at Marcia. She too had seen the gesture, but her face registered no change. If that had been an Italian mother, Elliott would have been torn to pieces, Ricardo surmised. Just then he saw a rat half the size of a Tuscan cat streaking down the dock. '*Madonna buona*,' he hissed, horrified.

He stifled a scream. If the passengers had been Italian, they would have all screamed. Now the scream was stuck in his throat and would give him a bad stomach. He reached into his pocket for his indigestion tablets. That woman who strode ahead so confidently, who accepted her son's relationship with a much older woman so calmly, had ruined his manhood. Of course, all skippers screamed. Screaming was good for you; all Italians did it. Screaming gave vent to the feelings that swirled inside any decent red-blooded Italian man. Now he'd been descreamed, and the cause of it was standing on the dock talking to Helen.

'*Dio mio*, how did I get into this? *Sono porco miserabile*; I'm a miserable pig,' he told himself. The angelus tolled the closing of the day and Ricardo crossed himself. They were off to find the filters so they could leave the next morning. 'Where's romance these days? Where are emotions?' Ricardo realized as he followed the two women locked in their own world that he very much missed his beloved Italy and he couldn't wait to be back there. The remembrance of the smell of a hot Italian cup of coffee assailed him, leaving him with a hunger that was like a long-lost love affair.

Chapter Seventy-six

Helen stood on deck in her usual position, her arm around Toby. They both shared a deep sense of sadness: this was their last port. The last time they would dock, the last evening out. Hopefully they would have a good Greek meal at last?

Helen squinted as the boat came near enough to the island to get some sort of understanding of the geography and the topography of Ithaca. 'Oh, do look, darling, isn't that lovely?' They'd turned the corner into the harbour, and before them lay Helen's perfect vision of a Greek island. 'I'm so pleased we saw this, Toby, otherwise I would have left Greece so disappointed. Elba is such a hard act to follow. Elba has such a brooding, mysterious air about her. But Ithaca is just what I've always dreamed a Greek island should be like.'

'I'm glad, Mum.' Toby kissed her lightly on the top of her head. 'I feel the same way. Half upset because we're leaving, but excited to hear how our demo tapes went. I'll phone Rollo as soon as we get in.' Helen could hear a deeper tone in his voice. His voice didn't swoop and glide quite so much. The trip had steadied Toby in just the way Helen had hoped it would.

She felt it was worth all those extra times and hours at the bar to give him this chance to move out of little parochial England and gain experiences in a much wider world. As for herself, she had found a contentment, a serenity, and now she knew what real peace was again. Yes, she was looking forward to hugging Fats and flirting with Charlie. But now she felt a lot more secure in who she felt she was.

She was in no hurry to rush into a relationship with any man. Maybe not ever again, but still she had her freedom. Her ability to make decisions about herself. A chance to enjoy being selfish. For the first time in her life she was nobody's child and nobody's wife. That in itself was a liberation.

They were moored against a rough stone wall, and there was no electricity, but the fridge still ran on either gas or electricity, so Elliott's last bottle of champagne was in there chilling. In the morning they would leave the little boat at her moorings and the charter passengers would take over with their own skipper. He wouldn't be like Ricardo, Helen thought affectionately. Ricardo was like having Father Christmas with you all the time. She would miss him, his funny jokes, and most of all his snoring.

Later, after Ricardo had led them to a small taverna at the peak of the quaint town, Helen sat next to Marcia and lifted her glass of retsina to her lips. On the table lay a delicious dish of chicken swimming in a rich garlic and rosemary sauce. Also, long wooden sticks with fat chunks of pork and bright red and green bell peppers lay like discarded rapiers. There were two bowls, one filled with crisp green lettuce, and the other with the white thick yoghurt they all loved so much. Chunks of coarse Greek bread were stacked neatly by Ricardo's elbow.

Ricardo gazed at his crew through a haze of wine. His eyes betrayed him and warned they were going to leak tears of regret at losing these people he had so come to love. 'I get English wife,' he declared, and cleared his throat.

'I'd stick to Italian women if I were you,' Marcia said, laughing. 'At least they look after men.' Her eye was captured by an unusually tall man. He was obviously the owner. He glanced towards her and there was an invitation in his eyes. Marcia signalled back. '*Nay*,' she telegraphed. He smiled happily at her and Marcia sat back, thinking how nice it would be to lie in his arms later and sample a Greek man as a lover.

Cricket, with his arm around Elliott, was arguing with Toby about music. 'Listen up, man . . .' he was saying.

Elliott, leaning contentedly against his chest, was thinking about her coming telephone call with Philip. Would he want her back? She felt as if she'd learned so much on this trip. Watching the little group through her long eyelashes, she realized that most of all she'd learned affection from women. Something she'd never really known before. Her friends, she knew, would always disappear into the woodwork if they met a man.

'Well,' Helen said as they opened Elliott's bottle of champagne, 'I feel as if I've been an old sock with the heel missing. Now, after this trip, I feel as if I know how to darn it. To make myself whole again.' She smiled at everybody.

Toby came back from the telephone. 'I've had a word with Dad and told him I'm on my way and I'll be seeing him at the weekend. But guess what, Mum? Rollo says he's got two appointments for us, and there is definite interest in the demo tapes.'

Helen got up and hugged him. 'That's wonderful,' she said. But what was much more wonderful for her was that Toby had not come back to the table looking like a beaten cur. He had obviously talked to his father in his new, confident voice.

Cricket and Toby were dancing around the taverna. The other guests watched them with amusement. Cricket was soon teaching them how to slap high fives.

Elliott leaned forwards and spoke to Marcia. 'Marcia,' she said, 'do you think men will ever be tender towards women?' She waited for the reply.

'If we let them, Elliott. If we let them,' Marcia replied.

Kisses

Erin Pizzey

The compelling story of three women, and the men in their lives.

Madeleine: pregnant at last, is on the verge of falling out of love with her faithless husband, Sy. But the child who might save their marriage proves to be as disruptive as she is beautiful.

Edwina: promiscuous and predatory, is the opposite of Maddie, and can teach her a thing or two about love, men and the wicked ways of the world. But will Maddie listen?

Germaine: good, solid and practical, has renounced men. But will her passion for the occult bring her happiness?

Very different yet joined by their affection, they seek answers to the questions which modern life throws at them - and in doing so discover that kisses aren't everything.

0 00 647719 4
£5.99

For the Love of a Stranger

Erin Pizzey

Money can't buy you love . . .

Mary Rose Buchan and Anna Kearney are two young Irish girls leaving a land where the English presence is still uppermost. Their nationality is their bond, yet their social status and temperaments contrast. For Mary Rose is rich, selfish, decadent and dissatisfied; Anna is poor but blessed with Celtic powers of second sight and goodness. This is the profound story of their entwined lives, and their thirty-year journey in search of love and friendship.

Set against a panorama of the Troubles, the rise of Fascism, the Second World War and the Italian Resistance, *For the Love of a Stranger* illustrates the emotional and physical awakening of two very different young women. It also combines their progression from childhood to maturity, and their journey from Ireland to England to America, land of dreams, and to Italy, land of joyous love and crippling loss.

Told with passion and eloquence, it also charts the dangerous territories of love inside marriage, love outside marriage, and the pleasure and pain that men and women visit on each other.

0 00 647331 8
£4.99

Unforgettable

William Gill

'A compulsive and evocative read by an excellent writer' ROBERT GODDARD

She is a legendary beauty, the woman every man wants to have - but none can keep.

He is a shy, would-be film-maker, young enough to be her son, living under the shadow of the father he never knew.

But time makes no difference to them. They live - and love - only for the moment. Until he glimpses the first, haunting clue to a mystery that takes him half way round the world, and into a labyrinth of deception leading back across the years.

And as curiosity turns to obsession, he realises that neither of them can ever escape the past. For at the heart of the labyrinth lies a murder - and a tragic secret to which she alone holds the key.

0 00 649003 4
£5.99

Lynne Pemberton

Eclipse

'Rising star in the blockbuster firmament' *Observer*

Lucinda Frazer-West: daughter of Lord Nicholas and Lady Serena, a young actress with a glittering future beckoning.

Luna Fergusson: daughter of West Indian businessman Royole, reluctantly accepted by his wife Caron, and developing a high-flying business career.

Two successful young women, unaware of the bond that links them. They are twins, the product of a one-in-a-million biological chance, following a liaison between Serena and Royole: twin sisters, one white, one black.

Now, twenty-seven years later, events are destined to bring them together, and to unmask the secret of their birth.

0 00 649005 0

Olivia Goldsmith
Fashionably Late

'A bittersweet tale brimming with excitement'
Company

Wherever she goes, forty-year-old Karen Kahn is fashionably late. She can afford to be: the star of the New York fashion scene, with her own company, a handsome husband and a deal that could make her millions, she is the apple – and the envy - of everyone's eye.

But she is too late for the ultimate in creation: a baby. Motherhood is proving to be elusive – as elusive as her own parentage, and as difficult as the cut-throat business of couture. Yet Karen is not one to take no for an answer, and late is better than never . . .

'Full of wisecracks, and gossip . . . this is a book for the beach. Olivia Goldsmith can keep you reading'   *Cosmopolitan*

0 00 647972 3

£4.99 net

Judi James

Naked Angels

Their love is sweet poison . . .

Evangeline, ugly-lovely daughter of famous American artists, is a top fashion photographer. Mik, moody, Hungarian, would like to be. When they meet on a London shoot, they are immediately drawn together as lovers, but, both driven by ruthless ambition, their clash spells doom . . .

Each is haunted by secret tragedy. Both have sacrificed private happiness for public success. Both are victims who inflict their pain on others.

Naked Angels is their story, of greed and glamour, of suffering, destructive passion and, finally, of hope and unexpected happiness . . .

0 00 649046 8

£4.99 net

Elizabeth Harrington

Daddy Darling

From the seedy lowlife of London's East End to the glittering prizes of the international art market, an innocent woman is caught between two very different worlds . . .

Gus is young, brainy and beautiful, a newly qualified barrister with a high-flying career ahead of her. When she is assigned her first big case - a notorious murder trial - she resolves to show everyone what she is made of, especially her father, the prominent and wealthy art dealer Piers Lawrence, whose attention she craves.

But Gus's search for justice is sabotaged at every turn. Determined, and with the help of journalist Tom Silverthorn, she digs deep into the dark underworld of the East End, where she uncovers a criminal network which began thirty years ago: ruthless, deadly and - horrifyingly - linked to her own mysterious past. Even worse, Gus realises that the enemy is getting closer, and that someone who knows everything about her will do anything to keep her silent . . .

0 00 647328 8